Ludic Feminism and After

Critical Perspectives on Women and Gender

Critical Perspectives on Women and Gender brings books on timely issues and controversies to an interdisciplinary audience. The series explores gender-related topics and illuminates the issues involved in current debates in feminist scholarship and across the disciplines.

Series Editorial Board

Titles in the series

Michelle Fine
Disruptive Voices: The Possibilities of Feminist Research

Susan D. Clayton and Faye J. Crosby
Justice, Gender, and Affirmative Action

Janice Doane and Devon Hodges
*From Klein to Kristeva: Psychoanalytic Feminism and the
Search for the "Good Enough" Mother*

Jill Dolan
Presence and Desire: Essays on Gender, Sexuality, Performance

Judith Newton
Starting Over: Feminism and the Politics of Cultural Critique

Jill G. Morawski
Practicing Feminisms, Reconstructing Psychology: Notes on a Liminal Science

Mary S. Gossy
Freudian Slips: Woman, Writing, the Foreign Tongue

Teresa L. Ebert
*Ludic Feminism and After:
Postmodernism, Desire, and Labor in Late Capitalism*

Ludic Feminism and After

Postmodernism, Desire, and Labor in Late Capitalism

Teresa L. Ebert

Ann Arbor

THE UNIVERSITY OF MICHIGAN PRESS

For Mas'ud Zavarzadeh

Copyright © by the University of Michigan 1996
All rights reserved
Published in the United States of America by
The University of Michigan Press
Manufactured in the United States of America
♾ Printed on acid-free paper

1999   1998   1997   1996   4   3   2   1

A CIP catalogue record for this book is available from the British Library.

Library of Congress Cataloging-in-Publication Data

Ebert, Teresa L., 1951–
    Ludic feminism and after : postmodernism, desire, and labor
in late capitalism / Teresa L. Ebert.
        p.   cm.
    Includes bibliographical references and index.
    ISBN 0-472-09576-5 (alk. paper). — ISBN 0-472-06576-9 pbk. :
alk. paper)
    1. Feminist theory. 2. Postmodernism. I. Title.
HQ1190.E24   1995
305.42′01—dc20   95-4333
                                                CIP

Acknowledgments

Parts of this book have appeared in earlier forms. Grateful acknowledgment is made to the following authors and journals for permission to reprint previously published materials.

College English for an earlier version of "The 'Difference' of Postmodern Feminism," *College English* 53, no. 8 (December 1991), published by the National Council of Teachers of English.

Cultural Critique for "Ludic Feminism, the Body, Performance, and Labor: Bringing *Materialism* Back into Feminist Cultural Studies," *Cultural Critique* 23 (winter 1992–93), published by permission by Oxford University Press.

Genders for "The Crisis of (Ludic) Socialist Feminism," *Genders* 21 (spring 1995). By permission of New York University Press.

Kostas Myrsiades and Jerry McGuire for "Subalterity and Feminism in the Moment of the (Post)modern: The Materialist Re-Turn," reprinted from *Order and Partialities: Theory, Pedagogy, and the 'Postcolonial,'* edited by Kostas Myrsiades and Jerry McGuire (Albany: State University of New York Press, 1995). By permission of the State University of New York Press. © 1995.

Rethinking Marxism for "Surplus Enjoyment in the Post-al Real," *Rethinking Marxism* 7, no. 3 (fall 1994).

Transformation for "(Untimely) Critiques for a *Red Feminism*," *Transformation* 1 (spring 1995).

Women's Review of Books for "The Politics of the Outrageous," *Women's Review of Books* 9, no. 1 (October 1991); and for response, *Women's Review of Books* 9, no. 3 (December 1991).

Contents

Preface

There will be . . . no future without Marx.
                                        —Jacques Derrida, *Specters of Marx*

One of the questions I ask in this book is why the dominant feminist theory in the postmodern moment—ludic feminism—has largely abandoned the problems of labor and exploitation and ignored their relation to gender, sexuality, difference, desire, and subjectivity. It has done so at a time when "two-thirds of all labour in the world is done by women. . . . In the Free Production Zones in South-East Asia, Africa and Latin America, more than 70 percent of the labour force is female[,] . . . the majority . . . young women (14–24)" who are highly exploited and underpaid (Mies 117).

The other side of this question is what ludic feminist theory has substituted in place of the economic. How does it explain social relations and the emerging world reality? Most importantly, does this explanation make transformation of the social possible? Following Foucault, Lacan, Derrida, and other poststructuralist theorists, ludic feminism, including much recent socialist feminism, has articulated the social as discourse/textuality and posited desire/pleasure as the dynamics of the social. In so doing, it has displaced economics, labor, and class struggle. The cost of this displacement has been enormous for feminist politics, especially for socialist feminism.

This, then, is clearly a moment of crisis for revolutionary politics, specifically feminism. Stanley Aronowitz, in a long essay, declares that the "socialist movement deserves a decent burial" ("Situation" 58). Socialist feminists, like Michèle Barrett, are abandoning Marxism and a socially transformative politics altogether, and turning instead to a discursive, cultural politics founded on the anti-Marxist writings of Michel Foucault and other ludic postmodern theorists. In the preface to her *Politics of Truth*, for instance, Barrett announces her anti-Marxism: "I am nailing my colours to the mast of a more general post-Marxism" (vii). But as Renate Bridenthal points out in her review of Barrett, "[W]here is this ship sailing to? This is not a time for intellectuals to be sailing away on a sea of indeterminacy" (220).

Under the pressure of the dominant discourses of Postmodernism, Marxism and historical materialism are becoming lost revolutionary knowledges for the current generation of feminists. Now, in place of a historical materialist analysis for social change, feminists are provided with models for "the care of the self," for "performing" and "remetaphorizing" difference, for "power feminism," and for "sexual-agency feminism," all of which trivialize the situation of women: reducing it to matters of textuality, desire, or voluntarism. But Marxism continues to haunt these practices. Jacques Derrida (from whom all post-Marxists have learned the deconstruction of the social) has arrived at a very different relation to Marxism—after devoting most of his philosophical writing to occluding Marxist knowledges. He now contests the new global *"dominant* discourse" that "proclaims: Marx is dead, communism is dead, very dead, and along with it its hopes, its discourse, its theories, and its practices" (*Specters* 51–52). Derrida declares, "Upon rereading the *[The Communist] Manifesto* and a few other great works of Marx . . . I know of few texts in the philosophical tradition, perhaps none, whose lesson seemed more urgent *today*" (13). He goes on to claim that "It will always be a fault not to read and reread and discuss Marx . . . It will be more and more a fault, a failing of theoretical, philosophical, political responsibility" (13).

The irony for feminist and left theory and politics today is that the ludic displacement of Marxism has been so pervasive that, for many, it is only Derrida's injunction to *re*read Marx that will open up a space for a reconsideration of Marx and Marxism in the post-al moment. Thus while feminists have largely silenced the Marxists in their own ranks, many may now heed Derrida's call to engage the "specters of Marx" and disclaim the "dogmatics" that

> is attempting to install its worldwide hegemony in paradoxical and suspect conditions. There is today in the world a *dominant* discourse . . . striving in truth to disavow, and therefore to hide from, the fact that never, never in history, has the horizon of the thing whose survival is being celebrated (namely, all the old models of the capitalist and liberal world) been as dark, threatening, and threatened. (51–52)

Derrida's reconsideration of Marxism, however, is itself caught in the contradictions of ludic politics: it continues to deconstruct Marx, turning his fundamental concepts into tropes, at the very same time it affirms the necessity of Marx's theories. As Derrida declares, "[I]f there is a spirit of Marxism which I will never be ready to renounce, it is not only the critical idea or the questioning stance . . . It is even more a certain emancipatory and *messianic* affirmation" (89). Marx and Marxism are reduced to a "spirit," a "specter," and such fundamental concepts as capital, money, and surplus labor are articulated as tropes. For instance, Derrida writes that "The whole movement of idealization . . . whether it is a question of money or of ideologemes, is a production of ghosts, illusions, simulacra, appearance, or apparitions" (45). In short, revolutionary critique, for Derrida, becomes the effort to "*conjure* (away) the ghosts" (47) to "chase away, or exorcise the specters . . . by means of critical analysis" (47). But to "read" Marxism as "messianic affirmation" is to revert to the most commonplace dogma. Marxism is not a utopian hope but a revolutionary theory and praxis devoted to the very real historical struggles to emancipate all people from exploitative relations of production and the unequal divisions of labor, property, power, and privilege these produce.

In this highly contested moment in the history of revolutionary politics, I will be arguing for a revolutionary reunderstanding and engagement with historical materialism for feminism in postmodernity. I do so at a time when feminism, for the most part, has lost the revolutionary knowledges of historical materialism so necessary to understand the exploitative relations of labor and production and to transform them. As a result, feminism has severely reduced its ability to build effective collective struggle for the emancipation of *all* people from exploitation: women and men of color, lesbians, gays, workers, colonized peoples and children. In fact, not only the possibility but the very issue of emancipation has been occluded in ludic feminism: dismissed as itself a totalizing (read totalitarian) metanarrative. Judith Butler, for example, following the post-Marxist Ernesto Laclau, proclaims the "loss of credibility" of "Marxist versions of history" and "the unrealizability of emancipation" ("Poststructuralism" 3, 8). But as Derrida quite rightly says, "There will be . . . no future without Marx" (*Specters* 13). For Marxism *is* the theory of emancipation in global patriarchal capitalism, and there is no emancipatory future, no emancipatory politics without Marxism. I am thus writing to reclaim the critique-al knowledges of historical materialism for feminism in postmodernity and to help revive a revolutionary theory and praxis for third-wave feminism.

As one of the readers of my manuscript wrote, "Ebert is, I fear, swimming against the tide." Not only am I politically contesting the ludic turn in feminism, but I am also challenging the very mode of canonic feminist theory. This mode over the years has become a more and more restricted, ahistorical, and localist genre of descriptive and immanent writing. According to the codes of this mode of writing, feminist theory, first of all, has to be written in a "feminine" language. In other words, it has to avoid abstract concepts (if it does deploy them, they must be quickly deconstructed into an indeterminate series of open-ended stories) and instead rely on anecdotes, memoirs, confessions, "little narratives," and other forms of intimate self-writing. The debilitating assumption behind this injunction is that concepts are in and of themselves panhistorically masculinist. The unsaid of such an understanding is, of course, that women are essentially aconceptual. I write against this assumption.

The code for writing feminist theory also requires that the theorist begin with women's experience, continue with women's experience, and end with women's experience, as if women's experience (whether understood empirically or tropologically) is economically, politically, and culturally autonomous, severed from larger socioeconomic practices. I write against this tradition. I believe that women's experiences are not given by nature or invented—whether by a sovereign self or by the play of significations. Instead, women's experiences are constructed historically through formations of material forces. As Marx and Engels said, "[P]eople won freedom for themselves each time to the extent that was dictated and permitted not by their ideal of man, but by the existing productive forces" (*German Ideology* 431). These forces, of course, operate through highly complicated and elaborate mediations to establish nuanced networks in culture and politics. For feminism to limit itself to these nuances—that is, to the *effects* of local mediations—to focus on the subject and on the utopian hope of "an ideal" and idealistic theory, as the prevailing mode of writing feminist theory increasingly requires, leads feminism to forget the conditions that produce these ideals and effects and to end up with a limited and limiting cultural analysis. Such an analysis may assure many women of the singularity of their experience, but it will never explain how that singularity becomes singular: as the effect of social totality.

In this book, therefore, I have transgressed the common code of feminist theory and mixed what in the contemporary academy is called "high theory" with "feminist theory," indicating the historical imbrications of the two. I have discussed canonic texts of high theory, as in the writings of Derrida, Foucault, Baudrillard, Lyotard, and Deleuze and Guattari, and feminist theory, including the work of Haraway, Butler, Cornell, Spivak, Barrett, Mies, Davis, Fuss, Gallop, Meese, Rubin, Young, Hartmann, James, and Dalla Costa, as well as Paglia, Wolf, and Roiphe, among others, along with such neo-Marxists as Jameson, Fraad, Resnick, and Wolff, and post-Marxists like Laclau and Mouffe. But I have also engaged the theoretical writings of Marx, Engels, and Lenin, who are excluded from the canon of both ludic theory and feminism: in fact, there is an unspoken injunction against invoking their names. I have engaged all these theories because I believe a truncated feminist theory (a theory only of women, by women, for women), no matter how reassuring and supportive it may seem, is in the long run complicit with the very economic and social forces of patriarchal capitalism that revolutionary feminists are struggling to overthrow. Feminist theory in this book may strike readers as quite different from the mode with which they are intimate. It defamiliarizes because it works to build a *global* theory for the emancipation of women and understands such emancipation to inevitably include *all* oppressed peoples. This book, then, is not a recitation of local genealogies of feminine/feminist discourses and the micropolitics of power and gender, nor is it a tabulation of the diversities and unrepresentable excesses of women's experience. *Ludic Feminism and After*—in its themes, argument, and mode of inquiry, as well as in its form of writing—is a contestatory book that attempts to recast feminist theory now. Like all attempts at recasting, my efforts will be met with hostility, skepticism, and resistance by many of those who have grown accustomed to the dominant feminist theory and who have benefited from it in their academic or institutional lives. But it is my hope that for some readers, especially young feminists now coming of theoretical and political age, *Ludic Feminism and After* will be an enabling book: enabling the development of a transformative feminism (*after* poststructuralism)—a red feminism—for the beginning of a new century of transnational equality for all people of the world.

In writing this book, I have been especially grateful for the sustained intellectual support of Rosemary Hennessy, Donald Morton, Helen Regueiro Elam, LeAnn Fields, and, above all, Mas'ud Zavarzadeh.

PART 1
Theorizing Materialism

CHAPTER 1

Feminism, Critique, and the Matter of Materialism

This book is a critique of what I call *ludic feminism:* a feminism that is founded upon poststructuralist assumptions about linguistic play, difference, and the priority of discourse and thus substitutes a politics of representation for radical social transformation. Ludic feminism has become dominant in the Euroamerican academy in the wake of poststructuralism. The aim of this work is to supersede it by pointing to its historical limits and to move toward a revolutionary and dialectical feminism: a new *red feminism.* The issue of critique, however, has become a difficult and troubling one for feminism. It is often misrecognized as negative and destructive, even as an attack or "trashing"—especially when it involves one feminist critiquing another. As Marianne Hirsch has said of one of Toril Moi's public presentations, "[H]er paper was built on what appeared to me and others as the *trashing* of other feminists' work . . . [T]here is now a way of building a career on *trashing* feminist work" (Gallop, Hirsch, and Miller 350; emphasis added). These are serious charges, felt painfully and passionately by those making them. They are, in fact, the opening remarks of a well-known "conversation": the published transcription of a discussion among Jane Gallop, Marianne Hirsch, and Nancy Miller, called "Criticizing Feminist Criticism." Yet if we turn to the presentation in question (a version of which is Moi, "Patriarchal Thought"), we are hard pressed to find any trashing. While Moi's essay is one with which I find much to disagree, it is a thoughtful and rigorous critique of what she sees as some of the underlying presuppositions, limits, and consequences of a rather wide range of feminist criticisms of "male science" or "male theory" by such critics as Evelyn Fox Keller (coeditor with Hirsch of the volume, *Conflicts in Feminism,* in which "Criticizing Feminist Criticism" appears), Susan Bordo, Nancy Chodorow, and Hélène Cixous. In contrast to these feminists, Moi argues for the theories of Michelle Le Doeuff, as providing a productive alternative to the limits in the other theories. Such critical engagements are

3

not only valid but also, I would argue, quite important for the intellectual and political vitality of feminism. Why then such distress over critique?

What is in question for Hirsch and many others is not feminist critiques of male theorists, often seen as both necessary and effective, but critiques of other feminists. It is important to note that we are not dealing here with direct or vulgar personal attacks (which should not be regarded as critique), but rather with a serious analysis of a writer's historical practices and intellectual positions and their effects. Yet this negative view of critique within feminism is so frequently voiced that it may be counted as the dominant view. To take an example from a quite different forum, a feminist reviewer in *Socialist Review* praised Hazel Carby's *Reconstructing Womanhood* for being "so courteous" because "the demolition or reworking of others' interpretations remains secondary" to the book's "positive agenda" (Kubitschek 148), which the reviewer evidently sees as opposed to critique (as demolition). We thus need to ask why critique, when aimed at other feminists, is misrecognized as trashing, as uncourteous demolition. What is at stake in this misreading, and can critique be understood in more productive terms?

I will attempt in this work to open up a constructive space for engaging in critique within feminism because I believe critique is crucial to producing those knowledges and practices that will enable us to understand and transform the exploitative operation of social relations and power that constitute capitalist patriarchy. I am, of course, aware that the concept of patriarchy is largely absent these days from most feminist and left analyses, dismissed as a reductive and totalizing notion, on the one hand, or as erasing class and the economic, on the other. But patriarchy, I believe, is a necessary "struggle concept" (to use Maria Mies's term [36]) for any transformative politics. Like ideology, essentialism, and even women, patriarchy is among a body of necessary struggle concepts for feminism that have been displaced by postmodernism and have to be reobtained from the perspective of materialist postmodern feminism and from our situation in the continuing struggle for emancipation. In the following chapters, I elaborate on patriarchy as a regime of exploitation that naturalizes socially constructed gender differences in order to deploy the social relations of production in class societies in ways that reproduce and legitimate the domination and exploitation of one gender by another. Patriarchy organizes asymmetrical, unequal divisions of labor, accumulation, and access to economic resources that guarantee not only the political privilege (domination) of male over female but, more important, the economic subjugation (exploitation) of the "other" gender as the very grounds of social arrangements. In other words, patriarchy—as a historically diverse ongoing system of gender differences for exploitation—is necessary to the very existence of class societies, including contemporary global capitalism. Feminism challenges this naturalization, including socially produced differences and the exploitation it reproduces and legitimates.

I believe materialist critique is one of the most effective means through which such a challenge can be carried out. I need to emphasize here that critique in itself is not an end: it is simply a means for producing the historical knowledges of social totality that are necessary for any coherent praxis for a radical transformation of patriarchal capitalism. To act effectively to construct radically different social arrangements (without the utopian mystifications that haunt some contemporary feminisms), we need to know *what* we are acting on. In other words, we have to have reliable knowledge of the social relations and institutions we seek to change. It is, of course, common knowledge now that poststructuralism and ludic feminism deny the possibility of such reliable knowledge. In the following chapters, I will address the politics of such epistemological maneuvers. Here I want to state that critique, far from an act of trashing, is in fact the most trustable ally of transformative feminism because it produces knowledge of the social totality by examining existing practices. Critique enables feminism to arrive, by democratic, public contestations, at a collective understanding of historical social relations and thus to act both knowledgeably and collectively. Critique, in short, provides guidelines for social change, not through dreams and mystical visions of cyborgs, goddesses, the "unpresentable Other," "pure difference," and other idealistic schemes, whose main effect has always been to bracket existing forms of exploitation in favor of some utopian community, but through collectively thought-out theory. The popularity of utopianism in ludic feminism is the effect of its complicity with the dominant social relations: utopianism—of any kind— is popular because it disregards existing social contradictions and points to a "beyond." No serious transformative social change can come about without knowledge of the existing social contradictions. Critique produces such knowledge. Furthermore (contrary to its perception as a negative act), it produces positive knowledge without positivism and other forms of essentializing. It is this positivity without positivism that Marx has in mind when he refers to critique-al[1] knowledge as that knowledge that does not "dogmatically anticipate the world" but finds "the new world through criticism [critique] of the old one" (Marx and Engels, *Collected Works* 142) [dass wir nicht dogmatisch die Welt anticipiren, sondern erst aus der Kritik der alten Welt die neue finden wollen (*Gesamtausgabe* 1, pt. 2:486). The "old" (the accumulated contradictions of capitalist practices) cannot simply be superseded through utopian visions; instead, critique provides a dialectical knowledge through its interrogation of the two. It is my argument that only through such critique-al, dialectical knowledge can feminism seriously engage the existing social arrangements and transform them.

Through critique, in short, the subject develops historical knowledges: she acquires an understanding of how the existing social institutions (motherhood, child care, love, paternity, taxation, family) have come about, how they have been located in exploitative relations of difference, and how they can be changed. By critique, then, I mean in part the refusal to take any practice or position as given; critique inquires into the seemingly self-evident and points up that what appears to be the natural order is in fact a social construct produced under determinate historical conditions. The purpose of critique, however, is not to simply point out the constructedness of ideas, practices, and theories. To simply argue for constructedness, as the theoretical work of ludic feminists demonstrates, cannot do more than problematize the seemingly natural. In fact, ludic postmodern theory has reached an epistemological impasse in its emphasis on the (discursive) constructedness of practices. For many ludic critics in the 1990s, constructedness signifies a form of constraint, if not determinism, and a denial of ethical subjectivity. Some ludic feminists who would like to show the ethical and the activist dimensions of poststructuralism have now more or less abandoned constructivist theories and have instead started to think about social practices in terms of "invention." I will analyze this move in the following chapters, but here it is important to note that invention is an ideological alibi for the bourgeois individual, who is, in fact, the site and source of invention—in spite of all the postindividualist epistemological detours these theorists make. The most famous trope for this displacing of constructedness by invention is, of course, Donna Haraway's "cyborg," followed more recently by Drucilla Cornell's "remetaphorization" and Judith Butler's "performativity," or what she now calls "citationality." Other recent texts, such as Pamela Benson's *Invention of Renaissance Woman* and Lynn Hunt's *Invention of Pornography*, are examples of the impasse of apolitical invention.

In its place I am proposing a historical materialist critique in the Marxist tradition. Such a critique moves beyond deconstructing the "natural," showing that the constructed and the invented (the "cyborg") is always

[handwritten margin note: Advocates of. in favor of. a Historical materialist critique]

limited by the social relations of production and their social contradictions. A historical materialist critique is not simply immanent (as in ludic critique) but connects various seemingly autonomous social practices to one another and to the global economic situation, thereby producing a historical knowledge of social totality. Materialist critique clearly differs from poststructuralist practice, which denies the reality of social totality and thus the possibility of knowing anything other than "metanarratives" or discursive effects of discrete and incommensurate localities.

Historical materialist critique is that knowledge practice that historically situates the possibility of what exists under patriarchal capitalist relations of difference—particularly the division of labor—and points to what is suppressed by the empirically existing: not just what *is*, but what **could be**. This "could be," however, is not a utopian dream: it is a possibility (owing to the development of the forces of production) that is suppressed (because of the dominant relations of production—the existing relations of private property and class). Materialist critique foregrounds the contradictions between the forces of production and the relations of production, what is historically and materially possible but is repressed. In short, materialist critique indicates that "what is" is transformable. The role of critique in what I will be calling *resistance* postmodern feminism is exactly this: the production of historical knowledges that mark the transformability of existing social arrangements and the possibility of a different social organization—an organization free from exploitation.

[handwritten margin notes: defn of critic of what is in place (and whether could be by that system in place) ↓ developing notions of "what is" transform able.]

Quite simply, then, materialist critique is a mode of knowing that inquires into what is not said, into the silences and the suppressed or missing, in order to uncover the concealed operations of power and the socioeconomic relations connecting the myriad details and representations of our lives. It shows that apparently disconnected zones of culture are in fact materially linked through the highly differentiated, mediated, and dispersed operation of a systematic logic of exploitation. In sum, materialist critique disrupts "what is" to *explain* how social differences—specifically gender, race, sexuality, and class—have been systematically produced and continue to operate within regimes of exploitation, so that we can change them. It is the means for producing transformative knowledges.

Critique of Ideology

Fundamental to a feminist critique is a critique of ideology (another concept suppressed in ludic feminism), for ideology is the means by which social differences are signified and maintained or contested. Ideology responds to the contradictory social reality that is the outcome of the divisions of labor, which restrict access to social and economic resources through class. Material contradictions produced in the economic practices of capitalism (such as the divisions of labor, unequal economic access) are "solved" ideologically in the cultural imaginary by naturalizing social differences. After innumerable contesting theories, from those of Marx's contemporaries to those of our own (Bell, Žižek, Fukuyama, Butler), Marx's classic theory of ideology still offers the most dynamic understanding. Ideology, Marx argues, is the discourse of the cultural imaginary (philosophical, aesthetic, legal, political, and religious texts and practices) through which people "become conscious" of the material contradictions of social life and "fight it out" (*Contribution* 21).

It is through ideology that practices and subjectivities are situated in specific social differences and these relations are naturalized as inevitable. Elaborating on Marx, Nicos Poulantzas argues that "ideology has the precise function of hiding the real contradictions and of *reconstituting* on an imaginary level a relatively coherent discourse which serves as the horizon of agents' experience" (207). To the extent that *ideology* is still deployed in contemporary feminism, it is a purely descriptive (not explanatory) term derived, through many attenuating mediations, from Althusser (esp. "Marxism" and "Ideology"). Even this descriptive notion is now frequently overwritten by a Foucauldian reading of ideology (Foucault, "Truth") and displaced by the notion of discourse (Foucault, *Archeology* and "Politics"; also see Laclau, "Populist," and Barrett, *Politics*). Displacing ideology by discourse is, of course, a move undertaken in order to replace social contradictions (explained by ideology) with social "difference": a concept that isolates difference in a locality and cuts its relations to other differences and, most importantly, to the cause of difference. In so doing, it renders all differences the same. Ironically, difference, which is instituted to free us from universalizing concepts, itself ends up a neouniversalist regime. Discourse blurs the hierarchies of power; we cannot distinguish the powerful from the powerless, the exploiting from the exploited. It represents the social in a way that all persons are at the same time powerful and powerless, exploiting and exploited, a social in which the privileges of the (upper) middle classes are mystified. Ideology critique, on the other hand, explains how differences are constructed socially and naturalized to legitimate the interests of a few. Ideology, then, is not simply representation: it denies social contradictions. Critique of ideology is an understanding of the materiality of these denials and the interests they serve: through the critique of ideology these naturalized relations can be exposed and contested.[2]

Patriarchal ideology, for example, operates through romance narratives, among other places, to mystify the social contradictions and material conditions of women's exploitation in patriarchal capitalism.[3] It seductively covers over male violence against women and the growing poverty of women (especially single women who are heads of households) by constructing narratives of female empowerment. The celebration of female empowerment is a prominent concern of romance writers—most of whom "consider themselves feminists" (Krentz [aka Amanda Quick, Jayne Castle, Stephanie James] 3). However, empowerment in romances is the ideological fantasy in which the woman, according to Krentz, "always wins: with courage, intelligence, and gentleness she brings the most dangerous creature on earth, the human male, to his knees. More than that she forces him to acknowledge her power as a woman" (5). The power women are allowed is limited to the power to tame the male, to entice him to capitulate to his place as a reliable sexual mate and protector. Another writer of romances, Susan Elizabeth Phillips, argues that romance novels provide a much needed "fantasy of command and control." But female power remains dependent on the male.

> [B]ecause [the hero] has been tamed by our heroine, because she exerts such a powerful emotional stranglehold over him, his almost superhuman physical strength is now *hers to command.*
>
> Shout hallelujah, Sister! No more fear of dark alleys! No more worries about things that go bump in the night! And best of all, no more males who are unable to understand the emotional needs of the female. The romance novel has—Abracadabra! Zap! Pow!—produced . . . a new female—a heroine who possesses all the softer qualities traditionally assigned to women but who has none of a woman's physical limitations because *his strength now belongs to her.* (58)

This is a very telling notion of power: not the power to transform existing social inequalities and end male violence and oppression; not the power to transform gender divisions and the condition of women's lives, but only the highly constrained and distorted "power" patriarchy has historically ascribed to the other gender. It is the power of woman to secure her place as woman, as sexual other, and to acquire the limited privileges provided by her association with the male-phallus. Critique of ideology exposes these limits, explains the reasons for them, and unmasks the ways romance novels naturalize male hegemony, particularly control of wealth and the relations of production. Critique of ideology disrupts these seductive imaginary identifications and demonstrates how they create a "false consciousness," that is, a distorted or partial understanding or identification that not only does not resolve the contradictions oppressing women but serves to resecure women in the subject positions and meanings required by the existing relations of exploitation. The process of critique of ideology is a means to enable women to produce oppositional subject positions and positive knowledge of their material conditions so that they can change them.

If feminism, as an ensemble of contesting ways of knowing and political practices, is to continue to develop, it must be self-critical. It needs to understand that a materialist critique of its own historical situation and limits is vital to its ongoing struggle against patriarchy—especially at a time when patriarchy is intensifying both its appropriation of feminism and its backlash against it.

The appropriation and backlash are signs that patriarchy is in crisis. It is being divided by its own difference: by the conflict between emergent forms of patriarchy and more traditional modes. In the spaces of these social fissures, contemporary feminism has built the site in which to articulate social change. Obviously, feminism has played a crucial role in displacing key aspects of traditional patriarchy (such as rigid gender roles or male domination of the professions). But what has been the effect of our efforts on emergent forms of patriarchy? We have seldom turned to see whether feminist strategies and knowledges are being appropriated on behalf of postmodern patriarchal practices, whether we have unwittingly helped these new forms to take shape.

For instance, feminism has helped bring about increased gender flexibility, allowing women to more easily take up the attributes of power and authority, while encouraging men to take up nurturing and child-care responsibilities. These gender shifts and the increased presence of women in professional and management positions, however, are largely confined to the middle and upper middle classes because they serve the interests of a late-capitalist, postmodern patriarchy. First of all, they maintain the middle-class (patriarchal) nuclear family that now requires two incomes, and second they fill the expanding need for a highly educated professional and managerial labor force from the pool of white, middle-class women, while most people of color, the working class, and the poor continue to be excluded from these positions. We need only look at the recent statistics on medical-school graduates to see that there have been significant increases in the integration of women, with many graduating classes evenly divided between men and women, some with women in the majority. Meanwhile, "the inclusion of blacks," according to the president of the Association of American Medical Colleges, shows "a backward drift" (Robert E. Tomasson, "Goals for Racial Inclusion Elide Latest Crop of Young Doctors," *New York Times*, 1 April 1992 C12). The percentage of medical graduates who are minority students has remained quite low, around 10 percent, while the proportion of Blacks and other minorities in the population is increasing. Within this overall low figure Black women have benefited slightly from the more general integration of women and have showed a small but steady increase (502 Black women enrolled in medical schools in 1986, 621 in 1991), while the number of Black men entering has dropped (from 489 to 441 in the same period; down 23 percent since 1971). In other words, access to economic (educational) resources has not changed: it remains monopolized by the dominant class. What has changed is a shifting of the resources that the dominant class has allocated to the "other." My argument is that feminism should not be about simply shifting the allocation of resources but should seek to increase access to resources for all people: regardless of gender, race, sexuality. Feminism, in other words, needs to go beyond its own contemporary limits and include class in its struggle. This is especially the case when we look at the total economic situation of women in this country. While many middle-class women, especially white women, have been benefiting from feminist advances, the overall access of women in the United States to socioeconomic resources is declining: women are increasingly becoming impoverished, single heads of households—the *feminization of poverty* (Sidel 15)—with disproportionately higher numbers of African-American and Latina women and their children being affected.

Feminists have to ask themselves a difficult set of questions: in what way have our knowledges and practices contributed to this situation or, at the very least, hindered us from seeing the relation between (white) middle-class privilege and choice and the constrained conditions and exploitation of poor women and most women of color at home and globally. What is the relation between the historical condition of different groups of women and feminist theory and practices? Materialist critique examines these relations and demonstrates the linkages among seemingly disparate events. Feminism needs to ask itself difficult questions about how its ideas circulate; such critiques are fundamental to any social theory. *Why then do so many feminists regard critique as trashing?* Perhaps we can find some insight into the problem by returning to the Gallop, Hirsch, and Miller conversation.

It is especially telling that all of them misrecognize critique, in Nancy Miller's words, as "judgment, a negative judgment" and, even more disturbing, as an issue of power of one woman over another. For instance, Hirsch responds to Gallop's critique of her (now part of Gallop's *Around 1981*) by saying, "My response to your piece has to do with power" (Gallop, Hirsch, and Miller 357). "Reading people's work in that way puts you in a position of power . . . Your revealing things to me about the unconscious of my writing places you in a position of superior knowledge" (360). This exchange shows that what is most problematic about critique in feminism is the unproductive way it is understood and, above all, the way feminism is itself informed by the larger social contradictions of patriarchal capitalism, which foregrounds the ideology of the unique, autonomous individual in competition and conflict with others.

Second, it seems that what is really at issue here is a misrecognition of critique as criticism. For criticism is indeed that mode of reading that is based on "judgment," whether aesthetic or moral: criticism is the practice of evaluation and interpretation, in that we judge a text according to a (transhistorical) norm or standard.

But critique is not judgment. As Barbara Johnson says in her introduction to Derrida's *Dissemination*,

> It is not a set of criticisms . . . [I]t is an analysis that focuses on the grounds of that system's [or text's] possibility. The critique reads backwards from what seems natural, obvious, self-evident, or universal, in order to show that these things have their history, their reasons for being the way they are, their effects on what follows from them, and that the starting point is not a (natural) given but a (cultural) construct, usually blind to itself. (xv)

In short, critique is not judgment but explanation; its concern is to explain how what we know, what we see, is related to what we do not see, to the historical limits of our knowledge and subjectivities and to the concealed material relations of power that produce them.

The issue, here, is how we understand these limits on our knowledge.

For Gallop, Hirsch, and Miller, who are largely situated—in spite of their poststructuralist protocols of reading—in the humanist space of bourgeois ideology, limits are largely understood as being individual and personal: the result of individual inadequacies of intelligence, talent, education, or experience. Thus any critique of limits is read as a judgment of personal (in)adequacy. But in critique, limits are understood quite differently.

Here I need to distinguish two modes of critique because of their different explanations of limits. What Johnson articulates is an immanent critique, which reads the text or system in its own terms and sees its limits or blind spots—its aporia—as the result of the contradictions or self-division within the text or system itself. Deconstruction is, of course, an exemplary instance. The problem with reading solely in terms of the system itself is that it becomes an ahistorical, formalist understanding unable to explain the existence of the system and its own terms or the relation of the system to the larger social and historical series. In contrast to immanent critique, a historical materialist critique traces its genealogy through such writings of Marx as his exemplary critique of Hegel ("Critique"), his reading of Proudhon (*Poverty*), and especially his more advanced critique-al treatment of capitalism (*Grundrisse, Capital*). A historical materialist critique begins with immanent critique but refuses to confine its inquiry to the internal contradictions and differences of the text or system. Instead, it argues that the contradictions within a system are always the articulation of the larger social contradictions, specifically the struggle over gender, race, and class inequalities, which are finally situated in the contradictions of the social division of labor. Thus the aporia or blind spots in feminist theory are not simply the effects of the logical contradictions of the system (for instance, of rationality or logocentrism), as deconstructionists argue, but rather the articulation of the historical contradictions of gender relations and class conflicts in patriarchal capitalism.

In other words, the limits of feminist theory are historical—that is, they are the **effects** of the operation of the social relations of production as relayed through the dominant ideology and power relations that constrain and restrict what it is possible for us to see and know. To the extent that historical materialist critique deals with individual practices, it examines them as conjunctural moments that display the working of the larger historical forces producing knowledge. The personal is always, as far as this critique is concerned, the political and as such transsubjective: an effect of social and economic contradictions and conflicts.

Theory and Experience

Part of the current feminist unease with critique, especially among ludic feminists, is rooted in the current conflicts in theory. It has become customary among ludic postmodernists to dissociate themselves from theory: theory is seen as an act of totalizing that has become synonymous in ludic circles with totalitarianism. For instance, Judith Butler—who is, in spite of her personal disclaimers, one of the elite theorists in the U.S. knowledge industry—distances herself from theory by assuming the familiar pose of ignorance: in ludic postmodern discourses, not knowing has become following Lacan, the genuine mark of knowing. Butler states, "I do not understand the notion of 'theory,' and am hardly interested in being cast as its defender" ("Imitation" 14). Gallop prefaces her book on Lacan by not only proclaiming her "inadequacy" but also granting it a special status as "both Lacanian and feminist" (*Reading* 20). Such acts of distancing have become part of a ludic ritual among those elite theorists who command considerable power and prestige in the academy precisely because they are theorists. Nor is this ceremony of denunciation confined to ludic feminists. It is shared by such prominent nonfeminists as J. Hillis Miller, another ludic theorist who regards himself as a "local" reader—a producer of pleasure, or what he calls the "joys of reading"—and claims that he is a "theorist" almost by accident. He practices theory, as the title of his recent book indicates, only "now and then." But we should not take these ludic theorists' distancing of themselves from theory literally. This gesture is itself theoretical in that it puts in question one notion of theory—theory as explanatory critique—and favors another one: theory as play and as a playful (vigilant) reading of the play of immanent differences in the text/system. This theory-as-play aims to affirm what exists rather than transform it; it seeks to show the incoherence of the seemingly coherent and implies that an explanatory critique is the embodiment of the will to totalization. Since I argue against the notion of theory as play and argue instead for *theory as explanatory critique*, I need to say more about the role of this different kind of theory that contests the notion of theory as play.

To begin with, theory as explanatory critique is not simply a different kind of theory. *Different* is often an alibi for extending the existing social relations under the guise of the "new." The quickness with which the postmodern knowledge industry appropriates, commodifies, and incorporates different theories indicates that they are no more than local and internal readjustments of elements necessary for the continuation of existing social relations. Explanatory theory is fundamentally different from theory as play in that the latter addresses itself exclusively to cultural politics, understanding cultural politics as the theater of significations, resignification (Butler), remetaphorization (Cornell), and redescription (Rorty). In opposition to theory as play, theory as explanation goes beyond cultural politics and engages the material base of the social formation that in fact conditions cultural politics. For theory as play, culture (as the staging of conflicting chains of significations) is (semi)autonomous, while theory as explanatory critique regards culture to be always articulated by material forces.

Theory as play and theory as explanatory critique are not, as they are often treated in the contemporary academy, simply two different choices. They are contesting modes of understanding social and political arrangements and how gender, sexuality, race, and class are situated within such arrangements. In short, there are material and historical conflicts between these two views of theory. Theory as play or performance and theory as materialist explanatory critique should not just be pluralistically accepted as simply two (free) choices but rather rigorously examined so that their historicity and their roles in contemporary feminism are clearly articulated. But ludic feminism has reduced theory to theory as play and, in so doing, has displaced explanation (knowledge for social change) by resignification (which blurs the seeming transparency of cultural signs and points up the undecidability of the common sense, which is the ground for dominant identities).

Feminist theory, I believe, must be a politically transformative practice: one that not only disrupts the specific conditions and features of racist, patriarchal, and capitalist oppression but also transforms the systematic relations of exploitation that produce local oppressions. A transformative feminist theory moves toward producing nonexploitative social arrangements. At the same time, feminist theory needs to be especially self-reflexive and adept at critiquing its own historical situation and limits; at resisting the patriarchal appropriation and normalization of its oppositional logic; and at insuring that its alternative practices of knowing are used on behalf of an emancipatory agenda. While many may agree with this principle, its realization is the most difficult issue in feminist theory today. In addressing these issues in this work, I thus speak as a feminist engaged in a self-reflexive dialectical exchange with other feminists over a critique of the limits, aporias, and presuppositions, in short, the problematic of feminist theory as it struggles to end exploitation. As I will make clear in the following chapters, I am also speaking from an oppositional space within the postmodern that I call a *resistance postmodernism.*

Theory, for many feminists (cultural feminists as well as ludic feminists), is seen as masculinist, abstract, elitist, phallogocentric, and a form of instrumental reason. Above all theory is considered antithetical to women's (different) experience and thus a "betrayal of feminism," as Nina Baym puts it. This seemingly abstract theory is also considered Eurocentric and contrary to the knowledges of people of color, especially women. As Barbara Christian writes, "[P]eople of color have always theorized—but in forms quite different from the Western form of abstract logic . . . [O]ur theorizing . . . is often in narrative forms" (68). "Narration" is, of course, a denial of the possibility of a coherent explanation and an affirmation of the play of difference, contingency, and undecidability. Christian, who is often regarded to be opposed to postmodernism, poststructuralism, and other post-al theories is, in fact, their reliable ally in undermining explanation— the production of transformative knowledges. She offers a "resistance to theory" that is, in its outcome, if not in its argument, identical with Paul de Man, Judith Butler, and Hélène Cixous.

Ludic postmodern theory is, in fact, an antitheoretical theory. We need only look at Derrida's *Post Card*, Lyotard and Thebaud's *Just Gaming*, de Man's *The Resistance to Theory*, Gallop's *Thinking through the Body*, or Fish's *Doing What Comes Naturally* to see this opposition to theory (understood as a phallogocentric rationalism) and the use of such ludic strategies as the play of tropes, parody, punning, anecdote, and autobiography (what Ulmer calls "mystory" in his *Teletheory*) to deconstruct theory, its concepts and principles. This antitheoretical stance also informs ludic postmodern cultural studies as is demonstrated in the writings of Constance Penley, John Fiske, Andrew Ross, Stuart Hall, Homi Bhabha, Donna Haraway, Meaghan Morris, and others, which are programmatically collected in Grossberg, Nelson, and Treichler's anthology, *Cultural Studies*. In writing the postscript to the volume, in which she both sums up its major themes and comments on the current state of cultural studies theory, Angela McRobbie celebrates "the absence of the tyranny of theory" that has been displaced by a "speculative 'writerly' approach" (724).

But this view of theory, whether adopted by humanists (e.g. Christian), postmodernists (like Gregory Ulmer) or feminists (Judith Butler) is politically very disenabling. It substitutes the personal (playful meditation) for the political (historical explanation), and in so doing—as I will demon-

strate throughout this book—it legitimates, among other things, a pragmatic pluralism that tolerates exploitation (as one possible free choice).
Theory as play is an articulation and defense of the exploitative social order
of capitalist patriarchy in that people are encouraged to "meditate" on personal matters instead of having "principles" about (changing) the social
order. The implications of the notion of theory as play is nowhere made
more explicit than in Stanley Fish's *There's No Such Thing as Free Speech . . .
and It's a Good Thing, Too.* "I don't have any principles," he writes, "If I
believe in anything, I believe in rules of thumb." Fish's ironic tone here is
part of his "pragmatism," which accepts the world in its actually existing
order as a given. This is a world immune to the systematic knowledge that
is necessary for social transformation. In this reversible and highly opaque
world, all one can do is mend (reform) the existing social institutions
according to local rules of thumb. Like both McRobbie and Fish, Richard
Rorty is another pragmatist who regards theory to be a "writerly" practice
aimed at developing, not knowledge (since, according to him, reliable
knowledge is not obtainable) but an ironic and reversible turn of mind in
citizens *(Contingency).* Theory, according to Rorty, can only undertake a
"redescription" of the already existing world: by redescribing (through
writerly practices), theory produces new representations of the world and
these new representations are just about all one can do to modify the dominant social order. The purpose of the "resistance to theory" in McRobbie,
Fish, Rorty, and many ludic feminists, such as Donna Haraway, who have
taken similar paths in their own writings is to discourage radical social
actions aimed at reorganizing the existing socioeconomic order and instead
to accept the existing system and live in it according to pragmatic "rules of
thumb."

The resistance to theory is a resistance to a coherent understanding of
capitalism and patriarchy and, consequently, a resistance to the kinds of
knowledge of social totality that can enable us to change the actually existing world. According to these resisters to theory, we can never have access
to (an absolute) Truth—in the light of which we might rationally order our
societies. Therefore, we might as well adjust to what is pragmatically given
through the exercise of our common sense ("rules of thumb"). This antitheory theory seems, on the surface, to be progressive: it opposes the totalitarianism of reason and instead advocates reform through local communities
of resistance (rape counseling centers, prisoners' coalitions, support of bat-
tered women). But in actuality it is a postmodern fatalism that reifies the
existing world and, in so doing, protects the material interests of the pow-

erful and the propertied classes. Rape is not a local issue and has everything to do with the global socioeconomics of capitalist patriarchy: without
the transformation of those structures according to the critique-al knowledges produced by theory, rape will not be brought to an end.

In other words, antitheory theory (theory as play) is an affirmation of
the pragmatically existing world in that all one has to do is to "speculate,"
to engage in "writerly" practices of changing representations, and reform:
for pragmatists all possible social orders are equally unequal. McRobbie,
Fish, and Rorty, in the end, are simply erasing politics in favor of ethics as
care of the self. Contrary to such poststructuralist antitheory feminists as
Drucilla Cornell *(Beyond Accommodation)*, feminism cannot be simply an
ethics: feminism is a politics, and, like all politics, it needs knowledge of the
social totality in order to bring about a new social order free from the
exploitation of class, gender, sexuality, and race.

Instead of conventionally (and conveniently) dismissing theory as a
masculinist, rationalist instrumentalism that acts as an abstract metalanguage bringing a violent closure of meaning, we need to reunderstand theory as an explanation of historical intelligibility. By this I mean theory is
most effective as it is understood in resistance postmodernism: when it is
understood not in an idealist way (theory as metalanguage) but as a materialist explanatory critique of the ways in which meanings are materially
determined by the operation of relations of capital and wage labor, and
social reality is naturalized in response to the contradictions of the social
division of labor. This reunderstanding of theory enables us to acquire historical knowledge of social totality and the relations of power, profit, and
labor that render certain forms of daily practices legitimate or meaningful
and mark others as meaningless. Theory, in this sense, is a self-critical double operation: it is both the frames of intelligibility through which we make
sense of reality, and the critique-al inquiry into and contestation over these
modes of meaning making. It thus enables transformative knowledge:
practice, in other words, is inscribed in theory as articulated here. Thus theory is not simply a cognitivism but a historical site of social struggle over
how reality is represented, that is, how constructed in relation to existing
social relations of production and how it may be changed.[4] Theory, in
short, is a political practice, not simply a rationalist and ahistorical abstraction or discursive play. This means that even such a seemingly natural and
nontheoretical practice as common sense is, as Gramsci argues *(Prison
Notebooks)*, a frame of intelligibility, a theory, but one that conceals its own

constructedness and consequently represents itself as the way things naturally are.

At the core of the controversy over theory is the issue of the relation of theory and *experience*—whether the humanist notion of the experience of the moral self (as in cultural feminism and in much of the work of women of color) or the postmodern celebration of the experience of the ethical subject of pleasure, the *jouissance* of the body (as in ludic feminism).[5] The argument against theory is, with local modification, based on the notion that theory is universalizing and thus indifferent to specific, particular experiences of women and people of color. Experience, it is assumed, is self-intelligible: it is the limit text of the real. I shall argue, however, that experience is itself a highly mediated frame of understanding. While it is true that a woman, a person of color, a queer experiences oppression, this experience is by no means self-explanatory: it has to be explained in relation to other social practices. Experience, in short, only seems local; it is, like all cultural and political practices, interrelated to other practices and experiences, and as such its explanation comes from its "outside." Theory is an understanding of this outside and an explanation of experience. Theory demonstrates that the "difference" (of experience) is itself global, historical, and always already determined by the material forces of production.

The contesting theories and commonsense logic about rape demonstrate how theory operates as a frame of intelligibility for experience: how experience is not self-intelligible. In other words, rape is an *experience*, but contrary to the common sense, this experience cannot explain its own occurrence: the explanation, the way we make sense of rape, comes from "outside" experience itself. Common sense provides a "theory, a way of making sense, of rape that represents patriarchal power relations and the sexual domination of women as natural and justified by explaining rape in terms of "natural compulsion" (e.g., it is human nature or uncontrollable male need) and especially through the logic of blaming the victim ("she dressed provocatively," "she asked for it," "no means yes"). In contrast to this commonsense frame of intelligibility, which conceals its own constructedness, a number of feminist theories about rape, especially the more radical ones, engage in a self-critical double operation. They critically challenge and denaturalize these dominant theories and the way they reproduce patriarchal power relations: Catharine MacKinnon, for example, argues that "sexual abuse works as a form of terror in creating and maintaining" the "inequality between men and women" (*Feminism Unmodified*

7, 6). While MacKinnon is referring primarily to social and political inequality, historical materialist feminists, like Maria Mies, go further in their critique-al retheorizations to show the connections between (the experience of) rape and the relations of production, arguing that sexual violence is part of the systematic practices of power and coercion that enable the "superexploitation" of women's surplus labor (see esp. chaps. 2 and 5). In the second step of this double move, feminist theorists then articulate an oppositional frame of intelligibility or way of making sense of (the experience of) rape: establishing the logic of women's right to control over and determination of their own bodies ("no means no") and, more fundamentally, the need to overthrow patriarchal systems of exploitation. Each of these contesting theories explains rape in ways that enable or constrain quite different sexual, social, juridical, and political practices—from the act of rape to the terms of its legal prosecution and efforts at social change. To regard rape as an individual experience—an experience that is self-intelligible—is encouraged by mainstream feminism because it localizes rape. Rape is seen as a local accident and not as the inevitable effect of the systematic working of wage labor and capital and the way that such a system needs the superexploitation of women. Rape, however, is not an accident, nor is it simply a personal matter—although it is painfully experienced as such. Rather, rape is the effect of the global working of patriarchal capitalism. To reduce it to an individual experience and to resist theoretical explanations because theory erases the specificity of a particular rape is to accept the common sense of patriarchal capitalism itself. Capitalism has always privileged experience because the logic of experience (local and individualistic) distracts critical inquiry and transformative action away from the *system* of capital. Rape is assigned to rape crisis centers and individual counseling, on the one hand, and the court of law, on the other: rape becomes a matter between two persons and not the historically inevitable practices of power in a system that is founded upon the exploitation of the many for the benefit of the few.

Feminist theory (like any theory) is a site of social struggle. This aspect of theory becomes more clear in two recent developments. One is the (post)feminist attempt—notably by Camille Paglia and Katie Roiphe—to discredit feminist theories of sexual violence as the systematic enforcement of gender domination and inequality. Paglia, in particular, attempts to revive the dominant patriarchal naturalization of male aggression by arguing that "male pursuit is a natural activity in both human and animal species." From this she argues,

I don't feel that any changes will ever be made in this ritual pattern
. . . It's coming from the hormones . . . I am *not* supporting rape . . .
[but] women have got to realize that there are natural patterns going
on here, that men are being impelled to pursue. ("What's Wrong" 10).

She may not be "supporting rape," but she is certainly circulating a way of
making sense of male rape that feminism has by and large displaced. Katie
Roiphe contributes to the same process of relegitimating patriarchal justifi-
cations ("explanations") of rape, and, like Paglia, she does so in the name of
feminism. Her theory, however, resurrects the logic of "blame the victim"—this time by arguing that "rape-crisis feminists reinforce traditional
views about the fragility of the female body and will" ("Date" 30); this
leads to a "denial of female sexual agency that threatens to propel us backward" (68). As one letter to the editor of *New York Times Magazine*, from
Diane Welsh, President of NOW-NYC and Anne Conners, Coordinator,
Anti-Violence Committee, commented: "Katie Roiphe's article . . . is a perfect example of backlash thinking. She shifts the responsibility of men who
rape to feminists who are fighting rape."[6]

But it is not only (post)feminists who are updating and revalidating
the dominant naturalization of rape. Much more disturbing is the active
retheorization of rape itself by hegemonic institutions and agents of postmodern patriarchy. This is especially the case in the Bosnian war, in which
primarily the Serbian forces have changed the very frame of intelligibility
about rape. "Rape" has to be understood not simply in terms of male
aggression, but in relation to the entire Bosnian crisis, the latest theater in
which the social contradictions of postmodern capitalism are unfolding.
The war is not about ethnicity—ethnicity is a cultural explanation of an
economic reality. War is about access to economic resources. The Serbs
have moved from the common understanding of rape as an individualized,
"personal" act to a social redefinition and practice of rape as an *organized*
instrument of war: a deliberate policy of "ethnic cleansing," mass genocide
through repeated, systematic rapes and sexual torture followed by death or
forced impregnation of the "ethnic other." Part of the difficulty in the
struggle against these sexual atrocities are the conflicts over the frames of
intelligibility used to define these experiences. This is especially a problem
for the women's groups organizing protests and legal actions against the
mass rapes, as a writer for the *Village Voice* discovered when she reported
on these activities. Commenting on a program by MADRE, an internationalist women's organization, to bring together women from Croatia, Serbia,

and Bosnia with women from other countries to "deliver a simple message: *Rape happens in every war, and must be recognized as a violation of women's human rights,* she says, "I was quickly introduced to the ways in which this line was not exactly 'arguable,' but misperceivable" (Carr 25). In short, there are a number of conflicting positions based on contesting frames of intelligibility. One of the main questions, as Carr puts it, "is this about women or is this about ethnicity" (25)? Opposing theories are also held by two of the feminists heading lawsuits being brought "against Radovan Karadzic on behalf of women raped during ethnic cleansing in Bosnia-Herzegovina" (Carr 26): Rhonda Copelon, of the International Women's Human Rights Clinic, and Catherine MacKinnon. Copelon opposes efforts "to separate ethnic-cleansing rape and 'normal' rape," viewing it as a "male strategy" that "normalizes" rape (26). In contrast, MacKinnon distinguishes "genocidal rapes" from "everyday rape," and, according to Carr, she "characterizes this particular sexual violence as 'misogyny liberated by xenophobia,' part of 'an ethnic war of aggression being misrepresented as a civil war among equal aggressors'" (29). MacKinnon goes further and calls for us to "think about this war as being to everyday rape what the Holocaust was to everyday anti-Semitism" (29). In short, there is conflict over how to define (theorize) the Serbian crimes: are there "two crimes, rape and genocide," as Copelon contends, or are these rapes acts of genocide because of the scale, organization, and planning of the rapes "with extermination as its goal," as MacKinnon maintains (29)?[7] The experience of the rapes and the struggle to oppose them are thus not self-evident or auto-intelligible; rather, our understanding—both of the experiences and the grounds for political struggle—depends on the theories by which we make sense of the material conditions and historical determinates of these realities.

Theory, then, is not opposed to experience but is in a dialectical relation with it: theory historicizes experience and displays the social relations that have enabled it to be experienced as experience. Such a knowledge prevents us from essentializing experience and makes it possible to produce new experiences by transforming the dominant social relations.

The pressing issue for feminism is not to reject theory (knowledge) but first to *critique* how specific theories are produced and used, in the interests of what labor-power relations, and second to engage in the struggle to produce new opposing theories (contesting knowledges) to participate in the struggle over opposing ways of constructing and changing the world by producing transformative knowledges that can serve as guidelines for practice. This book undertakes such a critique of (ludic) postmodern feminism and engages in the contestation over theory: it seeks to contribute to the feminist and socialist efforts to produce opposing knowledges as means for social change.

My work is thus concerned with the class and race politics of feminism and postmodern theory: not so much with these issues as objects of study or as themes in feminism but with the relation of specific theories to the social inequalities of class, race, gender, and nationalities. I focus in this book on critiquing the dominant "new" theories in feminism and postmodernism, because these are given a special privilege and authority within the knowledge industry. They are not only widely validated and disseminated but also carry an inordinate institutional influence in determining which knowledges will be central and which will be marginalized. The impact of ludic theories is considerable: as the dominant knowledges produced and commodified in the West, they participate in the colonization of indigenous knowledges globally and are often deployed to marginalize more revolutionary knowledges, especially Marxism. Such critiques, as I am proposing here, are thus all the more important. For it is only through historical materialist critiques that it becomes possible to understand why class and class analysis are so violently erased from the range of legitimate knowledges in contemporary feminist theory and what is the logic through which, for example, sexuality as an "excess"ive knowledge is privileged over gender in the ludic analytics and what are the consequences of these theoretical displacements.

One of the pressing questions, then, is: why has so much feminist and postmodern theory—from poststructuralism and Foucauldian discourse theory to post-Marxism and "queer" theory—been preoccupied with disclaiming and distancing itself from issues of economics, labor, production, and exploitation, dismissing these issues as "oppression studies" or "economic reductionism"? Feminist studies of economics, labor, and class, of course, continue but are almost entirely confined along disciplinary lines. Feminist scholars in economics, sociology, labor studies, and other social sciences tend to undertake circumscribed studies of these issues within the boundaries of their own field. These inquiries are then largely relegated to the terrain of specialist knowledges and excluded from any integrated transdisciplinary inquiry into gender and sexuality, thus marginalizing these issues in feminist theory itself. The question, as I stated at the beginning of this book, is why feminist theory has largely abandoned the problems of labor and exploitation and ignored their relation to the concepts of gender, sexuality, difference, desire, and subjectivity. Why, in short, has feminism suppressed the revolutionary knowledges of historical materialism? I am writing to reclaim historical materialism for feminism in postmodernity and to contribute to the construction of a revolutionary theory and praxis for third-wave feminism—a new red feminism.

Materialism versus Matterism

But what does materialism, particularly historical materialism, mean for feminism? While ludic feminists have tried to bury "objective reality" beneath the priority of discourse and significations, they are, nonetheless, feeling (however indirectly) its pressures: the polarization of wealth, feminization of labor, and impoverishment of women in the world are historical processes whose objectivity cannot be denied. The issue of materialism—of a reality independent from the consciousness of the subject and outside language and other media—is thus gaining a new urgency for feminists after poststructuralism. Many are beginning to ask whether there is "an outside to discourse," as Judith Butler does in her *Bodies That Matter*, and attempt to articulate this material reality. The issue is especially pressing for Anglo-American socialist feminists, who by and large have substituted Foucault for Marx, discourse for ideology, and joined other poststructuralist feminists in embracing a cultural or discursive materialism while rejecting any positive knowledge (knowledge free from the consciousness of the subject and independent from language) as positivism. Perhaps the best-known socialist feminist to make this shift recently is Michèle Barrett, who announces in the preface to her *The Politics of Truth: From Marx to Foucault* that she is moving from Marx's *"economics of untruth"*—"being," as she says, "Marxism's account of ideology, used to show 'the relation between what goes on in people's heads and their place in the conditions of production'"—to Foucault's *"politics of truth*, being his own approach to the relationships between knowledge, discourse, truth and power." In so doing, she embraces "a more general post-Marxism" (vii).

My discussion of the conflicting theories of materialism and their consequences forms an overture of theoretical issues and political concerns that I will be returning to throughout this book. The current retheorization of materialism in postmodern feminism follows two related paths. The first is a reunderstanding of materialist feminism coming out of the Marxist tradition. But this is itself a contradictory and divided site—involving a conflict between those feminists reclaiming historical materialism and those who, following post-Marxism, marginalize it as positivism. These post-Marxist feminists largely subscribe to the continued dominance of post-structuralist knowledges and are caught in the contradictions between the political necessity of materialism and its displacement by the ludic priority of discourse. They end up substituting discursive determinism for an eco-nomic determinism, as Barrett does in *The Politics of Truth*. The second mode is non-Marxist and is developed entirely out of feminist encounters with poststructuralist theories (especially those of Derrida, Foucault, and Lacan) and rearticulates materialism as a mode of idealism, what I call *mat-terism*: the matter of the body, the matter of sexuality, the matter of race, and, above all the matter of language.

In its engagement with materialism, ludic postmodern feminism has reached a political crisis. But it attempts to represent and deal with this cri-sis as an exclusively epistemological question—as if epistemology itself is not partisan. We, therefore, need to examine some of the reasons why mate-rialism—after the serious epistemological and political challenges from poststructuralism, post-Marxism, post-Heisenbergian physics and New Historicism—continues to remain a fundamental issue in feminism and how ludic feminism (as the avant-garde of discursivist social theory) has theorized materialism in the postmodern moment.

As long as ludic feminism continues to address the question of women—and does not simply collapse into a merely philosophical enter-prise and occupy itself with logical and epistemological arguments—that is, as long as it follows the feminist imperative of praxis, ludic feminism (unlike other varieties of postmodern discourse) is pulled into debates over the actual conditions of the lives of women. But no serious engagement with these conditions can evade materialism as simply a question of epis-temology. Ludic feminism is thus constantly drawn into debates and coun-terdebates over questions raised by materialism and its epistemological other—idealism. Some ludic feminists, however, have tried to blur the problem of materialism and prevent a full critique of the issues involved. Ironically, this "new" debate replays an old and familiar strategy described by Lenin nearly a century ago in his critique of idealism (*Materialism* 196–255). Describing the writings of the Machians, Lenin says that one thread that runs through their texts is their claim that they have "risen above" materialism and idealism and "have transcended this 'obsolete' antithesis." This gesture, Lenin writes, is no more than an ideological alibi because in their actual practices they "are continually sliding into idealism and are conducting a steady and incessant struggle against materialism" (354). Like Machians, ludic feminists declare that the debate over idealism and materialism is an outdated binary and, in the ecumenical spirit of postmodernist eclecticism (which underwrites liberal pluralism), provide a reconciliation of the two. Butler, for instance, offers her theory of performativity to, in effect, "think through" the binary of what is "characterized as the linguistic idealism of poststructuralism" and a "materiality outside of language" (*Bodies* 27–31). Similarly, Cornell offers her notion of "remetaphorization" and the "performative power of language" as a way to avoid "pit[ting] 'materialist' feminism against feminine writing" (*Beyond Accommodation* 3). However, as Lenin writes, any such hybrid project is an alibi for the legitimization of idealism (350), as I will demonstrate in the following chapters.

The political and epistemological crisis that materialism has produced in ludic feminism has to do with its class politics. Ludic feminism becomes—in its *effects*, if not in its intentions—a theory that inscribes the class interests of what bourgeois sociology calls the upper middle class. Ludic feminism does not acknowledge the materiality of the regime of wage labor and capital. It does not acknowledge the existence of a historical series independent from the consciousness of the subject and autonomous from textuality. Such a recognition would lead to the further acknowledgment of the materiality of the social contradictions brought about by the social relations of production founded upon the priority of private property. Ludic feminism cannot accept a social theory that finds private property—the congealed surplus labor of others—to be the cause of social inequalities that can be remedied only through revolution. Ludic feminism is, in *effect*, a theory for property holders. Nor can ludic feminism simply revert to an essentialist position and posit the consciousness of the subject as the source of social reality. Such a move would go against the general poststructuralist constructivism and consequently would lead to, among other things, a reinscription of logocentrism and the phallocentrism that underlies it. Ludic feminism therefore needs to invent a form of materialism that gestures to a world not directly present to the consciousness of the subject (as classic poststructuralism has done), but not entirely constructed in the medium of knowing (language) either. It has simply become "unethical" to think of such social oppressions as sexism, racism, and homophobia as purely matters of language and discourse. Ludic feminism, in other words, is beginning to learn the lesson of Engels's *Anti-Dühring:*

the fact that we understand reality through language does not mean that
reality is made by language.

The dilemma of ludic feminism in theorizing materialism is a familiar
one. In his interrogation of Berkeley, Lenin points to this dilemma that runs
through all forms of idealism: the epistemological unwillingness to make
distinctions between ideas and things (*Materialism* 130–300), which is, of
course, brought about by class politics. Ludic feminism, like all forms of
upper-middle-class (idealist) philosophy, must hold on to ideas since it is
by the agency of ideas that this class (as privileged mental workers)
acquires its social privileges. Although posed as an epistemological question, the dilemma is finally a class question: how not to deny the world outside the consciousness of the subject but not to make the world the material cause of social practices either. Ludic feminism, like Berkeleyan
idealism, cannot afford to explain things by the relations of production and
labor. This then is the dilemma of ludic feminism: the denial of materialism
leads ludic feminism to a form of idealism that discredits any claims it
might have to the struggle for social change; accepting materialism, on the
other hand, implicates its own ludic practices in the practices of patriarchal
capitalism—the practices that have produced gender inequalities as differences that can be deployed to increase the rate of profit. This dilemma has
lead feminism to an intolerable political crisis: a crisis that is, in fact, so
acute it has raised questions about the viability of feminism as a theory and
practice itself.

Given its class politics, ludic feminism has attempted to overcome this
political and epistemological crisis by theorizing materialism in a way that
reconciles its contradictory interests. On the one hand, it is primarily a theory of upper-middle-class Euroamerican women, yet, on the other hand, it
claims to be interested in social change for all women. These solutions have
taken two historically determined forms.

In the early phases of its romance with poststructuralism—roughly
from the early 1970s (as in the writings of Hélène Cixous and Julia Kristeva) to the mid-1980s (as in such early writings of Teresa de Lauretis as
Alice Doesn't)—ludic feminism understood materialism mostly as a matter
of language. This idea of the material as the matter of language is perhaps
most comprehensively outlined in a book published at the end of this
phase of ludic materialism, namely, *Textualizing the Feminine,* by Shari Benstock (1991). Benstock's conventional reading of what I am calling ludic
feminism does not directly engage the question of materialism, but her

book is basically an account of the emergence (and decline) of the notion of (mostly Derridean-Lacanian) textuality in contemporary feminism. Such feminists as Mary Daly, who are not in any conventional sense poststructuralists, also have a ludic understanding of materialism as a matter of language, as is clear from such works as *Gyn/Ecology*.

In theorizing materialism as a matter of language, ludic feminism essentially deployed the concept of textuality in Derrida (for example in *Grammatology*, esp. 141–64), the idea of the sign in Lacan (*Ecrits*, particularly 30–113, 146–78), and also the notion of language as discourse in Foucault (*Archeology*, esp. 40–49, and "The Discourse on Language" 215–37). For Foucault discourse has an "exteriority of its own ("Politics" 60); it is a reality in its own right and not simply a reflection of an independent reality outside it. In his elaboration on this view of discourse, Ernesto Laclau goes so far as to say that "The discursive is not, therefore, being conceived as a level nor even as a dimension of the social, but rather as being co-extensive with the social as such" ("Populist" 87). Understanding materialism as a matter of language has led ludic feminism to rethink politics itself. If the matter of social reality is language, then changes in this reality can best be brought about by changing the constituents of that reality— namely, signs. Therefore, politics as collective action for emancipation is abandoned, and politics as intervention in discursive representation is adopted as a truly progressive politics. Since language always works in specific contexts, the new progressive ludic politics was also deemed to be always local and antiglobal. From such a perspective, emancipation itself is seen as a metaphysical metanarrative (e.g., Lyotard, *Postmodern Condition*; Butler, "Poststructuralism"), and social change becomes almost entirely a matter of superstructural change, that is, change in significations. Political economy, in short, is displaced by an economy of signs.

With minor local modifications in the works of various ludic feminists, this notion of materialism is maintained in ludic theory from the early 1970s to the mid-1980s. However, from the mid-to-late 1980s (around the time of publication of Jane Gallop's *Thinking through the Body* in 1988) the idea of materialism as solely a matter of language loses its grip on ludic theory. After the publication of Paul de Man's *Wartime Journalism*—when questions of ethics suddenly become foregrounded in contemporary high theory—and under the increasing pressures from New Historicism, ludic feminism has made new attempts to rearticulate materialism in a less discursive manner. The pressures on reunderstanding materialism as a nondiscursive force have not been entirely internal to theory. At the end of the 1980s, as a result of conservative social policies in the United States and Europe (for example, new tax laws), a massive transfer of wealth from the working class to the upper classes has taken place. Moreover, the working of postmodern capitalism has literally affected everyday life in U.S. and European cities (homelessness, crime in neighborhoods devastated by unemployment, abandoned children . . .). In the face of such conditions, the idea of progressive politics as simply a question of changing representations and problematizing the obvious meanings in culture has become too hollow to be convincing. As part of the emergence of ethics in critical theory and the decline of high theory itself, ludic feminism has been rethinking its own understanding of materialism. In the 1990s materialism is no longer simply the matter of language; rather, it has become the resisting matter of the nondiscursive, or as Diana Fuss puts it in her *Essentially Speaking*, "the body as matter" (52). The main theorists of this new version of materialism are writers such as Judith Butler and Elizabeth Grosz. (Increasingly the notion of materialism deployed by Eve Sedgwick and other queer theorists is to a very large extent influenced by Butler.) The idea of the nondiscursive ("the real or primary relations") is, of course, available even in the early work of Foucault himself (*Archeology*, 45–46, 68–69). Butler, whose recent writings are increasingly marked by her engagement with something called the non/extradiscursive is, of course, a close reader of Foucault. (Butler's doctoral dissertation, later published as *Subjects of Desire*, it is helpful to keep in mind, is focused, in part, on Foucault.)

What is of great importance in any theory of materialism is the relation of the material to the nonmaterial. In his earlier works such as *Madness and Civilization*, Foucault had posited a more causal relationship between the discursive and nondiscursive. The innovation in *Archeology* and in the writings that followed is that causal explanation (in fact any explanation) is dismissed as a modernist search for origin. In the writings after *Archeology*, the discursive and the nondiscursive exist side by side without any necessary relation between them. The Marxist principle that the extradiscursive explains the discursive ("It is not the consciousness of men that determines their existence, but their social existence that determines their consciousness" [Marx, *Contribution* 21]) is abandoned in favor of indeterminacy. In fact, the indeterminateness of the relation between the discursive and nondiscursive is central to the idea of the material in ludic feminism. Through indeterminacy, ludic feminism—like all idealist theory—argues *always framed in terms of class* for the freedom of agency and proposes a theory of the social in which the bourgeois subject is still the central figure. The subject in ludic feminism does not, of course, always appear in its traditional form. However, it is commonly affirmed through a trope or a practice, such as the practice of performance in Butler: it is, for example, impossible to think of a performance—no matter how performative—without a performer. It is, therefore, important to say here that Foucault and ludic feminism ostensibly reject any causal explanation in order to acquire the freedom of the agent but in actuality the only determinism that they are opposing is the determinism of the material (labor, class, and the relations of production). In spite of their formal objections to explanation and causality, they, in fact, establish a causal relation in their theories between the discursive and nondiscursive in which the Marxist theory of the social is reversed. In ludic theory it is the discursive that silently explains the nondiscursive. Dreyfus and Rabinow (hardly opponents of Foucault!) put it this way: "Although what gets said depends on something other than itself, discourse dictates the terms of this dependence" (64). In other words, not only is discourse autonomous, it is also determining: it organizes the nondiscursive. In short, the nondiscursive is more of a formal(ist) gesture toward an "outside" that might be regarded as material. The decidability/undecidability of the relation between the discursive and nondiscursive—and not the mere acknowledgment (as in both Foucault and ludic feminism) that there is an extradiscursive—is the central issue in theorizing materialism. The result of this ludic positing of a relation of indeterminacy is a materialism that does not act materially; it does not determine anything: it is an inert mass. For the poststructuralist feminist, such as Butler, Fuss, or Cornell, this nondeterminate relation is what makes the theory of the nondiscursive in postmodern feminism "progressive" and nonreductionist. However, it is, as I will show in the following chapters, a very conservative understanding of the nondiscursive and its relation to the discursive. The indeterminacy that it posits as a mark of resistance and freedom is, in actuality, a legitimization of the class politics of an upper-middle-class Euroamerican feminism obsessed with the freedom of the entrepreneurial subject and as such privileges the inventiveness of the sovereign subject—in the form of what Butler calls "citationality," Cornell calls "remetaphorization," and more generally is understood as creativity, agency—over the collective social relations of production. This individuality is materialized in the uniqueness and irreplaceability of each body.

The nondiscursive for ludic feminists in the 1990s, thus, becomes more and more a question of not simply that which exists outside the discursive but as that entity which is resistant to the discursive—and the body is put forth as the prime site for this resistance. What I have said so far about the history and theory of materialism in recent feminist theory should not conveniently be read to mean that, for example, no feminist theorist before the mid-to-late 1980s talked about materialism as a matter of the body or that no feminist theorists, at the present time, regard materialism to be a matter of language. My point is that, at the present time, the notion of materialism as language is, to use Raymond Williams's terms, a "residual" concept (writers such as Barbara Johnson, who have shown an interest in feminism in their more recent writings, for example, still regard materialism to be a matter of language). The idea of materialism as a matter of body—as, in short, a force resisting the discursive—is an "emergent" theory. We see the effort to bring these two theoretical tendencies together in the work, for example, of Judith Butler.

In his move from the project of archaeology (questions of language and knowledge) to genealogy (issues of power and practice), Foucault has concluded that the only possibility of social change is through an entity that can resist the all-inclusive and all-encompassing regime of the dominant episteme that he himself had so thoroughly analyzed in *The Order of Things*. Since the episteme defines and controls all that is intelligible, to move beyond its regime one has to appeal to an entity that is nonthinking and nonintelligible and has the power to resist the episteme. This entity, for Foucault, is the body, and the power of the body is acquired through its relentless seeking of purposeless pleasure: pleasure not as the reward for performing the task of reproduction. As Foucault elaborated in his later works, such as *History of Sexuality* and *Discipline and Punish*, the body has its own materiality which enables it to exceed and escape discourse and its associated regimes of power-knowledge. This, of course, does not mean that the body is not conditioned, inscribed, and molded by discourse. However, it does mean that power-knowledge never succeeds in completely overcoming the body: culturalization is never total and the body always exceeds the power-knowledge that attempts to completely control it. This exceeding is possible partly because of the internal conflicts and contradictions among the various discourses that attempt to control the body.

The notion of the body as a resisting site in Foucault, however, is a highly political one and is devised in part to inscribe a bourgeois ludic materialism (of pleasure) in place of historical materialism. Foucault himself is quite clear on this point. In his "Body/Power," Foucault states that

The emergence of the problem of the body and its growing urgency have come about through the unfolding of a political struggle. Whether this is a revolutionary struggle, I don't know. One can say that what has happened since 1968, and arguably what made 1968 possible, is something profoundly anti-Marxist. How can European revolutionary movements free themselves from the 'Marx effect' . . . This was the direction of the questions posed by '68. In this calling in question of the equation: Marxism = the revolutionary process, an equation that constituted a kind of dogma, the importance given to the body is one of the important, if not essential elements. (*Power/Knowledge* 57)

The politics of Foucault's theorizing the body as a site of ludic resistance materialism becomes even more clear when he says, "I wonder whether, before one poses the question of ideology, it wouldn't be more materialist to study first the question of the body and the effects of power on it" (58). The materialism of the body in Foucault, then, is specifically designed to oppose collective revolutionary praxis by substituting individual regimes of purposeless pleasure—pleasure as a mode of the Kantian sublime, a pleasure that is an excess of all systems of representation and an escape from discourse and all social meanings. Social meanings—it is assumed— are all ideological, and the true freedom of the subject is attained by transcending ideology: pleasure deconstructs ideology (the preordained obviousness upon which the metanarratives of a society are founded) and arrives at surprising encounters that can only be called novel experiences (Foucault's formal opposition to "experience" notwithstanding).

This legacy of Foucauldian inferential materialism has dominated the ludic feminist notion of the nondiscursive and the material. Materialism in ludic feminism (as in Berkeley and other idealist philosophers) is, in fact, more a theological category than a materialist one. It is a form of what Lenin in his critique of Berkeley called "objective idealism" (*Materialism* 23). The masquerading of this objective idealism—or what could, in the context of Lenin's discussion of Berkeley, be called spiritual materialism— as materialism in ludic feminism has not escaped the attention of ludic feminists themselves. Kathryn Bond Stockton, herself a poststructuralist feminist theologian, describes the prevailing mode of materialism in ludic feminism in this way:

I mean materialism in its strongest sense: the material onto which we map our constructions, "matter on its own terms" that might resist or pressure our constructions, or prove independent of them altogether. This materialism is the nondiscursive something poststructuralist feminists now want to embrace, the extradiscursive something they confess necessarily eludes them. (131)

Unlike historical materialism, which foregrounds the historical praxis of the materiality of labor, materialism, for the ludic feminist in the 1990s, is not an actual historical praxis that determines other practices; rather, it is a purely inferential entity. It is, in fact, the consciousness of the subject that creates (invents) this ludic matter. Any understanding of matter as a positive entity (labor) is dismissed in ludic feminism as vulgar determinism or positivism. The matter of ludic feminism, in short, is a nondetermining matter that depends on the subject. As such, it reinscribes traditional Euroamerican idealism—this time represented as postmodern (nonpositivist) materialism—to cover up the contradictions and crisis of patriarchal capitalism. Materialism becomes (through such practices as "performance") that which exceeds the existing systems of representation—an escape from socially constructed meanings. In ludic feminism, then, materialism (as a resisting matter) is an invention. The seemingly antitranscendental element that materialism is supposed to bring to bear upon social analysis for ludic feminists, as Stockton herself realizes, "only masks their deep dependence" upon "mystic unfathomable Visibilities" (132). Ludic spiritual materialism, in Stockton's words, "stands as a God that might be approached through fictions and faith but never glimpsed naked" (131). Stockton's analysis is a conservative and local one: she simply observes the striking similarities that exist between spiritual materialism in ludic feminism and Victorian theological thought. In so doing, she blocks a more global understanding of ludic materialism: ludic materialism is an outcome of the contradictions of the social divisions of labor in class society. Spiritual materialism is, in short, a strategy for managing the crisis of class relations.

Materialism, in other words, is invented in ludic discourses to bring back transcendentalism in a more postmodern and thus convincing rhetoric. I have already suggested that the trope of invention and theories of invention are introduced in contemporary theory as a means to overcome the impasse of constructivism. Constructivism effectively combated humanism along with humanist and essentialist notions of the subject, but it also left the subject and subjectivity too determinate: upper-middle-class ludic theorists have not been able to accept any theory that circumscribes the freedom of the subject (of capital). However, what is commonly represented, under the guise of invention, as materialism in ludic feminism, is merely a reinvention of the very familiar technocratic imagination so valorized in capitalism: materialism as *technoludism*. The most well-known example of technoludism—that is, the conjuncture of technocratic fancy, inventionism, and spiritual materialism—is Donna Haraway's "Cyborg Manifesto," which has become for many the manifesto of new, postsocialist ludic materialism. I will extensively discuss Haraway's cyborgian materialism in the next chapter, but, for now, an apt commentary on the writings of Haraway and other feminist technotheorists is provided by Marx and Engels. In their critique of idealist philosophers, Marx and Engels called them "industrialists of philosophy" who live on "absolute spirit" (Marx and Engels, *German Ideology* 27). This description remains valid for (techno)ludic feminists today. It is necessary to recall that Haraway's essay ends with what Stockton calls the trope of "Christian Pentecost" (138) as Haraway claims that "Cyborg imagery . . . is a dream not of a common language, but of a powerful infidel heteroglossia . . . a feminist speaking in tongues" (*Simians* 181). This spiritual materialism—this ludic matterism in its various forms from cyborgian technoludism to Butlerian citationality— is now the dominant theory of materialism in the postmodern knowledge industry. It is a materialism that does not determine the nonmaterial but is, in fact, determined by the consciousness of the subject that infers it and thus constitutes it. Ludic materialism, then, whether perceived as the matter of sign/textuality or as the matter of the body, is an invention to overcome the determinism of social constructionism: it is a device to return the freedom of the subject and the contingency and nonnecessity of the social with a newly legitimated force to the entrepreneur and patriarchal capitalism.

Materialism, however, is neither a matter of language (discourse/textuality) nor an ahistorical, inert, resisting mass whose existence can be inferred by "faith or fiction," by performativity, resignifications, or other ludic rituals. In its most radical rendering, ludic postmodern materialism leads to a form of Feuerbachian materialism: "As far as Feuerbach is a materialist he does not deal with history, and as far as he considers history he is not a materialist" (Marx and Engels, *German Ideology* 41). Materialism is not a matter of inference. It is a *praxis*: the praxis of labor through which humans act "upon external nature" and change it, and in this way simultaneously change themselves (Marx, *Capital* 284). As a praxis, it is historical, and as labor, it is conflictually structured between the owners of the means of production and those who have nothing but their own labor power to sell. Materialism, in short, is a historical praxis and a structure of conflicts that determines other practices. Unlike the Foucauldian and ludic nondiscursive, it does not simply exist side by side with the discursive: it make the *material* discursive possible; it explains the discursive. Explanation is, of course, the very thing that Foucault's theory of the autonomy of discourse is designed to erase. For Foucault all explanations (the why) are ideological: only description (the how) of discourse is a legitimate form of knowledge. Materialism in sum is not an inert resistance to discourse, which has to be inferred by fictions and faith. Instead materialism is (as Marx meticulously describes it in *Capital* 340–416) what confronts the subject of labor in "the working day": the working day is the site in which the material and historical process of extracting surplus labor from the worker by the capitalist takes place.

In the previous pages, I have offered a rather dense outline of the theories of materialism in contemporary feminism. Here I would like to return to a few of these points and make some of the assumptions and effects of these theories more explicit. Theories that approach materialism as a matter of language, as discourse, base their argument on the assumption that discourse or textuality has an opacity and density of its own, a physicality, that makes language mean not simply by the intention of the author and speaker but by its own autonomous and immanent laws of signification. *lang. + meaning* This understanding of materialism is transhistorical: it refers mostly to the material in the sense of inert matter, medium or thingness and is, in short, a form of matterism rather than materialism. Or as Marx and Engels say in the "Theses on Feuerbach," "The chief defect of all previous materialism"—and we can add poststructuralist materialism to the list—"is that the things *[Gegenstand]*, reality, sensuousness, are conceived only in the form of the *object*, or of *contemplation*, but not as *human sensuous activity, practice*, not subjectively" (Theses 6). And "human sensuous activity" is above all, for Marx, labor: the way people "*produce* their means of subsistence" and thus "are indirectly producing their material life" (*German Ideology* 31).

It is, then, especially surprising to see a socialist feminist like Michèle Barrett define materialism in Marxist thought as "the doctrine seeing consciousness as dependent on matter" without realizing that matter in Marxism is not inert mass but the praxis of labor and the contradictions and class conflicts in which it is always involved. Barret goes on to pose the poststructuralist debate over materialism as one between "words and things," "matter" and "meaning" ("Words" 202, 201). However, words and things, to use her terms, are not finished ahistorical entities: they are the product of the social relations of production. To pose the question the way Barrett does is to erase the dialectical project of Marxism and to occlude the structure of conflicts in capitalism. Historical materialism is an explanation of these conflicts. Barrett's misreading is symptomatic of a more serious problem over the issue of materialism within Marxist and socialist feminism. This is fundamentally the problem of the place of the relations of production in feminist theory and political practice. It is the question of whether feminist knowledge should give priority to the way people "produce their means of subsistence" (labor)—to the material reality and historical struggles of the relations of production—or whether, as Seyla Benhabib and Drucilla Cornell argue, "[T]he confrontation between twentieth-century Marxism and feminist thought requires nothing less than a paradigm shift . . . the 'displacement of the paradigm of production'" (1). This is not simply a debate among materialist feminists. The "displacement of the paradigm of production" by a majority of postmodern, Anglo-American socialist feminists has significantly contributed to the occlusion of the economic and suppression of the problem of exploitation in most other feminist theories and consequently in contemporary social theory in general. It has produced a ludic socialist feminism *without* Marxism, turning it into a general left liberalism, and has participated in the ludic substitution of a discursive politics of individual, libidinal liberation for a revolutionary politics of collective socioeconomic transformation.

Why should this displacement matter? The erasure of Marxism from feminism and ludic postmodern knowledges has become so pervasive that the importance of these issues has been largely suppressed, and the question itself can no longer even be asked without requiring extensive explanation. It matters because, as Marx and Engels say, "the free development of each is the condition for the free development of all" (*Communist Manifesto* 75), and there can be no "free development" unless the fundamental *needs* of each person are met: unless production fulfills needs instead of making profits (Marx, *Gotha Program* 10). Making profits, in short, is the denial of the needs of the many and the legitimization of the desires of the few. As a revolutionary (not a post-al) socialist feminist, Nellie Wong argues,

> Without overthrowing the economic system of capitalism, as socialists and communists organize to do, we cannot liberate women *and* everybody else who is also oppressed.
>
> Socialist feminism is our bridge to freedom. . . . Feminism, the strug-

gle for women's equal rights, is inseparable from socialism—but not identical to socialism. Socialism is an economic system which reorganizes production, redistributes wealth, and redefines state power so that the exploiters are expropriated and workers gain hegemony. ("Socialist Feminism" 290)

A revolutionary socialist feminism is based on historical materialism. It insists that the material is fundamentally tied to the economic sphere and to the relations of production, which have a historically necessary connection to all other social-cultural relations. The material, in other words, contrary to ludic theory, does not simply exist autonomously as a resisting mass, side by side with autonomous discourse. Materialism, as Engels puts it, means that "the degree of economic development" in a society "form[s] the foundation upon which the state institutions, . . . the art and even the religious ideas . . . have been evolved, and in the light of which these things must therefore be explained instead of *vice versa*" ("Funeral" 39). It is—to repeat what is so violently erased in idealist theory—therefore, not "the consciousness of men that determines their existence, but their social existence that determines their consciousness" (Marx, *Contribution* 21). In short, Marx and Engels argue that "the nature of individuals thus depends on the material conditions determining their production"—"both with *what* they produce and with *how* they produce" (*German Ideology* 42).

For feminism this means that issues about the "nature of individuals"—gender, sexuality, pleasure, desire, needs—cannot be separated from the conditions producing individuals: not just the discursive and ideological conditions but most important the *material* conditions, the relations of production, that shape discourses and ideologies. Thus the struggle to end the exploitation and oppression of all women, and in particular of people of color, lesbians, and gays, within the metropole as well as the periphery, is not simply a matter of discursive or semiotic liberation or a question of the resisting "matter of the body," but a global social relation: it thus requires the transformation of the material conditions—the relations of production—producing these forms of oppression.

Historical materialism thus means the primacy of women's and men's productive and reproductive practices—their labor processes—in the articulation and development of human history and in the construction of their own subjectivities. As Marx argues in *Capital*, through labor the subject "acts upon" external nature and changes it, and in this way the laborer simultaneously changes her or his own nature (283). Such a view of materialism also understands "reality" to be a historically objective process: reality exists outside the consciousness of humans. Ideas do not have an autonomous existence, and thus reality is not merely a matter of desire of the body, or the operation of language (or, on the other hand, of the "thing-ness" of things). This does not mean that reality, as we have access to it, as we make sense of it, is not mediated by signifying practices. But the empir-ical fact that reality is mediated by language in no way means, as Engels and others have argued, that it is produced by language. Social relations and practices are, in other words, prior to signification and are objective. The subjugation of women, then, is an objective historical reality: it is not simply a matter of representation by self-legitimating discourses. The extraction of surplus labor is an objective social reality in class societies, and all social differences are produced by it, whether directly or through various mediations. Transformative politics depends on such a view of reality because if there is no objective reality, there will be little ground on which to act in order to change existing social relations. Transformative politics, in other words, does not simply redescribe the existing social world through different discourses as does ludic politics (e.g. see Rorty, *Contingency* 44–69) but rather acts to change the "real" social, economic—the *material*—conditions of the relations of production exploiting women and determining our lives.

The Reduction to Discourse

It is by now commonplace among ludic postmodernists and feminists, including many socialist feminists, to dismiss the insistence on relations of production as economic reductionism and to discredit the concept of any determination of the superstructure (e.g., the cultural, ideological, repre-sentational, political, judicial) by the economic base. This is, for instance, the core argument *against* historical or dialectical materialism and *for* cul-tural materialism in Donna Landry and Gerald MacLean's *Materialist Fem-inisms* (e.g., 61–62). It is necessary to discuss this book at some length since it articulates many of the questions I have raised in this chapter—the prob-lem of feminism, critique, and materialism—in direct opposition to my own argument. A critique of their book, therefore, will provide a more open contestation between my argument and that of ludic feminism. Landry and MacLean's book attempts "to present a history of the debates between Marxist and feminist social and cultural theorists in the 1960s,

1970s and early 1980s, primarily in Britain and the United States, and to analyze what has happened to transform those debates in recent years" (ix). But as deconstructionists they are quite ambivalent about the very project of writing a history and end up with what they themselves describe as a "schematic and inconsistent" "chronological narrative." *Materialist Feminisms* is especially representative of the discursive, post-Marxist turn in socialist feminism and demonstrates some of the limitations of this ludic mode.

They begin their book by saying that "this is a book about feminism and Marxism written when many people are proclaiming the end of socialism and the end of feminism. . . . We find these claims to be both premature and misleading" (vii). However, the authors are deeply invested in poststructuralism, especially deconstruction, as the ground of their knowledges, and this leads them to turn Marxism into a *textuality* that they try to deconstruct. In fact, the book expends considerable energy trying to displace and erase Marxism altogether from materialism and from feminism. Thus, while the book begins by treating Marxist, socialist, and materialist feminisms as nearly synonymous, it concludes by saying: "Need materialism be only an alias for Marxism? We hope that by now the distinction between Marxist feminism and materialist feminism is clear" (229). But in writing a materialist feminism *without Marxism*, the book offers little more than a left-liberal, poststructuralist "identity politics of undone identities."

The core of Landry and MacLean's notion of materialism is an adaptation of Raymond Williams's notions of cultural materialism and green socialism that they graft onto deconstruction. While they continue to call their position "historical materialism" (following Williams's revisions), they, in fact, fundamentally break with the tradition of historical materialism and instead subscribe to the, by now, dominant *discursive* conception of materialism.

> [T]he production of signs, of signifying systems, of ideology, representations, and discourses is itself a material activity with material effects. Instead of arguing that the material or economic base produces certain effects, like culture and ideology, as part of its superstructure, a cultural materialist would argue that ideology and the discourses generated by social institutions are themselves located in material practices that have material effects that affect even the economic structures of the base. (61)

This issue of the "materiality of the many signifying practices" and whether or not cultural, ideological, and discursive practices (superstructure) are determined by the "material or economic base" is, as I have already indicated, the basic conflict between a cultural or discursive materialism and historical materialism. As Landry and MacLean explain, "[F]rom a cultural materialist position, arguments for the determinism of the 'base' suffer from economic reductionism" (61–62).

But it is not really reductionism that disturbs Landry and MacLean, because they seem to have no trouble at all in accepting the post-Marxist view of Laclau and Mouffe that "history and the real *are* discursive" (140), which is itself quite a reductionist and deterministic position. What Landry and MacLean, like other poststructuralists and post-Marxists, are doing is simply replacing economic reductionism with a discursive reductionism and calling it a new nondeterministic materialism.

Thus, Landry and MacLean claim that the "more adequately materialist feminist reading" is one that reads both Marx and the world "as texts," for the world and history are "always discursively constructed" (139–40). Their main argument against Marx (and for deconstruction) thus involves reading Marx's concept of value, following Gayatri Spivak, "as a catachresis or pun," which "not only shifts the grounds of debate from a tendency towards economic reductionism but opens potentially productive contradictions in Marx's texts" (64). But surplus value in Marx is the profit gained from the appropriation and exploitation of the contradictions in the social divisions of labor in production. To turn it into a linguistic pun not only erases a powerful explanatory concept, it "shifts the grounds of debate" from social contradictions over the exploitation of people's lives and labor to the play of textual differences. The ultimate goal of such readings of the labor theory of value in Marx is to turn it into a concept analogous to value in Saussure (Saussure 111–22). However, value in language is a local condition of meaningfulness (Saussure 116). Signs acquire their value by opposition, to use Saussure's own term, but this opposition is itself the outcome of prior *material* oppositions that Voloshinov effectively discusses as the oppositions of classes: language is "an arena of class struggle," that is, a site in the struggle over the extraction of surplus value (23). The meaning of the sign *black*, in other words, is not determined simply by a local, immanent opposition to *white* but by the way black and white are constructed and given meaning in the process of production. Immanently it would be difficult to explain why *black market* is a term of derogation and *white lie* is a term of justification and thus acceptance. Black in *black market* is negative because of what is *outside* discourse: the race and class antagonisms over the social divisions of labor and expropriations of surplus value—antagonisms that are made intelligible and fought out in the arena of discourse. Surplus value in the labor theory of value, in short, determines not only the value of the sign but of all systems of intelligibilities in class societies (Callinicos, *Race* 16–39).

However, for discursive materialists, in spite of their formal protests, discourse in their practices determines not only the "real" but also social and political change. Materialist feminism, then—as put forth by Landry and MacLean and the majority of ludic postmodernists and feminists—becomes a discursive "politics of difference" sensitive to the "leaky distinctions" among "questions of race, sexuality, ethnicity, nationality, postcoloniality, religion, and cultural identity, as well as class and gender" (90). Materialist feminism is reduced, in short, to what Landry and MacLean celebrate as a poststructuralist "identity politics of undone identities." But such an identity politics completely displaces the transformative struggle against "interlocking systems of oppression—racial, sexual, heterosexual, and class oppression" called for by earlier materialist feminists, such as those of the Combahee River Collective (Landry and MacLean 145). This substitution of a politics of difference reunderstands power relations, following Foucault (*History* 85–102), as reversible relations of difference and rearticulates binaries, oppositions, and hierarchies as discursive categories and practices that can be "reversed . . . [and] displaced" by a "deconstructive reading." But such a rhetorical displacement of binaries does not eliminate the *real* existing social and historical binaries between exploiter and exploited. It simply covers them over, concealing their grounding in the social divisions of labor and the relations of production.

How is making discourse or the matter of the body the ground of politics and social analytic any less reductive than the economic base? Yet, while economic reductionism is to be avoided at all costs according to ludic theories, a discursive reductionism or a theological matterism is widely embraced as a complex, sophisticated, and open multiplicity. The issue here is not whether "reductionism" is negative: it is not—ask any rigorous scientist (Weinberg). To articulate the relations connecting seemingly disparate events and phenomena is in fact a necessary and unavoidable part of effective knowledge of the real. Rather the question is why are some reductions—particularly those connecting the exploitation and gender division of labor to the accumulation of capital—suppressed and rendered taboo in ludic (socialist) feminism while other reductions—such as the discursive construction of sex-gender or a matterist resistance as performance—are championed and widely circulated? The answer, of course, does not lie in the logic of the argument, although that is the way it is commonly represented. On a purely epistemological or logical level both moves establish a necessary relation between two phenomena. Instead, the answer is in the economic, social, and political interests these two forms of "reductionism" support and the power of bourgeois ideology to discredit historical materialist knowledges.

Thus, what is at stake in this displacement of the economic by discourse is the elision of issues of exploitation and the substitution of a discursive identity politics for the struggle for full social and economic emancipation. Marx and Engels's critique of the radical Young Hegelians applies equally to ludic cultural materialists:

> [T]hey are only fighting against "*phrases.*" They forget, however, that to these phrases they themselves are only opposing other phrases, and that they are in no way combating the real existing world when they are merely combating the phrases of this world. (*German Ideology* 41)

This is not to say that the conflicts over ideology, cultural practices, and significations are not an important part of the social struggle for emancipation: the issue is how we *explain* the relation of the discursive to the nondiscursive, the relation of cultural practices to the "real existing world"—whose objectivity is the fact of the "working day"—in order to transform it. Obviously this relation is a highly mediated one. But for ludic materialists the relation is so radically displaced that it is almost entirely suppressed, and the actual practice of ludic cultural analysis is confined entirely to institutional and cultural mediations severed from the economic conditions producing them. The analysis of mediations becomes a goal in itself, and the operation of mediations is deployed to obscure the "origin" (surplus labor) and the "end" (class differences) that in fact frame the mediations. It is only in the context of historical materialism that one can point up the politics of this erasure of origin (arche) and end (telos) in poststructuralist theory. In ludic feminism the arche and telos are erased as if they were merely metaphysical concepts. My point is that the erasure of arche and telos serves a more immediate and concrete purpose: it makes it impossible to connect the mediated to other social practices, and consequently the inquiry into and analysis of the mediations, themselves, take the place of knowledge of the social totality in which mediations are relays of underlying connections. For historical materialist feminists, however, cultural and ideological practices are not autonomous but are instead primary sites for reproducing the meanings and subjectivities supporting the unequal gender, sexual, and race divisions of labor, and thus a main arena for the struggle against economic exploitation as well as cultural oppression.

To critique the contradictions, the blind spots or aporias in feminist theory; to relate what the theorist does say to what she does not say; to expose the hidden assumptions and power relations in her work, and above all, to relate her discourses to the suppressed realities of the contradictions over the social division of labor, is not trashing or one-upmanship or a power game, as Gallop, Hirsch, and Miller maintain. Rather, it is an effort to understand the way racist, patriarchal capitalism limits how and what we know and to try to articulate new frontiers, new parameters, for our knowledges. It is only through a rigorous critique exposing the hidden social relations of production underlying a theory that it is possible for us to begin to break through these historical limits. It is, I believe, only through a collectivity of critique that feminists can together rupture the historical and ideological constraints on our knowledges in order to perceive and explain the systematic operation of patriarchal capitalist exploitation and, out of this knowledge, act to change society and end social injustice.

This book is a contribution to building an oppositional critique and the transformative knowledges it enables. However, by critique I am not referring to the ludic notions of what Richard Rorty calls "conversations"—polite exchanges in which every point of view has a say. A politically effective critique cannot confine itself to the bourgeois notion of a dialogical or pluralist space in which a diversity of positions are represented with the complacent notion that they are all equally powerful. Pluralism, as it is widely practiced in postmodernism and, more generally, in the social and cultural relations of racist, patriarchal capitalism, is not simply a neutral, open space. Rather plurality, multiculturalism, multiplicity, and complexity have frequently been deployed to silence, suppress, occlude, and marginalize other positions and to suppress a *fundamental* or *radical* diversity: the differences of the social division of labor, of class antagonisms and the revolutionary struggle to overthrow the existing exploitative social relations. The dialogical, in short, masquerades as openness, but it is, in fact, a restricted, closed space in which the dominant frames of intelligibility—especially in ludic postmodernism—violently exclude not only oppositional knowledges but also suppress the "real" material relations of exploitation. In the face of such historical repression and silencing, the project of building an open space for critical exchange cannot be limited to a pluralistic dialogue *within* a single framework but rather requires a *dialectical* critique *in relation* to the dominant knowledges that are widely disseminated and celebrated. *Real* openness in an unequal society is not given: it must be struggled over and built through a dialectical contestation that challenges the violent exclusions and breaks the silence of the hegemonic frames of intelligibility. A collectivity of critique does not need polite conversation so much as it requires strong, rigorous advocacy of the silenced positions and sustained, rigorous critiques of the limitations and hidden assumptions and effects of the privileged discourses. A collectivity of critique, in short, is a productive site in which to participate in the social struggle over theory and to build, through dialectical contestations, the necessary and effective knowledges for an emancipatory praxis.

CHAPTER 2

Cyborgs, Lust, and Labor: The Crisis of Ludic Socialist Feminism

One of the urgent tasks of feminist theory is a critique of opposing ways of understanding materialism and their consequences for a socially transformative feminist praxis. But this critique has largely been suppressed because, in postmodern discourses, the priority of labor and the relations of production—and with them, Marxism—are readily dismissed, not only as economic reductionism but also as obsolete knowledges superseded by new post-al knowledges (poststructuralism, post-Marxism, postmodernism, posthistory, postlesbian and postgay queer theory, and so forth) or simply replaced by local, empirical, non-Marxist descriptions of existing conditions. I will use the concept of post-al for the discourses and practices that erase the relations of production and class struggle from contemporary knowledges.[1] Central to these post-al practices are ludic theories of desire, which substitute desire for labor as the basic process of late capitalism, and the ludic notion of politics as primarily cultural or discursive and autonomous from the divisions of labor. As I explain throughout this book, these practices deploy difference to violently displace class.

This erasure is especially clear in one of the collections of feminist theory aimed at taking stock of the state of feminism, namely, *Women, Class, and the Feminist Imagination*, which is based in large part on a yearlong forum on the "impasse of socialist feminism" in *Socialist Review* (which is singularly antagonistic to the "production paradigm"). The "production paradigm" is a term commonly used, especially in the debates in feminism in the 1970s and 1980s, to refer to the historical materialist argument that all social, political, cultural, and familial practices are conditioned by the mode of production. The editors of the volume, Karen Hansen and Ilene Philipson, rehearse a familiar narrative of two competing paradigms in the history of socialist feminism. In this story a flawed and inadequate dual-

45

systems theory—which represents the failure of feminist efforts to theorize the condition of women in terms of relations of production and reproduction—is successfully vanquished by Gayle Rubin's sex-gender system and her critique of Marxism. Quoting Rosalind Petchesky, who claims Rubin created "a genuine Marxist-feminist methodology . . . a kind of watermark for Marxist-feminist's theoretical growth," Hansen and Philipson go on to add that Rubin's paradigm of the sex-gender system offered a "truly materialist means of understanding how sex and gender are produced [that] transcended the specific content of Marxist categories" (22).

But how is materialism understood here? Rubin displaces the fundamental materialist categories of labor, class, and relations of production. Her effort to, as she says, "isolate sex and gender from 'mode of production'" ("Traffic" 203) is based—as Nancy Hartsock effectively argues in her critique of Rubin—on a misreading of Marx "that undermines the value of Rubin's theory: [her] inadvertent redefinition of production as exchange" (*Money* 297). This is then compounded by another "abstraction: [her] transformation of the kinship system into a symbol system" (298). As Hartsock argues, Rubin's

> summary of production and extraction of surplus value in capitalism is marked by an extraordinarily consistent focus on exchange. As a result, the material process of production involving interaction with nature, concentration on concrete qualities of real objects, and cooperation with others, vanishes. (296)

In other words, Rubin dissolves the relations of production into an abstracted notion of exchange that is then replaced—through analogy—with the symbolic production of gender in a kinship system of exchange. She thus offers a cultural understanding of the production of gender in place of an economic explanation and substitutes a version of cultural materialism for historical materialism.

There is no question that Rubin's concept of a sex-gender system has been very influential in feminist theory, informing the work of feminists as diverse as Sandra Harding and the post-Marxist Chantal Mouffe. Andrew Parker, for one, claims that it "has become nothing less than indispensable, forming indeed one of the cornerstones of the field of Women's Studies" (28). Rubin's work has been influential in part because of the role it has played in localizing feminism: isolating feminist understandings of gender construction from the material, economic conditions—the division of labor and relations of production—crucial to (re)producing gender and sexuality and determining the exploitation of women, lesbians, and gays. Such a separation of gender and sex from economic practices legitimates the class interests of ludic feminists, who would, for the most part, like to see some measure of gender equality but who argue for it within the existing class relations so as not to disturb their own class privileges. In other words, they want to modify and reform but not to transform the existing social relations. Any analysis that engages the material conditions of gender and sexuality is thus dismissed as supplying Marxist answers to feminist questions, as if feminist questions are somehow outside the history of relations of production.

Rubin is quite explicit in calling on feminists to cut off the analysis of sex from its material conditions. First she asserts that "the needs which are satisfied by economic activity even in the richest, Marxian sense, do not exhaust fundamental human requirements . . . [T]he needs of sexuality and procreation must be satisfied as much as the need to eat" ("Traffic" 165). Then she argues that analysis of "sex . . . as social product" requires that "we need to understand the relations of its production" (by which she means cultural and symbolic, not economic, relations) "and forget, for awhile, about food, clothing, automobiles, and transistor radios" ("Traffic" 166). This is an idealist argument. It covers over the basic issue: all needs, including sexuality and nutrition, are material, which is another way of saying that economic practices are the condition of possibility for all other human practices. Furthermore, her argument equates very different levels of needs: the fundamental needs of food and the protection of the body are not at all the same as the commodified consumer needs of automobiles and transistor radios.

Rubin's argument has been widely deployed by feminist theorists and academics (nearly all of whom are upper-middle-class professionals and, thus for the most part, deeply invested in maintaining the existing system of class relations by diverting attention toward superstructural practices and away from the material base of society). Following Rubin's lead, many of these feminists—especially in the humanities and cultural studies— have not just forgotten "for awhile" but have almost entirely suppressed any knowledge of the economic relations of production in their theories of gender and sexuality. If they deal with the economic at all, it is in terms of an ahistorical and abstract notion of commodity consumption and exchange or an abstract notion of technology cut off from economic relations of production.

Hansen and Philipson replay Rubin's idealist argument in their own history of socialist feminism. They assert, for example, that "as feminists have come to recognize that women's desire to marry and raise children cannot be explained in exclusively economic terms, socialist feminism defined as dual systems theory appears to be at an impasse" (23). Such statements employ the same false logic as Rubin's essay. The production model, it must be emphasized, even in the highly problematic form of dual-systems theory, does not try to explain subjectivity and desire "in exclusively economic terms"; rather, it insists on the necessity of historicizing them: understanding and explaining these desires in relation to the material conditions, the division and exploitation of labor, producing them. Such an analysis attempts to show that desire is historical and not a free-floating autonomous performance: desire is a practice, not simply a performance, and as such it is historical and material. The actualization of women's sexual desires—especially breaking the bounds of heterosexuality—is determined by the material conditions by which they produce the sustenance of their lives.

The formation of desire, in short, is not free; it is historical and material. As Marx and Engels write, "[T]he first premise of all human existence and, therefore, of all history . . . [is] that men must be in a position to live in order to 'make history'" or, we can add, to fulfill their desires. "Life involves before everything else eating and drinking, a habitation, clothing and many other things. The first historical act is thus the production of the means to satisfy these needs, the production of material life itself" (*German Ideology* 48). In other words, not only the fulfillment of bodily needs but also the *ways* in which these needs can be satisfied (the paths of desire) are contingent on the relations of production sustaining the body. Thus, a woman's very sexuality—the ways in which her desires are constructed and the ways in which she is able to act on them, to be heterosexual, to be lesbian, to be a mother or not—is conditioned by her position in the historically specific gendered division of labor. The parameters of desire and the possibilities for fulfilling them are quite different for a woman whose means of sustenance depend on her taking up a rigidly gendered position of domestic labor and (re)production in a heterosexual marriage (as in many precapitalist, or partially capitalist societies) than they are for a woman who is able to meet her needs in advanced capitalism through access to one of the relatively gender-flexible positions in wage labor (e.g., a highly paid professional, such as a university professor).

Cutting off gender and sexuality in idealist theories from the material conditions producing them has contributed to the ever greater proliferation of seemingly autonomous zones of social reality in ludic knowledges. This is especially evident in the way Chantal Mouffe deploy's Rubin's notion of a sex-gender system to displace the concepts of patriarchy, capitalist patriarchy and social relations of production in her articulation of a post-Marxist socialist feminism (140–41). At the core of her argument is the necessity "to get rid of the problematic of 'women's oppression' altogether and to formulate the question in a completely new way . . . to study the way in which women's subordination is constructed in different practices, discourses and institutions, and what I call the sex/gender system" (140). For Mouffe, the sex-gender system becomes the means for understanding the condition of women in terms of the localized pluralities of largely autonomous, overdetermined, and heterogeneous social processes. Mouffe maintains that any interpretation that "remains within the economistic problematic of the base/superstructure distinction" is "untenable" (141). Society—understood as a totality, as a "system of social relations," such as the relations of base and superstructure—is no longer "a valid object of discourse" for Mouffe and her collaborator, Ernesto Laclau (*Hegemony* 111). It has become, as Laclau argues, an "impossibility" (*New Reflections* 89–96), because knowledge of totality is itself an impossibility.

The ludic and post-Marxist arguments against totality break with the more traditional view that totality is so immense that no knowledge of it is humanly possible and that therefore all our knowledges, in practice, are partial. The erasure of totality in postmodern social theory is based on Derrida's argument in his reading of Lévi-Strauss's *The Raw and the Cooked*. In *Writing and Difference*, Derrida claims that the project of "totality" is doomed and should be questioned "no longer from the standpoint of a concept of finitude as relegation to the empirical, but from the standpoint of the concept of *play*" (289). Totality, in other words, is not viable, not because one can never get hold of its immensity (that is, an empirical impossibility) but because it is a construct of language and, like all such constructs, subject to the law of differential playfulness. "If totalization no longer has any meaning," Derrida argues, "it is not because the infiniteness of a field cannot be covered by a finite glance or a finite discourse, but because the nature of the field—that is language and a finite language— excludes totalization" (289). This is because, he explains, "This field is in effect that of *play*, that is to say, a field of infinite substitutions only because it is finite, that is to say, because instead of being an inexhaustible field . . . instead of being too large, there is something missing from it: a center which arrests and grounds the play of substitutions" (289). For Derrida, totalization and its effect, totality, are always supplemented by play, and, as such, totality is never self-same and self-identical but always at odds with itself: it is self-divided by an unstoppable slippage. In place of the social as a set of necessary relations, then, Mouffe puts forth a notion of the social as what she calls a "multiplicity of social logics which construct power relations irreducible to the expression of a fundamental contradiction" (142)—such as the contradiction of class and the social division of labor.

However, when Mouffe presented these views at a (West) German-British conference sponsored by the Marxist journal *Das Argument* (which published the proceedings as *Rethinking Ideology*, ed. Hanninen and Paldan), the relation of the sex-gender system to the project of socialist feminism was widely debated (139–51). In particular, Michele Barrett—who, at that time, had not yet changed her colors to post-Marxism—argued (according to the summary of discussions [149–51]) that "women's oppression was not only found" in the sex-gender system, "but also in systematic patterns such as families, factories, i.e. the division of labour, wages and so on" (Hanninen and Paldan 149). Others, such as Frigga Haug, were especially "concerned with the fertility of those Marxist concepts which Chantal Mouffe proposed getting rid of." Thus Haug argued, "with respect to the base/superstructure concept . . . that fundamental answers to the women's case could be gained by looking at women's oppression from the point of view of the reproduction of society" (Hanninen and Paldan 150).

Most ludic feminists and theorists have obviously rejected both the fertility of Marxist concepts and the systematicity of social relations. Instead they have joined Rubin, Mouffe, and others in embracing the ideas of autonomy, multiplicity, and overdetermination. Thus, recent ludic theories of sexuality—especially queer theory—try to separate sexuality itself into yet another autonomous realm, independent from any causal determinants. Again Rubin's writing is exemplary here. In her "Thinking Sex" she has largely repudiated her own concept of the sex-gender system" put forth in "The Traffic in Women" because, as she now says, "I did not distinguish between lust and gender" (307). She thus argues that "it is essential to separate gender and sexuality analytically to more accurately reflect their separate social existence" (308).[2]

Need and Desire

Not only does Rubin break off gender and sexuality from the material conditions of production, she now breaks off sexuality from gender and, in
effect, advocates a form of postgender feminism founded upon self-signifi-
cation and the autonomy of what Rubin identifies as "lust." Lust becomes
the allegory for the sovereignty of the subject of desire whose excess is
uncontainable within a historical category such as gender. The subject of
lust is truly the deregulated subject of late capitalism where there are no
limits upon her practices of desire.[3] Rubin's lust—as an allegory of the free,
enterprising subject legitimating the free market of no constraints—is very
closely related to another model of excessive subjectivity: what Lyotard
(following Kant) theorizes as the sublime.[4] Rubin's narrative of lust, like
Lyotard's notion of the sublime, is a strategy of crisis management in late
capitalism: positing the free subject as an excessive (autonomous) agent
erases any necessary connection between the subject and system, desire
and history. Rubin argues that "Feminism is the theory of gender oppression. To automatically assume that this makes it the theory of sexual
oppression is to fail to distinguish between gender, on the one hand, and
erotic desire, on the other" (307). Each form of oppression is thus understood as having its own unique, acausal genealogy distinct from all other
social and economic practices and requiring its own mode of separate (differend) understanding since they are all incommensurable. According to
Rubin, "[A]s issues become less those of gender and more those of sexuality, feminist analysis becomes irrelevant and often misleading . . . Other
areas of social life, their forms of power, and their characteristic modes of
oppression, need their own conceptual implements" (309).

Rubin's severing of sexuality (as the site of excessive desire that is
transgressive of all regulatory social injunctions) from gender (as the articulation of social arrangements and regulations) is symptomatic of a larger
move in postmodern theory that is aimed at theorizing a transsocial space
in which the freedom of the subject—beyond the regulations of the state
(and its ideology)—is guaranteed. Isolating sexuality as Rubin does, in
other words, is part of the more global move of ludic bourgeois theory to
disconnect the subject from the larger economic and historical series.
Rubin's sexuality, Lacan's desire, Lyotard's sublime (in his rereading of
Kant), Derrida's differance, Baudrillard's hyperreal, Butler's performativity,
Irigaray's speculum, and Michael Warner's queer, are all different articulations of this panhistorical site of unencumbered freedom of the subject.

Desire, has become the general trope for all these sites—from the sublime to the speculum—and its articulations are widely diverse in contemporary ludic theory. They range from vulgar ludic views that establish a very unpostmodern binary between desire and knowledge all the way to the more philosophically rigorous arguments in the writings of such theorists as Deleuze and Guattari (*Anti-Oedipus, Thousand Plateaus*) and Avital Ronell (*Telephone Book*). Given the privileging of desire in ludic theory, it may be helpful to briefly examine this highly valorized and seemingly inclusive concept.

The vulgar postmodern theory of desire is perhaps most clearly expressed by Diane Elam in her *Romancing the Postmodern*. Impatient with any rigorous critique, she sums up her views on desire in her discussion of "Theory's Romance"—"All of this is to say: knowledge will not put an end to desire . . . since knowledge will always be set astray by the wandering of . . . desire" (146–47). As support for her claim Elam offers not an argument but anecdotes—"small narratives"—since she believes postmodernism has buried epistemology. Thus any attempt to argue for anything is doomed by the fragmentation of the argument itself by the "wandering of desire."

Among the anecdotes that she narrates in order to persuade the reader—not prove to him or her—that desire is a resistant excess is one in which she pits revolution against desire and shows their incommensurability. She retells the "apocryphal story of Lenin in Geneva prior to the Russian Revolution, when he supposedly spent as much time chasing a cure for baldness around pharmacies as in the library studying Marx" (199). This demonstrates, for Elam, "the resistance of hair care"—that is the resistance of desire, in this case for the care of the hair—"to revolutionary Marxist analysis" (199). Part of what is at stake here is the post-al rewriting of the theorist of the revolution of production as simply another desiring consumer: to assert, in short, the post-al priority in which consumption supersedes production. The organization of Elam's discourse is itself an enactment of desire and consumption: argument is displaced by anecdote; knowledge by the pleasures of (consuming) a story. Not only does anecdote not claim to prove anything; it need not even be true—the Lenin anecdote is, Elam admits, apocryphal. And, of course, this is her other and perhaps more important point: there is no longer any use in talking about truth since it is a version of desire anyway. What matters is the performance or, at the very least, illustration of the circuits of desire.

The fundamental question for ludic theory is not so much to prove an argument—that is to establish and explain relationships—as to introduce tissues of texts into a conversation and, in so doing, provide zones of seduction that resituate (seduce) the subject in(to) these zones. The opposition of knowledge to desire in ludic feminism is, of course, a return of the older binary in cultural feminism: the very familiar opposition between experience and critique in a "new" language. This return is not surprising because idealist theory always needs a transcendental arena in which to justify (naturalize) the contradictions of class relations. Cultural feminism attempted to resolve the material contradictions of capitalism through experience. It regarded a local and localizing experience to be the ultimate test of reality and theorized experience as an excess that could not itself be explained by critique: it could not be made the subject of knowledge in which its (naturalized) contradictions would be exposed and related to the larger social totality. Experience, in other words, was incommensurate with critique. However, ludic feminism, as the gender theory of late capitalism, finds experience no longer a safe site for justifying social contradictions, because transnational capitalism has itself foregrounded the connections between the daily and the global social totality, thereby turning the experience (of the daily) itself into a visible site of unresolved contradictions. This has lead to a depriviledging of experience in classic poststructuralist theory. Ludic theory needs a more agile concept that is itself not yet overwritten by contradictions. Or, if it is marked by contradictions, the contradictions need to be of a higher level of abstraction and thus not easily detectable. Desire is thus a more elusive (trans)locality. The main task of ludic theory is to place desire beyond the reach of critique, which produces a coherent knowledge of social totality.

Elam is quite clear about the relation between desire and critique. She begins her subversion of critique by erasing the very notion of falsehood and deceit in theory, thus making it impossible to appeal to truth as the ground for knowledge. Instead of falseness and deception—which always imply that there is truth that can be unveiled (a rather logocentric position in her view)—she believes we need to move beyond truth and falsehood and instead talk about desire as manifested in seduction. It is, therefore, more productive, according to Elam, to "talk about the experience of watching TV or going to the movies as not simply one of being deceived, but one of being seduced" (146). The move is necessary so that the access of ideology critique to truth is blocked, and we are therefore spared the power that, she believes, is always disguised in knowledge. The most effective way to overcome power is to abandon epistemology and instead adopt a Rortian, pragmatic approach to discourses: the question is not whether the discourse is true or false but whether it works or not. The social and material conditions that make one discourse work and another not work are irrelevant—they are part of a metaphysics of truth and, as far as Elam is concerned, decidedly unpostmodern. Elam believes that there is no use in appealing to truth because it is "singularly ineffective" (146). What is effective, for ludic theorists, as I have already suggested, follows a very constrained notion of what works. It is based on pragmatism as the test of truth, but a pragmatism that merely enacts the desire of the subject: what works is what the subject wants (desires). "Ideology critique," Elam warns us, "can unravel the web of deceit which causes us to buy . . . products," but it is not pragmatic; it "has little purchase on us" (146). The "fact" that truth "has little purchase on us" is taken by ludic theory as a pragmatic given—the question of *why* this is so is of little or no concern. Any analysis of the conditions of the social division of labor producing the situation in which what works is regarded to be true—that is, any analysis of the material conditions of possibility by which what works is rendered true—are ruled out as simple instances of the will to knowledge and, as such, totalizing and totalitarian (14–174).

The cure for will-to-knowledge is desire as romance: the excess-ive, the aesthetic sublime that challenges the way we know history (12). Romance takes us to the essence of history as desire (behind historical lines and shows us the actual workings of desire and/as textuality. In fact history, itself, is an articulation of desire: like desire, it precedes, succeeds, and exceeds itself (12). One can see this reversible excessiveness in the play of the *post* in postmodernism. Like desire as history/history as desire, postmodernism has the paradoxical ability to come both before and after modernism (3). The excess of *post* is the excess of all forms of desire. In romance, to give another text of desire, it breaks genre boundaries and transcends all rules and regulations of normative narrative (12). What is important for ludic theory in this understanding of desire as romance is that such a concept enables ludic theory to substitute desire for explanation, play for history, and seduction for critique of ideology.

Elam's notion of desire as autonomous and thus incommensurate with knowledge is only one articulation of this tendency in ludic feminism (after Rubin) to segregate desire from knowledge, sexuality from gender, and gender from the mode of production. The most influential and philosophically rigorous articulation of this theory is in the writings of Gilles Deleuze and Felix Guattari. It is necessary to engage, however briefly, their theory of desire because their views have now become the conceptual frame for almost all versions of the ludic idea of desire.

In their *Anti-Oedipus: Capitalism and Schizophrenia*, Deleuze and Guattari offer a post-Lacanian theory of desire in which desire is regarded as an autonomous force that not only defies any social determination but, in fact, shapes the social in many ways. Desire, in their view, is the *real* material thing. It is important to emphasize that for Deleuze and Guattari, as for all other ludic theorists, materialism (as I discussed in the previous chapter) means that which resists social meanings (ideology). The "traditional logic of desire," they contend, is "to a certain degree . . . all wrong from the very outset" (25). What is all wrong (I put aside the curious use of "wrong" in a discourse that posits itself to be postepistemological) is that all theories of desire since Plato, they argue, have thought of desire as a lack. Even in Kant, who seems to be interested in a more materialist theory of desire, the dichotomy of production and acquisition continues to haunt the theory of desire. In all classical theories, according to Deleuze and Guattari, desire is placed on the side of acquisition ("a lack of the real object"), and, as such, it is regarded in idealist terms (25). They acknowledge that Kant took the productivity of desire into account but argue that it was nonetheless an idealist position in that it regarded the productivity of desire to be limited to such unreal things as fantasy, hallucinations, and superstition; it did "not question the validity of the classical conception of desire as a lack" (25).

In all classical theories, then, "[T]he reality of the object . . . in so far as it is produced by desire, is thus a *psychic reality*" (25). Such a view is best developed, according to Deleuze and Guattari, in psychoanalysis. Their critique of classical theories, then, is that, according to these theories, the real object that desire lacks is related to an extrinsic natural or social production, whereas desire is seen as intrinsically producing an imaginary object that functions as a double reality, "as though there were a 'dreamed-of object behind every real object' or a mental production behind all real production" (25–26). This, they maintain, denies the materiality of desire and consequently leads to an idealist theory: the world as not all material but as constituted by phantoms conjured up by desire. Deleuze and Guattari, following Clément Rosset, reiterate that

> every time the emphasis is put on a lack that desire supposedly suffers from as a way of defining its object, "the world acquires as its double some other sort of world . . . the world does not contain each and every

object that exists; there is at least one object missing, the one that desire feels the lack of; hence there exists some other place that contains the key to desire (missing in this world)." (26)

Deleuze and Guattari then propose desire as a material entity: "If desire produces, its product is real" (26). Such a view of desire, which is presented as an anti-idealist theory, is an ideological alibi for cutting the relation between need and desire. According to Deleuze and Guattari, desire should not be thought of "as something *supported* by needs" (26). Desire, in short, is both autonomous and productive in its own right. In proposing their materialist theory of desire, Deleuze and Guattari are undertaking a seemingly epistemological project—an anti-idealist theory of desire—but in actuality, their project is an alibi for inscribing and universalizing the interests of the dominant class in contemporary knowledge. In cutting the relation between need and desire, they are at the same time cutting the relation of support (i.e., dependency) between use value and exchange value, production and consumption. It is in the interest of the ruling class to render exchange value independent, to represent it as its own source or—to use Deleuze and Guattari's vocabulary—as a materialist force in its own right. The source of profit in such a revisionist understanding of the political economy is not labor but the managing skills of the owners of the means of production and their managers.

However, Deleuze and Guattari take this displacement even further. Not only do they sever desire from need but they reappropriate needs as the (dematerialized) effect—the "counterproducts"—of a now materialized desire as cause and producer. They claim that "Desire is not bolstered by needs, but rather the contrary; needs are derived from desire: they are counterproducts within the real that desire produces" (27). In making needs the effect of desires, they join with Baudrillard and other ludic critics in constructing a post-al political economy in which consumption (desire) is the productive force and source of profit, thereby suppressing production and labor. This double move—cutting desire off from need and then reappropriating need as the product of autonomous desire—frees desire from actual historical needs (use value) and posits desire itself as a self-propelling social force. It is now desire that produces the social in this post-al logic: "social production," Deleuze and Guattari argue, "is purely and simply desiring-production itself . . . [T]he social field is immediately invested by desire . . . [I]t is the historically determined product of desire" (29). This reversal entirely substitutes desire for production and erases the reality of class struggle. In class societies, economic resources are not distributed equally (to each according to his needs); thus there are unfulfilled needs that, in fact, produce desire. However, for the class that Deleuze and Guattari represent, there are no unfulfilled needs. It is, then, quite logical, from the perspective of this class, to posit a theory of desire as a material force: desire is, for this class, immediately materialized, and, therefore, there is no gap (the shadow world that they describe as idealist) between desire and the object of desire. That gap, however, materially exists in the actual world of class society—it is the gap that, in fact, separates the class for which they speak from the proletariat: the class whose needs are fulfilled from the class whose needs are unfulfilled. This gap, I emphasize, is not an idealist one: it is the very (historical) materialism from which Deleuze and Guattari, Rubin, Derrida, Butler, and other ludic theorists escape by inventing a materialism of matter outside the structure of class struggle. It is the materialism whose matter is not an inert mass or a desiring effect, but rather is the result of human practice (labor) in the evolving class struggle between those who have and those who have not.

What is at stake in theorizing desire as autonomous and productive, I must emphasize, is not so much a correction of previous theories as an erasure of class struggle through a concept of desire. The post-al theory of desire is, in effect, a new justification for the desires of those who have and an erasure of the needs of others as basically unreal (idealist). The actual historical reality of class societies in late capitalism is that lack is itself lacking from the affluent world articulated in Deleuze and Guattari's texts. Lack and need become superfluous concepts and, as such, have to be erased: this is a world (class) for which the problem is no longer the problem of poverty (need) but of liberty (desire). "Desire," according to Deleuze and Guattari, "does not lack anything; it does not lack its object . . . Desire and its object are one and the same thing" (26). This is the same as the post-Lacanian materiality that is reproduced in the post-Marxist writings of Slavoj Žižek. Deleuze and Guattari critique Lacan for still allowing a lack. However, Žižek takes this critique into account and turns the Lacanian lack, itself, into a materiality: a materiality that is identical with the materiality of the hyperreal of simulation in Baudrillard. It is the materiality of fiction that is necessary in late capitalism for a revival of the real (Baudrillard, *Simulations* 23–49) and the rendering of need as postdesire. It is in Baudrillard himself that the politics of the erasure of the opposition of need and desire becomes especially pronounced. Desire is the need of the affluent. In his famous text "Consumer Society," Baudrillard, through his reading of Galbraith's *The New Industrial State,* poses the problem of the "equivalency of satiable demands" (40). Quoting Galbraith, he writes,

> "There is no proof that an expensive woman obtains the same satisfaction from yet another gown as does a hungry man from a hamburger. But there is no proof that she does not. Since it cannot be proven that she does not, her desire, it is held, must be accorded equal standing with that of a poor man for meat." "Absurd," says Galbraith. Yet, not at all. (40)

For Baudrillard the needs of the wealthy woman and the poor man are indeed equal—equally the desiring production of pleasure. The post-al notion, then, of desire as material and autonomous is the ideological alibi for the freedom of the affluent class of late capitalism, as is the series of concepts in ludic theory that duplicate impetus of desire under various names such as *differance*, discourse, genealogy, and sexuality in opposition to contradictions, materialism, history, and gender. The opposition between these two sets articulates the fundamental opposition between the two basic classes in capitalism, and the elision and erasure of the concepts of materialism is the elision and erasure of the class whose labor supports the other.

The new post-al real, then, is a scene of desire and enjoyment that is postneed, postclass, postlabor, and postproduction. We see the articulation of this post-al real especially clearly in the work of Slavoj Žižek. Called "an extraordinary new voice" by Fredric Jameson and championed by such post-Marxists as Ernesto Laclau, Žižek is the hot new intellectual commodity on the post-al theory circuit. Žižek's basic project is to write a Lacanian ethics in the place of Marxist politics and, in so doing, to discredit Marxist knowledges; to replace critique with psychoanalytic narration; and above all, to substitute enjoyment—that is pleasure/desire—for labor as the fundamental locus for understanding ideology, the subject, and a conflicted social reality. However, contrary to the claims of his admirers, Žižek is not the vanguard of a new radical political thinking. Rather, his writings revive a regressive bourgeois idealism that suppresses the historical and revolutionary knowledges necessary for social transformation.

Žižek's argument consists of a series of rhetorical moves: a layered, multiple series of analogies and homologies that displace historical explanation with ludic description at every level, from the most fundamental principles to the numerous local anecdotes. The scope, diversity, and excessive incongruity of these analogies—from Hitchcock's films to Hegel, from Lacan to Chernobyl—seduce, shock, and titillate, making his work a mirage of the sharp edge of the new and original. But, in fact, Žižek's discourse is little more than the banalities of bourgeois philosophy (masquerading as deep thinking. Žižek's urlogic—what acts as his (arche)analogy—is, of course, his elaboration of the Laclau-Mouffe notion of the constitutive social antagonism—"a traumatic social division which cannot be symbolized" (*Sublime* 45)—in terms of the Lacanian Real: as "an original 'trauma,' an impossible kernel that resists symbolization, totalization, symbolic integration" (6). In so doing, he rejects the Marxist notion of class struggle over the relations of production—that is, over the exploitation of labor—and substitutes a notion of antagonism as an unknowable, unresolvable deadlock, a leftover, a surplus, paradoxically both outside the social-symbolic and a support of it. "Lacanian psychoanalysis," he claims in *The Sublime Object of Ideology*, "enables us to grasp" how the "irreducible plurality of particular struggles" are all "responses to the same impossible-real kernel" (4).

This move, which creates a "break with [the Marxist] logic" of "global revolution" (4), is itself based on a hidden homology to Althusser's reading of the epistemological break in Marx in which the writings of the late Marx eclipse the early works. Žižek's entire theory depends on constructing a similar epistemological break in which the late Lacan largely displaces the theoretical concepts of the earlier Lacan. As he writes in *The Sublime Object of Ideology* "With the development of Lacanian teaching in the sixties and seventies, what [Lacan] calls 'the Real' approaches more and more what he called, in the fifties, the Imaginary" (162). The "paradox of the Lacanian Real" serves as the basis of all Žižek's thinking, in which the impossible kernel of the psychic Real—desire, *jouissance*—becomes, through analogy, the impossible kernel of the social real. As he says, "If we define the Real as such a paradoxical, chimerical entity which although it does not exist, has a series of properties and can produce a series of effects, it becomes clear that the Real *par excellence* is *jouissance: jouissance* does not exist, it is impossible, but it produces a number of traumatic effects" (164). *Jouissance*, enjoyment, in short, is the impossible, traumatic real kernel of both psychic and social reality.

The purpose of this move is, of course, to deny the objective social reality—which in capitalism is surplus labor—and to reduce it to a series of effects. A real that is knowable only through its effects does not have objective and material existence. It is indirectly available in effects, which are themselves only knowable through the interpretations of the subject. The real—as effect—in other words is the real produced by the subject. This transference is, of course, a very familiar move in bourgeois philosophy. Marx calls it "logical mysticism" and discusses it at length in his *Critique of Hegel's Doctrine of the State* as an inversion of the subject and predicate (Marx, *Early Writings* 65–69, 98–99, 168–69). It is also a theological argument: God is not known as an objectivity but only through his or her effects. There is, therefore, no reliable way to produce knowledge of these effects, which means all interpretations are equally (in)valid, their truth relative.

Žižek argues by a strict homology between social reality (the objective) and psychic reality (the subjective) in which the social is considered to operate entirely according to the laws of the psychic economy—in particular its circulation around the unknowable, unrepresentable surplus-void of the "Real of desire." One of the basic issues here for any attempt to theorize a relation between psychoanalysis and Marxism is: does the theory explain the psyche in terms of the social, or the social in terms of the psyche? Žižek has clearly chosen the latter and in so doing erases a materialist understanding and institutes an idealist one that, like all idealism, sees the psyche—particularly its circulation around the surplus kernel of enjoyment—as constitutive of reality.

The problem with Marxism, for Žižek, is its failure to "take into account . . . the surplus-object, the leftover of the Real eluding symbolization" (50). The priority of this surplus as enjoyment leads Žižek to argue by homology in *The Sublime Object* that "surplus value [is] the 'cause' which sets in motion the capitalist process of production," just as "surplus-enjoyment [is] the object-cause of desire." In so doing he rewrites the fundamental principle of surplus value in Marx as "announc[ing] . . . the logic of the Lacanian *object petit a* as the embodiment of surplus enjoyment." In short, surplus value now means an excess of enjoyment, *jouissance*—and the Marxist principle of surplus value as the effect of the appropriation and exploitation of labor is completely elided. This enables Žižek to invalidate what he calls the "vulgar evolutionist dialectics of productive forces and the relations of production" (53) of Marxism, which, in Žižek's words, argues that contradictions or a "limit" of the "discord" of relations of production in capitalism "brings about the need for socialist revolution." Social contradictions are, in short, rewritten as an excess beyond explanation and available only as isolated events experienced by the subject—that is, as symptoms. Žižek thus dispenses with the necessity for socialist revolution by invoking the "coincidence of limit and excess, of lack and sur-plus" (53). In other words, in spite of his antipoststructuralist disclaimers (e.g., *Sublime* 7), Žižek tries to discredit the Marxist theory of revolution by deploying the poststructuralist move of differential reversibility. For the reversibility of limit and excess means that any limit or blockage is auto-matically—that is rhetorically, or in the case of Žižek, ontologically—superseded by its surplus. In applying this to capitalism, Žižek argues that this limit, "blockage," is an "excessive power" that "*drives capitalism into permanent development* . . . the permanent revolutionizing of its own condi-tions . . . [which] is the only way for it to resolve again and again . . . its own fundamental . . . 'contradiction'" (52).

In short, the "paradoxes of surplus-enjoyment" as the new post-al "Real" enable Žižek to dispense with the necessity of socialist revolution and to instead revive an idealized notion of capitalism as itself a permanent revolution, incessantly resolving its own contradictions. Žižek thus turns Trotsky's notion of permanent revolution (borrowed from Marx), an understanding of international socialism as the condition for the superses-sion of capitalism by a classless, stateless globality, into a strategy of crisis management for capitalism itself in order to produce another comforting narrative of the permanence of capitalism as untranscendable. In so doing he completely suppresses the objective *reality* of surplus value and the con-tradictions of capitalism as based on the exploitation and appropriation of labor. In claiming the surplus of enjoyment as the Real *par excellence*, Žižek puts forth as reality an imaginary ontological state of enjoyment caught in the closed circuit of *demand and desire* and completely cut off from the basic historical reality of the social struggles over fundamental *needs* in global capitalism.

Moreover Žižek turns this "non-sensical, pre-ideological kernel of enjoyment," as he calls it, into a transhistorical *universal*: it is he says, "the last support" of "every ideology" (124). In making these claims, Žižek is, of course, reintroducing a *base* for the ideological *superstructure*. He breaks ideology's relation to a materialist base—the forces and economic relations of production—only to substitute in its place a grounding of all ideology, in fact all reality, on the idealist base of enjoyment. In short, *desire becomes the base* of the real in all ludic theories. Thus while economic reductionism is to be avoided at all costs according to ludic critics, Žižek's psychic and rhetorical reductionism—which reduces all ideology, all reality to the cir-cuitry of desire and enjoyment—is widely embraced as complex, sophisti-cated, and innovative. As I pointed out earlier, the issue is not whether "reductionism" is negative—to articulate the relations connecting seemingly disparate events is in fact a necessary and unavoidable part of effective knowledge of the real. Rather, the question is why are some reductions—particularly those connecting the exploitation of labor to the accumulation of capital—suppressed and rendered taboo in post-al politics, especially ludic feminism, while other reductions—such as the post-al connections of desire to the real—are celebrated and widely circulated? The answer is in the economic, social, and political interests these two forms of "reductionism" support and the power of bourgeois ideology and its intellectuals to discredit materialist knowledges.

The traumatic kernel of the Real that Žižek mystifies as the unknowable, unsymbolizable surplus/void of enjoyment is nothing other than the reality of the unequal, unjust division and exploitation of labor: *surplus value in its historical materialist sense.* But this traumatic kernel—this *surplus of labor*—is precisely the necessary blind spot of bourgeois ideology. It is unknowable only in so far as the bourgeois intellectual is deeply invested in the *refusal* to know the basis of wealth, power, privilege, and pleasure in capitalism: the refusal to know the exploitation of labor and his or her own position in it.

refusal to know

Žižek secures this unintelligibility of the real by equating and completely restricting the Symbolic to the realm of bourgeois ideology, which is, for all its embrace of pluralism, still an ideology legitimating and concealing the appropriations of surplus labor—whether from race, gender, or class. Žižek thus makes the social-symbolic reality synonymous with the modes of sense making and subjectivities required by multicultural capitalism. Whatever is outside this sphere, whatever challenges or questions it, is rendered an unsymbolizable, unknowable void for political, not ontological, reasons. We therefore have to take a critique-al look at the consequences of Žižek's rewriting of ideology as the fantasy construction that functions "to offer us the social reality itself as an escape from some traumatic, real kernel" (*Symbolic* 45), while he denies any possibility for knowing and explaining that real kernel in his campaign against the critique of ideology. Ideological analysis, for Žižek, refuses to interpret this unknowable, traumatic kernel of enjoyment. As he says in *Looking Awry*, "The only proper attitude is that which . . . [does not] reduce the gap between the real and the symbolic by projecting a (symbolic) message into the real" (36), in other words, one that does not explain but simply describes.

Žižek thus gives priority to a supplemental mode of ideological analysis that "aims at extracting the kernel of *enjoyment*" (*Symbolic* 125) and substitutes an immanent, discursive, *symptomal* reading for Althusser's *symptomatic* reading. Žižek blocks any materialist or symptomatic explanation of the lacks, disruptions, and crises in the everyday as effects of the historical social contradictions—specifically the inequalities of the social divisions of labor—and instead asserts a mystical, ludic nonknowledge. Ideological analysis, as he develops it, is homologous with psychoanalytic narratives, wherein a "fundamental non-knowledge insists" (*Symbolic* 68).

Perhaps nowhere is Žižek's mystification of the Real so evident as in his discussion of the Chernobyl disaster. He reduces the crisis to radioactive rays and states that

> the rays are thoroughly *unrepresentable*, no image is adequate to them. In their status as real, as the "hard kernel" around which every symbolization fails, they become pure semblance . . . they are entirely chimerical objects, effects of the incidence of the discourse of science upon our life world. (*Looking* 36)

Žižek has indeed succeeded in getting rid of what he calls the unfortunate paradigm of relations of production. He has reduced the specific historical forces and relations producing nuclear energy—whether in the monopoly capitalism of the West or the state capitalism of the East—into the mystical rays of discursive effects. Nowhere does he acknowledge that such a nuclear disaster is a consequence of superpower contestations and the so-called cold war, which produced the conditions under which inadequate and poorly designed equipment were built and put to use. The Chernobyl disaster is thus cut off from human history, labor relations, and the international competition for markets. It is turned into a ludic, excessive object of discourses that are aleatory and can move in any (unpredictable) direction. Objective reality, in other words, becomes the subject of ludic meditation and is reduced to mystical eruptions. Thus Žižek ends up claiming that some presymbolic, empty "Thing erupted that shook the very ground of our being" (*Looking* 37).

What is fundamentally at stake here for Žižek is that "access to knowledge is paid for with loss of enjoyment—enjoyment . . . is possible only on the basis of certain non-knowledge, ignorance" (*Sublime* 68). Žižek's answer is, of course, to abandon critique and the explanatory knowledge it produces, to instead "go through your fantasy"-ideology to "identify with the *sinthome*": in short, "enjoy your symptom." This is the basic obsession of the bourgeoisie, is it not? Fear of losing its enjoyment, fear of any restriction on its individual pleasure. Freedom is the right to pursue individual desire unhindered by regulation. In fact, for Žižek the great social evil is not exploitation but bureaucracy: government constraints on the individual's pursuit of pleasure. In this he is no different from Ronald Reagan, Margaret Thatcher, or Rush Limbaugh: they all want to deregulate the social so that maximum profits and pleasure can be obtained by those in power without any constraints on their enterprises.

compare to

Theory, as Althusser says, is the site of class struggle—or more generally the social struggles over the exploitation of labor, including race, gender, and sexuality as well as class. Žižek is a prominent player in this struggle, for he manages to articulate the dream of bourgeois theory: to ban labor and exploitation altogether from our knowledges and instead to leave us entirely in the realm of enjoyment, pleasure, and desire—which has become the hegemonic arena of (non)knowledge in the moment of ludic post-ality—an arena articulated not only by Žižek but also by theorists and critics as diverse as Baudrillard, Rubin, Elam, and Teresa de Lauretis. The ludic motto may well be Žižek's proclamation: "Enjoy your symptom as yourself."

The theory of sexuality as an autonomous practice free from social regulations is articulated not only by Rubin, but also more recently by Leo Bersani in his *Homos*. Bersani understands gay desire as resistant not only to heterosexuality but to sociality itself—acommunal, arelational, acausal. Such theories are basically retrograde articulations of upper-middle-class desire-as-need. At stake in Rubin's notion of sexuality is, in the last instance, the political economy of need—another way of saying that sexuality cannot be separated from use value, from production, and from the social division of labor that produces and deploys gender to justify its injustices. To segregate sexuality from gender is to posit it as an autonomous transhistorical desire that produces its own object of desire across the ages. Sexuality, however, is historical and not simply genealogical: it is implicated in and produced by class struggle, as are all other practices in human societies. Sexuality cut off from gender follows the same reduction Rubin enacts in all her writings: she reduces use value to exchange value and then posits exchange value (as in Baudrillard) as autonomous, self-propelling, and independent from the limits of the history of production.

The domain of the symbolic is theorized in ludic theory (as demonstrated by Deleuze and Guattari, Baudrillard, Derrida, and Žižek, to name only a few) as an independent site of differential workings of the sign.

Within such a cognitive mapping of the symbolic, Rubin and other ludic feminists articulate sexual desire as the effect of internal slippages—that is, as the essential "queerity" of the sign itself, which exceeds all regulatory systems of "straight" representation. To posit desire as the autonomous queerity of the sign is to reinscribe essentialism. It makes no difference whether desire or biology is posited ahistorically as the essence of sexuality. The fact that desire is mapped as internally unstable and the effect of libidinal vicissitudes (by Butler, Deleuze, Guattari, Rubin, de Lauretis, Michael Warner) does not change the fact that it is essentialized and naturalized.

Even such theorists of sexuality as Jeffrey Weeks and Kaja Silverman, both of whom have refused to abandon the notion of ideology in favor of discourse and who still continue to acknowledge the material construction of the symbolic as essentially ideological, are, however, unwilling to see the causal relation between sexuality and the economic. They tend to dismiss a materialist understanding of desire as functionalist and argue that sexual desire is mostly a matter of ideology, understood as an autonomous site of cultural politics, and not the economic. In "Capitalism and the Organization of Sexuality," for example, Weeks acknowledges that the notion of sexuality is "itself an ideological construct" (13), but then he relaxes the force of his proposition by saying that sexuality, like all other social practices, has "a relative autonomy within the capitalist system and from the ruling class" (14). In other words, his materialism of sexuality collapses into a materiality of ideology without connecting ideology and the material base of culture in a necessary relation. If indeed the "swinging, self-confident affluent homosexual male who lives in the pages of *Advocate*" (11) is a new sexual type that is as "limiting as the old stereotypes" (11), it makes sense to ask, what is this logic that is constant to capitalism and never goes away? If it is the effect of an autonomous practice, why does this autonomy seem to be constructed by the constants of class society? There is, in other words, a structure to these limits, and the structure is the articulation of the social relations of production, which at any historical moment also constructs the object of desire. The subject always desires what is historically possible. The very emergence of the "queer" itself is the effect of the development of forces of production and shifts in the organic composition of capital (which I shall explain later in my discussion of the relation between production and reproduction of life). The emergence of the "homosexual" is, itself, characteristic of a historical moment in which the forces of production have reached such a level of sophistication in their productivity that heterosexu-

[handwritten marginalia: naturally homosexual when ridiculed to show means of production]

ality (as a means of maintaining the reserve army of labor at a relatively high level) is no longer necessary. The reason heterosexuality is naturalized, in other words, is historical: societies that need to maintain their labor force at a certain level while facing plague, famine, and other natural and social disasters secure heterosexuality as a natural and sacred practice and marginalize other nonprocreative sexualities. In advanced capitalism, what is marginal is losing its historical reason for being marginal. Thus, as Foucault and others have pointed out, the emergence of new surfaces of desire and new forms of sexuality. To relate the expansion of sexuality, in the classic anarchic mode, to the state (what constitutes the basis of Foucault's notion of control) is to find an alibi for capitalism. It is the development of the forces of production that makes the naturalization of heterosexuality relatively unnecessary and not the need of the state to control. Capitalism does that control through its regime of exchange and consumption much more effectively on the economic level. This is the reason for what Weeks calls the "explosive emergence of sexuality in capitalist society" (11) and not the ideology of the state. The fact that homophobia is an obstacle to full legal and social integration of lesbians and gays is more a matter of the contradictions between the social relations of production and forces of production, contradictions that are now the substance of what conservatives call "culture wars" (see Field). One has to keep in mind that the very concept of homosexuality and the emergence of a distinctly recognizable mode of queer life, as Peter Ray argues, is the outcome of the development of capitalism as a result of "the industrial revolution of the eighteenth and nineteenth centuries" (32). As the Marxist queer theorist John D'Emilio writes in his text "Capitalism and Gay Identity,"

[handwritten marginalia: homosexuality form of means of labor]

> I want to argue that gay men and lesbians have not always existed. Instead, they are a product of history, and have come into existence in a specific historical era. Their emergence is associated with the relations of capitalism; it has been the historical development of capitalism—more specifically, its free labor system—that has allowed large numbers of men and women in the late twentieth century to call themselves gay, to see themselves as part of a community of similar men and women, and to organize politically on the basis of that identity. (*Making Trouble*, 5)

It is this historical specificity of the material conditions of possibility of homosexuality and desire that is occluded in ludic queer theory.

Kaja Silverman's discussion of masculinity, like Weeks's discourse on homosexuality, opens with a very productive critique of dominant theories. She begins her book *Male Subjectivity at the Margins* by demonstrating how the ruling discourses obscure those modes of analysis that stand in their way. She writes:

> Twenty-two years since the French publication of Foucault's *The Archaeology of Knowledge*, which can be retrospectively seen to have effected a kind of epistemological "break" with the Althusserian tradition, the word "ideology" may seem to exude the stale aroma of a theoretical anachronism. I would like nevertheless to suggest that, far from having exhausted itself, the great ideology debate of the 1960s and 1970s was broken off prematurely, before a series of crucial issues could be addressed. (15)

Her discussion of masculinity, desire, and sexuality, however, fails to recover the historicity of sexual desire. Like Weeks and other neo-Althusserians, she deploys a theory of ideology based on the semiautonomy of the cultural. Subjectivity and desire become part of ideological belief without a rigorous analysis of the relations of these ideological beliefs to social relations of production. Weeks and Silverman, in spite of their emphasis on ideology, end up more or less in the position of Andrew Parker and others who have critiqued Marxism for "unthinking sex" (Parker 19–41).

Parker's mode of approaching the theory of gender and sexuality in Marxism is a predictable rehearsal of the general logic of ludic theory. Instead of addressing the concepts through which Marx and Engels explain sexuality and gender and dealing with these concepts in terms of their explanatory ability, Parker examines their rhetoric. His approach in "Unthinking Sex: Marx, Engels, and the Scene of Writing," is similar to the one I have discussed in the case of Elam. It assumes that Marx and Engels's argument is undercut by their rhetoric; thus, he examines their language in order to show how their sexuality permeates their argument. The *sex* of the theorist and his own sexual preferences (or what Parker attributes to him) become substitutes for his theory of *sexuality*. I leave aside here the unsaid of Parker's reading, which is founded upon the notion that the experience of the subject is what constitutes knowledge. One cannot go beyond one's own desire, and all knowledge is, in this view, in fact a performance of desire. For Parker, Marx's theory of gender and family is an expression of his (latent homoerotic) desires.

In developing this reading, Parker plays on Rubin's "Thinking Sex" and performs a deconstruction of the production paradigm, because, as he says, "Western Marxism's constitutive dependence on the category of production derives in part from an antitheatricalism, an aversion to certain forms of parody that prevents sexuality from attaining the political significance that class has long monopolized" (28). He attempts, in other words, to "map the (de)structuring effects of eroticism . . . [and] to explore some ways that sexuality . . . thinks Marx" (31). In so doing he turns the historical materialist theory of production into a parodic "tropology . . . where production has been modeled on procreation" (41). But such tropoerotic destructuring of Marx's texts does not provide a new explanation; in fact, through parody, it discredits all explanations. Parker, like Rubin, naturalizes the erotic as the excessive practice that moves history but is itself transhistorical. The "always already" world of lust that emerges from this anti-explanation is the one that pragmatically legitimates the interests of capital. It does not account for practices because lust (as the sublime) cannot be accounted for. Lust is an unexplainable force of what can only be called nature, since it is in itself and has no source other than itself: it is self-originating. This final return to the natural and the biological shows how, after a relatively long detour (what is usually read as subtlety in the ludic academy), Rubin, Parker, Fuss, and other ludic feminists and queer theorists arrive at reactionary and oppressive conclusions: biology (lust, desire) is once again the grounding truth of feminism. The new subject of biology is, of course, a self-reflexive one who has very little in common with the earlier experiential feminism. But the conclusions of both are the same: it is nature (self-origination) that transhistorically shapes human practices.

Parker's reading is really not so much an argument showing how Marxism "unthinks" sex as a demonstration of the way Parker himself occludes Marxism's emancipatory theory of gender and sexuality by substituting rhetoric for revolution on the ludic grounds that that *concept* is undercut by *language*. Such a move does not show how Marxism unthinks sex; rather, it stages a layered unthinking of class and exploitation. Rhetoric always performs in a specific historical context: to reduce Marx's language to a set of panhistorical tropes provides pleasureful reading for the bourgeois subject, but it does not explain Marx's materialist theory of gender and sexuality. In contrast, we need to emphasize the writings of such theorists as John D'Emilio who insist that desire is social and provide an important response to these all too familiar charges against materialist theories of

[margin annotation: Rhetoric *]*

sexuality. As D'Emilio demonstrates in his historical analyses, "Capitalism has created the material conditions for homosexual desire to express itself as a central component of some individual's lives" (*Making Trouble* 12). As part of these material conditions, capitalism, particularly the "free labor system," as D'Emilio argues, has led to the separation of sexuality from procreation. Human sexual desire need no longer be harnessed to reproductive imperatives, to procreation" (12).

What we are left with, then, in ludic theories of the social is an ever increasing localization and fragmentation of knowledge of gender and sexual production. Desire (lust) is not only considered autonomous but primary, and needs are radically suppressed. Ludic theories, as I have already discussed, serve the interests of the (upper) middle class: for only those whose basic needs are already comfortably fulfilled can afford to dispense with the necessity of meeting basic needs and focus instead on fulfilling desires.

[handwritten margin note: Bourgeois emphasize desire; disregard basic needs.]

Division of Labor, or Difference?

By restricting their scope to ever more limited localities and conjunctures, ludic theories sever any causal relations and systematic connections among diverse practices in the social. Rubin's demand for the autonomy of lust enacts Mouffe's and Laclau's erasure of society into multiplicities of heterogenous "social logics." "Society," Laclau proclaims, "does not 'exist'" ("Building" 16). In place of society, we are left with a series of incommensurable differences—differences that Rubin argues should be considered in their own autonomy as different terms. What exists, to go back to Laclau, exists "in the pragmatic." As I have already discussed, in Fish and Rorty the pragmatic is an affirmation of the actually existing and a withdrawal from the struggle for social change. Such a withdrawal only serves the class interests of the few who are well-off within the existing social order.

Hansen and Philipson's short history of socialist feminism demonstrates a common strategy for displacing (forgetting) historical materialism. By asserting the impasse of dual-systems theory, Hansen and Philipson implicitly equate one specific way of theorizing gender in terms of the relations of production with the production paradigm itself. They thereby project the limitations, the impasse, of the former onto the latter. Indeed dual-systems theory has been inadequate—not because it is materialist, but because it is not materialist enough. Dual-systems theory has posited patriarchy and capitalism as two independent systems and then encountered serious difficulties not only in theorizing their conjunction but also in articulating patriarchy.

Patriarchy has usually been understood as distinct from the relations of production and, thus, as a universal, transhistorical structure, particularly an ideological or psychoanalytic one, as Juliet Mitchell argued in *Psychoanalysis and Feminism*. When patriarchy has been given a more materialist reading, the various versions of dual-systems theory have either undermined their own dual nature or posited a separate-spheres model.[5]

For instance, in defining patriarchy as "a set of social relations between men . . . that enable them to dominate women," Heidi Hartmann argues that "the material base upon which patriarchy rests lies most fundamentally in men's control over women's labor power" (14, 15) and that "the same features, such as the division of labor, often reinforce both patriarchy and capitalism" (29). This means, as Iris Young points out in her critique of dual-systems theory, that "it does not seem possible to separate patriarchy from a system of social relations of production . . . [and] if patriarchy and capitalism are manifest in identical social and economic structures they belong to *one* system, not two" ("Beyond" 47). The separate-spheres version, on the other hand, has located patriarchy and women's labor in the private space of the family, and capitalism and men's labor in the public arena of the economy. It has thus been unable to deal with the oppression of women outside the family or the current move of large numbers of women into wage labor. As Hansen and Philipson point out, dual-systems theory, with its emphasis on the division between public economy and private, domestic work,

> was speaking to an increasingly outmoded reality, one in which a male breadwinner supported a wife whose sole responsibility was domestic labor. By the mid-1970s, however, 47 percent of all women aged eighteen to sixty-four worked outside the home, and that proportion would rise to 63 percent by the mid-1980s. (19)

The specific limitations of dual-systems theory, however, do not invalidate the production paradigm and its explanatory power or its necessity for building a transformative theory and praxis of gender and sexuality.

As I will briefly discuss below, Marxist feminists have analyzed and understood the impasse of dual-systems theory and have contributed in quite rich and effective ways to the production of knowledges and transformative practices, but Hansen and Philipson omit this work from their story and from their collection of essays. Instead, they focus the rest of their tale on those "socialist feminists within the academy [who] are continuing to explore new terrain, develop new insights, expand on and move beyond the framework that Gayle Rubin set forth in her work on the sex/gender system" (23). The "new" in their narrative stands for those theories that abandon socialism for a ludic notion of radical democracy and replace transformative explanation with ludic description. If the production paradigm is mentioned or discussed at all in their tale, it is only to be dismissed, displaced, forgotten (e.g., 24–25). Their story and their anthology, in short, put forth a socialist feminism without historical materialism—a feminism more accurately described as a ludic radical democracy whose main features are described by Stanley Aronowitz in his "The Situation of the Left in the United States." Hansen and Philipson (like Aronowitz) largely replace historical materialism with cultural materialism, which is the main frame for nearly all the essays in the collection, including the only essay on Marxism, Sandra Morgen's, which rejects the way "Marxist economic reductionism imbues the mode of production with such deterministic influence" (282). Morgen is concerned instead with issues of consciousness and agency: with incorporating into Marxism the "importance of feelings, the unconscious, language and the roles of childbearer and child rearer in the development of women's consciousness" (283). The essays that address economic relations (mostly in the section on "Women, Work and the Labor Movement") do not go beyond a local empiricism and descriptivism, primarily around the issue of "comparable worth."

This strategy of projecting the limitations, the impasse of a specific articulation (dual-systems theory) onto the project of historical materialism provides an effective alibi for marginalizing and silencing current Marxist feminist theories of (re)production. This is the case not only in the Hansen-Philipson anthology but also in the Landry-MacLean history of materialist feminisms, which supplants the "impasse of socialist feminism" with a "poststructuralist identity politics." It is, therefore, quite common to misrepresent historical materialist theories (when they are acknowledged at all) as past, as outdated, as superseded by newer ludic knowledges (especially discursive, cultural materialisms) and, in so doing, dismiss them from most feminist and socialist feminist discourses. But this logic of outdatedness is a convenient invention to conceal a political contestation: it covers over the social struggle in the site of theory. In this way it is able to represent ludic knowledges as new boundary knowledges that are self-evidently better and true—true not because they have access to any core of the real (a possibility already denied) but because they are new, exciting, pleasureful, and seductive. Contesting knowledges—such as those produced by historical materialism—are simply erased as nonseductive (outdated). Consequently, knowledge is itself represented as the newest discourse, regardless of what it explains and what it occludes: "new" is that which is at the "end" of thought.

I put aside here the contradictions in the ludic self-representation of itself: the fact that, on one hand, ludic theory denounces "progress" as a modernist metanarrative (e.g., Flax 3–33, 75–91), but, on the other hand, represents itself as the outcome of progress—the transformation of the old into the new. The ludic argument about the outdatedness of historical materialism wins in the postmodern academy not because of its *truth* but because of its *appeal*. In the academy where one's worth (marketability) comes from the newness of one's knowledges, there is little room for whatever is designated as old. Like capitalists, whose survival depends on their ability to out-new their competitors, the ludic academy constantly seeks new forms of commodifying knowledge. Erasing historical materialism from the scene, ludic theory is represented not as a historical construct that is ultimately a response to the contradictions of the social division of labor, but as a form of immanent knowledge produced by language in a panhistorical "always already."

We see the operation of this ludic dismissal in Donna Haraway's genealogy "Gender for a Marxist Dictionary," especially in her reading of Iris Young's earlier (socialist) writings. In the early 1980s, Iris Young wrote several essays that moved beyond dual-systems theory and helped articulate a very important way of retheorizing gender and the relations of production for a feminist historical materialism. Young argued, "We need not merely a synthesis of feminism with traditional Marxism, but a thoroughly feminist historical materialism, which regards the social relations of a particular historical social formation as one system in which gender differentiation is a core attribute ("Socialist Feminism" 181). The basis for such a global and at the same time gender-differentiating theory is the social division of labor. According to Young, although "the category of class is gender blind and hence incapable of exposing women's situation, we can nevertheless remain with the materialist framework by elevating the category of *division of labor* to a position as fundamental as, if not more fundamental than, that of class" ("Beyond" 50). Thus, Young proposed that a "feminist historical materialism might utilize gender division of labor as a central category" ("Socialist Feminism" 185) and went on to claim that

> feminist historical materialism should remain Marxist in the sense that it takes the structure of laboring activity, and the relations arising from laboring activity, broadly defined, as a crucial determinant of social phenomena . . . [I]t must also find a way of analyzing social relations arising from laboring activity in gender-differentiated terms. (186)

This focus on the primacy of the division of labor for a feminist historical materialism is profoundly enabling, theoretically and politically. It moves beyond the essentialization of class, race, and gender as separate but equal categories of difference. Young's theory is that this essentialized difference has created the real impasse in feminism: a political theory paralyzed by the pluralism of mutually competing distinct differences that cannot be adequately theorized in relation to each other or in terms of systematic relations of exploitation. Of course, ludic feminism and post-Marxism have turned this concept of autonomous differences into a virtue, redefining society as "a multiplicity of social logics" (Mouffe 142). Gayatri Spivak, in response to a question about whether materialist feminism could include "an anti-racist position as well," answers: "No, I don't think so. I think these movements are very discontinuous . . . [E]ach of these things brings the other to crisis." She then goes on to separate Marxism from feminism and to divide both by their "heterogeneity" (*Post-Colonial* 138). Not only does Spivak reify differences as irreducible and discontinuous, she reproduces the bourgeois depoliticization of social theory as "crisis": a condition in which the law of necessity is suspended and no explanation of the social series can be offered other than a description of unexplainability—that is, of crisis. Crisis, in bourgeois theory is the concept under which conceptualization itself is suspended. Crisis is beyond explanation. This is its privilege and valorization in ludic theory. By reading the historical relations of conflicting theories—whose conflicts articulate the social contradictions of diverse class interests—in terms of crises, Spivak substitutes excitement (the crisis of difference) for effectivity: the ability of a theory to offer the historical explanations and guidelines necessary for social change.

Politics as a series of proliferating discontinuities and crises of differences makes for a very problematic and ineffective praxis—if one's political agenda is to end social exploitation and inequality and not simply to expand the range of possibilities for the desires of the already privileged. In contrast, putting the processes of the production, division, and exploitation of labor at the core of historical materialist feminism provides the means for articulating a historically differentiated yet integrated theory and praxis of social oppression and emancipation globally. The theory of the division of labor also enables feminist historical materialism to overcome the debilitating break in ludic theories between the cultural and economic, for it provides the grounds for explaining the relation among the cultural and ideological processes producing meanings and subjectivities and the relations of production structuring exploitation.

Haraway offers a much different reading of Young's theory of the division of labor, a reading that has become the dominant one. In her genealogy of feminism she calls Young's theory

> a good example of strongly rationalist, modernist approaches, for which the "postmodern" moves of the disaggregation of metaphors of single systems in favour of complex open fields of criss-crossing plays of domination, privilege, and difference appeared very threatening. (*Simians* 139–40)

This is, in effect, a dismissal of rationalism and modernism, modes of knowing that are, according to Haraway, "threatened," that is, subverted and *superseded* by ludic "'postmodern' moves of the disaggregation of metaphors of single systems"—or, in other words, by the deconstruction of the social totality of patriarchal capitalism into a series of tropes and incommensurate textualities. "Rationalist and modernist approaches" (specifically, feminist historical materialist theories of the division of labor and relations of production) are displaced by "criss-crossing plays of domination, privilege, and difference," that is by a deconstructive understanding of the (linguistic) play of differences as multiple chains of slipping signifiers and as reversible ("supplementary") hierarchies of difference. In other words, the historical binaries of exploiter and exploited produced by the social division of labor and the unequal appropriation of surplus labor are reread as a simple play of power that can be deconstructed by textualizing chains of supplementary, shifting signifiers that will disallow binaries and thus (Haraway believes) liberate women. Haraway's model of the social is fashioned after the Foucauldian resignification of exploitation as domination, in which power is cut off from the relations of production and becomes an autonomous network of local, reversible, generative exercises of resistance and domination. It undoes the historical binaries of powerful/powerless, oppressor/oppressed, exploiter/exploited. Thus revolution and the struggle for emancipation are no longer considered necessary or even *possible* (as we shall see in Butler's recent writing), since power, for Foucault, is itself generative: it generates its own forms of resistance, immanently reversing the hierarchies of (difference) powerful/powerless.

In short, the new ludic ways of understanding reality in terms of a textual *differance* (redescription, remetaphorization) and regimes of power-discourse represent themselves as not only supplanting an obsolete modernism but also as superseding an outdated historical materialist theory of exploitation and emancipation. Such arguments, as I have already indicated, incoherently presuppose a modernist sense of progressive chronology and reproduce the common sense of commodity capitalism, in which the newest of the new is best. The dominant ludic discourses have, in fact, been so successful in discrediting historical materialism that many socialist feminists, from Michèle Barrett and Zillah Eisenstein to Iris Young, have now either abandoned Marxism and the theory of production altogether or have significantly marginalized them in their work. Such a distancing and renunciation of Marxism and historical materialism in contemporary feminist theory has become increasingly required if one's writings are to remain (academically) viable and not be dismissed as superseded: especially after the eclipse of socialism in the Soviet Union and Eastern Europe, an eclipse marked by that signifier the Berlin Wall. Knowledges are abandoned not because they are not truthful but because their truth is incompatible (pragmatically) with the winning side: free-market economy and bourgeois democracy. Thus, Barrett, as I have already suggested, has moved from her earlier position in *Women's Oppression Today*, in which she decries postmodern discursive politics as "discursive imperialism" (88), to a position embracing it in the theories of Foucault and post-Marxism. Eisenstein now declares that "I no longer think socialist feminism is an accurate naming of my politics" ("Specifying" 45), and Young, under pressure from post-al knowledges, has largely backgrounded the division of labor in her work in favor of a more ludic notion of the politics of difference, as in her *Justice and the Politics of Difference*.

The ludic displacement of theories of the relations of production—and a praxis committed to ending the exploitation of labor—as superseded by post-al multiplicities and deconstructed binaries becomes an elaborate alibi to conceal the increasing economic divisions (the very real binaries) between the haves and the have-nots. Ludic theories, in other words, resolve in the imaginary the very real contradictions of patriarchal capitalism. They provide the necessary theories that deconstruct praxical binaries in the discourses of the imaginary. Doing so has given ludic writings prestige (as innovative) and privilege (for subtlety) and turned them into hegemonic theories at the very time when *actual inequality* is gaining social popularity and legitimacy, especially in the United States, and is "now being widely defended as a source of productivity, economic growth and individual striving for excellence" (Dionne 13). The real economic inequality between the privileged classes in the West and the exploited classes—both in the West and globally whose surplus labor is appropriated to produce that privilege—is a severe problem. In the United States alone, according to the Economic Policy Institute, there has been a substantial redistribution of wealth.

> [T]he share of the nation's wealth owned by the top 10 percent of its households rose from 67.5 percent to 73.1 percent between 1979 and 1988. The share of after-tax family income earned by the top 10 percent rose from 29.5 percent in 1980 to an estimated 34.9 percent in 1990. In the same periods, the income share of the bottom 10 percent dropped from 1.7 percent to 1.4 percent.
>
> The broad middle class—the 60 percent of Americans between richest and poorest—saw its share of family income decline from 50.2 percent in 1980 to an estimated 46.5 percent in 1990. (Dionne 13)

Such disparities, especially between the "overdeveloped" and "underdeveloped"[6] countries, have led to a resurgence of historical materialism among Third World feminists. For example, Norma Stoltz Chinchilla, one of the editors of a special issue of *Gender and Society* devoted to Marxist feminism, points to the historical conditions that have made Marxist feminism an urgent issue in Latin America, while it is occluded in the United States and Western Europe. As she argues,

> During the 1980s, . . . work on dissolving the hyphen and transforming Marxist-feminism into a political project languished on the back burner in the United States and Western Europe . . . In contrast, by the end of the 1980s, the synthesis of ideas from contemporary Marxist and feminist traditions and their transformation into a concrete politi-

cal strategy for social change had become a high priority for a growing number of Marxists and feminists in Latin America, especially in Mexico, Nicaragua, Peru, Brazil, Chile, and the Dominican Republic . . . This difference in emphasis in the Latin American and North American feminist movements is directly related to the different political and economic contexts within which social movements in the two areas have developed over the last decade. Conservative governments in the United States and Britain have reduced or dismantled social programs that benefit the poor and increased investment and tax incentives for the rich while maintaining the illusion that capitalism will continue to provide for all who are deserving. Events in the Soviet Union and Eastern Europe are generally interpreted by the press in those countries as definitive proof that socialism is terminally ill while capitalism is eternally young.

Meanwhile, the basically capitalist Latin American economies are undergoing one of their worst crises in history, with devastating effects on the living standards of the majority of people. (291–92)

The high priority many give Marxist feminism in the Third World and its marginalization and suppression in the First World raise serious questions about the priorities of feminism in these two arenas. For all its concern with differences and the exclusion of others (people of color, lesbians, gays), ludic feminism in the West primarily understands social change as an identity politics aimed at extending middle-class privileges—especially the free consumption of pleasures and fulfillment of desires—instead of engaging social change as the fundamental restructuring of the relations of production in order to end exploitation and provide all people with equal distribution of social resources.

A. Sivanandan, the editor of *Race and Class*, makes an important critique of Western (particularly British post-Marxist) identity politics and the way it substitutes a discursive "politics of hegemony" for class struggle. Sivanandan asks,

How do you extend a "politics of food" to the hungry, a "politics of the body" to the homeless, a "politics of the family" for those without an income? How do any of these politics connect up with the third world? . . . Class cannot just be a matter of identity, it has to be the focus of commitment. ("All" 18–19)

This is because, as Sivanandan has argued, "[T]he colour line is the power line is the poverty line . . . In South Africa, one might even say, race is class and class race, and the race struggle is the class struggle" ("Address" 65–66). Historical materialist feminism needs to move beyond Sivanandan here to insist that is not just an issue for South Africa, but for the world struggle against global capitalism.[7] The global system of exploitation is based on the appropriation of surplus labor according to social divisions of labor—that is, according to class. These class differences are themselves based on the historical division of labor in terms of the construction of gender and race differences: "race is class and class race"; gender is class and class gender, and the race struggle and the gender struggle are the class struggle. In short, the gender, race, and class struggles are all fundamentally the same struggle to end the social division and exploitation of labor: they are the struggle for international socialism.

Chandra Mohanty speaks to this problem in *Third World Women and the Politics of Feminism*. She not only refers to Sivanandan's critique of identity politics but also foregrounds his commitment to, as she says, "build our politics around the struggles of the most exploited peoples of the world" and his questioning of "'discourse' as an adequate terrain of struggle." Mohanty thus argues that "while discursive categories are clearly central sites of political contestation, they must be grounded in and informed by the material politics of everyday life, especially the daily life struggles for survival of poor people—those written out of history" (10–11).

But how is materialist politics understood here? Is it simply another form of discursive or cultural materialism? If so, it will not take us very far toward fundamentally changing the conditions of the poor but rather will leave us with variations on the "politics of food," "the politics of the body," "the politics of the family," as indeed has been the case in ludic feminism. Only when feminists understand material politics as *historical materialism*, as struggle over the relations of production, will it be possible to build an effective collective politics of emancipation around the struggles of the most exploited peoples of the world—an international socialist feminism.

It is thus important to emphasize here that in spite of the ludic turn taken by so many socialist feminists and the campaigns against the production paradigm, feminist historical materialism is not only not over, it is the site of some complex and effective theoretical work and a new historical urgency. The German Marxist feminist Frigga Haug, for example, has recently argued that historical conditions since the fall of the Berlin Wall have convinced me of the need to revive the debate on the relationship of women's oppression and the mode of production. In these days when capitalism seems to be the only alternative worldwide, I think that it is more urgent and strategic to turn to this question: how does capitalist patriarchy reproduce itself? ("Boys' Games" 51)

Haug's call for a return to the problem of the mode of production is especially important because much of her previous work—particularly the "memory work" she has done on the socialization of sexuality with the feminist collective associated with the Marxist journal *Das Argument*—has tended toward a cultural and discursive materialism.

Some of the most important work in feminist historical materialism is the "German School" of feminist theorists (Omvedt 40), Maria Mies, Veronika Bennholdt-Thomsen, and Claudia von Werlhof, who have retheorized the relations of production and gender inequality. The major articulation in English is their collaborative project, *Women: The Last Colony*, and Mies's *Patriarchy and Accumulation on a World Scale*. Their work contests the priority given the "narrow, capitalist concept of 'productive labor'"—that is, the wage labor production of surplus for capital—as "the most formidable hurdle in our struggle to come to an understanding of women's labour both under capitalism and actually existing socialism" (Mies, *Patriarchy* 48). Instead, they argue for a more general concept of the *productivity of labor*: "labour can only be productive in the sense of producing surplus values as long as it can tap, extract, exploit, and appropriate labour which is spent in the *production of life* or *subsistence production* . . . which is largely non-wage labour mainly done by women . . . producing use values for the satisfaction of human needs" (*Patriarchy* 47). The production of life is understood here as not simply the reproduction of human beings, but as the production of all forms of subsistence goods and use values necessary to meet basic human needs. While I have critique-al differences with this account (as I will discuss more fully below) its importance for materialist feminism is its argument for the production of life as the "perennial precondition of all other historical forms of productive labour" (47)—that is, the production of surplus value—and of all forms of accumulation. As Mies argues,

It is my thesis that this general production of life, or subsistence production—mainly performed through the non-wage labour of women and other non-wage labourers as slaves, contract workers, and peas-

ants in the colonies—constitutes the perennial basis upon which "capitalist productive labour" can be built up and exploited. Without the
ongoing subsistence production of non-wage labourers (mainly
women), wage labour would not be "productive." In contrast to Marx,
I consider the capitalist production process as one which comprises
both: the *superexploitation* of non-wage labourers (women, colonies,
peasants) upon which wage labour exploitation then is possible. I
define the exploitation as superexploitation because it is not based on
the appropriation (by the capitalist) of the time and labour over and
above the "necessary" labour time, the *surplus* labour, but of the time
and labour *necessary* for people's own survival or subsistence production. It is not compensated for by a wage . . . but is mainly determined
by force or coercive institutions. This is the main reason for the growing poverty and starvation of Third World producers. (48)

Building on the broad concept of productive labor in Marx as the
transformation of natural matter and his theory of primitive accumulation,
Mies understands the production of surplus values and the accumulation
of wealth as based, in part, on the appropriation and exploitation (the
superexploitation) of subsistence labor. In so doing, she, along with
Bennholdt-Thomson and von Werlhof, provides an important means for
theorizing the oppression of women, people of color, workers, and the colonized across various modes of production and historical social formations, but especially in global, imperialist capitalism. Their work opens up
a new way to explain the construction of social differences in relation to the
unequal divisions and appropriations of surplus labor (not only of the
wage worker but also of the subsistence worker) as part of an integrated
system without having to posit differences, such as gender, as a separate
ideological sphere distinct from the economic. It enables understanding the
relation of these different forms of productivity to each other and the subject's multiple and contradictory place within them. This is especially
important for socialist feminism because it moves beyond the binary of
public/private and does not simply equate the production of life with
domestic labor; yet it still accounts for household work.

Their work also enables an integrated understanding of gender, race,
and class differences as interrelated effects of the same process of exploitation of labor. It thus overcomes the deadlock of essentialized differences
that arises when they are understood as separate identities. The gender
division of labor is, for Mies, the precondition of all appropriation of sur-

plus value and accumulation, and thus of class differences, in any economic system. Materialist feminists can use this theory to explain the
importance of the division and exploitation of labor around race with the
development of capitalism, first through slavery, one of the primary means
of capitalizing the industrial revolution, and then through colonization and
systematic economic racism.[8]

The work of Mies, Bennholdt-Thomsen, and von Werlhof provides a
basis for explaining the collective exploitation of women—*in different
ways*—around the gender division of labor. I will address some of the problems and limitations with this theory below. Before doing so, however, it is
important to recognize that Mies's *Patriarchy and Accumulation* also contains an undeveloped, but potentially effective, concept of the subject for a
feminist historical materialism. The subject, including the body of the subject, is produced through the activity of labor according to its position in
the division of labor. Mies argues that women

> can experience their *whole* body as productive . . . It is of crucial impor-
> tance . . . that women's activity in producing children and milk is
> understood as truly *human*, that is, *conscious, social activity* . . . the activ-
> ity of women in bearing and rearing children has to be understood as
> work . . . [not] as purely physiological. (53)

The subject—its body, consciousness, meanings—is produced by and
through labor. For example, as women learned to invent "the regular cultivation of grains and tubers" and to breed animals (55), they also cultivated
a socially productive relation with their own bodies vis-à-vis the conditions
of production. Thus slave women in the Caribbean acted on (transformed)
their bodies to produce a birth strike as a form of resistance to the exploitation of their labor (90–92).

As promising as this theory is for feminist historical materialism,
Mies's own work is quite contradictory. She does not develop the consequences of her own understanding of the relations of production and elides
some crucial aspects of the Marxist notion of productive labor, class, and
surplus value. As a result, Mies sometimes abandons the powerful insights
of her own historical materialism. For example, Mies is quite right to argue
for the importance of the uses of violence and coercion in enforcing the
exploitation of subsistence labor—contrary to Foucauldian, nondeterminate power. However, her articulation of this issue and the origins of the
gender division of labor in terms of a male "predatory mode of produc-

tion" and masculine aggression tends toward culturalism. More problematically still, she gives priority to consumption over production (second part of *Patriarchy;* and esp. Mies and Shiva, *Ecofeminism,* which turns to middle-class voluntaristic consumerism as the agency of social change).

The work of Mies, Bennholdt-Thomsen, and von Werlhof is just one instance of the dynamic theorization of gender and relations of production among Marxist and socialist feminists. Their writings are an important contribution to an ongoing critique in contemporary feminist theory of the questions of production and reproduction as well as the problematics of patriarchy. Especially useful are Mies's earlier writings, which try to theorize patriarchy as a material force through the social division of labor. Although such a move is promising, she ends up by theorizing along more familiar paths and understands reproductive practices (what she and other theorists of the German school call the production of life) as a semiautonomous and transhistorical sphere. The production of life is regarded as a mode of production different from production for wages and profit and to be a mode of production for subsistence. It is, in short, a form of production not subject to the laws of the mode of production of capitalism. Mies's notion of the production of life draws upon the writings of earlier Marxists such as Rosa Luxemburg, who also considered capitalism as the effect not only of wage labor but also of a panhistorical primitive accumulation or form of surplus extracted from nonwage peasant workers on the periphery of the empire. This semiautonomous mode of production of life is also seen as having its own specificity.

However, what is a material practice and constitutes part of the social division of labor in Mies and other theorists of the German school becomes a question of desire in the writings of ludic feminists. In ludic theories, the mode of production and such other concepts as the social division of labor and class disappear, and the feminine becomes a sign subject to the differential laws of representation. The feminine, in short, becomes an aleatory sign whose surprising swervings put in question the stable signs and representations of patriarchy. The feminine, therefore, for ludic theorists, is not only not determined by the mode of production but, in fact, renders the laws of the mode of production undecidable. The production of life is seen as a question of desire, which is situated independently from the mode of production, and any analysis that renders desire as determined by the mode of production is dismissed as reductive (see, e.g., Nicholson, "Feminism and Marxism"; Cornell, *Beyond Accommodation* and *Philosophy;* Flax, *Thinking;* de Lauretis, *Technologies*). For ludic feminists, desire is itself treated as a material force.

In theorizing desire not as a lack (as classical psychoanalysis has done) but as a materiality in its own right, ludic feminism has deployed some of the theories put forth by Deleuze and Guattari in *Anti-Oedipus* and *A Thousand Plateaus*. In a famous passage in *Anti-Oedipus* (which I have already discussed), Deleuze and Guattari argue that desire should itself be "conceived of as production" (25) because "Desire does not lack anything" (26). Most importantly, they emphasize that "Desire and its object are one and the same thing" (26).

> The truth of the matter is that *social production is purely and simply desiring production itself under determinate conditions.* We maintain that the social field is immediately invested by desire, that it is the historically determined product of desire, and that the libido has no need of any mediation or sublimation, any psychic operation, any transformation, in order to invade and invest the productive forces and the relations of production. *There is only desire and the social and nothing else.* (29)

[handwritten marginal note: call for desire production is a form of desire]

I must point out that when Deleuze and Guattari mention determination, they have in mind not the forces of production, which are outside desire, but self-determination: an immanent determination of desire by its own working. Since the social in their theory is an effect of desire, to talk about socially determined is in fact a roundabout way of talking about the determination of desire by its own inner working. This is, in spite of its claims, an understanding of the social in a Hegelian mode: the social as alienated desire. Ludic feminism deploys the notion of desire as a materiality destabilizing the laws of the mode of production, and in so doing it, in effect, posits the production of life (i.e., human reproduction) as an independent domain, the domain of desire. The mode of production (to the extent that it survives in these mediated forms in the ludic theories of Haraway, Fuss, Butler, Cornell, Irigaray, and others) not only does not determine the practices of reproduction but is itself undermined by the excessive slippage of desire that is the (ludic) law of reproduction.

Production, Reproduction, Patriarchy

Positing reproductive practices as a semiautonomous sphere—whether in the theories of Mies and the German school along the lines of feminist historical materialism or in ludic feminism as a mode of desire—is done in the name of overcoming the flaws of Marxist notions of family, sexuality, and gender. Both such theories present themselves as politically progressive undertakings that aim at freeing theories of women and gender from the yoke of masculinist, rationalist, and totalizing notions such as the mode of production, which do not respect the specificity and difference of women. Theorists of autonomy regard themselves as progressive in their claims to avoid universalizing and their attention to localities of oppression and the nomadic (to use Deleuze and Guattari's term) difference of the feminine (see Jardine; Haraway, *Simians*; Barrett, *Politics*; Miles; Suleiman).

It is argued by ludic feminists and queer theorists as well as by socialist and dual-systems theorists (e.g., Schor, "Dreaming"; Eisenstein, "Developing"; Weeks) that oppression according to gender and sexuality is not specific to capitalism. Instead, it is the feature of all modes of production known to us. The exploitation of women is, in other words, panhistorical and as such must be theorized through such other practices as patriarchy, desire, mode of human reproduction, or (as has become popular through postmodern eclecticism) as a combination of all these, and thus as autonomous from the mode of production. These questions are, admittedly, extremely complex and have been the main issues in feminist theory over the last quarter of a century. To address them in their surface variations and discursive differences would require another full-length book in contemporary intellectual history and the politics of the concept. Obviously such an undertaking is beyond the scope of this project; however, I would like to outline here a historical materialist understanding of the relation of production and reproduction and the problematics of patriarchy in order to provide a general context for my contestation of the idea of the autonomy of the "reproduction" of life from the mode of production without, of course, erasing a historically specific and materialist concept of patriarchy. I begin with the commonly shared premise that gender and sexuality are not natural but the effect of history and the outcome of social practices. It is true that the issue of how gender and sexuality are constructed (by discourse or by class, for example) is the subject of considerable contestation, but postmodern feminist theory, by and large, is committed to the broad understanding of gender and sexuality as constructed. In my discussion of Lyotard, Cornell, Butler, and other postmodern thinkers, I will demonstrate how constructionism itself has reached a political and historical impasse for ludic theorists and is being displaced by the discourses of "invention," but for the moment I will work with the widely shared view that gender and sexuality are not pregiven and are produced in the social practices in which the subject is involved.

Feminism, in all its various forms, is a political (as well as philosophical) movement, and at the core of its formation is the idea that the existing social practices and organization of social life are such that they subject women to excluding practices, to oppression, and, most important, to superexploitation. Women are not given equal economic access to social resources. Feminism, in short, is committed to social change. Depending on how change is theorized, one finds a further difference within feminism. If change is theorized as the reform of current practices within the existing socioeconomic structure, we get one kind of social theory, and if change is understood as transformation—overthrowing existing structures and not simply amending and repairing them, we end up with a completely different form of social theory. My second premise, then, is that not only are gender and sexuality socially constructed, but in order to change this construction, we have to change the structures that construct gender and sexuality along the dominant axes. This means that I believe change should be transformational: what is needed is the total revolutionary transformation of all the structures of society. Local reforms stay within capitalism and simply attempt to organize a neocapitalist state: capitalism with a human face. Since capitalism is founded upon profit and since profit is the direct outcome of the exploitation of the many by the few (the extraction of surplus labor), there can never be, I believe, capitalism with a human face.

In order to act in the direction of a total transformation, one has to know what one is acting on: after several centuries, patriarchal capitalism has become a highly complex and agile system that is adept at managing its crises and presenting itself as the most natural form of social organization. No *praxical* knowledge can be a local knowledge. I make a distinction between practical, reformist, and local ameliorations and total, praxical transformation. In order to act upon the existing social arrangements and change them, one has to have a knowledge of social totality: how various parts and practices relate to each other. Such a knowledge cannot be obtained eclectically or piecemeal (as localist and nomadic theorists argue) but has to be obtained by a theory that can give a rigorous, coherent, and total account. Such a theory must foreground a concept that can provide an understanding of all social practices and show how they are connected beyond their immediate localities. It should, in other words, not only give a historical and specific account of the operation and working of practices but also show how these various, seemingly autonomous, practices are, in fact, related to each other, at a higher level of generality, as part of a historical and social totality.

Historical materialism provides such a knowledge through the concept of mode of production. It explains the seemingly differential workings of localities and accounts for their appearances (autonomous practices) and their connections to other sites. Ludic theory—as the theory of the ruling class—has since the early 1960s attempted to discredit such knowledges of social totality as totalitarian and rationalist metanarratives. The politics of such discrediting is, of course, not to allow the articulation of causal relations (which are an integral part of any knowledge of social totality) in order to establish a relation between the haves and have-nots; between the desires of some—which are obtained at the cost of the erasure of the needs of others—and between the pleasure of the few and the pain of the many. Ludic theory has localized pleasure and pain and focused on desire and need as nomadic, independent, autonomous micropractices that are not causally related to any other practice. The welfare of the ruling class, thus, has nothing to do with the ill-fare of the subordinated and exploited. This discrediting, in short, is a political one and not a theory founded upon truth: how could it be, when ludic theory has already ruled out the truth of social totality? The antitotality project of ludic theory presents itself as progressive because it rescues the difference of the locality. But in actuality, it is a political tactic of crisis management: it allows exploitation to go on without relating it to other social practices.

I argue that praxical knowledge has to be knowledge of social totality, and such knowledge has to be able to offer explanatory critiques of all social practices. The mode of production is such an explanatory concept: it offers a coherent understanding of historical, economic, and social practices and includes an account of desire, sexuality, and reproduction. Coherence (another discredited concept in ludic discourses) is a necessary condition of praxical knowledge. One cannot act productively on what one knows only dimly, tentatively, or incoherently; the celebration of incoherence and the fragmentary is not the result of some discovery, but simply the politics of occlusion of totality. To sum up, I argue that all social practices need to be studied in relation to the history of production and exchange.

In *Capital*, Marx reopens the argument that he and Engels had put forth in their early text, *The German Ideology* (42–43), and after a long argument, he concludes that "The conditions of production are at the same time the conditions of reproduction . . . If production has a capitalist form, so too will reproduction" (*Capital* 711). Reproduction here does not simply mean the reproduction of the conditions of production of capital, the means of production and class relations, but also the reproduction of labor power and thus of the laborer. It, therefore, involves questions of sexuality, domestic labor, and fertility and thus population. To separate the reproduction (of life) from the reproduction of the conditions of production is to regress to an idealist, bourgeois social theory in which (for the purposes of protecting the interests of the ruling class) all social practices are posited as simply different from each other without any necessary (causal) connections to each other.

The ludic differential (acausal) theory of the social makes, as I have already suggested in my references to Laclau's writings, the very idea of society an impossibility (society is seen as a coerced totality) and in so doing renders any knowledge of social totality a form of metaphysics or metanarrative, to use the term Lyotard has made popular. Without a knowledge of social totality, without knowing what one is dealing with, no radical social change is possible. To read the social as the site of infinite differences, each with its own laws of immanent operation, in short, is an ideological alibi for rendering revolution itself an impossibility and substituting for emancipation the project of local reforms that leave the existing structures intact. The politics of the erasure of society in favor of a number of differential and autonomous social practices becomes quite clear in Judith Butler's erasure of emancipation in her "Poststructuralism and Postmarxism." I will return to this issue and a critique of Butler's essay in chapter 4. The route that Laclau, Butler, and others have taken in renouncing the idea of society and emancipation is a Foucauldian one. Foucault not only rejected the notion of power as constructed in the site of production, he also replaced the exploited and exploiter as two antagonistic classes with the notion of simply two different kinds of holders of powers and denounced the idea of emancipation as an Enlightenment myth. Emancipation means the possibility of moving to an "outside," but if power is so pervasive that there is no outside to it, there is no emancipation: one is always inside the system. A version of this theory is circulated by such pragmatists as Fish, who talks about the impossibility of being nonprofessional, the impossibility of ever doing work that is not already coded by professional protocols. All that one can do in a system is to put up a resistance against it. Resistance, in its Foucauldian sense, however, accepts the unchangeability of the system and simply attempts to make that system more accommodating and more inclusive. This ludic resistance, contrary to its representation, is not a strategy of transformation but rather one of reform: it attempts to give capitalism a human face.

To recapitulate: in order to undertake revolutionary praxis and transform the dominant structures, one has to acquire knowledge of social totality. The only way to acquire such a knowledge of social totality is to theorize diverse social practices in relation to each other and through the laws that foreground their necessary relations. No eclectic theory (dualism, semiautonomy, full autonomy) can provide such knowledge. In fact, all eclectic knowledges provide not an understanding of the social but a conceptual stalemate. They represent all social levels as different and thus equally important in their own terms and are thus unable to account for (that is, to *explain* and not simply describe) the relations among diverse practices: why, for example, does the institution of the family change in different moments of history, and (what is more important) why does such a change take place at a time when the social relations of production are changing under the pressure of the forces of production? Why does the institution of dowry appear and disappear? Why does what was "normal" (rape within marriage) become a nonnormal practice, and why do the codes of laws change? These changes are neither the result of the ideas of thoughtful subjects nor the outcome of aleatory ("haphazard" to use Foucault's term) events: they are changes that take place because the determining structure of production changes.

All social practices are, through various and very complicated mediations, determined by the workings of the mode of production. Their apparent locality (and that is what it is—an apparent locality and not a real one) should not be taken as a sign of their independence. Instead they need to be studied in order to show that what seems, on the local level, to be autonomous is part of the larger and more general laws of determinacies. Patriarchal practices, for example, cannot be studied in and of themselves as if they were self-determining and subject only to their own immanent laws of signification and representation. Rather, they should be examined in relation to the social practices that deploy patriarchy to further the material and ideological work needed for the reproduction of society. To treat patriarchy as an autonomous institution that has existed across the ages, independent of the mode of production, is to posit an ahistorical social institution that places men in control of women's desire, labor, and fertility and that is always parallel to and not dependent on the laws of motion of class societies. Patriarchy, I argue, is much more effectively understood not as a system of transhistorical power (in a Foucauldian sense), but as a form of organizing labor that complements the social division of labor by naturalizing the role of gender in such division. Idealist theories of patriarchy, such as the one put forth early on in feminist theory by Juliet Mitchell in *Women's Estate*, for instance, make patriarchy a universal, transhistorical level of the unconscious that finds particular and historically contingent expressions in specific modes of production. In such theories, which have by now become the matrix of ludic feminism, consciousness (or in a psychoanalytical twist, the unconscious) once again, as in all bourgeois idealist theories, is seen as producing the material world.

By positing reproduction as an autonomous mode, idealist theories mystify global structures as micropolitical practices that are the effect of the playfulness (in the Derridean sense of the absence of transcendental signifieds) of local economies, which is another way of saying that they reify nomadic and molecular micropolitics. Most neomaterialist/neo-Marxist theories (Mitchell's writings are an example of an earlier form of this tendency, while such texts as Kaja Silverman's *Male Subjectivity* and Žižek's *Sublime Object of Ideology* are examples of more recent articulations) have argued for the (semi)autonomy of reproduction. In one way or another, they have been influenced by Althusser's notion of the semiautonomy of various levels of social formation and his concept of overdetermination, which is taken from classical psychoanalysis. However, even though Althusser's theories often focus on reproduction and thus valorize the processes of reproduction, he is himself keenly aware of the global connections between production and reproduction. In the opening of his "Ideology and Ideological State Apparatuses," which has popularized the idea of overdetermination and semiautonomy (of ideology in this case), Althusser understands the social, at least initially, as a determinate totality in which the logic of production explains the workings of other social levels. Although his main interest in the essay is on reproduction, unlike many of his followers and critics, he begins by locating reproduction and establishing its necessary connections to production. In so doing, he acknowledges the logic of totality when he declares,

> To simplify my exposition, and assuming that every social formation arises from a dominant mode of production, I can say that the process of production sets to work the existing productive forces in and under definite relations of production.
>
> It follows that, in order to exist, every social formation must reproduce the conditions of its production at the same time as it produces, and in order to be able to produce. (128)

It is as part of this historical process of production of the conditions of reproduction that a materialist theory of patriarchy should be developed. To argue that patriarchy is a phenomenon across the ages and that one has to theorize it as an autonomous and panhistorical process in order to attend to the "difference" of woman and to women's issues is to confuse specificity with segregation. The specificity of the woman/feminine does not mean its segregation from other social processes.

Marx and Engels, as is well known, regarded patriarchy as a transitional mode. They believed that patriarchy was a precapitalist practice that would be abolished by the development of capitalism. In the *Manifesto of the Communist Party*, they wrote:

> [T]he more modern industry becomes developed, the more is the labour of men superseded by that of women. Differences of age and sex have no longer any distinctive social validity for the working class. All are instruments of labour, more or less expensive to use, according to their age and sex. (62)

In other words, in advanced capitalism, age and sex (among other "natural" features of workers) become commodities that are deployed in capitalism depending on their cost as elements of labor power: they lose the naturalness that marked their status in feudalism (sexism, ageism, racism might become too costly for capitalism, in which case they will be discarded as nonfunctional entities under the alibi of enlightened reform). However, I believe that gender, sex, race, and age are still functionally effective in this stage of capitalism, and patriarchy is a material practice through which gender is naturalized in order to bring down the cost of labor power of women and in so doing increase the rate of profit for capitalists—as is so aptly demonstrated by the overwhelming numbers of women now employed in wage labor globally. In other words, I read Marx and Engels's text in more general terms (not simply capitalism but private property) and, in so doing, follow Engels's own later writings (*The Origin of the Family*, for instance). I argue that capitalism in and of itself does not abolish patriarchy. As long as there is private property (which is the congealed surplus labor of the alienated other), patriarchy continues. Patriarchy, as Marx and Engels argue, is a residual social practice, but this practice is constantly renewed and made an emergent practice under ever more innovative forms of capitalism because it is still profitable.

Patriarchy, in other words, is a feature of class societies. Class societies are marked by social divisions produced through the process of production (social division of labor). Class societies naturalize the social division of labor by means of pregiven ("natural") human attributes such as sex, race, age, gender. Difference in class societies is the difference of economic access, which is determined by the position of the subject in the social relations of production. Difference, in other words, is socially produced at the site of production. However, it is secured and legitimated by reference to the natural features of the workers (age, race, sex, gender) in order to keep down the cost of labor power (the only source of value) and thus increase the level of profit.

Thus, in the production of the conditions of its reproduction, capitalism (like all class societies) naturalizes its socially produced differences through the local regime of patriarchy. I refer to patriarchy as "local" because it is not, as dominant feminist theory claims, the cause of women's oppression: it is a historically specific practice in specific social formations. Marx and Engels's notion that gender becomes irrelevant to capitalism is correct: capitalism seeks the least expensive labor power it can obtain, and in this calculation gender, as such, does not figure. However, capitalism, through patriarchy, produces sexism, which places women in a hierarchical relation to men (privileging men over women) and, as a result of this operation, represents the labor of women as less desirable (less efficient, less effective) and in so doing purchases it at a lower cost. Patriarchy is, in other words, a material practice through which economic access is controlled, and this control, in turn, maintains profit at the highest rate that is historically possible. Patriarchy, through its material operation, makes the superexploitation of women a natural act: it is a historical mode of organizing labor in such a way that the labor of women is always seen as naturally less desirable than the labor of men.

Patriarchy is only secondarily a regime of power of men over women. The privileging of power ("domination" over "exploitation") is one of the hallmarks of ludic theory—such a prioritizing obscures the materiality of the conditions of women (exploitation at the site of production) and renders the situation of women an effect of discourses. Patriarchy is primarily a material practice of labor in which the labor power of women is made available to capital for a fraction of the expense of male labor. The only way that the labor of men and women becomes of equal value is when they are deployed to satisfy human needs (use value) and not profit (exchange value): in other words, when labor is not commodified, which is another way of saying patriarchy ends when the labor practices that it justifies are historically obsolete, that is, when capitalism is transformed into international socialism.

Some neo-Marxists and feminists, as I have already mentioned, argue that, far from being a secondary regime, patriarchy is, in fact, the central form of oppression of women and is autonomous from capitalism. One of the more familiar arguments put forth to support this view of patriarchy is the one first outlined by Heidi Hartmann and later developed by Isaac D. Balbus (78–80). Following Marx, both critics argue that capitalism is gender blind. But as Balbus puts it,

> That capitalism requires a reserve army of labor, private reproducers of labor-power, authoritarian socializers, and "expressive" nurturers, does not mean that capitalism requires that women monopolize these tasks. That they become the preserve of women is a function not of the capitalist mode of production but rather of the way in which this mode of production is obliged to adapt to a preexisting and persisting sexual division of labor in which men dominate women. It is patriarchy, not capitalism, that determines the sexual identity of those who perform the various functions that capitalism demands and, for this reason, it is precisely patriarchy that remains completely unexplained after an analysis of capitalist functions has been completed. (79)

In Hartmann's words, capitalism creates "empty places," and patriarchy determines who occupies them. Contrary to both Hartmann and Balbus, the determination of who occupies the empty place is not determined by a transhistorical (preexisting, that is, panhistorical) regime of power but by material practices in response to specific historical needs of forces of production. The argument of both Hartmann and Balbus (and numerous other critics) is itself historically rendered irrelevant. Balbus's point that capitalism needs a nurturer, but it does not have to be a woman, and it is patriarchy that places a "woman" there is not quite true in the 1990s. One of the results of the emergence of the "queer" has been that men can indeed now occupy traditional labor positions (nursing, for example), which in an earlier stage of capitalism was assigned to women. The occupant of the empty space in the capitalist social division of labor is determined by the historical forces unleashed by the forces of production and not by preexisting and transhistorical structures of domination. Men are now routinely in nurturing labor positions, and women are now serving not only in the army as nurses and support staff but also in combat zones—as pilots, for example, a role that at an earlier stage of capitalism was reserved for aggressive and authoritarian men. "All are instruments of labour," as Marx and Engels wrote, "more or less expensive to use."

As evidence for the priority of patriarchy over capitalism in the oppression of women and the inadequacy of a purely economic explanation, Balbus asks why, "given the relative cheapness of female labor," female participation in the labor force is not at least equal to male participation. The difference here is not, as Balbus suggests, an indication of extraeconomic factors but, in fact, a support for them. Capitalism cannot have a greater or equal participation of women in the labor force as long as it also needs another economic institution: the family. Women's participation in the labor force depends on the historical necessity of the family in the production of the labor force: as the family becomes less and less important in this process (through new technologies of fertility, for example, and also new forms of food technologies and child care that displace the family), women participate in the labor force more and more.

[margin note: family is means of product]

Patriarchy is a historically shifting material practice through which men control women's sexuality and fertility and also (especially in the domestic sphere) their labor, not because of some transhistorical attribute of men but because this control is necessary for maintaining an acceptable rate of profit. Men do this, not as free agents, but as "personifications of economic categories, the bearers [Träger] of particular class-relations and interests" (*Capital* 92). The control of sexuality and fertility is the main material local practice of patriarchy carried out in the "everyday" by men but determined by the mode of production. This control, to repeat, is required for maintaining an acceptable rate of profit.

The key question in realizing how the mode of production produces the conditions of its own reproduction is what Marx calls the organic composition of capital: C/V, the ratio of constant capital (machinery, equipment, buildings) to variable capital (V) (the part of capital used to purchase labor power). The rate of profit is an outcome of this relationship.

It is through the historical needs of this ratio that the mode of production, through the workings of patriarchy, controls the supply of labor (namely sexuality, fertility, gender relations). To again quote Marx, "[T]he conditions of production are at the same time the conditions of reproduction . . . If production has a capitalist form, so too will reproduction" (*Capital* 711). In other words, "The capitalist process of production, therefore, seen as a total connected process, i.e. a process of reproduction, produces not only commodities, not only surplus-value, but it also produces and reproduces the capital-relation itself; on the one hand, the capitalist, on the other the wage-laborer" (724). An integral part of this process is the relation of capital and laborer (the organic composition of capital). Marx elaborates on this:

> [I]n all spheres, the increase of the variable part of the capital, and therefore of the number of workers employed by it, is always connected with violent fluctuations and the temporary production of a surplus population . . . The working population therefore produces both the accumulation of capital and the means by which it is itself made relatively superfluous; and it does this by an extent which is always increasing. This is a law of population peculiar to the capitalist mode of production; *and in fact every particular historical mode of production has its own special laws of population, which are historically valid within that particular sphere.* (782–84; emphasis added)

Reproduction (population), in other words, as Marx argues is determined not by differential slippages of a transhistorical desire, but by the historical needs of the organic composition of capital.

Materialist analysis along the lines I have outlined is routinely dismissed in both contemporary mainstream feminism, which places the experience of the daily at the core of feminist theory, as well as in ludic theory, which, although it problematizes empirical experience, brings it back in terms of the sensible (as opposed to the intelligible), and I include here post- and anti-Marxist socialist feminists. With some variations and differences, these bourgeois feminist theories, as Roberta Hamilton demonstrates, have resisted historical materialist theory and insisted that feminist theory should be about "quintessentially feminist struggles around abortion, rape, birth control, battering, the control of sexuality, the sharing of housework, and childcare" (150). For them the real issue is "the struggle within the working class family between the sexes, a struggle clearly based on male domination and female subordination" (148). They find it hard to believe that there is much of a connection between "expectations and experiences of sexuality that men and women (including teenagers) have," with "the exigencies of waged work under capitalism" (150). Sexuality, is an autonomous realm of desire; family is the site of the unfolding of the transhistorical and primal forces of patriarchy, and wage labor is, well, wage labor! To attempt to account for these in their interconnections is to make the world (which is supposedly knowable in its sheer transparency) fit the theory (146). This is a populist approach to feminist issues that, in spite of its concerned, committed, and progressive language, has served the interests of the dominant social relations by segregating what it calls quintessentially feminist issues from what, according to such a binary, are nonfeminist issues.

This form of localism, as I have indicated, dominates ludic feminism, which, although it no longer mentions quintessentially feminist anything (for fear of being accused of essentialism), insists on the autonomy of desire and sexuality as, in fact, quintessentially feminist issues. (Cornell's notion of the feminine is an embodiment of this localism and seemingly nonessentialist quintessentialism.) In spite of their seeming differences, what relates the experiential feminism of cultural feminists, radical feminists, liberal feminists, ludic feminists, and many (non-Marxist) socialist feminists is that for all of them, the most important question is the matter of subjectivity or, as Hamilton puts it, "the psychological underpinnings of the relations of domination and subordination" (152). Feminism, in these theories, becomes a narrative about the subject and subjectivity; a subject of feelings whose impressions of the world should be the limit text of feminism. In this, it actually becomes an ally of another theory that reduces the social collectivity to subjectivity: capitalism. The subject of feminism, around whom the world evolves, following the established tradition of bourgeois ethics, is a self-reliant and resistant subject: she has initiative and against all odds always triumphs: "A husband who reacts violently to suggestions that he participate in domestic chores is left; a woman who really wants to work convinces her husband to move to another town. And less dramatically, on a day-to-day basis, women plan and work, scheme and compromise, to create satisfying lives for themselves and their families" (Hamilton 147). One wonders why then Hamilton calls for a study of uniquely female forms of oppression: the subject she admires and celebrates is anything but oppressed. She is an entrepreneur who uses every opportunity in order to organize the world to her benefit. What Hamilton reads as resistant woman is, of course, the bourgeois woman projected upon the working class. The actual life of women in need is very different from the one depicted.

In the context of dominant feminist theory, to suggest that sexuality, desire, and other "quintessentially feminist issues" are related to such abstract notions as the organic composition of capital is seen as a violation of a sacred bond. It is, however, much more helpful to a praxical theory to understand the underlying connections among appearances and to construct a nonsegregated knowledge of social totality. In such a connected knowledge, for instance, the prevalence of heterosexuality (which, in terms of reproduction, means fertility) or homosexuality (which, in the same terms, means lack of fertility) is seen not as the effect of the autonomous working of desire but as the working of the laws of motion of capital. The queer nation is not an independent movement created by the errancy of the sign and queerness of representation, which deconstructs and undermines phallocentric straight (realistic) representation, or by the rise of a sexual consciousness or by the need for individual freedom (as ludic and liberal theories put it). It is, rather, the effect of the working of the organic composition of capital. The question of teenage pregnancy, often treated ahistorically either as immorality or as the clearest sign of the working of desire and the rule of patriarchy, is also part of the law of motion of capital and its need for a surplus population, a product of accumulation on a capitalist basis. Sexuality is, in short, an articulation of profit. As such, it is determined by the mode of production.

This protection of the interests of upper-middle-class women and men, this resistance to theory and to a structural analysis of women's situation in capitalism, is perhaps nowhere more evident than in the response to what is known as the "domestic labor" debate. Ludic feminists and experiential feminists of different kinds are, once again, united in bracketing this debate and rejecting it as "economistic," classifying it as outdated and superseded by new knowledges. However, the issues raised in domestic-labor theory are as vital today as they were before the debate was so violently interrupted—in the same way that the debate over ideology was excluded from the scene of theory. Ludic theory tolerates only those issues for open discussion that do not threaten its epistemological foundation and political interests.

The most significant contribution of the domestic-labor debate was its *materialist* analysis of women's exploitation; it brought together feminist issues in a cohesive manner. It argued that male dominance was not simply a matter of abstract power relations, as New Left theorists and (somewhat later) Foucault formulated it, but was the material control of men over women's labor, fertility, and sexuality within the historical specificity of different modes of production. These relations were to be understood, therefore, not in terms of ahistorical man-woman relations ("patriarchy"), but historically, within the social relations of production in which they were articulated. The domestic-labor debate demonstrated that in sexuality and fertility, experienced as private and personal, the effects of global structures of economic relations and the social contradictions they produced became apparent. The private or personal, it was made clear, should be understood historically and materialistically and not as an isolated, autonomous chain of events in an aleatory genealogy. Theory was needed, proponents of the debate argued, because it allowed an understanding of these global structures, which were not available for inspection through sheer personal experience. To analyze these structures (so that one can act on them and transform them), one had to focus on a site where their effects were most visible. This place was the home, in capitalism structured as a private space segregated from the public. Women's oppression was produced in the family, and its specific form was household work.

The focus on household labor was not limited to labor in its reductive sense in bourgeois theory: simply acting on the external world, getting things done. Rather, labor is as Marx theorized it (*Capital* chap. 6), a process through which human beings make not only their world but themselves. Labor, in the domestic-labor debate, was an integral part of the personal. However, mainstream feminists suppressed this understanding of the subjective as historicized: the subject was not the monadic bourgeois subject, her identity formed by experience of the personal (desire), but the subject formed historically in the social relations of production. After all, as Eli Zaretsky had demonstrated in his *Capitalism, the Family, and Personal Life*, these social relations of production had constructed the household and family as private and had confined woman to them (23–55). Zaretsky argued that subjectivity itself was an effect of "proletarianization," which was the effect of capitalism (56–77). What Hamilton regards as autonomous, as a private "struggle between the sexes" (148), is demonstrated in domestic-labor theory to be structured by the global social relations of each mode of production. The quintessentially feminist issues, such as wife battering, child abuse, and rape within marriage, were all related to the privatization of the relationship between men and women within the household. Without a historical and material study of the household, these issues were apt to be essentialized and understood transhistorically. There was no primeval natural aggressiveness in men that caused patriarchy. Rather, patriarchy was theorized by the domestic labor theorists as the particular historical shape the relations of men and women took within specific social relations of production. Postmodern patriarchy is articulated by late capitalism. The household is not private and segregated from the public, but constructed by the laws of the motion of capital. Domestic-labor theory placed feminist theory, for the first time, on a solid material basis: it showed that privatized domestic labor is the historically specific form that women's superexploitation (and oppression) has taken under capitalism.

Such a materialist theory inevitably relies on class analysis and raises questions about the class interests legitimated by feminist theories. It follows that bourgeois feminism, the institutionally recognized form of feminism, would declare the domestic-labor debate reductive, abstract, and theoreticist.

The most revolutionary theories of domestic labor, following Marx and Engels, argued that through household work women were cut off from the public sphere of production and that this was the main cause of their oppression. However, the domestic-labor debate was not a monolithic theory but a debate, and more radical ideas were contained, not only from outside Marxism, but also from its inside. For example, Margret Benston not only opposed classical Marxist views on the emancipation of women through their joining public industry as put forth by Engels, she revised the fundamental concept of class (as the position of the subject of labor in the relations of production) and posited women as an autonomous class. The most sustained subversion of domestic-labor theory, however, came from such neo-Marxists as Mariarosa Dalla Costa and Selma James.

Dalla Costa and James were influenced by Italian social-capital theory (Baldi; Negri, *Revolutionary Writings* and *Marx*), in which the differences between wage labor and nonwage labor, laborer and manager were erased through such concepts as new social strata. In these theories, class struggle itself was replaced by political and ideological struggle in the form of the refusal of labor to capital. Dalla Costa and James argued that there was no need, as Marx and Engels had argued, for women to move out of the household and join public industry in order to become productive workers because their work at home was productive. (*Productive* is used here in the Marxist sense of producing surplus value.) Women at home produced labor power and thereby contributed to the production of surplus labor. Such a revision of the concept of productive work, which looked progressive and inclusive, posited the household as an autonomous site that through the reproduction of life (i.e., by producing laborers) controlled capitalism and could through the refusal of labor bring down capitalism. In this neo-Marxist reading, desire—the reproduction of life—determines capitalism, and the agency of the subject is the most important part of social transformation.

The conservative aspect of this reading of the labor theory of value becomes clear when we consider that, for Dalla Costa and James, because household labor was productive, it was a form of social labor. Consequently, socialism was not needed to make household work collective and public. Women were oppressed because their productive work was not paid for, and Dalla Costa and James (following Negri and others) demanded wages for it. In Dalla Costa and James's theory, the state (politics) replaces capitalism (economics). The state not only organizes labor but becomes the agency required to pay wages to women for their unpaid labor inside the household. Should the state refuse to pay, women should strike and refuse to labor (as Negri had argued ["Workers' Party"]). The "revolutionary" idea here was that because the state cannot possibly pay all household workers a fair wage, it will go bankrupt. Through their demand for wages, women will be able to bring down the state and put an end to its oppressive role in the management of social labor for capitalism.

Although presented as a materialist analysis, Dalla Costa and James's theories are essentially political subversions of the state and ideological interventions in cultural politics—not a revolutionary praxis. In spite of their progressive rhetoric, these neo-Marxist theories, in effect, reify the family and household and end up placing women permanently inside the isolated space of the household. Their program of liberation, in other words, accepted the inevitability of exploitation; it just demanded that the exploitation be made more fair by the compensation (not emancipation) of women. Dalla Costa and James's conclusion that women must reject the "myth of liberation through work" (49) is identical with the conservative demand that women withdraw from the labor market. In the name of freeing women and ending the sexual division of labor, their project actually institutionalized men's work separate from women's work—the project so dear to the heart of conservatives. I leave aside here their lack of analytical attention to recent developments in the labor force that have resulted in the employment, for example, of more than 50 percent of the women in the United States—an indication that capitalism needs women, not just at home, but also in the workforce because the work of women usually is paid for by lower wages. Rather than focusing on pay for household work, the attention should be on such issues as unequal pay for equal work and the superexploitation of women by capitalism, as well as on efforts to disestablish the family as an economic unit serving capitalism. The demand for wages for domestic labor conceals the fact that women, as Eli Zaretsky has argued, work for capital and not for their husbands.

My critique of Benston, Dalla Costa and James, and other New Left or neo-Marxist theorists in the domestic-labor debate is undertaken, of course, from a (classical) Marxist position. Bourgeois feminists, on the other hand, criticize their work for its focus on capitalism. Thus Heidi Hartmann, for example, reduces feminism to a theory of panhistorical "sexual inequality between women and men, of male dominance over women" (3) and then rejects Dalla Costa and other domestic-labor theorists for focusing on the role of housework in the perpetuation of capitalism. For Hartmann a truly feminist theory will show that "the importance of housework as a social relation lies in its crucial role in perpetuating male supremacy" (9)— as if this supremacy does not take place within a specific historical mode of production. Such a theory of patriarchy as an autonomous power leads Hartmann to a localist analysis of the relation between women and men. She rejects, for example, Zaretsky's view: "While Zaretsky thinks women's work *appears* to be for men but in reality is for capital, we think women's work in the family *really is* for men" (7). Hartmann's analysis makes sense only if the family is treated as an autonomous space composed of homogeneous practices: a space in which diverse practices converge and form a coherent totality in the service of men. But Hartmann's argument is contradictory here. For if we are consistent with the logic of autonomous localities, the family is not a monolithic unit but a site of incommensurate practices. For example, if one treats the care of children as an autonomous practice, one must conclude that women work for children. If a woman's mother is unable to take care of herself and lives with her daughter, the daughter taking care of her works for a woman. Child care, mother care, food care, emotional care, then, cannot be autonomous practices emanating from a central dominance, working for a man. Understanding each social practice *in its own terms* means that one cannot consider the family as a unit. Thus Hartmann's statement that "women's work in the family *really is* for men" (7) suppresses various micropractices in the family that by her logic must be equally autonomous. In her theory, there is no referent for the word *family,* only a divergent and incommensurate set of micropractices.

In contrast, I argue that the only way to produce knowledge of the family is to see it in its relations to social totality. It then becomes clear that capitalism has been the *cause* of women's exploitation; exploitation is only mediated, not caused, by patriarchy. When Hartmann pluralizes the beneficiaries of patriarchy, asking, "Who benefits from women's labor? Surely capitalists, but also surely men, who as husbands and fathers receive personalized services at home" (9), she is finding an alibi for capitalism. She simply juxtaposes the two beneficiaries, failing to show that men benefit only because of the economic relations that capitalism produces. I have already shown that it is not just men who receive "personalized services" at home. Hartmann's logic is self-contradictory and mystifies the political economy of domestic labor.

Domestic labor, as Paul Smith demonstrates, is a necessary labor; it secures the conditions of existence of capitalism. However, it is not productive labor. As Marx points out: "There are works and investments which may be necessary without being productive in the capitalist sense, i.e. without the realization of *surplus labour* contained in them through circulation, through exchange, as *surplus value*" (*Grundrisse* 531). Domestic labor remains a concrete labor that cannot be transformed into abstract labor (the substance of value), which is the necessary form it should take to become part of the exchange against capital. In other words, domestic labor, in its concreteness, does not "achieve equivalence with other forms of labour qualitatively" in capitalism (P. Smith 208). Domestic labor is not an abstract labor and part of commodity exchange because it does not follow the laws of value. For example, fluctuations in the price of labor power do not affect the performance of domestic labor. Or to take another characteristic, there is no competition "between 'domestic units' to minimize the labour time embodied in their products; inefficient households do not fail to sell their commodity" (208). If we try to regard the product of domestic labor as a commodity ("labour power") sold on the market, other problems arise. In other words, we run into problems if we regard domestic labor not as concrete, *necessary* labor but as abstract, *productive* labor—producing a commodity (labor power) for exchange for capital. For example, what exactly contributes to the production of labor power? If cooking is an integral part of the labor necessary to turn materials purchased by wages into consumable food, why should not eating also be counted as labor? Since sleeping is also an integral part of replenishing labor power, one should, according to this logic, also count sleeping as a productive labor. Such considerations, as Smith points out, lead Marx to ridicule the view that the "labour of eating . . . produces brain, muscles, etc.," a view that Marx thought stems from "the stupidity that consumption is just as productive as production" (Marx, *Theories* pt. 1, 185–86; see P. Smith 208, 217).

Marx's critique of the conflation of production and consumption not only points up the idealistic frame of Dalla Costa and James's project but also marks the underlying assumptions in the ludic paradigm. The conflation of production and consumption is the foundation of the theories of such postmodernist thinkers as Baudrillard (*Mirror* and *Critique*), Haraway (the figure of the cyborg is an ironic deconstruction of the binary of pro-

duction and consumption), and the entire argument that writers such as
Stuart Hall have put forth in support of the emergence of "New Times,"
which I will discuss below.

The fundamental point to bear in mind in dealing with domestic labor
is that it is not simply labor, in and of itself, that produces value, but rather
that labor performed within specific social relations of production. If we
identify necessary labor with productive labor, we also find ourselves in
the rather absurd position of counting the necessary labor of "the police,
technological innovation, natural forces" as all "productive" (P. Smith 213).
The productivity of labor is derived not from its concrete usefulness but
from its social form, which is determined by the social relations of production. It is not labor that determines its productivity; rather, the productivity
of labor is determined by its situation within the mode of production.

While the domestic-labor debate has been excluded from mainstream
postmodern feminism, a few feminists on the margins have continued to
engage these issues. This more recent work includes Lindsey German's
Sex, Class and Socialism, which focuses on the "role that the family plays in
the reproduction of labour power" as the crucial explanation of oppression
(11); the Canadian socialist-feminist debate over class, gender, race, ethnicity, and divisions of labor (Hamilton and Barrett); and the writings of
Nancy Folbre. Among the more controversial of these retheorizations is the
collaborative work of the Marxist-feminist psychoanalyst Harriet Fraad
and the neo-Marxist economists Stephen Resnick and Richard Wolff, who
develop a nondeterminist theory of the class and gender structure of the
household ("Every Knight" and *Bringing*).

At the core of the Fraad-Resnick-Wolff thesis is their articulation of
class structure as "the organization of the production, appropriation, and
distribution of surplus labor" (Resnick and Wolff, "Every Knight" 12). By
"surplus labor" they mean the amount of labor appropriated over the level
of necessary labor, which is "the amount needed to produce the current
consumption of the producers themselves" (12). However, unlike the German school, which theorizes the construction of gender differences as fundamental to the relations of labor and accumulation, Fraad, Resnick, and
Wolff distinguish economic class processes from gender as "cultural or
ideological processes."[9] This return to the theorization of gender as an
ideological process analytically distinct from the economic is, from the point
of view I have put forth in my discussion of production and reproduction, a
theoretical and political regression. Fraad and her colleagues attempt to
answer this by positing "gender processes as conditions of existence for

class processes"; thus they believe that gender processes "participate in determining them. At the same time, gender processes in any society are in part determined by the class processes there" (Resnick and Wolff, "Every Knight" 15). Their basic thesis is that class processes take "different forms of producing, appropriating, and distributing surplus labor such as the feudal, slave, capitalist" (12 n. 2). The household follows the "feudal form," in which the surplus labor produced by the wife is appropriated by her husband "in the form of household use-values" (16, 17). This thesis has generated considerable controversy. Some, like Julie Matthaei, find its theoretical formulation similar to dual-systems theory, particularly in its "problematic view of the household and the capitalist economy as separate modes of production" (70, 72). Others regard it as highly original. Kim Lane Scheppele, for one, finds that "by emphasizing the basic social form of a *class process* (rather than a class with specific content that cannot be generalized across settings) . . . they open up a new range of possibilities for Marxian thought" (86).

Taken together, these diverse theories and debates show that feminist historical materialists have been producing important theoretical work and a significant reunderstanding of the production paradigm and theories of the social division of labor. It is work with which I have theoretical and political disagreements, but it warrants considerable critical analysis of its effectivity and limits, and it needs to be at the center of the debates over feminist theory and praxis.

New Times?

Why, then, the almost complete marginalization and suppression of historical materialism among most feminists, particularly ludic socialist feminists? Donna Haraway's dismissal of Iris Young's early writings on labor theory as modernist and outdated suggests one explanation. But why is this logic—of the supersession of (ludic) postmodernism—so readily accepted as given and thus so widely disseminated? One obvious answer is because post-al knowledges have acquired such hegemony in the academy and, increasingly, in the culture at large in advanced capitalist societies: a clear indication that their theories support and legitimate the dominant social organizations of life. I will be challenging this hegemony throughout the rest of this book as I articulate the opposition between ludic and resistance postmodernism; rewrite the relation of feminism and postmodernism, and critique not only poststructuralist notions of difference, but also the deconstruction of social totalities; the erasure of emancipation, and the Foucauldian regime of power-discourse informing most ludic feminism.

Another explanation that ludic feminists and post-Marxists offer—and the one I want to take up here—is historical: the economic, social, and cultural realities of capitalism, according to these theorists, have radically changed, requiring new knowledges and new politics. This new reality is variously called "New Times" (particularly in Britain), postindustrialism, post-Fordism, postmodernism, and so on. New Times is both the name for this new reality and the mark of an extended debate—launched by the now defunct British publication, *Marxism Today*—over how to articulate and explain it. Stuart Hall and Martin Jacques (who have collected the various texts of this debate into a widely circulated anthology) have succinctly defined the New Times issue, and it is worth quoting them at some length.

> The "New Times" argument is that the world has changed, not just incrementally but qualitatively, that Britain and other advanced capitalist societies are increasingly characterised by diversity, differentiation and fragmentation, rather than homogeneity, standardisation and the economies and organisations of scale which characterised modern mass society. This is the essence of the so-called transition from "Fordism," which defined the experience of modernity in the first two-thirds of the century, to "post-Fordism." In economic terms, the central feature of the transition is the rise of "flexible specialisation" in place of the old assembly-line world of mass production. It is this, above all, which is orchestrating and driving on the evolution of this new world. However, this must not be understood as exclusively an economic development . . . [P]ost-Fordism is also shorthand for a much wider and deeper social and cultural development . . . which has over the years served to disrupt, if not entirely displace, the old distinctions between production and consumption, production and social reproduction. (11–12)

According to its advocates, the New Times call for new politics: especially the displacement of theories of production, labor, and class, in short, the rejection of Marxism. This has led, especially in Britain, to the development of post-Marxism—theorized by Ernesto Laclau and Chantal Mouffe—and in feminism to a post-Marxist, ludic politics exemplified in the recent writings of Michèle Barrett, Judith Butler, and Drucilla Cornell.

Post-Marxism also marks the frame for some of Gayatri Spivak's arguments. At the core of post-Marxism and ludic feminism, as I have already
indicated, is the rejection of the priority of the relations of production and
issues of labor and class. Thus when Haraway dismisses Young's theory of
labor as modernist, she is implicitly drawing on New Times logic: theories
of the social division of labor no longer explain postindustrial realities.

Socialist feminism, according to this logic, needs a new political theory. Haraway attempts to provide this in the form of "an ironic political
myth" (149) in her essay "A Manifesto for Cyborgs," widely regarded as
the exemplary socialist feminism for the New Times. It was first published
in *Socialist Review* in 1985; since then it has been reprinted frequently (e.g.,
Weed; Nicholson, *Feminism/Postmodernism*). Even more indicative of its
popularity among ludic theorists, Haraway's cyborg manifesto marks the
future of socialist feminism for most ludic feminists. Landry and MacLean,
for example, give the essay considerable attention in the final chapter of
their genealogy of materialist feminism, and Hansen and Philipson reprint
it as the culminating essay in their reader, where it is the last word in the
final section, "The Future."

Haraway claims to "build an ironic political myth faithful to feminism, socialism, and materialism" in a "blasphemous" way ("Manifesto"
149) in order to deal with the "extent and importance of rearrangements in
world-wide social relations tied to science and technology" (161).
"Advance capitalism," according to Haraway, "is inadequate to convey the
structure of this historical moment" (160). She thus calls

> for a politics rooted in claims about fundamental changes in the nature
> of class, race, and gender in an emerging system of world order anal-
> ogous in its novelty and scope to that created by industrial capitalism;
> we are living through a movement from an organic, industrial society
> to a polymorphous, information system . . . to scary new networks I
> have called the informatics of domination. (161)

In addition to drawing on the current post-Fordist logic, Haraway is
replaying here the older, more common notion of the postindustrial society, only in an updated, more ecologically sensitive version. Originally
articulated by the neoconservative critic Daniel Bell in *The Coming of
Postindustrial Society*, the argument for a postindustrial society is an argument for displacing the economic and suppressing Marx's theory of the
mode of production and labor value. It is a conservative strategy for

removing capitalism from critique. Bell argues for the (semi)autonomy of social practices: "Rather than assume a single linkage between the social relations and the forces of production," we should *"uncouple* the two dimensions" (xi), the "socio-technical dimension of society" from the socioeconomic dimension, that is, capitalism (x). Bell replaces capitalism with a technological determinism; changes in technology, especially in communications and the knowledge industry, produce a shift from production to service, from an industrial to an information society, from labor to knowledge. Bell's emphasis on the technical ("sociotechnical" dimension) later becomes part of the larger ludic theory of invention through the technocultural and technicist deconstruction of social constructionism that I shall discuss in the following chapters.

Haraway follows this same logic. Her new global technoculture, the "informatics of domination," replaces advanced capitalism with a "world system of production/reproduction and communication" based on "the social relations of science and technology" (163). However, Haraway is sometimes ambivalent about such displacements and occasionally denies or qualifies them. She claims, for example, that when she deploys the phrase "the social relations of science and technology" that she is "not dealing with a technological determinism, but with a historical system depending upon structured relations among people" (165). Since Haraway—in a Nietzchean mode and following Foucault, in particular, and poststructuralism, in general—has dispensed with causality, she has supposedly erased determinism. But she comes as close as possible to reinstating it in this essay. She argues, for example, that the "homework economy as a world capitalist organizational structure is made possible by (not caused by) the new technologies" (166). Haraway's essay substitutes a de facto technological determinism for what she regards to be a Marxist economic determinism, a technological matterism for a historical materialism.

Bell's and Haraway's moves are important in that they rewrite technology as technocultural rather than economic. Bell claims that "if capital and labor are the major structural features of industrial society, information and knowledge are those of the post-industrial society. For this reason, the social organization of a post-industrial sector is vastly different from an industrial sector" (xiii). While the progressive Haraway would consider herself quite the opposite of the neoconservative Bell, it is important to stress that the progressive Haraway, like the neoconservative Bell, rewrites technology as a sociocultural entity. The convergence of ludic and neoconservative technicism is telling not only epistemologically but also politically. Haraway severs technology from the relations of production that produce it: technology and its sociocultural relations become the abstracted ground of all other social, cultural, and economic realities. Her rather detailed descriptions of economic issues do not deal with the economic ground of technology so much as use the "largely economic reality to support [her] claim that these sciences and technologies indicate fundamental transformations in the structure of the world for us" (165). Her examples, in other words, demonstrate how technology is the (social) cause of these new economic arrangements, such as the homework economy or "the projections for world-wide structural unemployment," which she describes as "stemming from the new technologies" (168). Haraway, like Bell, rewrites the economic as caused by the social relations of technology, thereby occluding capitalism.

Haraway erases the very real material conditions of science and technology: she obscures the fact that they are *capitalist* science and technology. As the socialist thinker Michael Harrington pointed out (following Harry Braverman), "[C]apitalist technology was *capitalist* technology, that is . . . it was designed not simply according to engineering priorities but in keeping with social values, and incarnated the inferior position of workers"—especially women, we need to emphasize—"in the production process" (108). This occlusion of the capitalist relations of production grounding technology erases the exploitation of labor involved in producing the technology, on the one hand, and, on the other, the uses of technology to further increase the expropriation of labor. It is the issue, in short, of the way capitalism deploys science and technology to produce profit rather than to meet human needs.

Haraway takes this displacement of production even further by dematerializing technology as "coding," that is, as discourse. As she argues, "[C]ommunications sciences and modern biologies are constructed by a common move—the translation of the world into a problem of coding (164). Haraway thus has not moved beyond determinism; she has simply reversed it: the economic is determined by technology as code; discourse determines the material nondiscursive. What are the consequences of this reversal? Bell argues that "a post-industrial society is characterized not by a labor theory but by a knowledge theory of value" (xiv). For Haraway the labor theory of value is displaced by what we could call a "discourse theory of value" in which coding is the privileged term: thus we find Haraway asserting "technologies that write the world, biotechnology and microelectronics—that have recently textualized our bodies as code problems" (175).

Or, as she says in regards to the informatics of domination, "The entire universe of objects that can be known scientifically must be formulated as problems in communications engineering (for the managers) or theories of the text (for those who would resist). Both are cyborg semiologies" (162–63). The politics of change, as I will discuss more fully below, thus becomes the question of semiotic recodings, of writing other stories: "[F]eminist cyborg stories have the task of recoding communication and intelligence to subvert command and control" (175). Haraway's celebrated new "route for reconstructing socialist-feminist politics" (163), then, substitutes a technicist and discursive matterism for a historical materialism as the ground of feminist theory and practice and, in so doing, occludes production and marginalizes labor. She displaces revolution with reform and transformation with subversion. The similarities between Haraway's recoding as a politics of liberation and Judith Butler's "resignification" (*Bodies* 109, 237–42) as a politics of self-subversion and resistance raise the question: is there any difference between Haraway's discursive socialist feminism and poststructuralist textual or performative feminism?

Given the popularity of Haraway's work among feminists, my critique may seem harsh, even distorting. After all, Haraway describes the homework economy, cites "the international division of labor," mentions "export-processing and free-trade zones." But the issue is not whether a critic *catalogs* these realities—the question is how she *explains* them. What kind of connections does she make among various social practices; what kind of political interventions and social transformations does her explanation enable? It is important to again stress the obvious: the limitations of Haraway's theory are not personal but *historical*. Haraway's displacement of labor and the production paradigm is part of the class struggle in theory; it is part of the bourgeois disenabling of radical oppositional knowledges.

In fact the amount of intellectual and political energy that has been deployed, particularly since World War II, to discredit and displace the production paradigm and with it Marxism is truly extraordinary. The repetition of these efforts and the haunting of theory by the specter of labor speak powerfully of the eruptions of the objective reality of exploitation and the class struggle in the field of theory. What is most significant about this ongoing project of suppression is the way the politics of the post-al Left becomes identical with that of the post-al neoconservative Right. Both the post-al Left and post-al neoconservativism aim to erase class struggle from the social scene and replace it with a version of Rorty's "conversation."

Haraway's texts become the symptomatic site of convergence for the logics of the post-al Left and post-al neoconservatism: her argument weaves together the tissues of texts of Bell and Habermas—both of whom are arch-enemies of the working class and have attempted, in their writings, to displace the immediate producers with information managers.

Habermas quite specifically argues, in *The Philosophical Discourse of Modernity*, for the "obsolescence of the production paradigm" in the "paradigm shift from productive activity to communicative action and the reformulation of the concept of the (experiential) lifeworld in terms of communications theory" (76). This move to "communicative action," of course, underwrites both Haraway's recoding and Butler's resignification. In an earlier work, *Toward a Rational Society* (which Haraway cites), he claims that as

> technology and science become a leading productive force, rendering inoperative the conditions for Marx's labor theory of value . . . when scientific-technical progress has become an independent source of surplus value . . . the labor power of immediate producers . . . plays an ever smaller role. (104)

Such arguments contribute to the bourgeois efforts in the ongoing class struggle to marginalize the immediate producers. They lead Habermas to conclude that "the emancipatory perspective proceeds not from the production paradigm, but from the paradigm of action oriented toward mutual understanding" (*Philosophical Discourse* 82). This logic is, in fact, quite close to Haraway's argument for "a conscious coalition, of affinity, of political kinship" (156) based *not* on the shared commitment to end exploitation arising from the division of labor but on a mutual understanding of a "postmodernist identity of otherness, difference, and specificity" (155).

The convergence of both the post-al Right and post-al Left in claiming the shift from labor to knowledge/discourse, from production to communication and consumption, gives these theories the cultural status of truth and insures that they are not only widely disseminated in the academy but are commonly taken for granted as "what is" in the contemporary knowledge industry—from think tanks to the daily newspapers and TV informatics, like *Nightline*. Thus Haraway can easily critique "Marxian socialism" in which "Labour is the pre-eminently privileged category" (158) without providing any argument why this should not be the case: why labor should not indeed be privileged. She is excused from making any argument because her position is the site of a recycled obviousness in ludic theory. She simply dismisses what she calls Marxism's "essentializing move," as if her own theory of codes is not itself essentializing. She describes Marxist essentialism as "in the ontological structure of labour or of its analogue, women's activity" (158), but it is Haraway, not Marxism, that renders labor "an ontological category" (158). For historical materialism, the extraction of surplus labor is an objective historical practice in class societies: it is *historical*, not *ontological*. In class societies, all social differences are produced by the extraction of surplus labor: an extraction of labor that takes different historical forms. The test of the objectivity of surplus labor as the foundation of class societies is simply this: if surplus labor is abolished, the existing social relations will fundamentally change (Marx, *Capital* 240–416). Surplus labor is the unsurpassable objective reality of class societies, and on this objective reality (which is not subject to—that is, not changeable by—discursive interpretation) depends the oppression of women, workers, people of color, and lesbians and gays, as well as the struggle for emancipation.

Is Haraway describing new realities for us? Certainly she describes some important changes in the social and cultural relations of contemporary society, but whether these are, as she claims, "fundamental transformations in the structure of the world" (165) is highly debatable. What is at stake is whether these changes constitute fundamental transformations in the structure of capitalism. By subsuming the economic to the technological and then arguing for extensive social changes stemming from technology, Haraway misreads diverse social and cultural—that is, *superstructural*—developments as basic changes in the relations of production and the exploitation of labor: the economic *base*. When we look more closely at economic issues, we find a very different situation.

All of these theories and efforts to describe New Times, the postindustrial, post-Fordism, Jameson's "postmodernism as the logic of late capitalism" and Haraway's "informatics of domination," are based on the notion of a *break*, a fundamental transformation, in capitalism. But as Alex Callinicos argues in *Against Postmodernism*, such arguments resort to a "ferocious . . . reductionism . . . To read the accounts of 'New Times' in *Marxism Today* is to be confronted with an almost caricatured version of the kind of expressive totality criticized by Althusser, down to contrasted lists of the characteristics of 'Modern Times' and 'New Times'" (135), to which we can add Haraway's taxonomy for the informatics of domination (*Simi-

ans 161–62). Callinicos argues that the idea of postindustrial society (especially as formulated by Bell) "is, of course, nonsense" (121). While Callinicos may minimize some of the superstructural changes that are occurring, he effectively demonstrates the important point that many of the arguments describing the shift to postindustrial and post-Fordist societies are based on misinterpretations and exaggerations of economic trends. These exaggerations, we need to recognize, grow out of the need to maintain dominant class interests and suppress the class conflicts arising out of the social relations of production.

Callinicos calls for a "far more careful analysis" of the process of deindustrialization in Western economies and of the misleading claims that are made about it—such as "the disappearance of the industrial proletariat." He points out, for example, that "the rise in the proportion of output and employment taken by services, which is indeed one of the major secular changes in twentieth-century capitalism, has taken place primarily at the expense of agriculture rather than manufacturing industry." It is true that manufacturing—the production of goods—in advanced industrial societies has been "involved in a fall in the share of employment," but Callinicos argues this has been "primarily a *relative* change—typically industry's share of the workforce fell rather than the absolute number of industrial employees" (122). This decline in employment has also been accompanied by "considerable rise in manufacturing productivity" (123). In short, fewer people are producing greater output. Thus, while the numbers of people employed in industrial and manufacturing jobs—especially well-paying union jobs—in the West is declining, it has not been accompanied by a significant decline in overall manufacturing productivity. Obviously there has been considerable deindustrialization of specific economic sectors, such as the steel industry, in particular regions, such as parts of Pennsylvania and Ohio. But the overall "contraction of manufacturing employment in the advanced economies has been exaggerated," according to Callinicos, and, more important, it "is counterbalanced by the expansion of the industrial working class on a global scale" (127).

David Harvey, in his comprehensive critique, *The Condition of Postmodernity*, is more supportive than Callinicos of the claims of post-Fordists, and he subscribes, in part, to the importance of the flexible accumulation of capital and flexible technologies in production. He maintains that it is "dangerous to pretend that nothing has changed, when the facts of deindustrialization and of plant relocation, of more flexible manning practices and labour markets, of automation and product innovation, stare most workers in the face" (191). But he also questions the limits of these trends and acknowledges that the "insistence that there is nothing essentially new in the push towards flexibility, and that capitalism has periodically taken these sorts of paths before, is certainly correct (a careful reading of Marx's *Capital* sustains the point)" (191).

The basic issue at stake is whether these developments are surface changes or are more structural. How this question is answered, as I will elaborate in the following chapter, marks the distinction between ludic and resistance postmodernism. For ludic postmodernism, such as Haraway and the New Times critics, these surface changes are seen as a fundamental *break* in capitalism. For resistance postmodernists, however, there is *no break*. Instead, resistance postmodernists argue as Harvey does: "Even though present conditions are very different in many respects, it is not hard to see how the invariant elements and relations that Marx defined as fundamental to any capitalist mode of production still shine through, and in many instances with an even greater luminosity than before, all the surface froth and evanescence so characteristic of flexible accumulation" (187–88).

What are these invariant elements in capitalism that continue to "shine through . . . all the surface froth" of superstructural changes? The most fundamental element is *profit*. As Harvey states, "[W]e still live, in the West, in a society where production for profit remains the basic principle of economic life" (121). Capitalism is, of course, expanding globally with little or no constraints, so that the organization of all social life according to profit is more and more becoming the structure of relations throughout the world. Equally fundamental, the reality of profit, the "growth in real value *rests on the exploitation of living labour in production . . .* Capitalism is founded, in short, on a class relation between capital and labour" (Harvey 179–80; emphasis added).

The most important point to be made about the shifting patterns of production and employment is that they are all still grounded on the basic structural relations of capitalism—*the expropriation and exploitation of living labor (surplus labor) for profit*. Moreover, the exploitation of surplus labor is increasing, whether it is goods, services, information, or microelectronics that are being produced, here or globally. As Callinicos argues,

> The fact that manual industrial workers no longer form the majority of wage-labourers does not of itself imply the beginning of the end of the "work-based society." Wage-labour has if anything become a more pervasive feature of social experience in the past half century, with the decline of peasant agriculture and the growing involvement of

women in the labour-market. The fact that much of this labour now involves interacting with other people rather than producing goods does not change the social relations involved: one striking feature of contemporary industrial relations is the spread of trade unionism to the "caring professions" (health, teaching, social work, etc.). (127)

What changes there are in the economy, then, are changes concerning *how the extraction of surplus labor is taking place, not over whether it is taking place.* As long as there is surplus labor, there are class and other social divisions of labor (according to differences of gender, race, sexuality). This is the inevitable and fundamental structure of capitalism. Instead of a fundamental change in the structure of capitalism, there is an intensification of its structural processes. The increased productivity of fewer workers, on the one hand, and the rise in low-paid, part-time and temporary jobs, along with the revival of piecework and sweatshops, on the other hand, both contribute to increasing the rate of expropriation of the surplus labor of these workers. This "devaluation of labour power," as Harvey points out, "has always been the instinctive response of capitalists to falling profits" (192). Central to this process is the regulation and control of labor. This means that, contrary to Haraway's ludic dismissal of "labor" as essentializing, the social struggles over the division of labor—in short, the class conflicts between labor and capital—are at the very core of the sociocultural and economic changes variously called New Times, postmodernism, postindustrialism, or the informatics of domination. Harvey makes this important point when he argues that

We can . . . trace back many of the *surface* shifts in economic behaviour and political attitudes to a simple change in balance between Fordist and non-Fordist *systems of labour control,* coupled with a disciplining of the former either through competition with the latter (forced restructurings and rationalizations), widespread unemployment or through political repression (curbs on union power) and geographical relocations to "peripheral" countries or regions and back into industrial heartlands in a "see-saw" motion of uneven geographical development. (192; emphasis added)

Not only is there no *break* in capitalism, as ludic socialist feminists and postmodern critics argue, but the conditions Marx describes in *Capital* are still operating today and are still as devastating as they were in 1867:

[W]ithin the capitalist system all methods for raising the social productivity of labour are put into effect at the cost of the individual worker . . . [A]ll means for the development of production undergo a dialectical inversion so that they become means of domination and exploitation of the producers; they distort the worker into a fragment of a man, they degrade him to the level of an appendage of a machine, they destroy the actual content of his labour by turning it into a torment; they alienate *(entfremden)* from him the intellectual potentialities of the labour process in the same proportion as science is incorporated in it as an independent power; they deform the conditions under which he works, subject him during the labour process to a despotism more hateful for its meanness; they transform his life-time into working-time, and drag his wife and child beneath the wheels of the juggernaut of capital. (799)

This harsh reality is illustrated in a recent *New York Times* profile of a Kansas City, Missouri, worker, Craig Miller, his wife, Susan Miller, and their four children. The deindustrialization of jobs and increased productivity and exploitation of labor has certainly come at the *cost* of workers like the Millers. In 1992 Miller was laid off from his job as a sheet-metal worker for TWA earning $15.65 an hour. He is now working two part-time jobs for about $5 an hour—one at McDonald's "hustling orders for Quarter Pounders and chicken fajitas," the other driving a school bus—and "on the side he has started a small business, changing furnace filters," but without much success. Susan Miller works part-time as a stock clerk at Toys R Us for $5.95 an hour (Dirk Johnson, "Family Struggles to Make Do after Fall of Middle Class." *New York Times*, 11 March 1994, A1). According to the report, "[C]ounting all their part-time jobs, the Millers will make about $18,000 this year, less than half what Mr. Miller alone earned as a union sheet-metal worker" (A14). The Millers are now working four times as hard for less than half of what Craig Miller earned for one job. Their surplus labor is now being appropriated at a rate that has more than doubled. As he says about the new jobs: "Sure, we've got four of them . . . So what? So you can work like a dog for $5 an hour." Is pointing to this family's circumstances an act of *essentializing* labor?

This issue of the increasing exploitation of surplus labor is especially important in evaluating one of Haraway's most celebrated theses: "The actual situation of women is their integration/exploitation into a world system of production/reproduction and communication called the informatics of domination" (163). In this polymorphous new world, according to Haraway, communications and biological sciences along with micro-electronics and biotechnologies mediate "translations of labour into robotics and word processing, sex into genetic engineering and reproductive technology" (165). In other words, in Haraway's informatics of domination, production/reproduction is the province of technology, and labor is replaced by robotics (as she also indicates in her taxonomy for the informatics of domination [162]).

But this is a distorted understanding of labor: labor has not been translated, transformed, or replaced—it has only been occluded by Haraway's social analytics. Not only is the use of robotics largely confined to the production of a very few complex consumer products, but the production of robots and microelectronics, the practices of word processing and genetic engineering, are all based on the expropriation of surplus labor—increasingly women's surplus labor. Haraway's logic erases the fact that robotics and other automated machinery—the means of production—are, for the most part, *congealed labor*. As Ernest Mandel demonstrates, "[T]he price of machinery consists to a large degree of labor (for example, 40%) and raw materials (for example, 40% also)" (*Introduction* 26). But he also shows that, for example, "60% of the cost of raw materials can be reduced to labor . . . [T]he rest of the cost of raw materials breaks down into the cost of other raw materials—reducible in turn to 60% labor." In other words, "the share of labor in the average cost" not only of machinery, but also of any commodity, is successively greater: "the further this breakdown is carried, the more the entire cost tends to be reduced to labor, and to labor alone" (25–26). In short, all of these new technologies and practices involve the same old capitalist relations of labor. The integration/exploitation of women "into a world system of production/reproduction" and new communications technology is still an integration into capitalist technology, whatever its forms, and thus into the capitalist labor relations of the *exploitation of surplus labor*. What has changed is the increasing degree and extent to which *most* women globally are now being *superexploited* by capitalism.

Haraway has largely displaced capitalism as a mode of production from her new technological realities. This is not to say she does not use the term; obviously she does. In discussing the homework economy, for instance, she briefly cites the concept of capitalist and addresses issues of work and jobs (166); But she treats *capitalism* largely as an adjective, occluding its relations of production and labor. Her analysis rarely leaves the realm of the superstructure: the market, the paid workplace, the state all become, in her words, "idealized social locations" in which "there is no 'place' for women . . . only geometrics of difference and contradictions crucial to women's cyborg identities" (170). As a result, her richly detailed descriptions do more to obscure than to explain the existing economic realities of women. For example, the homework economy is indeed a new way of organizing work (or rather the contemporary revival of piecework), but it is still structured according to the same old appropriation of surplus labor. These new technological—superstructural—changes have not transformed the fundamental structural relations of the capitalist mode of production: there is no break in capitalism. The homework economy is an instance of what Alain Lipietz has termed "bloody Taylorization"—a concept he has used to describe the "'bloody' exploitation" occurring in the largely unskilled, "fragmented and repetitive" jobs in the manufacture of exports, especially electronics and textiles (74–76). These conditions pertain to the unregulated work places not only of homework but also of the new industrial sites of the export processing zones and sweatshops that are becoming the mainstay of manufacturing both in the Third World and in the deteriorating city centers of the First World. As Mike Davis and Sara Ruddick say of the local or "sectoral deindustrialization" of Black Los Angeles, "[T]he old Eastside manufacturing belt of auto, steel, rubber and electrical plants . . . has been entirely restructured . . . L.A. industry has been turned back from 'Fordism' to 'Bloody Taylorism' of an almost East Asian standard" (48). The conditions in the underground economy in the United States—especially for immigrant workers in such jobs as day laborers, garment workers, restaurant help—amount to "consistent, recurring abuse," as one New York lawyer describes the scene in New York City (Deborah Sontag, "Emigres Battling Abuse," *New York Times*, 2 June 1994, A1). Employers refuse to pay back wages (which are well below the minimum wage); workers are frequently injured or maimed on the job, and some are even held in indenture.

Women, in particular, are being crushed "beneath the wheels of the juggernaut of capital" not only through the exploitation of their subsistence (nonwage labor) but increasingly through their direct participation in despotic wage-labor relations—usually at even higher rates of exploitation than men since women tend to earn only "77 percent of what men do" (Peter T. Kilborn, "Job Security Hinges on Skills," *New York Times*, A24). But in areas of considerable unemployment and underemployment, the difference is even greater. According to both state and local studies, the median income of a woman working full-time in Pennsylvania is "approximately 63 percent of that of her male counterpart . . . [F]or poor women who head households in Pittsburgh the gap is 45 cents to the dollar" (McAllister 34). Most women are working in low-paying, part-time, and temporary jobs. According to the Labor Department, "[T]wo-thirds of all part-timers and nearly 60 percent of all temporary workers are women" (Kilborn A24). The differences between low-paying temporary jobs and well-paying, secure permanent work, with full benefits, are dividing a few privileged women from the deteriorating economic situation of the majority of women in this country and globally: The *New York Times* reports that, in the United States, "About 15 million working wives hold well-paid executive or professional jobs, anchoring their families to the middle or upper classes. But far more— 37 million—are working for lower wages as clerks and cashiers, nurses' aides and bank tellers, secretaries and maids. Their wages serve as a cushion between welfare and getting by" (Kilborn A24). One of the main consequences of the new technologies, then—and one that Haraway occludes— is the deepening class divisions of labor. According to Harvey, "[N]ew technologies have empowered certain privileged layers . . . [and] open up the way to high remuneration of technical, managerial, and entrepreneurial skills . . . presaging the rise of a new aristocracy of labour as well as the emergence of an ill-remunerated and broadly disempowered under-class" (192).

The Class Politics of Feminism

One of the most pressing questions in evaluating the class politics and social consequences of feminist theory is where and how feminists are situating themselves and their work in the class struggle. Obviously, most feminist theorists (including the writer and most readers of this book) are knowledge workers and, most likely, university professionals, and thus part of the privileged aristocracy of labor. How does this privileged class position affect the way feminists and postmodern critics understand and explain the real and participate in its transformation? When ludic theorists displace issues of class, labor, and exploitation by epistemological arguments about foundationalism and textuality—substituting instead a politics of desire (lust) and multiple "undone" or "cyborg" identities in the name of difference and a (Foucauldian) notion of power as nondeterminate, shifting, and reversible, are they not misrecognizing some of the historically specific effects of class privilege as *universal* conditions, which they impose on the very different class realities of others, and doing so in the name of an antiuniversalist difference? The issue here is, what is the level of our own class consciousness?

Post-al politics displaces class consciousness into identity politics, which underlies most postmodern social movements—movements of people of color, women, and queers, among other marginalized groups. But identity politics makes it impossible for the subject to speak for the other because the "authenticity and moral legitimacy" of one's politics, in Ellen Willis's words (xv), derive from one's experience as a member of such a group. A white lesbian, for instance, cannot speak for an African-American or, to take the logic of identity politics seriously, even for any other lesbian. She can only speak for herself. This logic of identity politics is not only dominant in the more traditional activist and humanist communities but also among poststructuralists, post-Marxists, and other ludic postmodernists. In his interview with Deleuze, Foucault articulates this injunction against speaking for the other through his concept of the specific intellectual (*Language, Counter-Memory* 203–17). In the moment of the postmodern, the formation of the intellectual is different from the traditional universal intellectual. The postmodern, nomadic intellectual is "aware of the necessity for confined individuals to speak for themselves" (208). A free person thus cannot "speak for the prisoner" since there is no universal common bond. Experience, in both the contemporary humanist and ludic postmodern formulations, separates people into autonomous entities. Autonomy is presented by both the activist humanist and the poststructuralist as a mark of freedom and liberation. It is not. The injunction against speaking for the other only looks progressive and liberating. In actuality it posits everyday experience as a limit text and, in so doing, occludes what, in fact, does form the common bond among people: their class relations. Class relations are questions of the social relations of production: they are open to conceptual knowledges and cannot be mystified as the experience of a separate, nomadic individual. It is here that Marx locates one of the functions of theory: to overcome the empirical limits of experience and construct knowledge of the structures that make experience itself possible as experience. By making speaking for the other taboo, poststructuralism and ludic theory, in general, have naturalized experience, and in so doing, have become complicit with the ruling social relations. The injunction against speaking for the other allows the upper-middle-class feminist to speak for herself and cut herself off from the other, for in ludic theory any solidarity not based on experience is a false one, a violent usurpation. An increasingly popular solution to this dilemma—offered by Donna Haraway ("Manifesto"), Diana Fuss *(Essentially)* and others—seeks connections on the basis of "affinity." In so doing, it posits a form of sentimentality and (self-)interestedness still grounded in experience as the basis for local and discontinuous connections, which reinforce rather than challenge the isolation, privilege, and priority of the (upper-)middle-class feminist's class interests and desires.

Not only can and should one speak for the other and *with* the other, but the *other is not other*. Rather, the other is connected to all others (including those at the center) by the relations of production. All others are constructed, in spite of all their surface differences, by the same laws of motion of capital. It is the recognition of these laws—and our shared determination by them—that enables us to speak for and with the other and not retreat into our own internal choreography of desires and interests. The question—what is our own class consciousness?—is a fundamental question. It is based on the objectivity of the historical reality of exploitation and profit, the laws of value in capitalism. To ask, What is the level of our own class consciousness? is, thus, not a personal and experiential question, but a historical question. It is fundamental to any political movement. Class consciousness—knowledge of the relations of production and exploitation of capitalism—and not the experience (identity) of the subject is the basis of revolutionary praxis. Marx and Engels make this quite clear in the *Communist Manifesto* (64). Knowledge of how class struggle articulates social totality, in what Marx calls the "decisive hour" (i.e., a knowledge that is not a construct of isolated consciousness but the product of the historical and material formation of the forces of production and their contradictions with the relations of production) makes it possible for the members of one class to cut itself adrift from its own class and speak for/with the other by joining the revolutionary classes. Does ludic feminism provide such knowledge of social totality or does it in fact repress any solidarity with the other under the ideological alibi that any such speaking for the other is unethical? Is not ethics itself a device used in ludic theory—in the name of respecting difference—to systematically prevent the formation of a united humanity against capital? Difference, it is now clear, is not simply an epistemological practice to unfound universalist foundations, it is a political apparatus to perpetuate the regime of nomadic, molecular subjects, and in so doing keep the existing social structure intact. Difference, in fact, is deployed to legitimate oppression in the name of respect for the other.

What kind of politics, then, does socialist feminism need for these

New Times that are, after all, new only in their appearances but still subject
to the same laws of capitalism? Haraway's technological and discursive
materialism eclipses the struggle against economic exploitation and its necessary connection to cultural politics and critique of ideology. Instead, she
puts forth a "cyborg politics" that "is the struggle for language and the
struggle against perfect communication, against the one code that translates all meaning perfectly, the central dogma of phallogocentrism" (176).
But her poststructuralist notion of the struggle for language cuts it off from
the relations of production and is unable to engage language, the sign—
what Marx and Engels call "practical consciousness" (*German Ideology*)—as
"an arena of the class struggle" (Voloshinov 23). Cyborg politics is "freed
of the need to ground politics in 'our' privileged position of oppression that
incorporates all other dominations" (Haraway, *Simians* 176); it rejects the
efforts of "Feminisms and Marxisms" to "construct a revolutionary subject
from the perspective of a hierarchy of oppression" (176). But such a cyborg
politics is indeed a political myth, as Haraway calls it, for it relies on a discursive sleight of hand—a recoding—to wipe away the objective historical
realities of the fundamental oppression of women and others through the
appropriation of their labor. There is indeed an objective, historical hierarchy of oppression: preventing people from meeting their basic human
needs by appropriating their labor and denying them equal distribution of
social resources is the fundamental oppression. Only those whose basic
needs are sufficiently fulfilled can afford the luxury of forgetting this hierarchy of primary reality. As the African-American Marxist-feminist Angela
Davis has argued, "[T]he most fundamental prerequisite for empowerment
is the ability to earn an adequate living" (*Women, Culture* 8).

The "cyborg perspective" is basically a bourgeois perspective that
obscures the class politics of its own privileged condition by grounding
itself in an identity that suppresses the commonness of exploitation under
the laws of capital. It suppresses its relation to the extraction of the surplus
labor of others, especially women of color. Haraway's "complaint about
socialist/Marxian standpoints is their unintended erasure of polyvocal,
unassimilable, radical difference made visible in anti-colonial discourse
and practice" (*Simians* 159). But what is this "unassimilable, radical difference"? Is it a historical remainder? How is it formed? Is it outside the relations of production? If so, how? To be more specific: is it the difference of
"women of color"—Haraway's representative cyborg, "Sister Outsider"?
How are these identities formed? Are not such reifications a post-al form of
colonialization and Eurocentric essentialization of the racial other as again

the unassimilable outsider—this time in the name of the other? The radical, unassimilable difference in racist, patriarchal capitalism is not the postmodernist identity of women of color but the conditions oppressing them. The radical, unassimilable difference is *surplus labor*—a difference whose assimilation dissolves capitalism itself, and the manifestation of this unassimilable difference in the everyday is *poverty*. Poverty—that radical difference—is the effect of production of profit and privilege for the few out of the expropriation of the labor of the many (the others). Poverty cannot be assimilated within bourgeois society, that is, within the existing labor relations of capitalism, without transforming that society into socialism. Poverty—*need*—is the radical, unrepresentable, suppressed other to bourgeois pleasure. The project of ending poverty, eliminating this radical difference, requires a revolution in the relations of production: a socialist revolution. But such revolutionary struggle is all but eliminated in Haraway's reconstruction of socialist feminism as "cyborg semiologies" and recodings that require a "subtle understanding of emerging pleasures, experiences, and powers with serious potential for changing the rules of the game" (Haraway, *Simians* 172–73). The objective in revolutionary social change is not "changing the rules of the game," which is little more than reformism and, in its ludic sense, reduces the social to gaming (Lyotard), to hyperreality and seduction (Baudrillard), or to a politics of dissemination (Derrida), in which changing discursive rules is equated with significant social change. Revolutionary change is concerned not to change the rules of the game but to overthrow the game, that is, to transform the existing system of racist, patriarchal capitalism.

This shift from revolutionary struggle to a politics of emerging pleasures and recodings of rules is the basis of Haraway's appeal. As one commentator, Christina Crosby says,

> The irony of the "Manifesto" is, I believe, the pleasure of the text, the pleasure of the unexpected turn . . . For those readers who have been active in socialist and feminist politics, there's the pleasure too, of the politically "incorrect," the break with the solemnities of left politics and the reductive dualisms which are all too familiar. (Weed 206–7)

What are these "solemnities of left politics and the reductive dualisms" it is so pleasurable to be freed from? They are, of course, the difficult and *unpleasurable* insistence on the historical reality of exploiter and exploited and the need to struggle against the exploitation of surplus labor, that is, against poverty. The *unpleasure* of predictable poverty shatters the complacencies of the cyborg. Poverty is monotonous and takes few surprising turns. Crosby is right: it cannot give pleasure to the bourgeois feminist, who delights in escaping the boredom of the everyday through the twists and turns of the sign, the play of fantasy. As the "struggle for language and against perfect communication," cyborg politics is primarily a discursive politics in which "contests for the meanings of writing are a major form of contemporary political struggle" (Haraway, *Simians* 175). Central to this struggle are the border writings, the "other" stories of women of color, of Sister Outsider, who in Haraway's "political myth . . . is the offshore woman" (174). But what stories does Sister Outsider tell us, or rather, what stories is cyborg (socialist) feminism willing to *hear?* Haraway tells the stories of Cherrie Moraga, Chela Sandoval, and such science fiction writers as Octavia Butler and Vonda McIntyre, which rewrite the myths of identity and consciousness as nonoriginary, border-crossing stories that are "not just literary deconstruction, but liminal transformation" (177).

But the issue is not simply "about access to the power to signify," as Haraway claims. Nor is it simply a matter of "recoding communication and intelligence to subvert command and control" (175) or a matter of "subversive rearticulation" or "resignification" of the symbolic, as Butler calls for (*Bodies* 109). These practices are no more than discursive politics, "cyborg semiologies." None of the texts that Haraway refers to as examples of liminal transformation have transformed anything in the social relations of production. Certainly they have made tales of the other available to bourgeois readers, who have consumed them for their unexpected turns, which generate tremendous pleasure. The texts of the other cited by Haraway and other ludic theorists are valorized not because they have brought about any change (or are capable of bringing about any change) but because they are new sources of pleasure for upper-class readers. (Their status as new best-sellers is a testimony to their harmlessness to the material relations of production.) These surprising tales that deconstruct the solemnities of bourgeois culture are quickly assimilated by bourgeois culture itself. They are, like Haraway's cyborg politics and Butler's "performatics," seductive, nonthreatening political fantasies for the already privileged. They will do little to emancipate women of color and all oppressed women from the very real conditions of exploitation. What is missing, what is silenced by cyborg feminism's vigorous suppression of production and labor are the most urgent and radical, the most fundamental, root stories of Sister Outsider: the offshore woman and the one who lives onshore (the one who immigrates and the one who is already here). Her primary story is not a literary deconstruction nor a liminal transformation; it is not simply a recoding of pleasurable boundary myths. The silenced story is a *historical materialist critique* of economic exploitation, including a critique of bourgeois feminists for their class interestedness and complicity in the expropriation of the surplus labor of others. It is the story, as Margaret Prescod-Roberts says, "about being here for the money" (13). It is the story

> about the mammy [in slavery] and about her work, that housework, because it has everything to do with the way capital—meaning big British and American money—was able to accumulate the vast amount of wealth and fortune that it did. It's important to talk about that, and it's specially important for us as Black women to talk about that when we say we're here for the money, because what we're saying is that we helped to create that wealth, that we were *pivotal* in creating that wealth. Don't tell us that we have to stay in the West Indies, that we have to work three times as hard to create new wealth for the West Indies. Because we have done three hundred years or more of labour—labour that I have done, my mother, my grandmother and people before me have done. When we look around, when I looked around my village, when I looked around Barbados, the wealth wasn't there. It was some place else. It was in London, it was in New York, from the French-speaking West Indies it was in Paris, from the Dutch-speaking West Indies it was in Amsterdam. (18)

Margaret Prescod-Roberts, an émigré from Barbados and cofounder of Black Women for Wages for Housework, U.S.A., and her fellow Sister Outsiders are struggling first over money, not meanings. In spite of the readings of Spivak, Haraway, and Barrett, money and meanings are not identical: they form a hierarchal binary. Money (need) always comes first. What is needed, what Prescod-Roberts calls for, is a material struggle over the exploitation of their labor—over all oppressed people's labor—and equal distribution of the wealth produced by their labor. The struggle over meanings, over language, over cultural practices and politics of representation (cyborgs) must be grounded in the priority of economic struggles and serve the collective struggle for the emancipation of all peoples from economic inequality. But Haraway and other ludic feminists respond to the call for the priority of money over meaning by a rereading of Saussure in which linguistic *value* is analogically written into labor *value* (see chap. 1). Money and meaning, in other words, are inscribed into each other as an example of the postmodern hyperreal.

What is at stake is clearly voiced by Salvadoran refugee women. As one refugee, Miriam Galdemez, a representative in the 1980s of the Democratic Revolutionary Front in Europe, says:

> The social structure in El Salvador is inhuman . . . [E]ven though *machismo* is a real problem, nothing's ever going to change until we have the basic necessities of life: housing, education, health care and economic security. At the moment, most of us are denied these basic necessities, and I don't think we'll ever get them until we change the whole power structure in El Salvador. (New Americas Press 33)

While the class war in El Salvador may have temporarily been halted by the violent intervention of imperialism, it has not brought a significant restructuring of the social order, and thus it has not brought social and economic justice. The poor today continue to be denied the basic necessities and feel betrayed and abandoned by the former guerrilla leaders who have become post-al guerrillas adopting the bourgeois project of coalition, conversation, and compromise as they sit in parliament ("Salvador's Poor Still Poor, and Angry," *The New York Times,* 15 April 1995, A1). Thus the hopes of another refugee, Maritza, a displaced housewife who became a supplies coordinator in the Mesa Grande refugee camp, still hold true today. She says simply of her dream for the future: "No more exploiters and exploited. We will work, of course, but we will all share equally. We want to be the ones to benefit from our work" (New Americas Press 227).

Ludic, cyborgian socialist feminism has become an "ethical" socialism for the bourgeoisie: a displacement of collectivity by intersubjectivity. No matter how much it may describe and decry the condition of women in the homework economy, the feminization of poverty, or the growing structural unemployment (as Haraway indeed does), unless it directly connects its cultural politics to the revolutionary struggle to fundamentally change the conditions of production, appropriation of surplus labor, and unequal distribution of wealth, it is simply playing with the boundaries of middle-class privilege and pleasures: expanding them here and there to include this or that small segment of the excluded. Haraway's cyborg politics—with its declared purpose of creating "an argument for *pleasure* in the confusion of boundaries and for *responsibility* in their construction" (150)—has helped justify the current move of many middle-class, professional, and academic socialist feminists and leftists away from revolutionary struggle, which requires that they break with their own class interestedness. Her cyborg myth validates the post-Marxist turn to the more comfortable pleasures of a postclass ludic politics aimed at semiotic freedom.

However, on the margins of the newly hegemonic ludic politics and cyborgian fantasies, other feminists have continued to work for revolutionary knowledges and praxis. I want to especially note one effort from a new generation of feminists struggling to break the silence around the problem of labor and build a collective revolutionary feminism for the third wave. In a rigorous critique of ludic feminism, Jennifer Cotter argues that

> Feminism's political effectivity . . . must be determined in relation to this global framework [of capitalism]; feminism must be a project that is concerned not with the personal liberation of a small group of relatively privileged women, but with the economic, social, and political emancipation of all oppressed and exploited women on the planet. Hence, the measure of success for feminism must always be determined in relation to its capacity to advance the material interests of the most oppressed segments of the female population on the globe. (121)

Socialist feminism cannot afford the luxury of cyborgian political fantasies; it must return to the necessity of collective struggle against the exploitation of surplus labor in order to "advance the *material* interests of the most oppressed" (emphasis added). And in so doing, socialist and materialist feminisms—indeed all feminisms—need to join in the struggle for international socialism. As Angela Davis has told us:

> If we are not afraid to adopt a revolutionary stance—if, indeed, we wish to be radical in our quest for change—then we must get to the root of our oppression . . . Our agenda for women's empowerment must thus be unequivocal in our challenge to monopoly capitalism as a major obstacle to the achievement of equality.
>
> I want to suggest . . . that we link our grassroots organizing, our essential involvement in electoral politics, and our involvement as activists in mass struggles to the long-range goal of fundamentally transforming the socioeconomic conditions that generate and persistently nourish the various forms of oppression we suffer. (*Women, Culture* 14)

It is important to add to Davis's call to action that we must also link our theoretical and cultural work to this long-range goal. In the second part of this book, I critique-ally engage ludic feminism and attempt to radically rethink the politics of the most advanced theoretical and cultural knowledges in feminism and postmodernity in relation to the revolutionary project of international socialism.

PART 2
Beyond Ludic Politics

CHAPTER 3

Feminism and Resistance Postmodernism

Why does feminism need to be concerned with postmodernism? A common answer is that it is an unavoidable issue for feminist activists and theorists alike. Not only has postmodernism—at least in its dominant ludic forms—erased the issues of labor and production, it has called into question the concepts grounding feminism: from identity, difference, and the category of woman/women to the very nature of politics and the real. As I have already indicated, it has so changed the frames of knowing and politics that a number of feminists, including socialist feminists, have abandoned the fundamental precepts of transformative politics. Michèle Barrett, for one, finds that her *Women's Oppression Today* (1980) "could not be written in the same way now"; its basic terms, like *oppression*, she comments in the revised edition, "look rather crude" in light of recent theoretical developments. "Now," for Barrett, is the moment of the postmodern. She thus goes on to say, "[P]ostmodernism is not something that you can be for or against . . . [I]t is a cultural climate as well as an intellectual position, a political reality as well as an academic fashion."

I want to argue here for a very different way of understanding postmodernism and feminism's relation to it. In so doing, I will be retheorizing both postmodernism and its fundamental concept—difference—in relation to historical materialism. How feminists understand postmodernism is central to the kind of politics we build and the kind of social interventions we can make: at the core of theorizing postmodernism is the question of the status and level of the changes that, we are told, have made the metanarratives of modernity incredulous. An understanding of the level at which these changes have taken place should also enable us to, at least tentatively, theorize the *post* itself. Is the post simply a moment in a linear history (after) as traditional humanist historians argue, or is it a transhistorical moment of crisis of the founding concepts of all phases of history, as put forth by (mostly) ludic theorists, who regard history itself to be a form of

129

writing and postmodernity simply a rewriting of modernity, which is itself a rewriting of a rewriting of a rewriting and (finally) an originality without origin. To be more precise, are these changes, as Haraway says, "fundamental transformations in the structure of the world" (*Simians* 165), or are they unfamiliar mediations on the level of culture (superstructure)? I raise this issue because the question of the relation of feminism to postmodernism cannot be answered outside a previous question, that of capitalism. As Fredric Jameson has pointed out, "[E]very position on postmodernism in culture . . . is also at one and the same time, and *necessarily*, an implicitly or explicitly political stance on the nature of multinational capitalism today" (*Postmodernism* 3).

We first need to move beyond the common reification of postmodernism as a homogeneous construct to understand the way it is produced and divided by the social contradictions of capitalism. Paraphrasing Jameson (*Postmodernism*, 398–99), I will begin by proposing that any analysis of postmodernism is explicitly or implicitly a contribution to a theory of the mode of production and its place in social theory. Postmodernism, I propose, is the articulation on the level of the *superstructure* of changes in the social, cultural, political—"in short, ideological forms" (Marx, *Critique* 21)—which have come about as a result of new forms of deploying capital and extracting surplus labor around the world. As such, postmodernism is not simply a series of isolated, shifting aesthetic and architectural styles, proliferating commodifications, philosophical deconstructions, split subjectivities, or multiple identities and differences. Instead, postmodernism is a contradictory historical condition, and its contradictions are those of the material base: both postmodernism and the theories that try to explain it are divided by the social contradictions of capitalism itself—by the contradictions of the forces and relations of production. To understand this condition, we can distinguish between quite different ways of theorizing postmodernism—what I call *ludic postmodernism* and *resistance postmodernism*—depending on how they account for these contradictions and the resulting changes.

One very common poststructuralist strategy to marginalize my theorizing of postmodernism in terms of ludic and resistance is to appeal to the deconstructive dogma and write it off as "binarist." According to such post-al orthodoxies, what I call ludic postmodernism is the effect of my violent exclusion of difference within postmodernism itself. Resistance postmodernism, in this protocol of reading, is not an outside to ludic postmodernism but in fact its difference from itself—its untotalizable remainder.

The two are, according to a post-al reading of my reading of postmodernism, versions of an archiform, and, as such, they are inscribed in each other.

Such a post-al reading (of my reading) will make it impossible to bring to the fore the class politics of dominant postmodernism because it normalizes the contradictions of the inside and outside by erasing the very opposition of the two. The binary of ludic and resistance, as should be clear from my argument so far, is not a textual or a hermeneutic opposition—one that can simply be deconstructed by a reading maneuver. This, and all binaries that I have discussed so far, are reproductions at the superstructural level of the fundamental binary of two antagonistic classes that are the outcome of capitalism's relations of production. To erase binaries, like many other hermeneutic moves of postmodern theory, looks progressive and inclusive. However, in actuality, it is an act of complicity because it obscures the founding binaries of class societies. By insisting on the difference between the ludic and resistance, then, I am insisting on bringing to the fore the binaries that are now routinely covered up in the name of a progressive politics. Binaries will lose their historical existence not through reading protocols but by abolishing class. Thus the role of a revolutionary theory is to always bring the binaries to the fore and, in so doing, to pressure the contradictions and fissures that bourgeois theory covers up whether in the name of the sublime, experience, or *differance*.

My reading of postmodernism as an effect of the contestation between the ludic and resistance would also be marginalized by such Hegelian neo-Marxists as Fredric Jameson, who would regard any discussion of difference to be the dominion of a (monolithic) postmodernism ("the cultural logic") and thus would exclude the category of resistance postmodernism from the scene of theory. For Jameson, there is a modernism (articulated by the universal norms of Enlightenment) and a generic postmodernism (the fracture of those norms and the emergence of the nomadic, differential subject and depthless surfaces). As I have already implied and will make more explicit in the following discussion, difference is the boundary practice of modernity and postmodernity. To reduce difference to the immanent laws of the sign, the errancy of tropes, and the playfulness of the hyperreal is to leave the theory of one of the most significant sites of social contradictions of capitalism to the normalizations of conservative theories that read difference as the excess-ive sublime and, in so doing, occlude the difference of class. Jameson's resistance to resistance postmodernism is a mark of such an uncritical acceptance and surrender of critique itself. To regard postmodernism monolithically, as Jameson does, is to allow the contradictions of the regime of profit to be formalized as immanent differences that are, according to the protocols of ludic readings, not just a characteristic of capitalism but of *all* systems of meanings. Resistance postmodernism deformalizes difference and shows how postmodernity is itself the effect of the most recent unresolved and unresolvable contradictions of capitalism. To reduce ludic and resistance postmodernism to a single logic is to accept the idea that difference is ontological. Difference is, I argue, historical, and the concept of resistance postmodernism is put forth to account for its historicity and to resist the idea of difference as always (only) within the very practice of culture and signification. Resistance postmodernism is thus a theory of the contradictions of the new flexibilities transgressing modernist forms of crisis management in capitalism. To confine the inquiries into postmodernism to a monolithic postmodernity, as Jameson does, is in fact to become complicit with "break" theories and to end up, as Jameson does, with a notion of the end of critique. Resistance postmodernism, then, goes against both the neo- and post-Marxist and the ludic readings of post-al New Times, of a break in capitalism—as articulated by Haraway, Hall, Laclau, Baudrillard, and those, like Lyotard, who reject the idea of a break but posit the break of metanarratives as a marker between modernism and postmodernism. Jameson formally disagrees with Lyotard and seems to dissociate himself from theories of the break (*Postmodernism* xxi), but he proclaims, "I have pretended to believe that the postmodern is as unusual as it thinks it is, and that it constitutes a cultural and experiential break" (*Postmodernism* xiii). He thus asserts as a hallmark of postmodernism a break that eliminates any distance between the critic and culture and thus makes any critique of the dominant culture impossible.

Resistance postmodernism is an effort to show the continuity within the ever more innovative forms capitalism takes in its search for profit. My insistence on resistance postmodernism is also an attempt to overcome the end-of-century fatalism that marks Jameson's surrender to the most acute forms of consumerism (the articulation of novel forms of acquiring profit within capitalism) as an apocalyptic cultural logic.

I have already critiqued many of the basic assumptions of ludic postmodernism in the previous chapter, but it may be helpful to briefly review the main issues here. Ludic postmodernism takes what it regards to be the unprecedented new social, cultural, and technological forms in contemporary societies as evidence of fundamental structural changes in capitalism and in the world. Consequently, it articulates the emergence of what it considers to be entirely new social configurations: New Times, postindustrial society, consumer society, post-Fordism, all of which are seen as postproduction, postclass, postgender, and, frequently, posthistory. Ludic critics conflate the economic with the cultural, social, and technological and to misread the considerable changes in the superstructure as indicative of profound economic changes, constituting a break in capitalism and the existing relations of production. This move is clear in Donna Haraway's cyborgian informatics of domination, but it also characterizes Baudrillard's concept of consumer society and Lyotard's postmodern condition. It even marks Jameson's notion of postmodernism as the logic of late capitalism.

Base and Superstructure

In contrast, resistance postmodernism articulates a historical materialist understanding of the changing sociocultural conditions. It argues that there is *no break* in capitalism, only new articulations of the relations of production. The extraordinary superstructural changes that we mark as postmodernism are simply new mediations of the fundamental social contradictions resulting from the division and exploitation of labor. Resistance postmodernism, in short, is a contesting way of explaining new crises of the material relations and new strategies for managing them in imperialist and racist, patriarchal capitalism. Resistance postmodernism takes as its point of departure the fundamental, objective reality of capitalism: the extraction of surplus labor for profit. As long as surplus labor is the base for the accumulation of capital, capitalism cannot change structurally. And since capitalism cannot survive without profit, its structures will never change. They will be made more subtle and flexible in order to keep the rate of profit as high as the level of class struggle in each era allows, but without surplus labor there will be no capitalism. The extraction of surplus labor, as Marx shows in *Capital* (e.g., chaps. 9, 11, 16), takes different shapes, but these shapes are not signs of structural changes, as ludic thinkers from Negri to Baudrillard to Aronowitz argue. I have demonstrated at length in the previous chapters that this is indeed the case: that surplus labor continues to be the *primary* base of accumulation in global capitalism.

Resistance postmodernism does not deny the emergence of new *cultural* forms (variously called hyperreality, cyberspace, and virtual reality to indicate that they are constructed by information) nor does it dismiss

excess-ive cultural significations, discursive performances, textual reproductions, and fragmentations of subjectivities. What it does argue is that
these are *not* autonomous and aleatory events, as Foucault would call
them. For resistance postmodernism, these are highly mediated, flexible
and layered articulations *on the level of the superstructure* of the continuing
social contradictions that arise out of the existing property relations. In
short, they are newer forms of the contradictions caused by the expanded
social divisions of labor in late capitalism.[1] Resistance postmodernism foregrounds the importance of difference. But in so doing, it radically
regrounds difference itself: difference, as I will elaborate below, is always
difference in relation to the system of exploitation—that is, in relation to the
international divisions of labor. Social differences, in short, are material
effects of the changing contradictions in the divisions of labor. Resistance
postmodernism argues that in order to keep the rate of profit high in late
capitalism, with the continuing development of the forces of production,
there are more and more subtle divisions of labor that are ever more
exploitative. Labor in the cyberspace of late capitalism, in other words, is
more, not less, exploitative, which is another way of saying that the cyborg,
the hyperreal, the simulacra are not autonomous practices and realities created out of knowledges, discourses, and codes, as argued in ludic theories
of post-al society. Instead, they are articulations of the newer, more subtle
divisions of labor.

For instance, Haraway argues that her "cyborg myth is about transgressed boundaries" (*Simians* 154) and that her informatics of domination
is the "movement from an organic, industrial society to a polymorphous,
information system—from all work to all play" (161). But late capitalism
has not moved, nor is it about to move, from all work to all play. Quite the
opposite. Except for the most privileged, leisure time in late capitalism is
not only increasingly commodified but is more and more another arena for
the superexploitation of subsistence labor (as in do-it-yourself projects and
volunteer work). And most important, leisure time is severely curtailed for
the increasing numbers of people (like the Millers [chap. 2]) who now must
work longer shifts or hold down two, three, or four part-time jobs to
replace the one well-paying job they have lost. Haraway mistakes superstructural forms, which are indeed changing, for a transformation in the
mode of production. The mode of production (the laws of motion of capital) continues to be the extraction of profit from surplus labor. Haraway's
cyborgian informatics of domination are superstructural *mediations* of the
underlying divisions of labor. The transgressed boundaries she celebrates

are effects of the new divisions of labor, especially between mental and manual work, and the new diversities within intellectual and cultural labor. New mediations of the division of labor include, for example, flexibilities in traditional gender boundaries of work between public and private, enabling large numbers of women to engage in wage labor. At the same time, gender inequality in wages and benefits and in access to privileged jobs is maintained while women *continue* to work a second shift at home. The current divisions of labor intensify the class and race differences among women, enabling a small minority of (mostly white) women access to secure, high-paying professional jobs while restricting the majority of women to temporary, part-time, underpaid, labor-intensive work. In short, late capitalism is marked by complex, expanding multilayers of mediation, not a break. It is ruled by the imperative of accumulation, and its new forms are new modes of searching for profit.

Mediations are nothing new in capitalism: at every stage in capitalism, labor is mediated, especially by exchange value. Accumulation takes new forms, but the cultural changes brought about by new forms of accumulation and the ideological justification of profit do not in any way herald the only break that will usher humans into a new era: a termination of accumulation. Capitalism is driven by its constant law of M-C-M: money, commodities, more money. Each new ensemble of mediations articulates the deployment of labor, the public sphere, and business-government relations differently and lasts as long as it maintains profit and promotes accumulation. There are, then, historical limits on any mediation. To confuse these mediations with a fundamental change in the nature of capitalism is itself part of the ideological justification of profit—a role that bourgeois theorists play in the capitalist knowledge industry.

The *difference* of the latest form of capitalism lies primarily in the expansion of the layers of exchange and the multiplication of the levels of mediations between labor and capital: for example, new ("Japanese style") participatory workers' teams; conversion of the "elementary" labor force in the Third World into advanced centers of production almost overnight; emergence of the electronic market, cybertransactions, and instantaneous trading; internationalization of finance; management of demand by the state (e.g., new forms of subsidizing business); and so on. But in all these changes, the fundamental principle of production for profit remains dominant. Whether it is in the regional small manufactory that Adam Smith referred to as the earliest form of the new division of labor in capitalist production (7), or national steel manufacturing (in Korea, Japan, the United

States), or such transnational cyberfactories as Intel, production under the regime of capital follows the same structure: production for selling, and selling for profit. This means the appropriation of the labor of the many by the few, and thus the dominant form of exploitation is the appropriation of surplus labor. The changes that Haraway, Negri, Jameson, Baudrillard, and others refer to are changes in the way profit is made, not in the regime of profit itself (see Mandel, Onimode, Boll, Heilbroner, Drucker, Beaud, and Dobb). These mediations involve an ever-expanding commodification not only of culture but of nearly every aspect of our daily lives, including subjectivities. Our bodies are more and more densely mediated. (One of the more visible marks of this commodification is the laser-splash tattoo, in which a corporate logo—such as for Pepsi—is tattooed onto the consumer's ear, making the consumer herself a permanent extension of the commodity. Each time the consumer purchases the product, her earlobe will be scanned, making her eligible for price discounts.) The problem with ludic theories, especially those focusing on consumer society (Baudrillard, Fiske, Penley, Ross) or the commodification of culture (Jameson), as I will discuss more fully below, is that they lose sight of the connections between new forms of commodification and "consummativity" (to use Baudrillard's term) and the labor producing it. The mediating forms themselves become the new ground and limit not only of knowledge but of reality itself. One of the issues, then, in the contestations between resistance and ludic postmodernism is how these diverse mediations are understood.

In resistance postmodernism, then, postmodernism, in all its diversity, is basically the extraordinary proliferation of mediating forms and practices in late capitalism in every arena of the superstructure and the considerable expansion of the superstructure itself. Resistance postmodernists try to theorize and explain the ways in which this diverse range of cultural, social, political, institutional—in short, *ideological*—mediations are connected to the fundamental relations of production. The superstructure is the scene in which people become "conscious of this conflict" between labor and capital, which is occulted in new mediations, and "fight it out" (Marx, *Critique* 21). Critique of ideology is the means of deoccultation.

Ludic postmodernism, on the other hand, represents these diverse mediations as autonomous emergences, cutting off their connections to the *base,* to the relations of production. They dispense with the classical Marxist concept of base and superstructure as binary, outmoded, dysfunctional, and reductionist. They read the ideological as a mode of semiosis and representation and thus regard discursive, cultural, social, technological, and institutional processes as autonomous, with no necessary connection to any other series. In short, ludic critics cut off the modalities of *exchange* from their grounding in the mode of production (chap. 2). They argue that in postmodernism "Capital is freed from Labor" (Sivanadan). Ludic social- *avoids* ist feminism relies on a *discursive* or *cultural materialism* and substitutes *the* semiotics for labor. It is, as Baudrillard says, not production but "the code *labor* that is determinant: the rules of the interplay of signifiers and exchange value (*Political Economy* 146).

The fallacy of substituting consumption for labor as the basis of capitalist accumulation is demonstrated by Ernest Mandel, who offers a logical "proof of the correctness of the labor theory of value" (*Introduction* 27), in the form of a "proof by reduction to the absurd."

> Imagine for a moment a society in which living human labor . . . has been completely eliminated from all forms of production and services. Can value continue to exist[?] . . . [S]uch a situation would be absurd. A huge mass of products would be produced without this production creating any income, since no human being would be involved in this production. But someone would want to "sell" these products for which there were no longer any buyers! . . . Expressed another way, a society in which human labor would be totally eliminated from production, in the most general sense of the term, with services included, would be a society in which exchange-value had also been eliminated . . . [F]or at the moment human labor disappears from production, value, too, disappears with it. (27–28)

The other side of the ludic valorization of consumption is the erasure of needs. This is especially evident in Baudrillard's hyperreality of simulations, signs, and simulacra. Needs, for Baudrillard, "are *nothing;* there is only the system of needs," defined as "the product of the system of production" ("Consumer Society," 43, 42). But the system of production, for Baudrillard, as we have already seen, "is itself hyperreal" (*Simulations* 44) and enmeshed in the semiotic codings of commodities and simulacra. Needs, in other words, are themselves local simulations of ·

> desire, which is insatiable because it is founded on a lack . . . A need is not a need for a particular object as much as it is a "need" for differ-

ence *(the desire for social meaning)*, only then will we understand that satisfaction can never be *fulfilled*, and consequently that there can never be a *definition* of needs. ("Consumer Society" 45)

Baudrillard's consumer society not only deploys semiotics to supplant capitalism, but socialism as well. For socialism, as a society organized to fulfill real, material needs, becomes both unnecessary and impossible when needs are seen as merely the insatiable need for difference: part of the unending chain of significations covering over the lack that is desire.

This ludic postmodern consumer society and commodified culture of simulated needs—described by Baudrillard and embraced by such other postmodern critics as Arthur Kroker—is primarily the affluent world of the privileged. As Baudrillard says, "[W]e are everywhere surrounded by the remarkable conspicuousness of consumption and affluence, established by the multiplication of objects, services, and material goods. This now constitutes a fundamental mutation in the ecology of the human species" ("Consumer Society" 29). Is this a fundamental mutation, or is it a continuation and intensification of the class inequalities of capitalism globally? The new society of "consummativity" is a society of consumers whose basic needs are already met and whose practices of consumption are thus concerned with the circulation of desire through the codes of commodities and simulated needs. Feminism cannot limit its practices to a Baudrillardian consumer society.

The severe limits of Baudrillard's consumer society and much of the post-Marxist logic of New Times are effectively described by Neil Lazarus.[2] Even though Lazarus does not use the concept of ludic postmodernism, many of his observations are applicable to it. For instance, the ludic concept of consumer society is, as Lazarus says of Baudrillard, based on an "unwarranted generalization entailed in his redefinition of a putatively dominant cultural practices—consumption—as *constitutive of society itself.* Once society is defined exclusively in terms of consumption, those who are not consumers become invisible" (97). In other words, by making a *cultural* practice constitutive of society, ludic critics not only engage in a highly reductive overgeneralization, but they erase labor itself. As Lazarus says, they "exclude all those who are not 'consumers,' but whose labor makes 'consummativity' possible" (97). They exclude both those who produce commodities as well as those who produce subsistence—neither of whom have access to the value, the profits of their surplus labor, the exploitation of which provides the surplus value, the capital, for those who do consume.

Lazarus convincingly argues that the claims for New Times are replaying the same old Eurocentric imperialism. He contends that the "deficiency in postmodernist theory" consists in "the tendency to generalize from specific forms of (Western) social existence to *social existence as such*, thereby ignoring not only the *fact* of 'the international division of labor,' but, more significantly, *its concrete constitutive effects*" (96). With the "hypothesis that the world has undergone drastic and accelerating change . . . today's influential champions of postmodernism (or 'post-Marxism' or 'New Times') operate in strict though unwitting accord with the ideologues of the New World Order . . . an imperialist and capitalist world-system . . . [that is] disturbingly reminiscent of the old world order" (95).

The complicity of ludic postmodern critics with these ideologues is all the more disturbing because it occurs in the name of a progressive left politics. Fredric Jameson's theory of postmodernism as the logic of late capitalism is a case in point. Although coming out of a Marxian tradition, it does not escape many of the problems of ludic postmodernism because it embraces postmodernism uncritically. In fact, it duplicates much of the reactionary ludic logic, particularly Baudrillard's simulacrazation and displacement of the mode of production and the marginalization of struggles over the exploitation of labor.

In *The Political Unconscious*, Jameson argues that "the 'problematic' of modes of production is the most vital new area of Marxist theory" (89) and in *Postmodernism*, he states that "my analysis of postmodernism claims to make a contribution" to "the notion of a 'mode of production'" (399). Given Jameson's commitment to the "Marxist intellectual tradition" (*Ideologies* 1: xxvi), one would expect that such a focus would provide a critique-al (if not a resistance) understanding of postmodernism. However, his actual theorization of the mode of production, and thus the way he explains postmodernism, is far from being critique-al: it absorbs ludic theories of signification and consequently offers a view that is mystifying and conservative. Jameson's "version of all this," as he says, "owes a great debt to Baudrillard" (*Postmodernism* 399).

In *Postmodernism* Jameson argues that "postmodernism, as an enlarged third stage of classical capitalism," has led to "the gradual repression of . . . conceptuality," particularly "globalizing or totalizing concepts like that of the mode of production itself" (405). But instead of intervening in the suppression of such fundamental historical materialist concepts, Jameson abets it. That "a 'mode of production' model is not a production-ist model," he declares, "always seems worth saying" (406). But what is he saying? What is a mode of production that is not productionist? Jameson is saying implicitly what Baudrillard says explicitly: that consumption rather than production—in other words, consumption rather than surplus labor—is the basis of capitalist accumulation in postmodernism. Both Bau-drillard and Jameson commit what Marx called "the stupidity that con-sumption is just as productive as production" (*Theories* pt 1., 185–86). Jame-son offers a model of the mode of production that erases the appropriation of surplus labor just as thoroughly as does Baudrillard's hyperreal semiotic system.

The priority of consumption over production in Jameson's account is evident in his reification of the mediating forms of the market and com-modification. Jameson collapses the economy into the market, which he turns into a trope or figure disseminated throughout his work—and neglects the core issue of the mode of production: the problem of (surplus) labor. Tellingly, the one chapter treating economics in *Postmodernism* is on the ideology of the market. True, Jameson is critical of the expanding process of reification in postmodernism, including the "effacement of the traces of production" (*Postmodernism* 314) and points out that "this kind of 'effacement' is surely the indispensable precondition" on which consumer society is constructed; reification "generates a radical separation between consumers and producers" (315). But having insisted on this point, he treats these practices as causes, not symptoms: as autonomous, unprece-dented events. The ludic descriptions and narratives Jameson provides acquiesce rather than intervene in this effacement. His work foregrounds the standpoint of the consumer and excludes and eclipses the standpoint of labor.

Jameson textualizes the mode of production. Following Baudrillard, he deploys it as a trope or figure, and like any figure, it acquires a fluid, indeterminate meaning: it becomes a set of equivalences in a sliding chain of signifiers. At one point, Jameson specifically designates the mode of production—the "organizing unity" of the "social system—as a new object—code, sign system, or system of the production of signs and codes," which he designates "as a *mode of production*" (*Political Unconscious* 89). The most common of Jameson's semiotic equivalences is his use of production and productivity as tropes for *cultural production*—both the production of specific cultural products and a more general creative (productive) activ-

ity—as in his discussion of "form production" and "the production of theoretical discourse" (*Postmodernism* 317, 391–99). It is important to note that
in his discussion of the latter, he characterizes such production as a process
of transcoding and claims that Baudrillard provides "the paradigm gesture
of the new production process" when he "links the formula for exchange
and use value (rewritten as a fraction) with the fraction of the sign itself
(signifier and signified), thereby inaugurating a semiotic chain reaction"
(395). Moreover, he asserts that in this production of "theoretical discourse,
it is always the superstructure that is determinate" (396). Jameson even
extends his own "semiotic chain reaction" to encompass "postmodernism" itself, which he says, is "designed to name a 'mode of production'
in which cultural production finds a specific functional place" (406).

 What is this special function? In his earlier essay on postmodernism,
Jameson argues that postmodernism is "unthinkable without the hypothesis of some fundamental mutation of the sphere of culture in the world of
late capitalism, which includes a momentous modification of its social
function," and which should be "imagined in terms of an explosion: a
prodigious expansion of culture throughout the social realm, to the point at
which everything in our social life—from economic value and state power
to practices and to the very structure of the psyche itself—can be said to
have become 'cultural'" (*Postmodernism* 47–48). For Jameson, then, the
mutation of culture can take place autonomously, since he, at least formally, admits that we are still living in capitalism. The notion of culture
changing radically while the material base of society and its property relations remain the same is a profoundly un-Marxist and deeply idealist one.
Jameson theorizes culture, in the ludic mode, as a set of practices with a life
of their own. This, however, is a rather weak description of Jameson's claim
for culture because in his next move he claims that the material base itself
is cultural. For Jameson, the momentous change in the function of culture
in the postmodern mode of production is the subsumption of the economic
by the cultural: the mode of production becomes *cultural production.*
Entirely missing in Jameson's ludic logic—just as in Baudrillard's—is production as source of the extraction of surplus labor—the source of accumulation and profit. This occlusion of labor enables Jameson to claim that the
"new and final horizon" of the mode of production "may be designated
. . . as *cultural revolution* (*Political Unconscious* 95). Cultural revolution, in
other words, replaces economic revolution.

 What we find in both Jameson's notion of production and his theory of
postmodernism is an extraordinary reification of culture and the super-

structure. Jameson is quite right that there is a "prodigious expansion of culture" in postmodernism. But it is a ludic fetishization of the cultural to argue that "everything in our social life—from economic value and state power to practices and to the very structure of the psyche itself—can be said to have become 'cultural'" (*Postmodernism* 47–48). Such a notion of the cultural becomes a form of cultural imperialism, dissolving production into a series of mediating tropes. Jameson justifies this cultural imperialism as itself a historical effect of postmodernism. However, resistance post-modernism critiques this cultural imperialism as an effect of the ludic reification of superstructural mediations as autonomous series.

In addition to textualizing the mode of production, Jameson engages in another ludic move by pluralizing it as well. In *The Political Unconscious*, he defines it as "heterogeneous": as consisting of multiple levels or "horizons" and containing "the co-existence of *several* modes of production all at once" (95). He sums up this argument in *Postmodernism*: "[A] mode of production is not a 'total system' . . . [I]t includes a variety of counterforces . . . 'residual' as well as 'emergent' forces" (406). But Jameson's rewriting of the mode of production as *multiple* modes of production simply renders it nondeterminate and undecidable: it is *all* modes of production and *no* specific (determining) mode of production. Thus late capitalism is, for Jameson, a confluence of multiple, indeterminate modes of production. The effect of this pluralistic notion is to entirely suppress and displace the basic mode of production in *all* stages of capitalism, which—it is important to again stress—is the extraction of profit from surplus labor. Jameson's notion of heterogeneous, multiple modes of production thus justifies his erasure of labor and his culturalization of production. The limits of Jameson's ludic logic are especially clear when we examine his explanation of its usefulness for feminism. He claims that

> The notion of overlapping modes of production . . . allow(s) us to short-circuit the false problem of the priority of the economic over the sexual, or of sexual oppression over that of social class . . . sexism and the patriarchal are to be grasped as the sedimentation and the virulent survival of forms of alienation specific to the oldest mode of production of human history, with its division of labor between men and women . . . The analysis of the ideology of form . . . should reveal the formal persistence of such archaic structures of alienation—and the sign systems specific to them—beneath the overlay of all the more recent and historically original types of alienation—such as political

domination and commodity reification—which have become the dominants of that most complex of all cultural revolutions, late capitalism, in which all the earlier modes of production in one way or another structurally coexist. The affirmation of radical feminism, therefore, that to annul the patriarchal is the most *radical* political act—insofar as it includes and subsumes more partial demands, such as the liberation from the commodity form—is thus perfectly consistent with an expanded Marxian framework, for which the transformation of our own dominant mode of production must be accompanied and completed by an equally radical restructuration of all the more archaic modes of production with which it structurally coexists. (*Political Unconscious* 99–100)

This is a very telling passage: it not only equates late capitalism with cultural revolution—that is, with the superstructure—but it segregates the sexual from the material and represents sexual oppression and the patriarchal as autonomous from and *other* than a capitalist mode of production. As I explained in chapter 2, such segregation of patriarchy as an independent, ahistorical form of oppression that is not determined by capitalism is the hallmark of neoconservative ludic social theory. For Jameson, such "archaic" modes may be said to coexist *with* the capitalist mode of production, but they are, nonetheless, distinct, autonomous, residual forms: the "division of labor between men and women" is thus understood to be a "virulent survival" of the "oldest mode of production of human history" rather than fundamental to the expropriation of surplus labor and superexploitation of women in capitalism. Jameson makes this sexual apartheid disturbingly clear when he distinguishes between "the transformation of *our own* dominant mode of production"—that is, capitalism (emphasis added)—and the "radical restructuration of all the more archaic modes of production"—such as patriarchy. This is a serious step backward for feminism. As I have already indicated in the previous chapter, materialist feminist texts, such as those by Maria Mies, have been articulating the fundamental necessity of the gender division of labor *in* capitalism—not as a residual effect or archaic mode but as the very basis of capitalist accumulation. This is not to say that the gender division of labor has not also been basic to previous modes of production—but to read it as a residual mode of production *coexisting* with capitalism is to negate the ways in which the gender division of labor has been radically *reconfigured by* capitalism and is fundamental to the mode of production and division of labor that *is* capitalism. In the famous passage in *The Communist Manifesto*, which I have already quoted and analyzed, Marx and Engels discuss patriarchy as a practice that has its origin in precapitalist modes of production—a practice that capitalism, at its highest moment of expansion, will have no use for. But their reading of patriarchy—as long as it survives in capitalism—is not a segregationist one: they show how in fact capitalism commodifies sex and uses "differences of . . . sex" as an "instrument of labor" (62). In Jameson the ways in which differences of sex are deployed in capitalism are simply relegated to the ahistorical margin of the residual.

Jameson does not so much "short circuit the false problem of the priority of the economic over the sexual, or of sexual oppression over that of social class" as transcode it: reducing the material and historical to the semiotic and formalist. This is a "false problem" not because the base, the economic, is not prior to the sexual and sexual oppression, but rather because it is *not separate* and distinct from them. As I have been arguing, gender and the sexual are direct effects of the material conditions of the social formation: the mode of production and labor processes in global capitalism. The other disenabling implication of Jameson's argument follows from his representation of the mode of production *as itself a cultural revolution*. In making such a case, Jameson is subsuming the economic to the cultural—that is, the base to the superstructure—and then positing (cultural) change as a function of capitalism itself. Thus there is no need to change capitalism: there is no need for any social revolution because cultural change has been substituted for the radical transformation of labor relations. Superstructural revolution subsumes the struggle to end the exploitation of labor. Feminism, for Jameson—specifically radical feminism—is seen as a *supplement* to Marxism, and as such it is basically the cultural and ideological struggle against an archaic mode of (cultural) production. Jameson thus completely occludes materialist and Marxist feminism as the struggle against the exploitive labor relations and mode of production that *is* capitalism by privileging a mode of feminism that is more focused on the difference of woman as naturally pregiven than on the social revolution to change the fate of all human beings.

Jameson's work is divided by a fundamental contradiction: he claims the position of historical materialism, but he deploys a ludic logic that ends up completely erasing it, subsuming the economic to culture, the base to the superstructure. For example, Jameson occasionally criticizes the theories of power in Weber and Foucault as well as the theories of postindustrial society and consumer society (especially those of Baudrillard), because, as he says, "the economic finds itself in both reassigned to a secondary and nondeterminant position beneath the new dominant of political power or of cultural production" (92–93). Yet Jameson's writings reproduce the very same problems because he reifies cultural production and reassigns and marginalizes the economic as "secondary and nondeterminant" just as much as the ludic theories of Baudrillard or Foucault.

This problem is a serious contradiction in Jameson's work: a contradiction that articulates his contradictory class politics, which at times he also seems to be quite aware of in a disingenuous way. In the introduction to *Postmodernism*, for example, Jameson follows the historical materialist position that there is no break in capitalism. He says, for example, that "postmodernism is not the cultural dominant of a wholly new social order . . . but only the reflex and the concomitant of yet another systemic modification of capitalism itself" (xii). At the same time, he says that he has "pretended to believe that the postmodern is as unusual as it thinks it is and that it constitutes a cultural and experiential break" (xiii). What is the theoretical and political status of such *pretense?* Is it possible to pretend to believe in the claims of postmodernism—especially its cultural imperialism—without also having to *suspend* belief in the fundamental concepts of historical materialism? Does such pretense not also involve a substantial acquiescence to the terms and conditions of (ludic) postmodernism and a reproduction of its frame of intelligibility? Jameson's reification of the superstructure would certainly suggest so. There is a telling evasiveness in his discussions of base and superstructure: he neither disavows nor affirms the necessity of the base in relation to the superstructure. Instead, he puts forth such circumlocutory statements as the following: "[T]o say that my two terms, the *cultural* and the *economic*, thereby collapse back into one another and say the same thing, in an eclipse of the distinction between base and superstructure . . . is also to suggest that the base, in the third stage of capitalism, generates its superstructures with a new kind of dynamic" (*Postmodernism* xxi). In no way does he specify *how* he understands this "new kind of dynamic" of the superstructure. I have already demonstrated the way Jameson understands the superstructural mediations in such expansive terms that they dissolve the economic into the cultural. Thus, when he says " 'base and superstructure' is not really a model of anything, but rather . . . an imperative to make connections . . . a heuristic recommendation simultaneously to grasp culture (theory) in and for itself, but also in relationship to its outside" (*Postmodernism* 409), we have to recognize the degree to which these connections are *not* made in Jameson's work: "culture (theory)" is not "grasped" in dialectical relation to the mode of production and exploitation of labor. Instead, in pretending to believe (and thus to promote) the claims of (ludic) postmodernism, Jameson ends up emptying the concepts of historical materialism of their radical explanatory value. Indeed, "base and superstructure is not a model of anything" in Jameson's work—rather it becomes a sliding trope for the ludic primacy of the cultural. When Jameson calls postmodernism the cultural logic or dominant of late capitalism, we thus need to understand it in terms of his pretense—his *suspension* of historical materialism.

In contrast to this ludic logic, resistant postmodernism insists on the need for the model of base and superstructure and asserts the priority of the mode of production, especially since the economic has been so fundamentally eclipsed by ludic logic. Displacing the base, as ludic postmodernists have done, has not lead, as they have claimed, to greater historical understanding and complexity, but rather has meant that our social, political, and cultural analysis does not move beyond the bounds of superstructural mediations: the connections between the material conditions of our labor and the cultural practices, meanings, and subjectivities we produce have been severed. Resistance postmodernism's insistence on the economic, on the relations of production and labor, however, does *not* deny the way the superstructure effects and acts on the economic. Rather, it seeks to understand the *dialectical* nature of this relationship. It is useful to recall here Engels's comments on this problem in his letter to Joseph Bloch (21–22 September 1890).

> According to the materialist conception of history, the *ultimately* determining element in history is the production and reproduction of real life. More than this neither Marx nor I have ever asserted. Hence if somebody twists this into saying that the economic element is the *only* determining one, he transforms that proposition into a meaningless, abstract, senseless phrase. The economic situation is the basis, but the various elements of the superstructure: political forms of the class struggle and its results, to wit: constitutions established by the victorious class after a successful battle, etc., juridical forms, and then even the reflexes of all these actual struggles in the brains of the participants, political, juristic, philosophical theories, religious views and their further development into systems of dogmas, also exercise their influence upon the course of the historical struggles and in many cases preponderate in determining their *form*. There is an interaction of all

these elements in which, amid all the endless host of accidents (that is, of things and events, whose inner connection is so remote or so impossible of proof that we can regard it as non-existent, as negligible) the economic movement finally asserts itself as necessary . . .

We make our history ourselves, but, in the first place, under very definite assumptions and conditions. Among these the economic ones are ultimately decisive. (Marx and Engels, *Reader* 760–61)

To engage the interaction of various elements while insisting on the decisive role of economic forces enables resistance postmodern feminism to hold on to the *objective reality* of the material conditions of women's lives and the lives of other oppressed peoples. It provides the means for understanding the way the conditions of their working day, the exploitation of their labor, their unequal access to social resources determine not only the complex meanings, practices, and desires of their daily lives, but also their relation to their own subjectivities, to their bodies, to others, to the society as a whole, and especially, to the class struggle over economic and social justice for all. Resistance postmodernism produces historical explanations of the *dialectical* relations between the mode of production, the social divisions of labor, and the proliferating superstructural mediations in late capitalism.

The differences between ludic and resistance postmodernism come down, in short, to their opposing ways of theorizing the role of mode of production and thus the relation of base and superstructure, and consequently, the mode of explaining the social, cultural, and political. At stake in the opposition between ludic and resistance postmodernism are two very different understandings of politics. Ludic politics is a cultural politics: it is a discursive practice that seeks open access to the free play of signification in order to dissemble the dominant cultural policy (totality), which tries to restrict and stabilize meanings. Donna Haraway's notion of ludic cyborg politics is exemplary of this logic and closely parallels more textualist or deconstructive feminists and postmodernists, from whom she is usually considered distinct. While Haraway is concerned with the problem of women's "integration/exploitation into a world system of production/reproduction" (*Simians* 163), she understands this situation in terms of communication and coding—what she calls cyborg semiologies. She thus defines "cyborg politics [as] the struggle for language and the struggle against perfect communication, against the one code that translates all meaning perfectly, the central dogma of phallologocentrism" (*Simians* 176).

In contrast, resistance postmodernism insists on a historical material-ist political practice that works for the equal distribution of social resources to all and for ending the exploitation of labor. Such social transformation can not result simply from a *semiotic freedom* but requires a radical restruc-turing of the social relations of production through class struggle. Resis-tance postmodernism integrates the problem of poverty into the problem of liberty, but the *effect* (not necessarily the intention) of ludic postmod-ernism is to isolate liberty from poverty. Ludic postmodernism acts to expand the range of liberty for those already freed from poverty—without acknowledging that the condition of such freedom (usually understood as choice) is the exploitation of the labor of others.

The crucial issue for feminism is how does it locate itself in the class struggle being acted out in the scene of theory? What kind of politics is feminism producing in postmodernism—that is, in the new superstruc-tural forms and practices of late capitalism? Is feminism a materialist polit-ical practice and theory that is able to explain and intervene in the exploita-tion of women's lives and labor? Or is it a ludic cultural politics that understands women's condition largely in terms of autonomous regimes of discourse (cyborg semiologies) and seeks a discursive freedom? Most feminists engaging postmodernism now are adopting a ludic logic. Some do so with enthusiasm (e.g., Rubin, Butler, Cornell, de Lauretis, Fuss, Iri-garay), others with reluctance (such as Spivak, Silverman, Moi). But the main reason for this ludic turn has been the historical dynamics of contem-porary class struggle, in which the ruling class has secured new advantages for itself and institutionalized these advantages through the state (the reign of Reagan-Thatcher-Kohl and their successors). The triumph of business in this era, climaxing in the conquest of markets in Eastern Europe, has been relayed by ludic discourses in discrediting historical materialism and dis-missing the necessity of labor and class struggles. My purpose in critiquing ludic postmodernism is to break the hegemony of ludic logic and to reclaim historical materialism for feminism in postmodernism.

Resistance postmodern feminism moves beyond the limitations of ludic feminism to explain and theorize the way diverse and *seemingly* autonomous social institutions, cultural practices, meanings, desires, and subjectivities in postmodernism (the superstructure) are dialectically related to the relations of production and expropriation of labor (the base) in global late capitalism. As part of this undertaking and its intervention in the patriarchal capitalist knowledge industry, resistance postmodern femi-nism returns to the problem of ideology and develops a materialist critique. The project of ideology critique, as Kaja Silverman shows in her *Male Subjectivity at the Margins*, was interrupted in the mid-1970s at the very time that a materialist theory of ideology—developed in Marxist feminist discourses—was putting pressure on ludic discourses. Silverman's own project, as I have already indicated, is ambivalent in its approach to ludic theory, but her recognition of the necessity of the critique of ideology for any interventionist knowledge of the social is very useful. Rosemary Hennessy has also argued effectively for the necessity of the critique of ideology for feminist theory in her *Materialist Feminism*. Both Silverman and Hennessy, however, will find my theory of ideology somewhat different from their own (and the two are not, of course, identical either). My point here, however, is not the differences in the theory of ideology, but an argument for bringing the problem of ideology and ideology critique back to feminist theory. In addition, resistance postmodernism engages in a radical retheorizing of basic concepts in feminism and postmodernism—such as difference—in terms of historical materialism.

Difference-within and Difference-between

Postmodernism is an articulation of the crisis of difference brought about by the contradictions of late capitalism and the demise of monopoly capitalism. The ensemble of legal, cultural, philosophical, and social forms we call modernism provided the justification for capitalism in the earlier stage of entrepreneurial capitalism and, to a large degree, during monopoly capitalism, as capital increasingly traveled overseas and, at the same time, became centralized. At the core of modernism (which has had such a profound effect on the emergence of feminism in the late nineteenth and early twentieth centuries) is the theory of Enlightenment with its principles of the equality of all human beings and universal human rights and its privileging of reason and rationalism as the means for realizing a just society. All of these principles are, of course, embodied in the notion of representative democracy, which formally recognizes equality in the principle of one person, one vote. The fundamental fissure in modernism arises out of a basic aporia: its blindness to the contradictions between this superstructural promise of (discursive) democracy (equality for all—that is, discursive sameness) and the actual material practices in capitalism of profit for some (economic difference)—which have included not only the daily expropriation of the labor of wage workers but also the exploitation of women's subsistence labor and the enslavement and colonization of people

of color. Modernism is divided, on the one hand, by its promise of universal equality, and, on the other, by its legitimation and reproduction
(through such ideological and sociocultural beliefs and practices as the free
market, individualism, public and private, separate spheres, and separate
but equal) of the divisions of property, resources, and labor according to
the differences between men and women, white and black, owners and
workers, colonizer and colonized.

The crisis brought about by this contradiction opens the fault lines of
modernism and in so doing undercuts it as the theory that has legitimated
entrepreneurial capitalism and the free market in the institutions of bourgeois democracy—notably the American and French revolutions. The
rhetoric and arguments of modernism, in other words, are simply no
longer adequate to deal with the accumulated contradictions of entrepreneurial capitalism. Postmodernism is the result of this inability of modernist theory to contain the contradictions of capitalism. Therefore, the historical role of postmodernism is to reconcile the contradictions of
capitalism (the incompatibility of discursive human rights and economic
rights) and to solve them in new ways. Postmodernism undertakes this
project of solving—in the imaginary of culture—the material problems that
cannot be solved in the actual practices of capitalism by normalizing material contradictions as difference (discursive diversity) and then legitimating difference itself as not only the hallmark of a developed civil society but
also as an integral element of the new human rights. In other words, having failed to solve the problem of contradictions in its actual practices, capitalism produces a theory that represents contradictions (born out of the
relations of wage labor and capital) as difference and difference itself as
part of enlightened citizenship. In this way it discredits the idea of (modernist) equality as the sign of a repressive universalism that Western
democracies have outgrown.

Ludic postmodernism is the height of this normalization of the contradictions of modern capitalism as difference and the justification of difference as the celebration of the uniqueness, irreplaceability, and excessiveness of human subjectivity and its rights (Drucilla Cornell's *Beyond
Accommodation* is exemplary of this position). Resistance postmodernism,
however, critiques human rights in this sense as a bourgeois project that
covers up the fundamental economic inequality produced under the
regime of profit. Resistance postmodernism insists on the collectivity of
humanity, on the universality of their needs, and on the necessity of fulfilling the needs of all people as the material conditions for the possibility of

any historically viable difference. In other words, resistance postmodernism rejects the normalization of contradictions as difference and points out that such a ludic notion of difference is an ideological alibi for defending the interests of the ruling class. Real difference—nonexploitative difference—is possible in historical human societies only after the abolition of the social division of labor (Marx, *Gotha* 8–10). In other words, the understanding of human rights now codified in ludic feminism is established upon a bourgeois notion of difference: it constructs, as Marx argues, a bourgeois right, which is inequality in disguise. Bourgeois right is, at most, a political emancipation or, in Marx's own words, an "emancipation within the prevailing scheme of things" ("Jewish Question" 221). This bourgeois human right is based upon the erasure of the "essence of community and inscription of the essence of difference." It is "the expression of the separation of man from his community, from himself and from other men . . . It is now only the abstract confession of an individual oddity, of a private whim, a caprice" (221). The difference in bourgeois modernism and embodied in human rights is "the right of man to private property" (229). Even in its most advanced form (in a socialist democracy or a "radical democracy," as Laclau and Mouffe call it), "This equal right is an unequal right for unequal labour," Marx explains, because it is based on "the same principle" that "regulates the exchange of commodities" (*Gotha* 8–9). Human rights thus cannot be established, as postmodern theory would like us to believe, by the pursuit and affirmation of difference. "Right," Marx points out, "can never be higher than the economic structure of a society and the cultural development thereby determined" (10). The radical path to a fundamental (nonexploitative) difference is, therefore, through a recognition of human needs: "From each according to his ability, to each according to his needs" (10). It is only through recognition of universal needs that difference can be materialized. It is also in such a moment that, as Lenin argues, in his reading of Marx, that the "state will wither away" (*State,* 75–92). The notion of difference here is not an apparatus for solving—in the cultural imaginary—the contradictions of practices in capitalism. Differences become historically viable and nonexploitative only after these contradictions have been solved *in practice* through the transformation of wage labor.

Postmodernism—in privileging a bourgeois notion of difference—becomes a regime that protects the contradictions of capitalism by providing the alibi of difference. The postmodern war against the universal occults the contradictions in modernity, since the breaking up of the universal into endless differential localities makes it impossible to grasp the incoherence (contradictions) of the social. As I mentioned in my critique of Jameson's homogenized postmodernism—in which there is no room for a resistance postmodernism and consequently a generic difference is set up as a mark of the postmodern dismantling of modernism—the real question is not that postmodernism foregrounds difference (Marxism had done this), but *what is* difference and also what is at stake in the discourse of difference? Ludic theory conceals the contradictions of modernism by declaring a new post-al state of affairs in which the accumulated contradictions of the "before" are left behind. Postmodernism uses difference (as a difference of signs, of identity/textuality) to discredit calls for collectivity and universality and, in so doing, justifies the interests of the ruling class, which is ruling only because of the difference of its access to economic resources. Resistance postmodernism critiques bourgeois difference in ludic theory and points out that the project of modernity fails not because it is wrong but because it is idealist and shows a way to materialize difference through Marx's theory of difference in his *Critique of the Gotha Programme.*

Feminism has long been at the center of the struggles over difference in modernism and now postmodernism. The current crisis of difference in feminism is both an effect of this history and a consequence of the larger contradictions in patriarchal late capitalism that are being fought out in the scene of theory. The more recent contestations over the difference of difference in feminism involve conflicts over the status of gender (whether the primary difference is gender or sex); over woman as the sexual other; over the differences within women, and the differences of desire (e.g., the feminine/maternal imaginary). Feminism, in short, is engaged in a debate over *how* to rewrite (theorize) difference and *what* to write as a difference in postmodernism. What is missing in these struggles over difference is the *difference of labor,* and it is this difference that materialist feminism reclaims. Certainly feminists have taken up a variety of positions in the contesting superstructural articulations of difference within both modernism and postmodernism. My concern here is to critically engage the main ways of understanding difference in modernist and postmodernist feminism and to propose a historical materialist retheorization of difference.

The ludic postmodern notion of difference as *difference-within* calls into question the very possibility of identity, which is grounded in a notion of *difference-between* and has been the philosophical foundation for most modernist modes of feminism, from liberal to radical and cultural feminism. Difference-within displaces and rewrites what had previously been seen as the prevailing issue in feminist theory—the conflict between equality and difference—as one between an essentialist identity and antiessentialist differences. I return to the problem of essentialism in chapter 5, but here I want to focus on the contestations among *difference-between, difference-within,* and, what I will be proposing as *difference within a system of exploitation.*

We need to critique the political effectivity of these conflicting theories of difference and to understand their historical limits: the ways in which they are linked to and are either complicit with or contest the social divisions and inequalities of labor, property, and resources in global late capitalism. Any politics and its theories are always historically constrained and circumscribed by the structures of exploitation they challenge. As I have already indicated, I believe the only way to overcome these limits is for feminism to engage in a collectivity of critique that continually interrogates the political effects and class politics of its theories and challenges any complicity with the relations of exploitation in capitalism. Such critique helps us to produce new sites of opposition and social transformation. My debate with various feminist theories, then, is always taking place within this commitment to a collectivity of critique and its necessity for emancipatory politics.

Various modernist feminisms, from Enlightenment and liberal feminism, on the one hand, to cultural and radical feminism, on the other, have understood their politics as an attempt to define women's position in society—as well as the basis of women's oppression and an agenda for change—in terms of either a basic equality with men or a fundamental difference *between* men and woman. The Enlightenment and liberal feminist argument for a natural equality between men and women depends on the belief in an inherent human nature based on a rational consciousness immanent in men and women alike. In other words, the selfhood of women is the same as, that is, it is identical, with their immanent human nature, specifically, their rational consciousness (which is the same as men's). Any differences between men and women are thus thought to be the result of the violence of an unjust society that prevents women from fully developing their innate (human) reason. By denying women access to education, to economic independence and legal responsibility, as is still the case in many parts of the world, or by continuing to restrict women's economic opportunities and individual rights (as in abortion), patriarchal society cripples and distorts women's innate capabilities—which they share with men—

and denies women their natural rights to fully develop their reason and achieve self-fulfillment, to use a favorite term of liberal feminists.

However, for other feminists subscribing to modernist discourses and social theory, the claims made by Enlightenment and liberal feminism for a sameness and identicalness or identity between men and women erases, or at the very least glosses over, social and historically constructed differences. A statement such as the Seneca Falls Declaration of 1848, for example, which "*Resolved,* That the equality of human rights results necessarily from the fact of the identity of the race in capabilities and responsibilities" (Schneir 82), has been seen by these feminists as erasing and subsuming women's difference into the dominant norm, which is viewed as masculinist. For feminists who believe in the existence of fundamental differences between men and women, equality is impossible, since it merely reproduces discrimination against women by failing to account for and include their difference in society. In order for equality to be achieved (which is often still the goal of those who subscribe to difference-between), women's separate needs, deriving from their different biological or social condition, must be considered. For instance, economic equality is seen not merely as an issue of open access to job opportunities but is also dependent on making special provisions for child care and maternity leaves. Usually left out of these feminist arguments for economic reform is the radical restructuring of capitalism itself—the elimination of profit (economic difference).

Obviously the contesting modes of feminism around difference-between and equality converge in places. Some notions of equality, for instance, do not argue so much for a sameness between men and women as acknowledge the differences between them and instead posit equality as the *indifference* to difference for the purposes of ending legal and economic discrimination. Or as Juliet Mitchell points out in her essay "Women and Equality," liberal and social democratic notions of equality in capitalism recognize that "there are differences but these should not count" (30).

Cultural and radical feminists, on the other hand, argue for and celebrate the fundamental differences between men and women, commonly treating these differences as deterministic and largely inherent traits. The explanations of these differences vary considerably among these feminists, ranging from biological causes, as in Shulamith Firestone's claims that "biology itself—procreation—is at the origin of the dualism" (8), to social and cultural factors. In environmental explanations, women's different modes of thinking, characteristics, and values are seen as developing out of women's nearly universal participation in, and often their confinement to, the domestic sphere and its duties and responsibilities, especially mothering and the care of dependents, whether young or old. As one of the main documents of contemporary radical feminism, Roxanne Dunbar's "Female Liberation as the Basis for Social Revolution" puts it, "'maternal traits'" are "conditioned into women." "Most women have been programmed from early childhood for a role, maternity, which develops a certain consciousness of care for others, self-reliance, flexibility, non-competitiveness, cooperation" (550). Thus, Carol Gilligan, for example, contends that women and men generate opposing forms of moral reasoning and ethics: women are concerned with an "ethics of care" and a "morality of responsibility," because their different socialization and experiences in the public world stress a "morality of rights."

Other feminists from Charlotte Perkins Gilman to Mary Daly and the women's peace movement find women as a group are creative, peaceful, nondominating, and healing, whereas men and the patriarchal institutions and practices they have produced are destructive, violent, exploitative and dominating. In addition, many feminists also elaborate related sets of differences: women are considered—whether by biological or social factors—to be situated primarily in the body and the contingencies of everyday reality (as in housekeeping and child care); thus women tend to be focused on the concrete and contingent and to be more sensuous, emotional, and associational in their thinking, while men emphasize the rational, abstract, scientific, and theoretical modes of knowing.

For poststructuralist and ludic postmodern feminists any form of difference-between is a mode of *identity*, and the binary oppositions between those feminists advocating equality—that is, identity or sameness between men and women—and those feminists claiming a difference between men and women is a false opposition. Equality and difference are seen as "supplementary," to use Derrida's term from his reading of Rousseau in *Of Grammatology*: they are "two significations whose cohabitation is as strange as it is necessary" (144). Thus ludic postmodernists read difference, as it is articulated by radical and cultural feminists, as an identity, and identity as difference. For instance, the female difference celebrated by cultural and radical feminists is seen by poststructuralists as constituting an identity that is just as determining and congruent—that is just as identical—with the selfhood of a woman as is the rational identity of Enlightenment and liberal feminists. The only distinction here is that this female identity is differentiated from, rather than seen as the same as, men's identity.

Resistance postmodernism shares in much of this critique of difference-between as producing reified, naturalized identities, whether under the name of equality or difference. But it understands the problem quite differently: as the result of an inadequately *materialized* theory of difference, rather than an inadequately *textualized* theory.

The main result of the postmodern critique of difference-between has been to expose the limits and complicity of these forms of feminism with many of the assumptions and practices sustaining the oppressive structures of difference they have struggled to change. Thus, while both those feminists believing in equality and those committed to difference have critiqued the generic modernist, humanist self—man as the universal, all encompassing figure—and revealed its exclusions and blind spots, they all still subscribe to such basic modernist tenets as the autonomy, uniqueness, and inviolability of the self, a self that is identical with itself or selfsame, whether that self is defined in terms of a coherent rationality or maternalism. All still believe, as Matilda Joslyn Gage put it in 1893, in "the political doctrine of the sovereignty of the individual" (240): in other words, the autonomous individual of free will and agency required by capitalism. Moreover, both modes of modernist feminism are alike in essentializing an identity for women—whether based on a sameness or on a difference between women and men—in terms of which women are defined as sharing the same set of traits and experiences, thus constituting a unified group. For Enlightenment and liberal feminists, this unity is the human race itself. For cultural and radical feminists, the differences between men and women constitute an identity, unity, and cohesion within the groups defined by the two categories, thereby erasing the *differences within* each category, specifically the differences of class, race, and sexual preference among women. Both modes of feminism—those advocating equality and those claiming difference—can be termed *identarian* feminism because of their commitment to an essentialized identity.

For materialist and socialist feminism the problem with most modernist feminist struggles over difference and equality is not so much its essentialism as its overemphasis on the superstructure and its neglect, by and large, of the relations of production of capitalism. Most forms of modernist feminism have not engaged the *difference of labor*—particularly the exploitation of surplus labor and thus the difference of profit. They have not sufficiently questioned the organization of society around profit and surplus labor; instead they have sought a more equitable distribution of profit—as in equal pay, comparable worth, the Equal Rights Amendment—as well as more support for the different needs of women within the existing labor relations, for example, better child care. Marxist and socialist feminisms, at least in their more radical forms, have tried to realize the promise of equality at all levels of society from the political and cultural to the economic. They have been especially concerned with ending economic difference: eliminating profit and the exploitation of surplus labor and insuring the equitable distribution of socioeconomic resources to all. It is the struggle for a revolutionary restructuring of society organized around fulfilling needs rather than creating profits: *from each according to her ability, to each according to her needs!*—to adopt Marx's famous proclamation. In short, Marxist and socialist feminists have been concerned with the dialectical relations between base and superstructure. Of special importance to the development of this dialectical feminism is the work of Clara Zetkin, Alexandra Kollontai, Rosa Luxemburg, Evelyn Reed, and Heleieth Saffioti.

Marxist and socialist feminism have historically been based on the modernist principle of difference-between. In fact, the difference between exploiter and exploited grounds all revolutionary struggles. But many socialist feminists have commonly substituted an essentialized identity or difference (e.g., the category of women) for a materialist and dialectical understanding of the categories of difference-between. Historical materialism does not understand differences as essentialized identities but rather as historically produced oppositions arising out of the class struggles over exploitation. It is important here to note how this confusion has made socialist feminists especially vulnerable to the poststructuralist deconstruction of difference-between. In fact, the recent ludic turn among a number of socialist feminists (notably, Donna Haraway and Michèle Barrett) and the abandonment of socialism altogether by many others (such as Zillah Eisenstein) is largely owing to this postmodern rewriting of *difference-between* as *difference-within*.

In opposition to modernist, identitarian feminism is what can be called *differential* feminism—those feminisms developing largely out of poststructuralism, that is, out of ludic postmodernism. Differential feminists conceive of difference not as an identity but as self-divided, as always split by its other: they are concerned not with the difference between but with the difference within. Thus no entity, whether an individual or the category of women, is a coherent, self-contained, selfsame identity; rather, it is always different from itself, divided by its other, which is produced through its own excess-ive signification.

But what is meant by identity and difference here, or rather what are the contested meanings attached to these terms? Difference, in the modernist epistemology, is always understood as the difference between one particular, individuated subject and another; one particular, unique category and another. Difference-between constructs identities by delineating the clearly marked boundaries between coherent entities or individuals that are selfsame, that is, identical with themselves, in their difference from the other. According to this logic of identity in which difference participates: A is always A because it is not B; a chair is always a chair because it is not a table. By positing separate, individuated, and bounded entities, the logic of identity creates a ground of certainty—if a chair is a chair and nothing but a chair, then we can at any given time rely on it as a chair. To simplify a complicated philosophical issue, we can say that difference-between is a quest for certainty. The contestation of ludic postmodernity with difference-between, then, is the contestation with certainty—with the unshakable grounds and foundations that give the traditional modernist epistemology a basis from which to know the real in a decidable manner. This is another way of saying that the ludic postmodern quarrel with the essentializing difference-between is a quarrel with decidability. As Drucilla Cornell says, "[U]ndecidability plays a necessary role in the reconceptualization of feminism as ethical feminism"—which is her name for a form of ludic feminism based on the "feminist alliance with deconstruction" and a Lyotardian notion of indeterminate justice (*Beyond Accommodation* 28, 107–18).

Ludic postmodern difference overturns identity and displaces the ground of decidability. And of course, the question for feminism is, how can it build a transformative politics on a postmodern difference that throws out certainty and destabilizes identity? Because in order to change a practice or a structure, one has to know what one is working with. Knowledge is the condition of possibility for transformative politics. Without knowledge, politics collapses into moral platitudes and activist self-righteousness—both of which are ahistorical and modes of subject maintenance. I will provide an answer to this question of transformative politics by showing how resistance postmodern feminism situates difference-within back in the social and reads undecidability not as a result of textuality but of social struggle. But first I want to specify this rewriting of difference as it is commonly articulated in ludic postmodernism, particularly poststructuralism.

Ludic postmodern difference is the difference within signification—it is the play, dispersion, and diffusion of distinctions circulating immanently in the relay of meanings. In other words, in ludic postmodernism, individuals are not self-contained and definite identities, possessing an irreducible quality, individual uniqueness, or a certain, decidable meaning. Rather, they are traversed and divided by a "weave of differences," that is, by differences within. Thus any specific entity is a "tissue of traces" of the endless dissemination of differences in the relations of signification. As Drucilla Cornell says of this process of difference or *differance* (as Derrida writes it in "Differance"): "Any reality, including the Law of the Father, established in and through the symbolic, is always already divided against itself as soon as it is *presented*" (*Beyond Accommodation* 108)—that is, as soon as it is *represented* in and through the signifying chain of differences.

To understand how this dissemination of differences destabilizes obvious meanings, we need to briefly recall some of the main presuppositions of Derridean deconstruction. Derrida radicalizes the idea of difference in Saussure, who argued that "in language there are only differences *without positive terms*" (Saussure 120), in other words, without identity. The sign, for Saussure, consists of a relation between a signifier and a signified, which anchors the signifier and thus meaning, but Derrida dispenses with any secured or stable signified—what he calls the "transcendental signified" (*Grammatology* 20). Stable meanings (the adequation of signifier and signified) is, for Derrida, the effect of violently stopping the play of meaning through the transcendental signified: as Derrida writes, "There has to be a transcendental signified for the difference between signifier and signified to be somewhere absolute and irreducible" (20). By play, however, Derrida does not mean "play *in the world*, as it has always been defined" (50). Rather by play, he means "the absence of the transcendental signified as limitlessness of play" of signs (50): in other words, the excessive proliferation of meanings that deprive the signifier of any single meaning. Difference, for Derrida, then, is the relation of signi*fiers* to each other in language, and language, in turn, is nothing but the play (dissemination) of difference. Meaning is, thus, the result of a chain of signifiers without stable signifieds or referents; what is taken as a signified is, in fact, a signifier stopped in its playful dissemination. Language, in short, is nonrepresentational: it means not because it refers to a world "out there" but because it is a system of differences among signifiers, without sameness, without transcendental signifieds. We thus have no direct access to what is commonsensically called reality; our knowledge of the world is always mediated by language and its system of differences. Since the sign always slips, we never get a secure knowledge of the world. As Cornell writes, "[D]econstruction challenges the rigid divide between the literal, the real and textuality. What is 'real' and what it means to be 'realistic,' to pay attention to the real, is always given to us in a text" (*Beyond Accommodation* 108). For deconstruction, this is not so much a denial of reality as a reunderstanding of our groundless and unfounded relation to reality: there can be no practice or arena outside the play of signifiers, or rather outside the relations of difference that constitute meaning. As Derrida says, "[A]ll experience is the experience of meaning," which is the effect of *differance* (*Positions* 30).

Herein lies the destabilizing of identities and the overturning of certainties. Meaning—and with it identity—is considered unfounded and undecidable because the play of signifiers constituting it can no longer be anchored in a referent or signified or secured in a reality outside language; rather, they are part of a slipping, sliding chain of differences. Since language is a nonrepresentational system of differences, our knowledge of the world becomes equally slipping, sliding, and differential: different and always deferred. Knowledge of social totality, which is necessary for any social praxis, becomes a logocentric narrative from such a perspective. In poststructuralist theory, as in any idealist theory, it is the meaning that invents the world and not the world that determines the meaning. Meanings are created by the consciousness of the subject, and to put meaning first is also to place the subject at the center of the world. It is, in short, the consciousness of the subject that produces the world and not the world that constructs consciousness, as historical materialists contend. Poststructuralist theory has put in question consciousness and the subject, but this should not be taken to mean their erasure from this theory. Poststructuralism removes one kind of subject (the Cartesian subject of consciousness), which has become historically irrelevant to late capitalism, and invents another kind of subject (the subject of the body). Consequently, it also puts in question one kind of consciousness (consciousness as divine), which has become dysfunctional, and in its place institutes another form of consciousness (consciousness as sensuality and pleasure).

Derrida rewrites difference itself—spelling it with an *a*, *differance*, to designate the postmodern inscription of a *difference within* difference itself. *Differance*, according to Derrida, marks the way difference is divided by "two apparently different values . . . tied together . . . to differ as discernibility, distinction, separation, diastem, *spacing*; and to defer as detour, relay, reserve, *temporization*" (*Margins* 18). *Differance* is thus both differing and deferring, both spatial and temporal. Moreover, *differance*, for Derrida, "is not a concept . . . not simply a word"; rather, it is "the playing movement that 'produces' . . . differences"—differences that themselves, accord-

ing to Derrida, "*play:* in language, in speech too" (*Margins* 11). *Differance*—
like *writing, pharmakon, supplement, hymen*—reflexively turns back on itself
and denies that it is itself, that it has an identity. Derrida's notion of *differance* is typographically a novel invention, but epistemologically it is
founded upon Heidegger's notion of *dif-ference*" (202). Heidegger uses the
concept in order to show that what he calls the "intimacy" of "the world
and thing is not a fusion"—a unity or a moment of solidified identity.
Rather, "Intimacy obtains only where the intimate—world and thing—
divides itself cleanly and remains separated. In the midst of the two, in the
between of world and thing, in their *inter,* division prevails: a *dif-ference*
(202). Heidegger, like Derrida, is careful to warn his readers that in such a
locution, difference no longer has its commonsensical meaning: "The word
difference is now removed from its usual and customary usage. What it
now names is not a generic concept for various kinds of differences. It
exists only as this single difference. It is unique" (202). In its new rearticulation by Heidegger, difference no longer refers to "a distinction established between objects" (202), which is another way of saying, "[D]iffer-
ence is not abstracted from world and thing as their relationship after the
fact" (202). Difference is thus constitutive of their very being: "In the bidding that calls thing and world, what is really called is: the def-ference"
(203). The means by which this bidding takes place is language: "Language
speaks. Its speaking bids the dif-ference to come which expropriates world
and things into the simple onefold of their intimacy" (210). Like Heidegger,
therefore, Derrida uses *differance* as a source that is not originary; *differance*
is what enables the playfulness of the sign—its endless and nonstoppable
substitutions.

Among the core concerns of ludic postmodernism and feminism, then,
are the various ways of insisting on the *play*—the unfounded slippage and
dissemination—of difference (hence my use of the term ludic) informing
not only deconstructionist theories of language and textuality but also
Lyotardian notions of justice and gaming; Baudrillardian discourses on the
political economy of the sign; Barthesian ideas of the writerly text; Foucauldian theories of noncausal, reversible power; Laclau and Mouffe's
post-Marxist notion of hegemony and post-Derridean interpretations of
the late Lacan; as well as the feminist extensions of these discourses,
notably in the works of Cornell, Butler, Haraway, Grosz, de Lauretis, *l'écriture feminine,* and queer theory.

Deconstructionists, and ludic postmodernists in general, contend that
this difference-within, *differance,* undermines the entire logic of identity

grounding Western thought. The nonrepresentational nature of signification makes it impossible to present an identity or entity as selfsame, as having an essence or presence that is the same as itself. The *same*, Derrida
argues,

> is not the identical. The same, precisely, is *differance* (with an *a*) as the
> displaced and equivocal passage of one different thing to another,
> from one term of an opposition to the other. Thus one could recon-
> sider all the pairs of opposites on which philosophy is constructed and
> on which our discourse lives, not in order to see opposition erase itself
> but to see what indicates that each of the terms must appear as the *dif-
> ferance* of the other, as the other different and deferred in the economy
> of the same. (*Margins* 17)

Any identity in Western thought is situated in relation to an other. But for
Derrida, all "othering," that is, all opposition, takes place in the "economy
of the same." Each term of a binary pair is not *opposed* to the other, but
rather is part of the *same* weave or chain of differences as the other. It is the
supplement of the other, which is another way of saying the it is the *differance* of the other.

What does this mean for how we understand the dominant concepts
and knowledges used to make sense of—that is, to construct—reality in the
West? On the one hand, they are all organized in terms of binary oppositions between two seemingly different, self-contained identities, such as
man/woman, activity/passivity, sun/moon, culture/nature, head/heart,
logos/pathos, to borrow a list from Hélène Cixous (63, 64). Yet, on the other
hand, they are all part of the economy of the same, and thus the play of *differance*. The organization of binary oppositions is both hierarchical and
patriarchal ("phallogocentric"). The first term of any binary pair is privileged and given priority over the second term, and this primary term, as
Derrida, Cixous, and others have demonstrated, is always associated with
the privileged position of the male, of the phallus, in Western society. The
certainty or truth of Western thought is thus determined by this hierarchy
in which the primary (male) term is not only privileged over its other
(female) term but is designated the defining term or norm of cultural meaning. However, the seeming priority and identity of the primary term is a
fraud. Poststructuralist and ludic feminists attempt to dehierarchize and
dismantle these dichotomies textually by exposing the difference within
signification, while historical materialists, as I will argue below, explain the

"fraudulence" of these binaries as the ideological effects of the struggles over the social divisions of labor. For Derrida, the difference of the primary term in any binary opposition is not outside but "within" the term itself: any identity is always *divided within* by its other, which is not opposed to it but is instead supplementary. However, the logic of identity banishes this difference within the privileged term by projecting its otherness onto a secondary term seen as outside, thus representing the difference-within as an external dichotomy. In so doing, the phallogocentric logic is able to assert its primary (male) terms as seemingly coherent "identities without differences," as self-evident presences, and to exclude and suppress the "dangerous supplement"—the (female) others on which these illusory identities depend.

In other words, it is only by excising the other (the female) inscribed within the male that the male acquires its primary status in the binary opposition male/female dominating patriarchal social relations and gains its presence and selfsameness, while the female is constructed as other, as lacking and as subjected or secondary to the primary male term. In short, "woman" is constructed in what Luce Irigaray calls the "specularizations" of Western patriarchal discourse (*Speculum*), in which woman is the mirror image, the negative reflection, of man. Male is thus not a clearly bounded identity *different from* female but is instead self-divided and traversed by its other, that is, by the female, which is its supplement, its difference on which it depends for its coherent meaning and full existence. Deconstruction is thus a critical operation that demonstrates how the binary other is always the suppressed supplement, the difference inscribed within a term, and concludes that there can be no decidable term, no self-present identity that can assert meaning with any clarity and certainty in culture. This undecidability—the inscription of difference into identity and the removal of its self-sameness—is the mark of ludic postmodern difference. Thus the position of Derrida and most poststructuralists, including many feminists, "is not against sexual difference. It's against the transformation, the identification of sexual difference with sexual binary opposition" (Derrida and Bennington 71). Such sentiments lead ludic feminists to advocate as the goal of change the removal of all restrictions, all limits on the *play* and *pleasures* of sexual differences. Drucilla Cornell's *Beyond Accommodation* is exemplary of this move: following Derrida, she calls for "a new choreography of sexual difference" that goes *beyond* the "divide of the sexes . . . seen as a scar . . . a limit on the proliferation of sexual voices, each with its own unique notes" (98). Such moves may seem liberating at first until we notice

that this "new choreography of sexual difference" and desire posits difference and a going beyond quite ahistorically. There is no accounting here of
how difference was materially instituted to begin with and how it forms
the historical matrix of our lives. It simply finds difference limiting, and
through the device of a new choreography moves beyond it. This is a political move to supplant the social differences of labor and suppress any
attention to the struggle to emancipate women from exploitative relations
of production. I return to this issue in my discussion of ludic politics later,
but first we need to examine how ludic postmodernism writes the sexual
difference of woman.

For Alice Jardine the inscription of (ludic) postmodern difference is a
process she calls "gynesis—the putting into discourse of 'woman'" as that
space of the other, of the excluded (25). However, the woman inscribed by
poststructuralism, according to Jardine, is "neither a person nor a thing,
but a horizon . . . a reading effect, a woman-in-effect that is never stable and
has no identity" (25). She is the unrepresentable excess, the trope, for all
that is excluded, unknowable, and other in phallogocentric discourse. Or as
Shoshana Felman puts it, she is "*the realistic invisible,* that which realism as
such is inherently unable to see" (6). Thus to disrupt mimesis, to dismantle
the representations that exclude her and to dehierarchize the binaries that
subject her, is seen as a subversive act. In this sense, all poststructuralist
writing, whether by men or women, engages in displacing phallogocentric
discourse. *L'ecriture feminine* participates in this deconstructive inscription
of difference, of woman into phallic discourse, and at the same time
rewrites the process. Irigaray, in fact, formulates a mode of deconstruction
she calls "mimicry" or "mimeticism": the act of mimicking or miming
women's assigned position in phallic discourse as the specular representative, the mirror image or mimic of the male (*This Sex* 76). As Toril Moi
describes Irigaray's practice, "Hers is a theatrical staging of the mime:
miming the miming imposed on woman, Irigaray's subtle specular move
(her mimicry *mirrors* that of all women) intends to *undo* the effects of phallocentric discourse simply by *overdoing* them" (*Sexual/Textual* 140). Drucilla
Cornell celebrates Irigaray's notion of mimesis as "a feminine 'capacity'
. . . to evoke the disruptive excess," but she uses it to argue for her conservative point that "we cannot simply declare ourselves freed from prison,"
for we are confined to "move within the gender hierarchy." The answer for
Cornell, the limited freedom she acknowledges is only the freedom to give
metaphors "new meanings" (*Beyond Accommodation* 148).

Irigaray's mimeticism—as well as the more general ludic focus on the parodic, pun-ful, playfulness of difference/*differance*—has had considerable impact on ludic feminists. Through such related strategies as Butler's resignification, Cornell's remetaphorization, Haraway's recoding, and Jardine's gynesis (which is "a new kind of writing on the woman's body" [52]), ludic feminists deconstruct and dehierarchize the dominant discourses through textualizing strategies that disturb representation. They demystify its naturalness, exposing its constructedness and showing its clarity and decidability to be a fraud based on exclusion of the other—variously named Woman, feminine, women of color, or, as Judith Butler argues, "the lesbian phallus." This deconstructive logic has become commonplace in a diverse range of postmodern discourses and feminism. Again Haraway is exemplary here, for her cyborgian socialist feminism—which is not identified as particularly textualist—follows a similar logic that foregrounds irony and "releasing the play of writing" in an effort to "build an ironic political myth" (*Simians* 175, 149).

There is, however, a difference among ludic feminists over how to disrupt the dominant representations. For many, an effective postmodern feminism is a radical negation. As Kristeva argues, if "A woman cannot be," that is, if she is always already the negative representation, the other, then "*It follows that a feminist practice can only be negative,* at odds with what already exists so that we may say 'that's not it' and 'that's still not it'" and "rejecting 'everything finite, definite, structured, loaded with meaning, in the existing state of society'" ("Oscillation" 166). I would like to emphasize that "negative" as it is used here does not carry its commonsensical meaning. It is essentially a Hegelian concept meaning negation and surpassing: "[I]n the negation the transition is made through which the progress through the complete series of forms comes about of itself" (Hegel 51). It is in this sense, for example, that Adorno engages the project of negative dialectic. Negation is a strategy of resistance against the certainty of the existing order.

Some other feminists insist on an affirmative deconstruction. This is especially the case with *l'ecriture feminine* and the way it is articulated by such American critics as Cornell, who seeks a "feminist alliance with deconstruction." For Cornell "the insistence, in what has come to be labeled the New French Feminism, on the affirmative writing positioned as feminine" enables "the affirmation of feminine difference, irreducible to being their Other, [and] is understood as 'truly new under the sun,' a future not identifiable as the evolution of the same" (*Beyond Accommodation* 12–13). In other words, Cornell's affirmative deconstruction (which I will engage more fully later) and *l'ecriture feminine* posit a sexual difference in excess—that is, beyond—the boundaries of othering and the logic of the same. However, in seeking to produce a feminine writing (whether out of the female body or out of a new troping of the feminine) that is not just a negative practice but a positive one, such affirmative ludic feminism risks reessentializing the feminine and constructing a new identity anchored in a reified notion of the body and language. This risk is especially evident in the uses and adaptations of *l'ecriture feminine* made by many of its followers; however, the inaugural theorists, notably Irigaray, have tried to guard against it. Irigaray in fact warns against trying to define woman and thus reproducing the logic of the same, or rather the logic of identity and decidability. Instead she claims women "must, through repetition-interpretation of the way in which the feminine finds itself determined in discourse—as lack, default, or as mime and inverted reproduction of the subject—show that on the feminine side it is possible to *exceed* and *disturb* this logic" (qtd. in Moi 139).[3] Thus woman, as Irigaray writes her, is not an individuated, coherent, selfsame identity, nor is she merely the specular surface on which the male projects his negative reflection. Rather, "'She' is *indefinitely* other in herself" (*This Sex* 28; emphasis added). Cornell considers Irigaray's mimesis—her miming of the feminine through repetition-interpretation—to be "explicitly utopian." Following Irigaray, Cornell attempts to posit a nonessentializing "affirmation of the feminine as performance, as a role that can be restyled, played differently" (*Beyond Accommodation* 19), but as I argue later, it is highly questionable whether Cornell or *l'ecriture feminine* succeed in moving beyond essentialism.[4]

Woman, for Irigaray, "(re)-discover[s] herself" in the multiplicity of her pleasures and desires—that is, in her *jouissance,* which is the surprising excess of her sexuality, of her being, of her desires that patriarchal discourses cannot represent and thus cannot know. She identifies "herself with none of them in particular"; thus she is multiple, plural, "never being simply one" (*This Sex* 31). Woman is thus self-divided, different from herself. This difference-within, dividing woman, derives, of course, from the feminist rewriting of Lacan's rewriting of Freud, who first exploded the unity of the humanist (modernist) self, showing it to be split by the divide between the conscious and the unconscious—a split, which Lacan argues (in such texts as "The Agency of the Letter in the Unconscious" and "The Freudian Thing," both in *Ecrits*) traverses us as we enter language or the symbolic order and distances us from the imaginary. By writing herself, woman, in *l'ecriture feminine*, engages in a double move that both "speaks" her excess—that which patriarchy cannot grasp, can represent only as silence, as absence—and simultaneously disrupts the very binaries and decidability of patriarchal discourse that has trapped her. As Cixous writes,

> A feminine text cannot fail to be more than subversive. It is volcanic; as it is written it brings about an upheaval of the old property crust, carrier of masculine investments; there's no other way. There's no room for her if she's not a he. If she's a her-she, it's in order to smash everything, to shatter the framework of institutions, to blow up the law, to break up the "truth" with laughter. (258)

The feminine text is, above all, woman herself; for woman in poststructuralism and most ludic postmodernism is a trope, a rhetorical or discursive effect; she is the product of textuality as the regime of difference (within), deferment, and differing.

How can this textuality, this writing of woman back into patriarchal discourse—whether through gynesis or *l'écriture feminine*—be subversive; how can it "blow up the law" and "break up the 'truth,'" as Cixous claims?

For ludic feminists, the textualization of social institutions is subversive, and subversion is change, because it empties the patriarchal representations of the phallogocentric discourse of their meaning—it rejects, as Kristeva says, "everything finite, definite, structured, loaded with meaning, in the existing state of society." The law or truth of patriarchal society is the law of the phallus, which is the logic of identity, the logic of the same, of the singular, inviolable One that suppresses its other. It is this patriarchal regime of decidable representations that produces the male as the privileged, empowered term and subjugates woman as the excluded other. Thus, according to Barbara Johnson, "Nothing could be more comforting to the established order than the requirement that everything be assigned a clear meaning or stand" (*World* 30–31). As a result, disrupting the clarity and certainty of meaning, dehierarchizing binary oppositions, inscribing the *difference-within*, celebrating undecidability, and speaking woman's unrepresentable excess (her *jouissance*) through such textual strategies as deconstruction, mimicry, parody, pastiche, free association, and so on, are all subversive acts for ludic feminists. These strategies denaturalize and expose the illusion of identity and certainty on which the regime of patriarchal representation rests and depose the male/phallus from its privileged seat as the primary term, as the One and the Same. Such deconstructive interventions in the dominant patriarchal cultural policy have become fundamental to ludic postmodern feminism, and much of the recent work in postmodern feminism is devoted to theoretical elaborations of these ludic strategies: most notably Judith Butler's theory of performativity (as articulated in *Gender Trouble*), which she rewrites as citationality and resignification in *Bodies That Matter,* and Drucilla Cornell's remetaphorization of the feminine.

The feminist deployment of deconstructive strategies and turn toward difference-within has in many ways been quite effective—*on the level of the superstructure*—in demystifying and denaturalizing much of the common sense of patriarchal ideology. But is it enough? And if such modes of writing are subversive, is subversiveness itself an effective intervention in the order of patriarchal capitalism? Subversiveness is, at the most, a rearrangement of the existing order within its ruling frame: it is a radical form of reform. The question for contemporary feminism is whether reform—through the channels that NOW (National Organization for Women) proposes or the subversions that Cixous puts forth—is an adequate means of transforming the dominant social arrangements that deploy sexual difference to justify social inequality. My argument is that subversion is the device of the feminism of the upper middle classes. Only a revolutionary praxis can bring about the kind of social organization of life in which gender and sexuality are not means of unequal distribution of wealth and power.

Even Irigaray admits that "A woman's development"—by which she means her inscription of the multiple, plural female imaginary suppressed by patriarchal discourse—"however radical it may seek to be would thus not suffice to liberate woman's desire," because traditionally "woman is never anything but the locus of a more or less competitive exchange between two men" (*This Sex* 31–32). In other words, she is produced in social and economic relations, in social struggle. But again, it is not sufficient to say that woman is part of a "competitive exchange between two men," for her place in such exchange itself results from the class, gender, and race divisions of property relations and appropriation of surplus labor, because (to continue with Irigaray's language) the two men are two historical men. They are embedded in the inevitable struggle between labor and capital and are part of the struggle over surplus labor and profit. In short, they are not just two *essences* of masculinity but are situated in "masculinity" in the history of the social relations of production.

An effective feminist theory, then, is one that is not simply concerned

Beyond ↓

to "liberate woman's desire" because desire is historical and, like all historical practices, part of the social struggle over the distribution of resources.
An effective feminist theory works, first and foremost, to transform property and labor relations in order to emancipate women and all oppressed
peoples from exploitation and to fulfill their *needs.* The ludic displacement
of difference-between and the corresponding rhetoricization and troping
of capitalism—reducing it to a superstructural arena of commodification,
consumption, and significations—has been especially detrimental to revolutionary feminism. The only effective way to address the fundamental fissure between equality and difference in capitalism and its superstructural
forms is to be able to explain and transform the historically produced divisions between the exploiters and exploited.

property of feminist theory

The concept of difference-between has had a contradictory history:
while it has been necessary for revolutionary struggle in order to foreground class antagonisms, it has also been dehistoricized and deployed in
an abstract mode in the ideological apparatuses of patriarchal capitalism to
legitimate socially produced differences as natural segregations. To resist
this ideological appropriation and naturalization of a historically produced
difference-between, on the one hand, and also to reclaim the historical and
radical aspects of the materiality of difference-within (not simply a difference-within that is the effect of textualization and hermeneutical moves),
on the other hand, I propose retheorizing historical difference as *difference
within a material system of exploitation:* that is, a historical materialist theory
of difference in postmodernity.

Differences in class societies are always exploitative. Thus the goal of
a transformative feminism in the moment of the postmodern should be to
end differences and not, in the mode of ludic theory, to enhance them. The
enhancing of difference—as proposed, for example, in identity politics,
which draws heavily on ludic theory—is, on the surface, a progressive
move: it recognizes differences (sexuality, color, nationality) and affirms
them rather than absorb them into an abstract universalism. But the other
of difference, contrary to what ludic theory argues, is not universalism but
collectivity—collectivity in the historically determined social relations of
production. To simply affirm difference without showing how exclusions
and oppressions based on difference have been the outcome of the social
relations of production obscures the fact that although oppression is felt as
an experience of difference from an abstract universalism (lesbian and gay
bashing, racism, the denial of medical services to illegal "aliens"), it is produced in a historically constituted system of production. At various

moments of its development, the social relations of production give meanings to such attributes as gender, nationality, sexuality in such a fashion
that the social meanings of these differences justify the system's use of
them in its labor force to maintain an acceptable rate of profit. Difference,
in the end, is always an alibi for increasing profits in class societies. In the
United States, the gay man who is discharged from the navy, the woman
who is denied combat duty in the army and thus cannot get the promotion
and economic rewards reserved for combat officers, the African-American
who is not given a managerial position in the baseball league, and the
immigrant who is confined to manual labor in the fields are all marked by
a difference that justifies their exclusions and exploitation. To simply fight
for abolishing discrimination against women, African-Americans, and people of other nationalities localizes global issues: it reduces problems of
exploitation to domination. It does not transform social arrangements; it
simply reforms local practices and, in so doing, allows the system constantly to shift the site of its exploitation to yet another difference. The
argument for enhancing differences does not end exploitation; at best it
changes its direction. The goal of transformative feminism should be to put
an end to exploitation and thus end difference: emancipating people from
difference will not come about before people are emancipated as producers. In short, although oppression is felt as an experience of difference, it is
not explainable by difference itself. Difference is explainable only by the
system of production that deploys that difference. The aim of transformative feminism, then, is not a society that is, in Laclau's mode, a radical
democracy of infinite differences (of incommensurate local experiences)
but a socialist society of united humanity.

Only in such a socialist society—a society in which the needs of all
people are met without regard to their differences—does a historically
viable notion of difference become possible: a difference that is achieved
after (and not in place of) common needs. This is the difference that Marx
theorizes in *Critique of the Gotha Programme* and sums up as: from each
according to her ability and to each according to her needs (10). Before difference there is collectivity based on commonality, and that commonality is
based not on experience but on the place of persons in the social relations
of production. Only the commonality of position in the social relations of
production makes possible the emergence of difference as a material and
historical practice—and not, as identity politics advocates, as simply the
commonness or affinity of experience.

Historically, Marxism and Marxist-socialist feminism have developed the only theory and praxis capable of maintaining a sustained commitment to revolutionary struggle to meet the *needs* of women and other oppressed peoples and to challenge the exploitative labor and property relations of capitalism. This is, in large part, because they have not confined the struggle for equality to the superstructure (the political, legal, cultural) but have instead linked it to the material base. Socialism and socialist feminism—in their classic, historical materialist forms—are fundamentally engaged in the struggle to end difference by establishing economic commonality: to end the profit of a few through the exploitation of the many. They are, in short, committed to the struggle for full equality at all levels of society and the elimination of the differences between exploiter and exploited, between owners of the means of production and those who own only their labor. This is ultimately the difference that makes the differences of man/woman, queer/straight, white/black socially significant. Without the difference between labor and capital, the other differences collapse and lose their significance, their difference. The necessary struggle is thus to eliminate the divisions of labor and social resources. Instead of a society organized around the profit of a few, historical materialist feminists struggle for the fundamental restructuring of society to meet the needs of all people: *from each according to her ability, to each according to her needs!*

While ludic postmodern feminism makes a contribution to the critique of dominant "phallogocentric" discourses and signifying practices, these critiques have also made the struggle over difference-between impossible by transferring "between" to "within." Ludic theory has argued that the difference-between is a violent erasure of difference-within. Class struggle between the bourgeoisie and the proletariat, according to such an argument, becomes the effect of the erasure of the struggle within the proletariat. The two classes, in short, are seen not as a relation of opposition but as part of the same economy of signification that projects the slippages and gaps within on to an opposition between. This is the argument that, of course, underlies the Foucauldian notion of power, Butler's idea of performativity, and the eclectic figure of Haraway's cyborg. Difference-between is a necessary concept for transformative feminism. However, it should be marked as a historical difference produced materially and not reduced to a difference originating in nature. While ludic strategies, based on difference-within, destabilize and disrupt dominant representations, they neither exceed nor do they transform the structure of gender-sexual differences. Instead, they occult the exploitative relations of capitalism itself, which are always the effects of a difference *between* historically constituted social classes.

The textual notions of language and discourse that dominate ludic postmodern and feminist thinking—from Derrida and Baudrillard to Foucault and de Man, and from Irigaray and Butler to Haraway—is based on the ideal of meaning as the effect of the internal laws and play of language or discourse as formal systems. Even when meaning is understood in terms of Foucauldian discursive regimes of power-knowledge, it is still posited as the effect of immanent, closed systems of symbolic laws and rules of discourse (*Archeology* 31–39). Butler's articulation of heterosexuality as a "regulatory regime" of discursive rules and norms is another example of this tendency in ludic thinking. No ludic theory—no matter how complex, subtle, and detailed its articulation of a specific discursive series—moves beyond the limits of the superstructural forms to engage the relation of meanings to the relations of production and labor. If they do engage the economic, as Baudrillard and Lyotard do from time to time, it is only after rhetoricizing and eroticizing it in a manner not unsimilar to Bataille's reading of materialism, expenditure, and use value, that is to say, turning it into a semiosis and/of desire. In the name of exceeding boundaries, ludic critics entirely restrict knowledge to the limits of the superstructure—entirely suppressing the base, rendering it unrepresentable and unknowable (see, e.g., Miller 309–27). The Kristevian strategy of emptying the world of meaning is little more than a cognitive act, confined to the problem of the consciousness of cultural forms. I am not interested in questioning the poststructuralist arguments that reality and individuals are always already mediated by language and made intelligible only through the operation of difference. What I am contesting is that, even if this is the case, the fact that reality is mediated through language does not in any rigorous sense mean that reality is, therefore, made of language. Furthermore, language, as Marx and Engels suggested, is "practical consciousness" (*German Ideology* 44)—it is produced through collective practices and is not reducible to the set of formal, textual, and semiotic rules and laws put forth by ludic theorists.

I am proposing instead a materialist understanding of the *dialectical* relation of language, discourse, and significations to the base: to the relations of production, private property, and divisions of labor and to the social struggles over these exploitative relations. Resistance postmodern feminism retheorizes postmodern difference—that is difference-within,

namely *differance*—as a *material differance*. I have already indicated how difference-between is always a historical difference constructed at the point of
production, but we also need to recognize how what ludic theory uses to
suppress difference-between—and posits as an autonomous difference-within that is supposed to exceed difference-between—is merely a
logocentric fiction that is itself historically produced. Difference-within is
not simply a difference of the same from itself because of an excess of signs,
and therefore it is not simply an epistemological question. The incoherence
within—what produces rifts and gaps in any given entity and creates the
instability that is taken by ludic theory as a mark of the unrepresentability
of the excessiveness of signs—is not, in other words, a question of immanent laws of signification but an articulation of the social contradictions of
class society. Difference-within is not a negation of difference-between but
is, in fact, a localized side of it. If the "masculine" is self-divided, its
self-division is not caused by the excessiveness of the codes of masculinity
that consequently spill over and inscribe the masculine into the feminine
and finally deconstruct the masculine. Rather the incoherence of the masculine is part of the incoherence of the social relations of production
founded upon profit. The social relations of exchange and profit (not the
semiotic codes of the masculine) produce a binary masculine/feminine
that is necessary for the ideological superstructure to justify not only the
divisions of labor but also the regime of the commodity. The regime of
wage labor needs a nuclear family based on the binary of masculine and
feminine, and the instabilities of these gender categories come not from
their representations but from a material base that is itself oscillating. It is
oscillating because it is the site of class struggle over the production and
distribution of social wealth.

Ideology of the Sign

Materialist feminism needs the notion of difference-between to argue for
class differences between antagonistic classes, and it also needs a retheorized concept of difference-within to show how gender subjectivities are
themselves produced by the very struggles and antagonisms that, in fact,
shape the social relations of production. Difference-within is not textual;
rather, it is the articulation of actual differences in class societies: its trajectory shows how class, the social relations of production and struggles over
them, in fact, produce all diverse levels of our lives.

    To be more precise, meaning (for example, "masculinity") in historical materialism is not a formalist question: it is neither a matter of *identity* (of correspondence or reference between the word and the world), as modernists contend, nor is it a matter of a *difference* of tropic slippage, of *differance* (that is, a lack of correspondence and nonrepresentation between word and world). Instead, meaning is a matter of *social struggle* over the relation between labor and capital as articulated through the determination of the relation between signifier and signified: in other words, the sign itself is an arena in which social conflicts fight it out.

> Existence reflected in the sign is not merely reflected but *refracted*. How is this refraction of existence in the ideological sign determined? By an intersecting of differently oriented social interests within one and the same sign community, i.e., *by the class struggle*.
>
> Class does not coincide with the sign community, i.e., with the community which is the totality of users of the same set of signs for ideological communication. Thus various different classes will use one and the same language. As a result, differently oriented accents intersect in every ideological sign. Sign becomes an arena of the class struggle. (Voloshinov 23)

The sign, as the arena of the class struggle, is thus the site for all the social conflicts over the exploitative divisions of labor, social resources, and private property—especially those of gender, race, and sexuality.

But what specifically does it mean to say the sign is the arena of social struggle? First, we need to retheorize the sign not as the correspondence between a single signifier and signified (as in formalist modernist linguistics), nor as a free-floating chain of signifiers (as in equally formalist poststructuralist theories). Instead, we can reconceive the sign as situated in an ideological process in which the signifier is related to a matrix of historically possible signifieds. The signifier becomes temporarily connected to a specific signified—that is, it attains its degree of determination as meaning—through social struggle in which the prevailing ideology and social contradictions insist on a particular signified (or set of signifieds). Such a relation is insecure, continually contested and changeable. Signifieds are challenged, struggled over, and displaced by opposing ideologies asserting other signifieds in relation to a particular signifier in order to support their own meanings and practices and to propose their own reality. The signified that acquires a necessary relation to a signifier is the one that, at that historical moment, most clearly articulates the level of class struggle. The relation between signifier and signified is, therefore, continually struggled over. The assertion of an oppositional meaning or signified can be readily displaced and appropriated by the dominant ideology, articulating the intensity or relaxation of class struggle. The history of the instability in the meaning of the family of signifiers—*Negro, Afro-American, Black, African-American*—is an example of the determination of the relation between the signifier and the signified (not by its internal semiosis) but by the forces of an outside: the outside of the social relations of production.

While a materialist theory of the sign has been largely absent from feminism, it has had much more of an impact in postmodern cultural studies, especially through the earlier work of Stuart Hall (see, e.g., "Rediscovery"). However, Hall's articulation of the social struggle over the sign, even in his early, materialist phase of writing, erases the signified and instead adapts Voloshinov's notion of the multiaccentuality (or accenting) of the sign and sutures it to the ludic theories of Roland Barthes, to the notion of an open connotative field, that is, in terms of a plurality or multiplicity. However, I think it is necessary to insist here on the concept of the signified as a historical, ideological relation—and not erase it—in order to clearly mark the way ideology attempts to secure and fix the meaning of signifiers by anchoring them to reified signifieds, which it then seeks to naturalize and represent as inevitable, even transcendental. The connotative field of a signifier then can be understood as consisting of historically determined matrices of possible signifieds, which are privileged, and frequently hierarchized, by the systematic relations of exploitation and social struggle.

Second, some of the most recent articulations of the social struggle over signs, especially postmodern cultural studies, are dematerializing the sign. As I have been arguing throughout this work, the notion of materiality itself, under the pressure of ludic textualization and post-Marxism in cultural studies, becomes more local and asystematic, more rhetorical and discursive (reducing it to the opacity, sensuousness, and indeterminacy of signifiers or the irreducibility of the body). Such moves marginalize, if not completely displace, the understanding of materiality as the historical forces of the relations of production—and it is these relations that are articulated and fought through signifying practices and relations of difference.

This displacement is especially clear in some of the essays in the *Cultural Studies* collection (Grossberg, Nelson, and Treichler), notably Kobena Mercer's text, in which he rearticulates the social struggle over signifiers—particularly signifiers of race—in terms of indeterminacy and a "radical polyvocality"; this leads to a rewriting of race as a "floating signifier," as

Angela McRobbie does when she comments approvingly on Mercer's (ludic) understanding of the social situation of the sign and uses it to read what she specifically identifies as the floating signifiers of race and sex in popular culture (727). Such reunderstandings of the sign omit the way signifiers are situated in and appropriated by the relation of labor and capital and thus are neither historically indeterminate nor simply free elements of possibility for resistance.[5]

Ludic theory's reading of the sign and the relations of signifiers and signifieds is performed through immanent critique. Such a critique, as is clear from my discussion of the materiality of signification, is not able to show how the sign means not only because of its internal laws but more importantly because of the political economy of signification, which is always determined by the outside of labor relations. An understanding of the political economy of signification, I believe, is more effectively developed by a critique of ideology than by an immanent critique.

Critique of ideology inquires into the social and historical struggles over meaning. It interrogates the operation of difference in relation to its outside, to the social contradictions of specific regimes of exploitation, paying special attention to the contesting ways diverse superstructural articulations of difference are related to the divisions of labor and property. It investigates how codes, tropes, and signifying practices are *used* to help achieve and maintain the social, cultural, political, and juridical forms—in short, the superstructure—required by the existing relations of production. It examines how they operate to secure ideologically necessary subject positions and how these subject positions are represented as natural. Ideology critique is itself a dialectical method aimed at articulating the dialectical relation between superstructure and base: it both examines the immanent operation of signifying practices within the superstructure and relates these to the operation of the mode of production. The dialectical nature of ideology critique means that it can effectively deploy immanent critique as *part* of its overall dialectical critique of the relation of base and superstructure. The difference, in short, between a materialist ideology critique and a formalist, immanent ludic critique is that ludic discourse analyses and deconstructive strategies, as I have already indicated, are limited to the immanent description of the superstructure, whereas materialist ideology critique moves beyond the bounds of the superstructure to articulate its relation to the relations of production. While an immanent critique of the sign offers an inspection of *how* the sign moves in its own terms and provides the reader with the pleasures of witnessing the opacity and complexities of meanings, ideology critique addresses the question of *why* signs mean what they are thought to mean. The purpose of ideology critique is not to provide pleasure but to develop class consciousness.

One of the points of fundamental break between ludic socialist feminism and historical materialist feminism has been over the issue of ideology. For historical materialists, the critique of ideology is a crucial aspect of a socially transformative politics: it is the means for developing class consciousness. The ludic turn toward a cultural or discursive materialism in feminism has entailed discrediting theories of ideology and the marginalization of critique. For most feminists, "[T]he word 'ideology,'" as Kaja Silverman notes "may seem to exude the stale aroma of a theoretical anachronism," but as Silverman goes on to argue, "[F]ar from having exhausted itself, the great ideology debate of the 1960s and 1970s was broken off prematurely, before a series of crucial issues could be addressed." However, rather than effectively contest this premature and unwarranted closure of theories of ideology, most of those socialist and materialist feminists who had significantly addressed the critique of ideology in the past, such as Michèle Barrett, have largely abandoned it in the present and joined the ranks of poststructuralist feminists and post-Marxists, who have dissolved the critique of ideology into a more general Derridean textual deconstruction or Foucauldian discourse analysis. This move is clearly marked by Barrett in the preface to her most recent book, *The Politics of Truth*, whose "main preoccupation," she declares, "is the concept of 'ideology'" (vi), and which she opens by affirming, "I had previously argued that one could not explain the oppression of women without taking very seriously indeed the role of ideology and culture in the creation, as well as reproduction, of that inequality" (vi). However, she immediately goes on to express considerable skepticism about the force of the concept of ideology, and to admit that in this book, "I conclude on a fairly lukewarm note as to the value of the concept of ideology itself for contemporary social analysis" (vi). In fact, as she clearly indicates, the title of the book itself marks her siding with the ludic postmodern shift away from Marxism and displacement of the critique of ideology: "In using Foucault's preferred term" (the politics of truth) "rather than entitling the book 'The Economics of Untruth'" (which she identifies with "Marx's account of ideology"), she indicates she is signaling her move "to a more general post-Marxism" (vii).

Under pressure of ludic postmodern discourses—from poststructuralism and the Foucauldian theory of (aleatory) power to the logic of New Times—the specific link of ideology to class interests and the economic in

Marxism is seen as invalidating the concept of ideology. "The distinctly Marxist definition of ideology (ideology = mystification serving class interests) is untenable" (167), Barrett argues, largely because it is not "applicable to understanding the cultural, ideational and subjective experiences of people in terms other than—if additional to—those of social class" (158), especially gender and race.[6] This ludic dismissal is underwritten by Foucault, who states that "the notion of ideology appears to me to be difficult to make use of" because it "stands in a secondary position relative to something which functions as its infrastructure, as its material, economic determinant" (*Power/Knowledge* 118).[7] The value of theories of ideology, however, lies precisely in their ability to critically engage the *dialectical* relation between superstructure and base. The efforts to discredit theories of ideology for their economic determinism is simply another version of the overall ludic attempts to suppress the economic base and reify superstructural forms (such as "cultural, ideational and subjective experiences") as autonomous and auto-intelligible. Moreover, the dismissal of the economic in theories of ideology, itself, becomes another alibi for rejecting ideology. As Barrett argues, there is little "force or resonance in the concept [of ideology] once its explanatory associations with class and its economic determinism have been stripped away" (vi). This leads her to conclude, following the lead of post-Marxism, that "in so far as one breaks with the 'class-belongingness' of ideology one is logically led to break with Marxism in general" (15). She then turns to a more Foucauldian, poststructuralist, and discursive notion of power and the social.

This whole move to break with class and the economic and thus with Marxism has become the new dogma of (ludic) postmodern discourses and of much recent feminist theory. The issue, as I have been arguing throughout, is not that class and the economic are reductive, since much of feminism and (ludic) postmodern discourses, including post-Marxism, have indeed embraced a reductive fetishization of the superstructural that erases any dialectical understanding of its connection to the relations of production. The real issue is that the charge of reductionism is used to get rid of the materiality of social antagonism. This has lead to a simplistic notion of class as a fixed social entity or identity separate from the divisions of gender and race. Ludic critics have isolated culture, ideology, and subjectivity from their groundedness in labor in the name of difference, plurality, and diversity. In so doing, they have obscured the way differences are historical effects of the division of labor: the way differences are always situated and the consequences of the systematic relations of exploitation, which are fundamentally economic.

We see this economic imperative of ideology especially clearly in India, which, as one of the primary sites of patriarchal capitalist development under imperialism, is an important exemplar of the brutal contradictions of global capitalism and the international division of labor, particularly around gender and race. In India, for instance, young girls, daughters, are sold into marriage, into indentured slavery, by their fathers (as in the recent case in Hyderabad concerning the thirteen-year-old girl sold to a Saudi Arabian as part of a common international trade in young girls) for economic reasons. It is important to note that this practice, as I suggested in my reading of Marx and Engels on patriarchy in the previous chapter, is not so much a residue of feudalism as it is a revitalized mode of capitalization and superexploitation of women in late capitalism. The selling, indenturing, and trade in women globally, but especially in newly capitalist regions (such as China, the Thai-Burmese border, Eastern Europe, Russia, and to a large degree, India) is the direct effect of unconstrained profit-making activities, not only around the growing commodification of sex, but more important, in terms of the radical reorganization (and breakdown) of previously socialist societies bringing back the exploitation of surplus labor. It is primarily girls who are being sold because of the systematic inequities of the gender division of labor and property relations upon which the cultural and social differences are constituted. In other words, the ideological differentiations of the subjectivities, meanings, practices, and institutions of everyday life around gender support and reproduce the very economic divisions that ultimately determine the ideological differences.

The ludic erasure of the relations of production and processes of labor blinds most theorists to these realities and suppresses the connections between the everyday privileges of most theorists, academics, and professional women, and this international division of labor. It forces us to ask: to what degree our theories (in spite of our good intentions) participate in the ideological mystification, justification, and legitimation of the international division of labor and obscure much of the exploitation of women and people of color globally and at home. As I have already indicated, the very concepts needed to explain and understand this process—base, superstructure, as well as class, labor, exploitation, ideology, totality, and system—have all been discredited and eliminated from the advanced theories in feminism and (ludic) postmodern social analytics in the West. The more effective the theory in displacing these concepts and concealing knowledge of the relations of production, the more institutional privilege, prestige, and profitability the theories and their practitioners garner within the academy and the culture industry. We need only remind ourselves of the star salaries, endowed chairs, and status accorded to the most prominent ludic theorists in feminism and in the humanities and cultural studies more generally. Feminists cannot afford to ignore the damaging effects to others of the blind spots and aporias in our most privileged theories. We can not take *pleasure* in the pleasuring play of ludic theories without confronting the cost to others of our pleasures, without critically engaging the connections between the theories most highly rewarded in the culture industry of late capitalism and the ideological work these theories perform in suppressing the very concepts most necessary to challenge patriarchal capitalism.

CHAPTER 4

Post-al Politics: Maverick Feminism and Emancipation

Ludic postmodernism articulates a diverse series of post-al notions that it sees as constitutive of new truths and realities—chief among these is a politics that subverts the very ground of transformative politics and substitutes a discursive or cultural politics in its place. Drawing on such (ludic) postmodern discourses as Derridean deconstruction; Foucauldian analytics of power; and Lyotardian logic of the differend, of incommensurability, ludic feminists—most notably Judith Butler, Drucilla Cornell, Donna Haraway, as well as Diana Fuss and Teresa de Lauretis—are articulating a "new" poststructuralist, post-Marxist politics that is postclass, postfoundationalist, postemancipatory, posthistory, postgender, postdialectical, postteleological, postpatriarchy, postessentialist . . . Moreover, ludic feminists are increasingly reconfiguring politics as ethics, turning it into a postpolitics. In fact, ludic feminists are taking the lead in retheorizing politics in terms of these various post-alizations. While such prominence for women and feminists within the culture industry is a matter of celebration for many, for others the widespread commodification and appropriation of ludic feminist politics requires a more careful scrutiny of its presuppositions and effects. We need to ask both what has become of feminist politics in (ludic) postmodernism and what is an effective politics for feminism in a racist, patriarchal late capitalism?

At the core of this post-alization of politics is the ludic displacement of material reality (the nondiscursive) by the discursive. I have already addressed this issue, in part, in the first chapter, but here I want to engage in a more sustained critique in terms of some of its consequences, particularly the substitution of ethics and semiotic subversions for the project of emancipation. What is at stake here for feminism is not only the question of how to effectively bring about social change but what constitutes social change. These are especially pressing questions when ludic theorists are commonly arguing, as the post-Marxist Ernesto Laclau does, that society itself "is an impossible object" ("Transformations" 40–41). Butler, following Laclau, declares the "unrealizability of 'emancipation'" because its "foundations are exposed as contradictory and untenable" ("Poststructuralism" 8). This discursive politics attempts to discredit historical materialism and confine politics strictly to the arena of the superstructure: reducing it, in effect, to simply a cultural politics concerned with changing cultural representations, signifying practices, and textualities—what Butler calls "resignification" and Cornell terms "remetaphorization." Post-al politics is the means for realizing the ludic priority of *semiotic freedom:* which, as I have discussed earlier, seeks the liberation of desires through the free, unconstrained play of codes, multiple significations, and pluralities of differences. In contrast, transformative politics, the project of resistance postmodernism, involves radical interventions in *both* the prevailing relations of production *and* its superstructural forms. It seeks to end the exploitation and divisions of labor, to abolish private property and restructure social relations to meet the *needs* of all people. It is based on a historical materialist theory and praxis and works dialectically, engaging the interconnections between base and superstructure, between relations of production and signifying practices. Resistance postmodernism does not reject the cultural or discursive as sites of political struggle but rather argues that these need to be understood in their specific historical connections to the relations of production and the class struggle in order to open up a space for an emancipatory politics.

The Diffusion of Power

The crux of all ludic postmodern and feminist theories, as I will discuss more fully below, is the rewriting of the social as largely discursive (thus marked by the traits of linguistic difference), local, contingent, asystematic, and indeterminate. In many cases, this move is accompanied by a rearticulation of power as diffuse, acausal, and aleatory—most notably by Michel Foucault and a number of feminists, especially Judith Butler. Such social systems (totalities) become, for ludic postmodernists, merely discredited metanarratives rather than social realities to be contested. According to this ludic logic (which is itself a meta-narrative that forgets its own meta-narrativity), not only history but also the social are seen in semiotic terms: as free-floating traces of textuality (Derrida), as "given by the universe of the phrase" (Lyotard), and as a regime or genealogy of discursive practices and power-knowledge relations (Foucault). In all these cases the social is without center or determination: for Derrida this is expressed as the absence of any grounding (transcendental) signified, such as God or experience, resulting from the play of *differance;* for Lyotard it is articulated in terms of the differend, while in Foucault it is accounted for by the acausal, aleatory nature of power. As Derrida puts it in a well-known passage in "Structure, Sign, and Play":

> Henceforth, it was necessary to begin thinking that there was no center, that the center could not be thought in the form of a present-being, that the center had no natural site, that it was not a fixed locus but a function, a sort of nonlocus in which an infinite number of sign-substitutions came into play. This was the moment when language invaded the universal problematic, the moment when, in the absence of a center or origin, everything became discourse—provided we can agree on this word—that is to say, a system in which the central signified, the original or transcendental signified, is never absolutely present outside a system of differences. The absence of the transcendental signified extends the domain and the play of signification infinitely. (*Writing* 280)

The political consequences of this idealist move are made clear by the post-Marxist political theorist Ernesto Laclau, who develops a ludic social theory "identifying the social with an infinite play of differences" ("Transformations" 39). Taking up this passage from Derrida, he argues that "to conceive of social relations as articulations of differences is to conceive them as signifying relations." Thus, not only is the social decentered, according to Laclau, but social relations, like all "signifying systems," are "ultimately arbitrary." As a result " '[S]ociety' . . . is an impossible object" (40–41). By reducing the social to signifying relations, that is, to a discursive or semiotic process, Laclau renders *social* relations "ultimately arbitrary" (like any sign). This means that social relations cannot be subjected to such determining relations as exploitation since they are "arbitrary." If social relations are not exploitative (determined), they no longer require emancipation.

Laclau and other ludic theorists are not just rewriting the "struggle concepts" (society, history, exploitation, emancipation) necessary for social change as a series of tropes or metanarratives. They are also turning the *realities* these concepts explain into indeterminate signifying relations. Ludic theorists, in short, are troping the social. In so doing, they *dematerialize* social realities, cutting them off from the material relations of production and turning them into a superstructural, textual play of *differance*.

Postmodern reality thus becomes a crisis of signification, what Lyotard has called a "crisis of narratives" (*Postmodern Condition* xxiii). All texts and signifying activities—including all social relations—can no longer provide reliable knowledge of the real. This textualized real (e.g., society, history) becomes unreliable, indeterminate, impossible because meaning (signification) itself is seen as self-divided and undecidable: the access of the signifier to the signified is delayed and deferred, divided by a *difference-within* or *differance*. Entities we might naively take to be the same—that is, identical with themselves and marked by their differences from (between) others—are shown instead to be *supplementary* to their others and different within themselves. It may be helpful to recall Derrida's account of *differance:* "The same, precisely, is *differance* (with an *a*) as the displaced and equivocal passage of one different thing to another, from one term of an opposition to the other . . . [E]ach of the terms must appear as the *differance* of the other, as the other different and deferred in the economy of the same" ("Differance" 17). Another way of writing of difference-within is Lyotard's *differend*, which marks the radical point of difference, of incommensurability among events and phrases located within heterogeneous language games. As a result of the play of the *differend*, as I will discuss more fully below, such fundamental principles as truth and justice are not only incommensurable, but indeterminate and undecidable.

Post-al politics is essentially a semiotic subversion emphasizing this traffic of differences, *differance, differends*, dividing and dispersing all social and cultural practices, including politics itself. It substitutes a politics of difference-within for a politics of differences-between. Politics, for ludic postmodernists, can no longer be grounded on clear identities and oppositions, nor can it be situated in a reality outside representation as a referent for action. As a result, any transformative or materialist politics—any emancipatory politics—based on the struggle against hierarchies of differences (such as the class struggle, peasants' or workers' movements, women's liberation movements, anticolonial movements; civil-rights movements) are seen as foundationless.

My deployment of the concepts of ludic and post-al politics to refer to a diverse range of theories, theorists, and political strategies within postmodernism and feminism is, of course, rejected by ludic postmodern feminists and critics who are devoted to the subtle distinctions among themselves. Drucilla Cornell, for one, rejects her own "earlier formulation of the relation between the modern and the postmodern as a constellation" because the terms are "code-words" that "function primarily to obscure subtle, theoretical differences between disputants" (*Philosophy* 11). Similarly, Judith Butler, in her essay "Contingent Foundations" (which, significantly, is the lead text in the anthology she has edited with Joan W. Scott) insists, "I don't know what postmodernism is" (17), because the "differences among . . . positions cannot be rendered symptomatic, exemplary, or representative of each other and of some common structure called postmodernism" (6). It is only possible, she claims, to focus on the "specificities" of each theory; the way "Lyotard's work is, for instance, seriously at odds with that of Derrida" (5). To do otherwise, to take a concept as exemplary of a shared set of assumptions would effect "a violent reduction of the field" (5). The injunction against symptomatic reading, which makes visible the common structure in diverse texts, is part of an attempt to make knowledge of the social totality impossible and render any revolutionary praxis founded upon such a knowledge an act of violence. Of course, this concern over reductionism by Butler and other poststructuralists is quite one-sided: they have no hesitation reducing the differences in the diverse fields of Marxism or Western philosophy to exemplary paradigms, such as phallogocentrism or economism. Moreover, Butler's valorization of the multiple local differences among theorists—such as Derrida and Lyotard—not only revives the notion of uniqueness (which deconstruction had displaced) but, more important, obscures the shared presuppositions among these diverse theorists: not the least of which, as I have already indicated, include their reification of the local, the contingent, the event, indeterminism, and a semiotic (textual, discursive) notion of difference (*différance, differend*).

The issue, however, is not the multiple differences among various theories, discourses, or writers. Rather, the issue is the necessity of moving beyond local, specific details to explain the underlying processes that link disparate concepts and events. It is not a question of avoiding reductionism: any theory that moves beyond simple *description* of details to explanation, analysis, or critique is involved in some form of reduction, that is, some articulation of relations among differences. Ludic theorists evade this problem by reifying description and invention: processes that simply replay the movement of tropes and signifying differences or invent new idioms (Lyotard), metaphors, and subversions of existing discourses (remetaphorization in Cornell or resignification in Butler). In so doing, they displace concepts, analysis, and explanation, leaving us to ask, what is the political and social effect of a theory that supplants explanation with description? More to the point, what are the consequences of a theory that substitutes the unrepresentable, excess, and beyond for historical understanding? Butler and other ludic theorists fail to see that their own reification of the local, the contingent, the excessive is itself reductive and exclusionary. The issue, then, is not whether a theory is reductive: *all theories*, all ways of making sense of the world (deconstruction, common sense, Marxism), involve frames of intelligibility that require specific reductions: specific relations among differences. The question is *how* they understand the relations connecting differences, linking the processes, events, and experiences of daily life—and *what* are the consequences of this understanding?

The ludic is not a rigidly defined category but a social logic articulated in a number of diverse, even conflicting ways by various theorists. My concern is not to write a taxonomy of ludic theories, but to critique-ally examine some shared presuppositions and consequent politics. It may be helpful to mark two basic orientations in the way the social and political are rewritten discursively, if we keep in mind that they share a basic frame of intelligibility. One tendency is somewhat more rhetorical in its concerns and focuses on the textuality of the social; it develops what is, in effect, a textual politics. Perhaps best exemplified by Derridean deconstruction and the Lyotardian theory of language games, it focuses primarily on the traces and incommensurability of significations, especially in linguistic texts and speech acts, from philosophy, literature, and the law to popular culture. It attempts to decipher the play of textual differences (*differance/differend*), that is, to subvert supposedly fixed meanings and grand narratives, what Lyotard refers to as "cultural policy" (*Postmodern Condition* 76). The other orientation attempts to develop a more social and historical *semiotics*, but it understands both the social and history in terms of discursive processes— as demonstrated in the works of Michel Foucault or Ernesto Laclau and Chantal Mouffe. In any particular instance of ludic theory, there is, obviously, considerable mixing of the theoretical discourses and presuppositions from these two related tendencies. For example, Laclau, whose writings are exemplary of ludic theories of the social, draws extensively on Derrida's logic of *differance* in order to rewrite the social as a series of signifying relations or semiotic process. Thus for Laclau, "[N]o social linkage can be constituted except as an overdetermination of differences" ("Transformations" 44). The core of this other side of ludic theory is the radical rethinking of power, especially as articulated by Michel Foucault. It attends primarily to the operations and institutionalizations of meaning in local networks of power and provides the basis for a post-al coalitional politics—as advocated, for example, by Diana Fuss, Donna Haraway, Chela Sandoval, and others.[1] This is not to say, however, that power is not also an issue for those focusing on textual politics. As Eleanor MacDonald has pointed out, "a deep suspicion of power" informs Derrida's theory—and, we can add, most ludic thought—in which there is an "ethical resistance" to power as a mechanism enforcing conformity, sameness, and a denial of differences (229). For deconstructionists and those feminists engaged primarily in textual politics, power tends to be understood largely as a constraint on the possibilities of meanings: it is a matter of interpretation and has very little to do with questions of production. It is, in short, a restriction on the play of *differances*—as in Drucilla Cornell's opposition to the "silencing" and exclusions of the "feminine difference" in the "masculine symbolic" (*Beyond Accommodation*).

Power in Foucault is not understood as primarily textual, although it is irrevocably linked to the operation of discourse and knowledge relations. Rather, power, according to Foucault, "must be understood in the first instance as the multiplicity of force relations immanent in the sphere in which they operate and which constitute their own organization" (*History* 92). Moreover, these force relations of power are self-constituting, immanent, local, and diffuse. Power, in other words, is aleatory (that is, marked by chance), contingent (not historically determined), heterogeneous (divided by difference-within), and unstable: by provoking resistance it undoes itself. Foucault's analysis of the local and contingent, however, is based on a static, ahistorical, and mystified concept of power: "Power is everywhere . . . comes from everywhere . . . is permanent, repetitious, inert." It is always already with us and always will be. Moreover, Foucault turns resistance into a nearly automatic, immanent response to the exercise of power: "where there is power, there is resistance" (95–96). For resistances "are inscribed in the [relations of power] as an irreducible opposite," rather like a natural resistance to a physical force (96). His theory substitutes contingency for social necessity. In so doing, it preempts any need for collective social transformation—any need, in other words, for emancipation. It dispenses with the necessity for organized social and political revolution to overthrow dominant power relations. All we need do, according to this ludic logic, is validate the "multiplicity of points of resistance" that power itself generates.

Perhaps the most appealing aspect of Foucault's theory for left critics and feminists is that it offers "a non-economic analysis of power," as opposed to the "economism in the theory of power" in Marx and in the juridical-liberal notion of power (*Power/Knowledge* 88–89). Foucault conflates these two quite opposed understandings of power by equating a trope with a theoretical explanation, following the ludic assumption that explanations and concepts are tropes. He characterizes juridical-liberal power as a form of economism simply because it relies on the trope of commodity exchange. Whereas in "the Marxist conception of power," he says, "one finds none of all that" (88). What one does find—and what Foucault's entire theory of power is an attempt to displace—is, as Foucault describes it: "an economic functionality of power . . . [P]ower is conceived primarily in terms of the role it plays in the maintenance simultaneously of the relations of production and of a class domination which the development and specific forms of the forces of production have rendered possible" (88–89). In opposition to a Marxist theory of power, which always insists on the *dialectical* relations of power and the economic, Foucault (the former student of the Marxist philosopher Louis Althusser) develops an unrelentingly *anti*–historical materialist theory of power. He severs power from its material connection to the social relations and contradictions of production and reduces it to an abstract force confined to the superstructure. His is an antidialectical theory that substitutes an analytics of localized, reversible domination for a theory of systematic global exploitation. This ludic displacement of historical materialism has made Foucault one of the main articulators of post-Marxism in late capitalism and given him an extraordinary influence among academics, professionals, and other middle- and upper-class knowledge workers, especially in the West.

In fact, the Foucauldian theory of power has become so hegemonic in feminism, so taken for granted as *the way things are*, that only a few materialist feminists, such as Nancy Hartsock and Rosemary Hennessy, have critiqued Foucault—not simply for his failure to address gender, which is a common complaint among feminists—but more important for the limitations of his localizing theory of power. As Hartsock points out, "[S]ystematically unequal relations of power ultimately vanish from Foucault's account of power—a strange and ironic charge to make against someone who is attempting to illuminate power relations" ("Foucault" 165). As she rightly points out, Foucault's "stress on heterogeneity and the specificity of each situation leads him to lose track of social structures and instead to focus on how individuals experience and exercise power" and "has made it very difficult to locate domination," since it denies any understanding of power as the domination of one group or class over another (168–69). Similarly, Hennessey critiques the "shortcomings of [Foucault's] commitment to the contingent and the local," which "makes it difficult to explain the workings of power in terms of antagonistic relations between oppressor and oppressed" (20). In short, Foucault's anti–historical materialism makes it impossible to explain systematic relations of exploitation in patriarchal capitalism. We are left simply with an overriding *localism:* a micropolitics that reduces complex dialectical processes to specific instances of differences and breaks up the systematic operation of power to find a diffuse and unsystematic force.

Both the textual and the more social modes of post-al politics dispense with class struggle and attenuate other social contestations: if there are no oppositions, only the "moving discord of different forces, and of differences of forces," as Derrida puts it ("Differance," 18), then there are no social contradictions and no social conflicts, only the eternal play of differences. Or, as Foucault argues, if power is a multiplicity of forces that produces its own resistance, there are no social contradictions, only local sites of differences. In other words, ludic postmodernism substitutes a nonhierarchal, pluralistic play of semiotic differences and aleatory power for exploitation, for the opposing material interests organizing socioeconomic relations in which differences are used to control access to social resources.

Among the more sophisticated articulators of post-al politics are such ludic feminists as Drucilla Cornell—with her synthesis of a Lyotardian theory of the social as language games, Derridean deconstruction, and *l'écriture feminine*—and Judith Butler, whose work provides a complex development of both deconstructionist textuality and a Foucauldian analytics of power. These two exemplary theorists also demonstrate especially clearly the problems and limitations of post-al politics. Butler's theory of performativity and her displacement of emancipation enacts the inadequacy of both a Foucauldian analytics of power-discourse and a deconstructionist logic, whereas Cornell's ethical feminism is especially illustrative of the limitations of textual politics. I will take up Judith Butler's discursive materialist politics later in this chapter, but first I want to address the problems of textual politics as articulated by Cornell and Lyotard.

The Politics of Invention

Textual politics seeks to problematize signifying practices and established
meanings and to demonstrate that in every entity there is a surplus of
meaning, an excess, a difference-within that prevents that category from
being a reliable ground for knowledge of reality in general and politics in
particular. Using such rhetorical techniques as parody, pastiche, and fragmentation, textual politics (obscures prevailing meanings;) it disrupts the
oppressive totality of the cultural policy through play, gaming, experimentation, and innovation—not only in writing but in signifying activities,
generally—as well as through transgressive readings (immanent critiques),
all of which are intended to subvert the rules of grand narratives and prevent the easy circulation of meaning in culture. As Derrida claims, "[D]iffer-
ance instigates the subversion of every kingdom. Which makes it obviously
threatening and infallibly dreaded by everything within us that desires a
kingdom" ("Differance" 22). Derrida's claim here articulates an important
and influential principle of post-al politics: if difference in-and-of-itself
"instigates the subversion of every kingdom," then there is no need for revolution or social struggle: change is the inevitable outcome of the infallible
subversions generated by *differance*. Moreover, *differance* provokes a series
or chain of subversions that continually subvert themselves; a play of differences that proliferates without foreclosure. For historical materialists,
however, such a textual politics forecloses fundamental socioeconomic
transformation and thus changes little. But most ludic theorists regard the
subversive politics of signification to be a liberating act, deconstructing the
totalities—that is the grand narratives—organizing reality. Obviously,
such textual politics has been the main impetus for ludic feminists like
Luce Irigaray and Hélène Cixous, but it receives one of its fullest elaborations in the work of Drucilla Cornell, who calls for a remetaphorization and
rewriting of the feminine to realize her project of a utopian, deconstruc-
tive-feminist ethics and theory of justice: "a dream of a new choreography
of sexual difference" (*Beyond Accommodation* 2, 18).

To clearly understand the limits of textual politics for feminism, especially as articulated by Cornell, it is useful to first critique-ally examine
some of Lyotard's basic precepts that have so influenced ludic feminists.
The main aim of Lyotard's work—as well as of textual politics as a whole—
can best be characterized by his declaration at the end of *The Postmodern
Condition:* "Let us wage a war on totality; let us be witnesses to the unpresentable; let us activate the differences and save the honor of the name"

(82). Lyotard's position is similar to those Fredric Jameson calls the "most strident of the anti-totality positions": these are based "on the silliest of all puns, the confusion of 'totality' with 'totalitarianism'" ("History" 60). But this has not prevented Lyotard from influencing ludic feminism, not only in its unrelenting localism but in the priority it gives to politics as representation, as naming, of the unpresentable. Lyotard's localism dismisses any attempt to understand the systematic relations connecting disparate events and instead reifies the radical singularity of events. He thus posits culture as a fragmented series of "different language games—a heterogeneity of elements. They only give rise to institutions in patches—local determinism" (*Postmodern Condition* xxiv).

What is at stake in the debate over totality and the local is the issue of where feminism should locate its theories and practices, in short, its politics. It is a debate over the most effective arena for social transformation and the aims of change. Should feminism focus on the totality of systematic social relations that is, on patriarchal capitalism? Should it try to understand the dialectical relations connecting events and diverse levels of social and cultural practices to the relations of production, in order to address the global relations of exploitation? Or should it be concerned with local, specific, contingent, and incommensurable differences, as Lyotard and other ludic critics argue? Ludic theorists, from Lyotard and Derrida to Foucault and Laclau deny the objective existence of totalities, arguing that social relations are heterogeneous and incommensurable, traversed by multiple differences (within). Moreover, they contend that the theories that articulate totalities—even to overthrow them—are themselves totalizing. Any assertions of unities or systematicity are seen as exclusionary and dominating, as is certainly the case with ludic readings of Marxism. But such a ludic logic conflates social totalities (such as capitalism or society itself) with the theories—or what Lyotard calls, the metanarratives—used to make sense of them. For Lyotard and other ludic critics, totalities are both constructed and legitimated by metanarratives, and to question these grand narratives is to undermine their credibility and to show that the totalities they describe and validate are merely reductive fictions. To resist a reductive social totality, according to ludic postmodernists, one need only resist the theory that legitimates it; one counters a totality's tyranny by being witness to the representations (signifiers, phrases) its metanarrative excludes and silences.

But totalities, such as capitalism, are not simply effects of metanarratives, reductive fictions imposed on the multiplicity of daily life. Rather, totalities are historical structures: the systematic relations that produce the material conditions and organizations of daily life, including the divisions of labor and distribution of social resources. To transform people's access to socioeconomic resources and to end exploitation requires a notion of totality in order to be able to critique the systematicity and global relations of oppression and to move beyond the limits of an immanent critique of local contingencies. For localizing theories do not so much end exploitation as elide it.

Given the widespread dissemination of the antitotality logic of Lyotard and others, it is by now a commonplace of ludic theories to rewrite the basic project of transformative politics, that is, emancipation—the collective struggle to end exploitation—as simply a matter of a metanarrative. Such a move textualizes politics and warrants a closer examination of Lyotard's notion of metanarrative and theory of incommensurability. According to Lyotard, a metanarrative is a story that attempts to legitimate and give meaning to other stories. In so doing, it founds and organizes the meanings for all stories in a field in terms of its own rhetorical figures and narrative of emplotment, thereby suppressing the heterogeneity of meanings and the singularity of events. For Lyotard, "the emancipation of the rational or working subject" is an "Enlightenment narrative, in which the hero of knowledge works toward a good ethico-political end" (*Postmodern Condition* xxiii–xxiv)—but, like all metanarratives, it "has lost its credibility" (37). Thus the only appropriate critical and political stance, for ludic theorists, is, in Lyotard's words, an "incredulity toward metanarratives" (xxiv): an incredulity, in short, toward emancipation as the necessary social struggle against systems of exploitation like patriarchal capitalism.

Not only does Lyotard designate metanarratives as totalizing and therefore totalitarian, but he also claims they are terrorist. As Lyotard explains, "[B]y terror I mean the efficiency gained by eliminating, or threatening to eliminate, a player from the language game one shares with him" (63). This notion is expanded in his other works (notably *The Differend* and *Just Gaming*, written with Jean-Loup Thebaud), in which he refers to the suppression not only of another player but of other phrases, statements, representations, and language games. The terror (totalitarianism) of metanarratives, for Lyotard, is a domination that imposes linkages on what he considers to be the incommensurable heterogeneity (differences) of disparate events and phrases: it not only excludes other possible meanings but, most crucial for Lyotard, it suppresses the radical singularity of events by establishing linkages among them. The act of linking always introduces a *differend*—a radical point of difference, of incommensurability between events and phrases located in heterogeneous language games. In effect, it is a *difference within* the speech act, metanarrative, or language game. According to Lyotard,

> In the *differend*, something "asks" to be put into phrases, and suffers from the wrong of not being able to be put into phrases right away. This is when the human beings who thought they could use language as an instrument of communication learn through the feeling of pain which accompanies silence (and of pleasure which accompanies the invention of a new idiom) . . . that they must be allowed to institute idioms which do not yet exist. (*Differend* 13)

Lyotard articulates an exemplary ludic logic here. By foregrounding the issues of language games and representation, Lyotard rewrites oppression (terrorism, totalitarianism), not as the *material* conditions of exploitation— the denial of people's needs and the appropriation of their labor—but as a matter of consciousness and language: the "feeling of pain which accompanies silence," in other words, the suppression of the heterogeneity of possible meanings. As a result, the necessary political act is the subversion of representations, the disruption of those metanarratives (and more broadly the symbolic order) that suppress the *differend*. "What is at stake . . . is to bear witness to differends by finding idioms for them" (13). Against the pain of silence Lyotard asserts the pleasure of invention of phrases, idioms, tropes. He is, in short, substituting a discursive invention for transformative politics.

This move is based on the ludic textualization of the real and contradictory rewriting of truth as (absolutely) relative. The true is considered to be always already relative: an incommensurable effect of the differing "phrase universes," language games, textualities, *differance/differends* used to describe, that is, to *establish*, the true. Such a logic undermines any transformative political activity by rendering the relation among the truth, real, and justice incommensurable and indeterminate. According to Lyotard and Thebaud,

> [A]ll politics implies the prescription of doing something else than what is. But this prescription of doing something else than what is, is prescription itself: it is the essence of a prescription to be a statement such that it induces in its recipient an activity that will transform real-

ity, that is, the situational context, the context of the speech act . . . among all these thinkers, not only Plato but Marx as well, there is the deep conviction that there is a true being of society, and that society will be just if it is brought into conformity with this true being, and therefore one can draw just prescriptions from a description that is true. (23)

In other words, for Lyotard there is an incommensurability, a *differend* between prescription and description, between justice and truth, that denies any possibility of founding justice and thus politics on truth. Lyotard's own logic is based on reducing politics to a speech act: to a series of relations between sender and receiver and between the communicative interaction and its abstract, localized context (*Differend* 139–40). Since the speech act is always already divided by *differends*, he finds an incommensurability between the prescribing or "norm-giving subject" and the receiver who has to "put himself in the position of the sender of the [prescriptive] statement . . . in order to work out all over again the theoretical discourse that legitimates, in the eyes of this sender, the command that he is issuing" (Lyotard and Thebaud 23). This difference within the communicative situation, for Lyotard, undermines the legitimacy of any prescription for social change, as well as any description of the "true," because it opens up the possibility of inventing other linkages, other meanings, other truths. Lyotard, in a manner reminiscent of Kant, regards any arrival at the concept of justice from the truthful or a decided good to be totalitarian. In short, any attempt to articulate a knowable good involves a *differend* and the suppression of other notions of good. Because the social, according to Lyotard, "is given along with the universe of a phrase . . . [and] depends upon the phrase by which one links onto the preceding one, and since this linking is a matter for differends between genres of discourse, the nature of the social always remains to be judged. In this way, the social is the referent . . . of a judgement to be always done over again" (*Differend* 140). Any judgment, in other words, one makes about the nature or truth of the social, of the good or about justice, is always a matter of specific, contingent, and incommensurable linkages that must be "always done over again," since any one linkage will suppress some *differend* and must be displaced by yet another linkage. Lyotard's position, then—as summarized by one critic—is that "a just politics can only consist in responding to the imperative 'be just' without claiming to know in advance what it is to be just. Politics is thus not a matter of devising strategies of arriving at goals so much as experimenting in search of an indeterminate law, the idea of justice" (Readings 110). It is important to stress here a point that I will return to in discussing other ludic theorists: the crux of the ludic logic is this rewriting of the social in terms of indeterminate discourse, language games, phrases, speech acts. Specifically this means that the material social contradictions are subsumed to a discursive tension, as Lyotard calls it: "[T]he tension, or rather the discord, of the social is . . . given with its phrase universe" (*Differend* 140). Politics, itself, is reduced to discursive alterations and subversions: what Lyotard calls the "invention of new idioms" for the *differend*. The post-al politics of invention is the local, contingent act of generating new phrases, idioms, linkages, and rules for judgment (judgments that have "to be always done over again") for each particular situation without any preexisting criteria.

Such a politics of invention no longer seeks to transform reality and rejects the possibility of social revolution, since there is no secure knowledge of the real or notion of justice on which to act—only the continual repetition of contingent acts of judging that invent their own idiom, their own criteria as they go along. For historical materialists, however, justice is not indeterminate; nor is politics foundationless. In contrast, for historical materialism the good is real but always obscured by the dominant ideology. In other words, the "knowable good" is not simply a rhetorical effect of language games marked by the play of difference. Rather the "knowable good" is a historical condition: it is the effect of the economic and sociocultural possibilities opened up by human production but at the same time restricted by the social contradictions of the existing relations of production and obscured by the operation of ideology in global capitalism. To be more specific, capitalism has developed the means of production and forms of technology to fulfill the basic needs of all people, for food, shelter, clothing, medical care, education, but it does not do so because of the imperatives of profit and the priority of private property. To take one quite obvious but largely overlooked example: thousands of tons of dairy products produced in this country are put in storage in order to artificially maintain a certain level of profit on dairy items, rather than distributing the food to the millions of hungry and starving children in the United States and globally.

The conflict between the priority of needs (feeding hungry children) and profits (for the dairy industry) is *not* simply the incommensurable effects of conflicting speech acts and language games, although certainly speech acts are involved in this conflict, especially in the ideological naturalization of hunger and deprivation as inevitable. Instead, this conflict is the historical effect, as Marx says, of "the material productive forces of society" (the technological capability to produce extremely large quantities of milk products and other foodstuffs), which have "come in conflict with the existing relations of production, or—what is but a legal expression for the same thing—with the property relations within which they have been at work": in other words, the production, commodification, and distribution of milk not primarily to feed as many people as possible but to maximize the surplus value or profit of those who own the means of production and distribution of milk products (*Contribution* 21). It is quite true, however, as Marx argues, that it is within the "ideological forms"—"the legal, political, religious, aesthetic or philosophic"—that women and men "become conscious of this conflict and fight it out" (*Contribution* 21). However, Lyotard's erasure of the issue of ideology and his focus instead on the singularity of speech acts and *differends* greatly mystifies the social struggles over truth and justice by confining them to language games—that is, to the superstructure—and cutting off their dialectical connection to the relations of production (base). Justice in Lyotard's logic seems to be an indeterminate competition of incommensurable, equal notions of good precisely because what is suppressed by his discursive localism is material necessity: the priority of *needs*.

For historical materialists, truth is not a universal given nor a metaphysical certainty, but neither is it simply a local effect of language games. Rather truth is a historically struggled over and constructed knowledge-effect. To assert the historical constructedness of truth, however, in no way denies the existence of objective reality (Engels, *Anti-Dühring*, 96–103) nor dissolves it into rhetoric or textual relativity. Instead, it refers to the way objective reality is made intelligible at any given historical moment: what is validated as making sense, what is represented as "what is," what is legitimated as true, are all effects of class struggles over meaning and the historical conflicts over knowledge. The relativity of knowledge is no way to be equated with relativism (Lenin, *Materialism and Empirico-Criticism* 134–36). Rather, these are questions of ideology, for ideology constructs the representations in terms of which we make sense of and live our relation to objective reality—to the material relations of production shaping our lives—and in terms of which we understand and relate to ourselves and each other.

The truth of hunger, for example, is not simply "given with its phrase universe," as Lyotard claims. Instead, it is the historical effect of the class struggle over the production and distribution of food. One of the main arenas of this conflict in patriarchal capitalism is the ideological fight over the meaning or causes of hunger—that is, over how it is represented and made intelligible. This means that the truth of hunger is indeed articulated in terms of phrases, genres, speech acts, but it is not *given* by them. These phrase universes need to be understood not simply in terms of the communicative situation or context, but *dialectically* in connection to the relations of production. In short, we need to know not only *what* are the conflicting meanings of hunger and *how* they are constructed but *why* these specific (mis)representations (phrase universes, metaphors) are produced at this historical moment. It is this last issue—*why*—that the localism of ludic thinking brackets. For the question of *why* is the question of the dialectical relation of the singular entity, event, or meaning to the larger social totality—to the relations of production. Thus the most common ideological misrepresentation, "the most common—and most misplaced—assumption," as one socialist critic, Mark O'Brien, points out, "used to explain starvation is that there is not enough food to go round." This misrepresentation conceals the actual conditions of production. According to O'Brien, "For 30 years, world food production has on average increased 16 percent faster each year than population size. . . . Enough grain is grown to make every man, woman and child fat on 3,600 calories a day" (6). In other words, the ideological misrepresentation of hunger as the result of scarcity naturalizes the consequences of production for profit: it conceals the *reality* that scarcity of food is now a result of *overproduction* for profit. In naturalizing production for profit, ideology operates to remove from critical scrutiny—that is, to render invisible and unknowable—the systematic capitalist relations of production creating this scarcity, such as the transformation of food into a commodity to be purchased, the substitution of cash crops for agricultural production for use (subsistence), and government subsidies for disposing of food. As Paul d'Amato reminds, not only are farmers "paid by governments to take land out of productive use—in order to keep prices competitive," but "during the Reagan years—when millions starved to death in sub-Saharan Africa—the U.S. Government built special grain storage tankers, fitted with special trap doors, to dump their contents into the sea" (11). Moreover, the commodification of food and demise of subsistence food production means that access to food in patriarchal capitalism is dependent on one's ability to buy it. The 1974 famine in Bangladesh, for example, resulted not from scarcity but from the inability of the poor to purchase food (Sen, *Poverty and Famines*). It resulted from the organization of the production and distribution of food for profit—which ideology conceals.

The fundamental material contradiction of patriarchal capitalism is deprivation (not only hunger but poverty, homelessness, lack of health care, illiteracy) amid overproduction and abundance. But the localism of ludic analytics—the fetishization of the contingent singularity and discursivity of events—mystifies the material reality. Justice, is not indeterminate; rather, it is very clearly determined by the historical conditions of possibility of human production: it is now possible to feed the world's population, to meet every person's basic need, and not doing so is unjust. Knowing the truth is neither a question of describing some true metaphysical or ontological essence nor a matter of negotiating incommensurable language games. Rather, it is the question of a dialectical understanding of the dynamic relation between superstructure and base: between ideology—(mis)representations, signifying practices, discourses, frames of intelligibility, subjectivities—and workings of the forces of production and the historical relations of production. Crucial to such a dialectical knowledge is the critique of ideology—a practice for developing class consciousness—which, as Henri Lefebvre has discussed,

> consists in studying the margin which separates what men are from what they think they are, what they live from what they think. It re-examines the notion of *mystification* more deeply . . . We must first denounce mystifications, and then proceed to a study of how they could have begun, of how they were able to impose themselves, and of how ideological *transposition* can operate in men's consciousness; for ideologies and mystifications are based upon real life, yet at the same time they disguise or transpose that real life. (146)

Perhaps one of the most serious problems with ludic knowledges is the way they mystify the material conditions of our daily lives: they develop "mystifications . . . based upon real life, yet at the same time they disguise or transpose that real life." Their (re)mystifications are all the more effective precisely because they are developed by demystifying the dominant common sense and some of the ideological forms necessary to earlier stages of capitalism. Ludic postmodernism, in short, plays a central role in generating many of the ideological (re)mystifications necessary to late capitalism, not the least of which are the erasure of class struggle and the occlusion of the relations of production.

This ideological remystification of the real is especially evident in Drucilla Cornell's textual politics, which is indebted not only to Lyotard's logic of the *differend* but especially to Derridean deconstruction (she seeks, as she says, a "feminist alliance with deconstruction") and to Irigaray's "refiguring of sexual difference" (*Beyond Accommodation* 16). Cornell both textualizes reality and offers a textual politics to subvert it. She argues that

> what is "real" and what it means to be "realistic," to pay attention to the real, is always given to us in a text. "Text" here is meant to refer not only to a literary text, but also to an established context of meaning through which we read ourselves . . . The "real," as either the literal or as the psychologically plausible, does not completely govern possibility. *Differance* subverts the claim that "This is all there is!" The trace of Otherness remains. As a result, *differance* also undermines the legitimacy of the attempt to *establish* any particular *context*, including the masculine symbolic, as a kingdom which absolutely rules over us . . . The shutting in of context, the denial of new possibilities yet to be imagined, is exposed as political, not as inevitable and, more importantly, as unethical and, ultimately, unjust. (108–9)

By reducing the real to what "is always given to us in a text," Cornell's textual politics—like all forms of post-al politics—subsumes the nondiscursive to the discursive and becomes yet another ludic rehearsal of idealism, as I discussed in chapter one. Her concern is primarily to subvert the "designations imposed by context"—which is pregiven, which "we do not control and which shapes us" (5). Chief among these is "gender identity, the most stubborn of contexts" (171). But by context Cornell does not refer to historical and material socioeconomic conditions; rather, she is indicating another form or level of textuality: "the established context of meanings" such as the law or the "masculine symbolic." Cornell's textuality sutures over the objective reality of the relations of production and division of labor, entirely suppressing it. She states that in writing what she calls "the mamafesta"—her ludic reinscription of manifesto, "a fable" for rewriting "feminine 'reality'"—"the opposition between literal and the textual is undermined" (2). But Cornell is putting forth a very reductive notion of the real: not only does she textualize it, but she also equates it with either the cognitive ("the psychologically plausible") or the "literal"—by which she suggests both that which seems to have a clear referent and that which is in binary opposition to the imaginary. Although she would deny that she is reviving a binary here, she clearly insists that her "fable emphasizes the deconstruction of a reality that stands in as the unshakable, literal truth" and is disrupted (opposed) by something "more (*mere/mehr*), not as what *is there* in the actual, but as what has yet to be rendered at all, as the repressed, as the disruption of the unconscious, as the explosive force of an imaginary . . . is the feminine as written in the letter" (2). The real (the literal) for Cornell is the arena of established (dominant) discourses—"the masculine symbolic, as a kingdom which absolutely rules over us"—while the site of resistance is the *imaginary* or, in Lyotardian terms, *invention*—that which exceeds the established bounds of discourse, which Cornell designates by "remetaphorization." What is obscured and sutured over by this binary of imaginary excess (invention) and dominant discourses (contexts)—and more important, what is omitted as the site of social struggle—is the objective reality of the material conditions of the relations of production and exploitation. Cornell "denies any rigid dichotomy between [her] utopian feminism and materialist feminism," but the only way such a statement can have any validity is by textualizing not only materialism but also reality itself, as Cornell does. In excluding the objective reality of the *base*, Cornell, like other theorists of post-al politics, has chosen to situate her understanding of reality in the space of the discursive/textual and to enclose politics entirely within the frame of the superstructure. She substitutes, in short, a discursive economy for a political economy.

It is especially important to recall here that in their history of Anglo-American socialist feminism Karen Hansen and Ilene Philipson proclaim Drucilla Cornell, along with Seyla Benhabib, an example of "socialist feminists who have begun to push against the limitations of a Marxist outlook in an even more radical way than Gayle Rubin did in 'The Traffic in Women'" (24). They quote at some length from Cornell and Benhabib's declaration in the introduction to *Feminism as Critique* that "the confrontation between twentieth-century Marxism and feminist thought requires nothing less than a paradigm shift of the former . . . the 'displacement of the paradigm of production'" (1–2). Cornell's subsequent work is not only exemplary of this displacement and the turn away from historical materialism in socialist feminism, but also of the eclipse in feminism of an effective socialist politics. Her work clearly demonstrates that abandoning the production paradigm in feminism has severely marginalized and even suppressed any adequate understanding and intervention into the material conditions of the exploitation of women and other oppressed peoples.

In place of the revolutionary struggle for emancipation, Cornell argues for an ethical feminism. However, instead of a concern with the radical transformation of the political economy of exploitation, Cornell attends to "the productive power of poetic signification that *gives* us the ethical significance of the feminine as a redemptive perspective . . . [which] gives significance to the 'discovery' of feminine specificity" (*Beyond Accommodation* 117). This specificity, this singularity of differences, is the crucial issue in Cornell's ludic ethics and theory of (unattainable) justice. According to Cornell, "Justice *remains*, as beyond our description, as the call of the Other, which Derrida, quoting Levinas, only dares to evoke as 'the equitable honoring of faces.' Such honoring would demand the recognition of each one of us in her singularity" (113). Justice, in short, is the impossible messianic project of the recognition (representation) of the singularity of the other—or, as Cornell quotes Derrida, it is the unpresentable "experience of absolute alterity" (112–13). But justice for historical materialists is not an impossible, messianic project. Instead, it is the transformation of the social relations of production to meet the needs of all people and eliminate the injustices of class differences and the priority of private property and profit. The privileging and mystification of the other is an alibi for placing class interests beyond the reach of change.

What is unethical and unjust in Cornell's textual politics is *not* the exploitation of the labor of the many by the few but rather the foreclosure of interpretation, of the plurality of textual possibilities, and the discursive denial of the other. The harm that primarily concerns her is a discursive "violence" that establishes a symbolic context that excludes the representation of the singularity of the mystified other. It is what Derrida calls "the war within discourse," in which "language can only indefinitely tend toward justice by acknowledging and practicing the violence within it. Violence against Violence. *Economy* of violence." Moreover, he declares that "the worst violence" is "the violence of the night which precedes or represses discourse" (*Writing* 117). Thus, following Derrida and Lyotard, Cornell is substituting a discursive economy of violence for a political economy of violence.

Cornell argues that women's "'reality' disappears within the legal system if it cannot be signified" and, to support her argument, draws on Lyotard's logic of the *differend*, which forms one of the cornerstones of her theory. In particular, she cites the *differend* as what "'asks' to be put in phrases and suffers from the wrong of not being able to be put into phrases right away" (*Beyond Accommodation* 60–61). For Cornell, "the silencing of women, because of *dereliction*"—a term she borrows from Irigaray to indicate the way "feminine difference cannot be expressed except as signified in the masculine imaginary or the masculine symbolic" (7)—"can be understood as the *differend*. The resultant harm to women either disappears, because it cannot be represented as a harm within the law, or it is translated in a way so as to be inadequate to our experience" (60). The issue of harm, for Cornell, is a return to the problem of the (in)adequacy of the *representation* of the specificity of feminine difference—the silencing, misrepresentation of feminine otherness by the dominant masculine symbolic. Cornell is not only foregrounding a textual harm but also textualizing harm itself: as both what is caused by the textual exclusion of feminine otherness and that which must be named (represented) in order to be known. We need to qualify the use of the term *representation* here, for while Cornell's ethics is indeed primarily concerned with the problem of the (in)adequacy of representation (recognition), she does not deal with it in terms of reality: the adequacy of representation's approximation to the real. Instead, she is concerned with the representation of the unrepresentable: the imaginary and utopian feminine that "we *are cut* off" from by the masculine symbolic (103), that is, the "dream of a new choreography of sexual difference" beyond representation in the "current gender hierarchy" (96, 168). Harm, by and large, is this exclusion of the alterity of the feminine: "violence to the feminine 'being,'" according to Cornell, "inheres in the very act of the repudiation of the feminine" (9).

Thus, the ethical-political act for Cornell is the subversion of this discursive violence through "the affirmation of feminine difference," which following Irigaray she defines as an affirmation that "dreams and then refigures the feminine as the difference that undermines gender identity." The strategies of affirmation for Cornell are processes of rewriting adapted from Irigaray (particularly her notion of mimesis). Among these strategies, the most important are remetaphorization and restylization. Remetaphorization puts into play the feminine as both the difference within gender hierarchy and the excessive, heterogeneous sexual differences beyond gender identity: "the infinite possibilities of"—the differences within—"feminine *jouissance*" (17).

However, this privileging of discursive violence and textual subversions in Cornell's work becomes an alibi for suppressing the material reality of socioeconomic violence and exploitation: the violence of appropriating people's labor and the violence of private property. It *cuts off* any understanding of the relationship between the representable/unrepresentable and the material relations of production; between symbolic constructions (exclusions) of sexual differences and the divisions of labor. Cornell's ethical feminism is aimed, in large part, at deconstructing the gender hierarchy in the legal system; she seeks a "messianic conception of justice, in which gender would no longer govern our rights" (116). But the "displacement of gender hierarchy" is not primarily a matter of the "affirmation of the feminine" through the play of tropes "refiguring the feminine" nor a rewriting of myths, as Cornell's nearly exclusive focus on feminine affirmation would suggest (13). What Cornell forgets is what Evelyn Reed has so clearly argued, that the "abasement of women has been a permanent feature of all . . . class society . . . So long as women led or participated in the productive work of the whole community, they commanded respect and esteem" (*Problems* 93). The central concept here is "productive work of the whole community," for once women were "dismembered," as Reed says, into separate "monogamous family life under the system of private property," they "were stripped of their economic self-dependence" (93–94). The issue is not that women's work within the home is not productive labor, but that the condition of women's lives and their rights depend on whether their labor *directly* contributes to *social* production (to the "work of the whole community") without being mediated through (and often *owned by*) the patriarchal family and its male head—and second, whether women have direct (unmediated) access to the products and value their labor produces. In patriarchal capitalism this means specifically whether women earn a wage for their labor and whether they own property—in short whether they have "economic self-dependence."

The determination of women's rights and the conditions of their lives by their place in the relations of production and division of property is dramatically demonstrated in Amartya Sen's global study of the ratios of women to men. He argued, as his title suggests, that "More Than 100 Million Women Are Missing." Sen contends that "the numbers of 'missing women' in relation to the numbers that could be expected [to be living] if men and women received similar care in health, medicine, and nutrition, are remarkably large. A great many more than a hundred million women are simply not there because women are neglected compared with men"— in short, their fundamental material *needs* are neglected (66). The reasons cannot be attributed simply to lack of economic development since, as Sen points out, "many poor countries do not, in fact, have deficits of women . . . sub-Saharan Africa, poor and undeveloped as it is, has a substantial excess of women" (62). Economic development, in itself, does not improve women's mortality; instead it is, as Sen notes, quite often accompanied by a relative worsening in the rate of survival of women" (62). Nor is this repudiation of women primarily a matter of cultural factors—of the masculine symbolic (the focus of Cornell's ethical feminism). Rather, the fundamental element in women's survival is her place in the relations of production. According to Sen, "[W]omen's 'gainful' employment"—her "working outside the home for a wage, or in such 'productive' occupations as farming"—and her "owning assets . . . can greatly influence what are implicitly accepted as women's 'entitlements'" (63). For example, "Punjab, the richest Indian state has the lowest ratio of women to men (0.86) in India; it also has the lowest ratio of women in 'gainful' employment compared to men" (64), while in the much poorer Indian state of Kerala, "the ratio of women to men of more than 1.03 is closer to that of Europe (1.05)" and is owing to women's gainful employment as well as to their increased "education and economic rights—including property rights" (66).

Missing women, however, is not simply a Third World problem. As another social scientist, Neera Kuckreja Sohoni, stresses, "[T]his crisis is truly *global* in scope." It is "far more severe among girls (defined as age 19 and under) than among adult women" and somewhat worse in *developed* countries. She writes that "according to United Nations estimates . . . in 1990, in the 'developing' world, there were just 954 girls age 19 and under for every 1,000 boys. The 'developed' world is actually missing more— there are only 952 girls per 1,000 boys" (96). For all its preoccupation to "dream beyond the boundaries" of the masculine symbolic, as in Cornell, or to play with cyborgian boundary breaking, as in Haraway, ludic feminist theory is largely incapable of looking beyond middle-class economic security to try to understand and explain what is imperiling the very survival of women and girls in advanced industrial countries and globally. The answer requires feminism to reclaim theories of production and return to the political economy of emancipation. Instead, Cornell substitutes an ethics of indeterminate justice for a politics of emancipation.

But justice is not indeterminate nor a utopian beyond: it is not, as Cornell asserts, "the possibility/impossibility of deconstruction and, therefore, of the beyond to what 'is' law" (*Beyond Accommodation* 116). It is not even primarily a question of the law and its limits. Justice is, first and foremost, an issue of women's place in the relations of production and the division of property. Cornell, however, not only rejects the necessity of any feminist engagement with the production paradigm, she entirely evades the problem of actual private property. The only mention Cornell makes of property in *Beyond Accommodation* is to cite one of Derrida's etymological era-sures of property as a signifier in a sliding chain of signifiers. She quotes the following passage from *Spurs:*

> As a result, the question, "what *is* proper-ty (*propre*), what is appropri-ation, expropriation, mastery, servitude, etc.," is no longer possible. Not only is propriation a sexual operation, but *before* it there was no sexuality. And because it is finally undecidable, propriation is more powerful than the question *ti esti*, more powerful than the veil of truth of the meaning of being. (98; Derrida, *Spurs* 111)

The actual, historical relations of private property are simply eclipsed and sutured over by reducing property to an abstract signifier that can then be deployed (and displaced) in a sliding chain of signifiers that transform it into an undecidable sexual operation ("propriation"), whose limit, Der-rida declares, "determines . . . the very limit of being itself" (*Spurs* 113). It is especially significant that this ludic operation transforms the material property relations—which are fundamentally class relations—into a sexual operation (desire), and moreover, one that sets the horizons of being. How-ever, as Marx and Engels said of Striner, who made similar "etymological connection(s)":

> All this theoretical nonsense, which seeks refuge in etymology, would be impossible if the actual private property that the communists want to abolish had not been transformed into the abstract notion of "prop-erty." This transformation, on the one hand, saves one the trouble of having to say anything, or even merely to know anything, about actual private property and, on the other hand, makes it easy to dis-cover a contradiction in communism, since *after* the abolition of *(actual)* property it is, of course, easy to discover still all sorts of things which can be included in the term "property" . . .
>   In a word, rent of land, profit, etc., these actual forms of existence of private property, are *social relations* corresponding to a definite stage of production. (*German Ideology* 231)

In other words, property—which is the objectified, congealed form of the social relations of the division of labor—is transformed by Derrida, Cor-nell, and other ludic critics into an abstract signifier cut off from any dialec-tical relation to the economic, to the relations of production. This severance demonstrates yet again how isolated and isolating is the ludic logic with its claims to *inclusivity*, but its actual *exclusive* focus on superstructural forms and a post-al, discursive politics.

Cornell, however, is very concerned that her deconstructive ethics and textual politics not be seen as "undermining the actual experience of suffering" of women (35). She makes similar proclamations at several points in her book and contends that "The material suffering of women is not being denied in the name of a process of writing that continually transforms the representation of the feminine as if the rewriting itself could put an end to patriarchy" (2). But the issue is not whether ludic feminism denies "the material suffering of women" (how could it?); indeed many like Cornell *recognize* the actual experience of suffering of women. However, recognition alone is not enough. Rather the issue is *how* we understand the condition of women and act to change the *material reality* of women's exploitation. In articulating her position, Cornell not only reifies textuality but also seems to fall back on a form of experientialism: she addresses the actual experience of suffering—in other words, the *results* of oppression. But her attention to the pain of suffering (to results) supplants and occludes the material relations of oppression that *cause* women's suffering. For Cornell, the central tenet of her post-al politics "is that the condition in which the suffering of all women can be 'seen' and 'heard,' in all of our difference, is that in which the tyranny of established reality is disrupted and the possibility of further feminine resistance and the writing of a different version of the story of sexual difference is continually affirmed" (2). Cornell's call to disrupt "the tyranny of established reality" does not refer to the transformation of socioeconomic conditions but to the subversion of the *discursive context* through deconstruction and invention—by "writing a different version of the story"—so that we can see and hear the pain. However, it is not enough to see and hear, that is, to name and represent women's suffering or to deconstruct the tyranny of established discourses that prevent suffering from being recognized (seen, heard).

Transformative politics is not simply a matter of *recognizing* or feeling the pain of the other. Instead, it is the necessity of *eliminating* the pain and suffering of people; of transforming the real material conditions—the divisions of labor and property—producing exploitation. Cornell claims that "the rewriting of the feminine can . . . be transformative, not merely disruptive" (2). But what does Cornell's remetaphorization and restylization of the feminine, her refiguration of Woman, transform? It is, as Cornell herself states, a metaphoric transformation: the refiguration of Woman and attempt to "discover the possibility of the 'way out' from our current system of gender identity" (169). This is, for Cornell, an affirmation of the unrepresentable, utopian possibilities—"the dream of a new choreography of sexual differences." Certainly such rewriting or invention of the feminine along with the practice of deconstructing the dominant logic of the masculine symbolic can help to change (reform) the prevailing codes and representations by challenging their seeming naturalness and generating new metaphors, idioms, and representations. While these do indeed disrupt existing significations, they are still very limited interventions in the ideological struggle precisely because they do not engage the connections underlying diverse representations and their relation to economic conditions of production. In other words, ludic feminists can be quite effective in articulating the *what* and *how* of specific representations and local instances of discursive contexts and even in radically rewriting (reinventing) some of these representations, as Cornell argues. But they are unable to explain *why* these representations and discursive contexts are being produced in this way at this historical moment. Textual politics is especially blind to the connections and the complicities between the oppression of the many and the comfort and pleasures of the few (including most feminist theorists). It does not, in short, confront the class and labor differences at the root of suffering so that these can be eliminated. Invention (rewriting) in the end is a form of immanent, textual description that reifies the local and the specific. In so doing, it displaces explanatory critique and occludes any historical or dialectical understanding of material conditions and global relations causing exploitation. It is precisely in her claims to inclusivity that we see just how limited and exclusive Cornell's feminist ethics is. As she says,

> The feminist project as I have described it involves the demonstration of the irreducible opening of gender identity, the most stubborn of contexts, which in turn allows us to dream of a new choreography of sexual difference. The mimetic writing of feminine specificity, including the reworking of myth, can then be combined with the articulation of the determinate situation of women within our legal and political context, and with the genealogical exposure of how we are formed as objects within the masculine symbolic. *The mistake is to think that we cannot engage in all three aspects of the project, and worse, that one excludes the other.* (171, emphasis added)

The problem is not that these three aspects cannot be combined, but that none of them moves beyond the boundaries of the discursive and superstructural. As I have already indicated, even the legal and political context has been textualized in Cornell's logic. Cornell's seemingly inclusive project for feminism is, in fact, highly restrictive, for it is only a series of disruptions of existing representations in the name of an imaginary, idealist utopianism. It substitutes a localizing ethics of representation for a global politics of emancipation.

Mystifying Materiality

The works of Cornell and Lyotard raise serious questions about the limitations and effectivity of a post-al politics of invention: a politics of discursive transformation that seeks to move beyond established codes into a utopian space of unencumbered (semiotic) freedom through the subversion of existing regimes of discourse and hierarchies of representation, language games, and signifying relations. Part of what is at stake in the emphasis on invention by ludic theorists is the crisis of social constructionism. Structuralism and, later on, poststructuralism critiqued traditional humanism for its metaphysics of presence—by which it secured its basic categories (self, consciousness, gender, sex, race) in nature. They offered, as a supplement to this theory of the subject, the notion that the subject was not naturally created but was socially constructed. By now, the idea of social construction as opposed to a natural essentialism has become the ludic orthodoxy, and the conflict between essentialism and constructionism has become one of the most contested scenes in feminism. Recently, however, the theory of the subject as socially constructed is turning into an impediment for ludic postmodern theorists and critics, for whom constructionism seems too deterministic and restrictive of the agency of the subject. Ludic theorists are thus attempting to problematize this determinism through the trope of invention—the multiple, indeterminate, reversible play of significations that subverts any stable, definite meanings. For these ludic critics, the subject's inventiveness—that is, her or his participation in the discursive play of language games, metaphors, significations—enables her or him to overcome the determinacy of social construction and move into the terrain of a utopian future. This move first to a semiotic constructionism and then to invention involves a double displacement of historical materialism. By construing social construction largely in terms of a discursive construction, structuralists and poststructuralists have substituted a linguistic determinism for a historical materialist concept of construction as determined by the forces and relations of production. Now the more recent ludic rejection of even linguistic determinism entirely eclipses the historical actuality of determinism without having to address its materialist and economic forms. This valorization of a liberating inventiveness and complete erasure of any form of necessary relation is clearly evident in Cornell's utopian feminism with its strategies of remetaphorization.

But perhaps one of the fullest articulations of this eclipse of historical materialism in the shift from constructionism to invention is developed by Judith Butler in *Bodies That Matter*. Butler's work, as I have already indicated, is among the most sophisticated attempts to bring together both the textual and more social modes of post-al politics through her combination of a deconstructive textualism with a Foucauldian analytics of power. She rewrites constructionism, specifically the construction of gender/sexed bodies, in terms of invention—what she calls performativity or citationality.[2] Butler specifically contests "radical linguistic constructivism," which "is understood to be generative and deterministic" and forms a "linguistic monism, whereby everything is only and always language" (6). According to Butler, what ensues "is an exasperated debate that many of us are tired of hearing" (6): a debate over determinism and agency, over essentialism and constructivism. She decries the way structuralist and radical linguistic theories reduce constructivism "to determinism and impl(y) the evacuation or displacement of human agency" (9). This is an especially important issue in Butler's work. She is committed to the preservation of agency; in fact, it is the priority of her post-al politics. But she rejects both the "voluntarist subject of humanism" and the grammatical subject of structuralist and classical poststructuralist theories. She thus dismisses those who construe construction along structuralist lines, because they "claim that there are structures that construct the subject, impersonal forces, such as Culture or Discourse or Power, where these terms occupy the grammatical site of the subject" (9). In other words, she objects to what she considers to be a personification of "discourse or language or the social" that posits a grammatical subject as initiating the activity of construction. Butler attempts to displace this grammatical logic of structuralist and "radical linguistic constructivism" (the logic of subject and predicate) with a more open rhetorical or discursive logic of agency as reiteration: in other words, with a notion of *agency as invention*, which she variously calls performativity or citationality.

Her work is heavily indebted to Foucault's view of power, which, she argues, should be "understood as the disruption and subversion of this grammar and metaphysics of the subject" (9); it is an analytics of power that, for Butler, accounts for the generation of subjectivities without in turn positing a determining subject. This enables Butler to understand construction as "neither a subject nor its act, but a process of reiteration by which both 'subjects' and 'acts' come to appear at all. There is no power that acts, but only a reiterated acting that is power in its persistence and instability" (9). In other words, subjects/agents are effects of the agency of a reiterative power that she calls "performativity." Butler is asserting a localized and localizing theory of power and construction (performativity) that is determinate yet indeterminate and involves subjectivities but not a "Subject" and an agency that constructs its own agents.

Invention or performativity enables Butler to posit a mode of inquiry—into the construction of the subject—that "is no longer constructivism, but neither is it essentialism," because there is, Butler asserts, "an 'outside' to what is constructed by discourse (8). However, this is an inventive rather than a conventional notion of outside.

> [T]his is not an absolute "outside," an ontological thereness that exceeds or counters the boundaries of discourse; as a constitutive "outside," it is that which can only be thought—when it can—in relation to that discourse, at and as its most tenuous borders. (8)

In other words, the very outside to discourse that allows us, according to Butler, to escape the dichotomy of constructivism/essentialism, is itself *invented* through the play of discourse. By this she means that "the extra-discursive is delimited, it is formed by the very discourse from which it seeks to free itself" (11). However, this is not so much a move beyond the "exasperated debate" as it is yet another ludic displacement of fundamental issues through a tropic play that conflates differences through a logic of supplementarity.

The limits of this discursive invention of the outside (the extradiscursive) are made especially clear in Butler's ludic articulation of matter/materiality. She reunderstands "the notion of matter, not as a site or surface, but as *a process of materialization that stabilizes over time to produce the effect of boundary, fixity, and surface we call matter*" (9). In other words, Butler is substituting "materialization" for construction, but in so doing, she puts forward a concept of materiality that breaks both with the commonsense understanding—where this term refers to a reality or referent *outside* language—and with a historical materialist understanding, in which this concept refers to the objective reality of the actual historical conditions produced by the mode of production. Instead, Butler rewrites materialization as a form of discursive practice: as she says, "*[M]aterialization* will be a kind of citationality, the acquisition of being through the citing of power" (15). Citationality—that is, the practice of citing, repeating, summoning sexual norms and laws—is, in turn, also a form of performativity. Performativity, a concept Butler originally developed in *Gender Trouble*, cannot be simply reduced to performance, especially theatrical notions of performance as role playing. Butler argues that "performance as bounded 'act' is distinguished from performativity insofar as the latter consists in a reiteration of norms which precede, constrain, and exceed the performer . . . further, what is 'performed' works to conceal, if not to disavow, what remains opaque, unconscious, unperformable. The reduction of performativity to performance would be a mistake" (*Bodies* 234). The meaning of performativity, in other words, slides into a kind of speech act that repeats or cites the norms of sex. In fact, one of the main concerns of *Bodies That Matter* is "the reworking of performativity as citationality," so that Butler now defines performativity as "the reiterative and citational practice by which discourse produces the effects that it names" (14, 2).

Butler's outside to discourse, in other words, is what discourse itself constructs through "exclusion, erasure, violent foreclosure, abjection." But this outside is itself supplementary: it is a "disruptive return" that constitutes what excludes it. For example, the primacy of masculinity in Western metaphysics is, Butler argues, "founded . . . through a prohibition which outlaws the specter of a lesbian resemblance" (the lesbian phallus); masculinity, then, is an "effect of that very prohibition . . . dependent on that which it must exclude" (52). The outside (the excluded lesbian), in other words, is the necessary ground constituting the inside of masculinity and heterosexuality. Butler is following here the classic poststructuralist erasure of the boundaries between inside and outside, that is, supplementarity (Derrida, *Of Grammatology*, 144–45). But this supplementarity—what Butler insists is the "indissolubility of materiality and signification" (30)—also locates us as always already in an infinite semiotic loop: a kind of discursive Möbius strip. Butler reduces materiality to the materiality of the signifier and the effects of signifying processes, notably citationality. As she declares, "[I]t is not that one cannot get outside of language in order to grasp materiality in and of itself; rather, every effort to refer to materiality takes place through a signifying process which . . . is always already material" (68).

Thus, sex, for Butler, is not "a bodily given . . . but . . . a cultural norm which governs the materialization of bodies" (2–3). The construction of sexual identity is an activity of performativity in which the body assumes or materializes its sex through a process of citationality—that is, a *speaking* in and through bodies in which the symbolic laws, norms, and discourses of heterosexuality are cited in the same way that a judge cites a law (14). There is in Butler's theory, then, an equivalency or rather a tropic sliding and linking together of materialization, performativity, citationality as all forms of discursive reiteration. In other words, matter (the body) is given its boundaries, shapes, fixity, and surface—it is materialized (sexed)—through the citationality of discourse, through the reiteration of norms. The materiality of sexuality, then, is not outside language but is the *effect* of discourse.

However, in a footnote, Butler specifically disclaims that materiality is "the effect of 'discourse' which is its cause" (251 n. 12). But, she is able to make this disclaimer only through a series of dissimulations that in turn validate dissimulation, itself, as the crux of her theory of materiality/materializations. She does so by deploying Foucault's theory of power, which, as I have already indicated, posits power as dispersed without an originary source. Foucault's notion of power enables Butler to, as she says, "displace the causal relation through a reworking of the notion of 'effect.' Power is established in and through its effects, where these effects are the dissimulated workings of power itself" (251 n. 12). Butler is, in short, deconstructing causality (following Nietzsche's rereading of causality through its effects in his *The Will to Power*) into a circuit of supplementary relations in which the cause, as Nietzsche claims, is itself the effect of its own dissimulated causality; the effect is itself the causality of its own dissimulated effects. This move enables Butler to rewrite materiality as the effect of power: "'Materiality' appears only when its status as *contingently constituted through discourse* is erased, concealed, covered over. Materiality is thus the dissimulated effect of power" (251 n. 12; emphasis added). In Butler's ludic argument, materiality is thus entirely confined to the level of the superstructure, to discourse. Moreover, this articulation of materiality, like Cornell's notion of the real, is an extended ideological remystification. In the name of openness, it puts forth an understanding of power as a closed, self-legitimating operation. It suppresses the material conditions of what Marx calls "the working day": the production of profit (surplus value) through the exploitation of our unpaid and subsistence labor.

Butler's mystification of the materiality of materialism—the materiality of labor—is quite explicit in two brief references she makes to Marx's historical materialism. The first is an offhand reference in which she attempts to appropriate Marx to her position by linking him to her rereading of classical notions of matter as temporalized and as positing the "indissolubility of . . . materiality and signification" (31). She attributes this temporalization to what she claims is Marx's understanding of "'matter' . . . as a principle of *transformation*" (31). However, Butler is able to appropriate Marx only by misreading him and completely excluding the issue of labor. She specifies that her reading is based on the first of Marx's "Theses on Feuerbach," in which, she says, Marx "calls for a materialism which can affirm the practical activity that structures and inheres in the object as part of that object's objectivity and materiality" (250 n. 5). In "this new kind of materialism that Marx proposes . . . the object *is* transformative activity itself and, further, its materiality is established through this temporal movement . . . In other words, the object *materializes* to the extent that it is a site of *temporal transformation* . . . as transformative activity" (250 n. 5). This is a remarkable act of idealist abstraction, for it suppresses the fundamental element in Marx's "new kind of materialism": this "practical activity," this "transformative activity," constituting the object *as   labor*. Marx's understanding of materiality in the first of the "Theses on Feuerbach" as "sensuous human activity, practice" is the insistence on materiality *as labor*. To reduce labor to mere temporality is to exclude its materiality and do exactly what Marx opposes: to substitute interpretation for transformation of the world. As Marx writes in *Capital*, "Labour is, first of all, a process . . . by which man, through his own actions, mediates, regulates and controls the metabolism between himself and nature . . . Through this movement he acts upon external nature and changes it, and in this way he simultaneously changes his own nature" (283). Labor, of course, takes place in a temporality, but this is a specific history (i.e., a particular articulation of a mode of production), not an abstract, idealist, immanent temporality of *differance*. However, Butler does indeed reduce this transformative activity to an abstract (and quite idealist) notion of temporal movement. Of course, the temporality informing Butler's concept of materiality—as well as her concepts of performativity and the differences within reiteration and citationality—is not a historical, materialist temporality but rather the deconstructive trope that is one of the core principles of the Derridean notion of *differance*.

In basing her theory of materiality on Foucault's notion of a diffuse, autonomous, contingent, and aleatory power, Butler, like Foucault, makes power the *constitutive* base of society and all social processes, substituting it for the Marxist concept of a *determining* economic base. But how effective is such a move, especially when we also consider that Butler has articulated Foucault's analytics of power in relation to a deconstructive logic of supplementary, thus generating a circular logic that quite outdoes Foucault? As I have already suggested, Butler constructs a supplementary circuit in which all the fundamental concepts of her social analytics are equivalent— or tropically slide one into the other. She declares not only that "'materiality' designates a certain effect of power or, rather, *is* power in its formative or constituting effects" (34), but also that "performativity is one domain in which power acts *as* discourse . . . [as] a reiterated acting that *is* power" (225). Moreover, Butler insists, as we have already seen, on the "indissolubility of materiality and signification" (30) and that *"materialization* will be a kind of citationality" (15), that is performativity. In other words, power is not only the constitutive base of the social, immanent in all processes, but, through a series of tropic slippages, *power is materiality is discourse is citationality is performativity.* Such a circular understanding of power and materiality borders on the ludicrous. It does not explain processes of power and social construction so much as *avoid* explanation altogether by inventing a series of tropic displacements. Butler is, of course, following Foucault, who claims that "power is everywhere . . . comes from everywhere" (*History* 93). But as Nancy Hartsock rightly points out, "Power is everywhere, and so ultimately nowhere" (170). Such a notion of power is so broad and idealist that it is both absurd and ineffectual. How much more absurd, then, is Butler's supplementary logic in which *power is materiality is discourse is citationality is performativity?* Not only is power everywhere and nowhere, but power is everything and nothing.

While this may be a quite ineffectual theory of power for any politics of social transformation, it is nonetheless a very appealing and popular one among ludic feminists and theorists, precisely because it provides an analytics of power in which we do *not* have to confront the global relations and systematicity of power; in which we do *not* have to deal with the most serious consequences of power operating in dialectical relation to the mode of production and division of labor—the consequences, in other words, of *exploitation.* By construing power as immanent in all processes, as operating *as* discourse, as citationality—and thus as a "reiterative acting" divided by differences-within—this ludic logic constitutes power as reversible, as generating its own resistances. The "compulsory power relations" that Butler argues operate through multiple local sites to "form, maintain, sustain, and regulate bodies" (34) are themselves unstable and indeterminate: generating and sustaining resistance along with regulation. Moreover, the privileged place ludic theories accord discourse means, as Foucault argues, that discourse transmits and produces power; it reinforces it, but also undermines and exposes it, renders it fragile and makes it possible to thwart it. The agency of change, in other words, is discourse itself or power *as* discourse. More, specifically, it is what Butler calls resignification.

The politics of such a ludic theory blurs the lines between the powerful and powerless, oppressor and oppressed, and produces a social analytic that turns the historical binaries of social class into reversible matters of discourse in which exploiter and exploited become shifting positions in the (Lacanian) Symbolic, open to resignification. This means that, through the play and invention of discourse (resignification), every subject, everyone, always already has access to the power imminent in discourse without any connection to the position of the subject in the social division of labor. In other words, in this analytics of power, the social relations of production—class relations—are covered up. Everyone is always already located in multiple sites of resistance no matter what their location in property relations may be. This view occludes the source of power: the fact that power is always constructed at the point of production. Power for historical materialists is always linked to relations of production and labor. In any society divided by the unequal division and appropriation of labor, power is a binary relation between exploiter and exploited, powerful and powerless, owner of the means of production and those who have nothing but their labor power to sell. Power, thus, cannot be translated into a plurality of differences as if all sites of power are equally powerful. The resolution of these binaries does not come about through a linguistic resignification but through revolutionary praxis to transform the system of exploitation and emancipate those it exploits.

We especially see Butler's assertion of the agency of invention (citationality) as a dematerialized site of reversible power in her efforts to account for the way "sex is both produced and destabilized in the course of this reiteration" of norms (10). Not only does citationality invoke the "chain of binding conventions," but it is also "by virtue of this reiteration that gaps and fissures are opened up," producing instability, and "this instability is the *de*constituting possibility in the very process of repetition, the power that undoes the very effects by which 'sex' is stabilized" (10). In other words, as supplementary processes, citationality, reiteration, and performativity, all simultaneously constitute and *de*constitute; regulate and *de*regulate; produce and *de*stabilize the materialization—sexing—of the body. The process of reiteration (citationality/performativity) is, *in and of itself*, a process of *invention:* the reversible, destabilizing, de/reconstituting play of significations that subverts definite meanings. The regulatory power of norms, established through reiteration, is itself reversible: it is also a *de*regulatory power.

However, contrary to ludic claims, this diverse deployment of deregulating invention by Butler, as well as by Cornell, Lyotard, Derrida, and others is not a progressive move beyond the bounds of existing systems and their material conditions. Rather, invention is a way of avoiding the consequences of the structural forces in society. Invention is a double move that attempts to displace exploitation. Again, it does so by first construing material structural forces either as discourse or as so heavily mediated by discourses as to be indissociable from them. Then it reinterprets these structures in terms of the trope of invention and a differential logic (*differance/differend/*difference-within), defining them as in themselves heterogeneous, indeterminate, self-deconstructing processes. In other words, within this ludic logic, structures are always already being *undone* by their own destabilizing processes, their own differences-within. This means, in effect, that there are no exploitative or determining *structures* or *systematic* relations, including production, because such structures would always already be in the process of *undoing* themselves and their effects. Of course, ludic critics do not deny oppression (understood as domination, as opposed to exploitation), but they largely confine oppression to local gestures of power that are, by definition, reversible, that generate their own resistances. This means that there is no need for revolution or class struggle since any oppressive structure is itself a deconstituting process that undoes its own effects of oppression. Domination in particular undoes its own attempts to regulate subjectivities. As Butler argues, "'[S]exed positions' are not localities but, rather, citational practices instituted within a juridical domain" that attempts to "confine, limit, or prohibit some set of acts, practices, subjects, but in the process of articulating that prohibition, the law provides *the discursive occasion* for resistance, a resignification, and potential self-subversion of that law" (*Bodies* 109). Liberatory politics, for Butler, is thus a matter of invention, of resignification: the difference within every citation or repetition of a norm that opens up a space for reinventing the norm and its symbolic regime, as in the regime of heterosexuality.

However, by trying to explain heterosexuality as regulatory regime of discourse, a compulsory symbolic law operating through citationality, Butler confines "the regime of heterosexuality" entirely to the superstructure, to a discursive order. She suggests *how* it may operate, but she is not able to explain in any way *why* it does so; why it has the social and historical power it does; *why* it deploys (cites) the norms that she thinks it does. In cutting off heterosexuality from the material conditions of production, she isolates the regime of heterosexuality from patriarchal capitalism. This enables her to substitute the *symbolic regime* of heterosexuality for the *social formation* of patriarchal capitalism (which she entirely occludes) as the structure constructing our lives, gender, and sexuality. Moreover, her post-al politics posits invention as the latest trope for the freedom of deregulated subjectivities and unbounded desire, unconstrained by the truth of needs. But in actuality, the deployment of invention justifies, normalizes and, in the name of deregulation, regulates the subjects of the New World Order. None of these ludic modes of invention—Butler's resignification, Cornell's remetaphorization, Haraway's recoding, Lyotard's ode to the pleasures of inventing new phrases—breaks the logic of the dominant ideology of capitalism, which produces subjects according to the needs of the moving forces of production.

Butler's own analysis points up the limits of her ludic privileging of the discursive. Class, labor, and the relations of production are the suppressed but constitutive outside of her own theory. Her notion of citationality, for instance, is unable to *explain* the material reality of lesbian and gay oppression. Thus, she briefly moves toward a class analysis of resisting sexualities in order to ask, "For whom is outness a historically available and affordable option? Is there an unmarked class character to the demand for universal 'outness'?" (227). However, following her notion of citationality, Butler regards class itself to be a performance: a quoting of the texts of power. In other words, class, for Butler, is based on power as access to discourse and is contingent and individual; it does not concern the position of the subject in the social relations of production. But class is not the effect of power; rather, it is the construct of production and, as such, it is a collectivity of practices.

For historical materialist feminists and lesbian or gay critics, however, outness, and the possibility of exploring alternative sexualities, is not simply a matter of individual desire, nor is class a series of individualities. This is not to deny that one experiences sexuality as an individual; rather, it questions whether sexuality can be *explained* on the level of experience. Butler's question about the affordability of outing both hints at and withdraws from dealing with the historical forces that, in fact, make individual experience socially possible. Peter Ray demonstrates how the industrial revolution of the eighteenth and nineteenth centuries broke down the traditional bonds and constraints of a society which had been tied to the land by economic necessity. Millions began to work in the cities for money wages, and for some at least the possibility arose of living outside the traditional family arrangements. Heterosexuality and homosexuality were concepts developed by the medical, moral and legal authorities at that time, in order to police the new society by demarcating acceptable and unacceptable behaviour. Male homosexuality was not specifically outlawed in Britain until 1885. (32)

Similarly, John D'Emilio's work (see chap. 2) develops a sustained argument for the way alternative sexualities are tied to the labor relations of capitalism (*Making Trouble*). In her intimate critique, "A Question of Class," the contemporary lesbian theorist and writer Dorothy Allison offers an explanation of alternative sexualities and class that is an effective intervention in the ludic reading of "queerity." She argues that "Traditional feminist theory has had a limited understanding of class differences and of how sexuality and self are shaped by both desire and denial" (15). Focusing specifically on lesbian sexualities, she writes:

> I have known I was a lesbian since I was a teenager, and I have spent a good twenty years making peace with the effects of incest and physical abuse. But what may be the central fact of my life is that I was born in 1949 in Greenville, South Carolina, the bastard daughter of a white woman from a desperately poor family, a girl who had left the seventh grade the year before, worked as a waitress, and was just a month past fifteen when she had me. That fact, the inescapable impact of being born in a condition of poverty that this society finds shameful, contemptible, and somehow deserved, has had dominion over me to such an extent that I have spent my life trying to overcome or deny it. I have learned with great difficulty that the vast majority of people believe that poverty is a voluntary condition. (14–15)

No matter how much ludic theorists try to erase questions of class, poverty, and the economic from their work, their analysis is haunted by the relations of production and divisions of labor. We find this return of the repressed of the relations of production in Butler's ludic analysis in the opening chapter of *Bodies That Matter*, in which she attempts to "discern the history of sexual difference encoded in the history of matter" through a "rude and provocative" rereading of Plato (54, 36). She begins by positing matter within the metaphysical binary of matter and form, and confines her argument to this metaphysical circuit. But at two points in her text, when she attempts to explain *why* Plato has constituted the category of the excluded in the way he has, she is forced to move beyond the domain of discourse to the *relations of production and the division of labor*. As Butler explains, "This xenophobic exclusion operates through the production of racialized Others, and those whose 'natures' are considered less rational by virtue of their appointed task in the process of laboring to reproduce the conditions of private life" (48). And again, she says, "There is no singular outside, for the Forms require a number of exclusions; they are and replicate themselves through what they exclude, through not being animal, not being the woman, not being the slave, whose propriety is purchased through property, national and racial boundary, masculinism, and compulsory heterosexuality" (52). All these exclusions are part of the same singular outside: the material relations of production that construct all of the social divisions and differences around labor and the appropriation of social resources. In other words, for all Butler's discursive displacements, the concealed, sutured-over *base* of her own theory is still the *economic base*.

We can see the consequences of these different theories of materialism by briefly examining the construction or materialization of female gender, what Butler calls "girling." To describe this process, Butler adapts Althusser's concept of interpellation, which means the ideological process of calling a person to take up (identify with) the position named.

> [M]edical interpellation . . . (the sonogram notwithstanding) . . . shifts an infant from an "it" to a "she" or a "he," and in that naming, the girl is "girled," brought into the domain of language and kinship through the interpellation of gender . . . The naming is at once the setting of a boundary, and also the repeated inculcation of a norm. (7–8)

Butler understands this naming ("girling") as placing the infant in a regulatory regime of discourse (language and kinship). But for historical materialists, ideological interpellation does not simply place the infant in discourse; more important it also places the child in the relations of production, in the social division of labor, according to gender, sexuality, race, nationality. Butler's theory of performativity eclipses this dialectical relation between ideology and the economic. Butler is concerned with changing how bodies matter, how they are valued. But without relating ideological interpellation to the relations of production, no amount of resignification in the symbolic can change "What counts as a valued body"—for what makes a body valuable in the world is its *economic value.*

This *truth* is painfully clear if we move beyond the privileged boundaries of the upper middle class in the industrialized West (for whom basic needs are readily fulfilled) and see what is happening to "girling" in the international division of labor—especially among the impoverished classes in India. Here the medical interpellation of infants or fetuses, particularly through the use of the sonogram, immediately places "girled" fetuses not only in discourse but also in the gender division of labor and unequal access to social resources. About 60 percent of the girled fetuses are immediately aborted or are murdered upon birth (female infanticide) because the families cannot afford to keep them. The citational acts and rituals by which individuals are repeatedly girled, such as expensive ear-piercing ceremonies and exorbitant bride dowries, are not simply acts of discourse, but economic practices. In India, under postcolonial capitalism, the appropriation of women's surplus labor is increasing to such an extent that these rituals and performatives of "girling" are becoming highly popular and widely exploited sources of capital and direct extraction of surplus labor, so much so that the unmarried woman's *family* is itself being "girled" in order for its combined labor to collectively produce the surplus value taken from the girled body (e.g., in bride dowries). Revolutionary praxis, not simply resignification, is necessary to end the exploitation and murdering of hundreds of thousands of economically devalued girled bodies.

Maverick Feminists and Marxism

The post-al politics put forth by Butler, Cornell, and other ludic feminists is basically an anarchic notion. Its primary objectivity is individual freedom from *authority* rather than emancipation from socioeconomic *exploitation.* The evocative figure of post-al feminist politics is the maverick feminist celebrated by Cornell and initially articulated by Derrida and Christie McDonald in "Choreographies." For Cornell, the maverick feminist is the agent of the "new choreography of sexual difference" based on invention, on the "performative powers of the metaphors of the feminine . . . to enhance and expand our 'reality,'" (83). In affirming what she frequently calls, following Derrida, the "power to dance differently," Cornell substitutes invention for revolution, as her lengthy quoting from the Derrida-McDonald interview demonstrates (part of which I repeat here).

Perhaps woman does not have a history . . . because all alone she can resist and step back from a certain history [precisely in order to dance] in which revolution, or at least the "concept" of revolution, is generally inscribed . . . Your "maverick feminist" showed herself ready to break with the most authorized, the most dogmatic form of consensus, one that claims (and this is the most serious aspect of it) to speak out in the name of revolution and history. Perhaps she was thinking of a completely other history: a history of paradoxical laws and non-dialectical discontinuities: a history of absolutely heterogeneous pockets, irreducible particularities, of unheard of and incalculable sexual differences. (83; bracketed phrase inserted by Cornell)

The maverick feminist, then, is one who breaks with the history of material social relations, and especially the history of revolutionary struggle, replacing it with invention—a nondialectical narrative (history) of paradox and discontinuities, of heterogeneity and differences, of dance (as Cornell's inserted phrase emphasizes). But what is this history that is so readily displaced, and who is this maverick feminist?

She has many ludic permutations—one of the most recent being Diane Elam's "Ms. en Abyme," whom she features in the subtitle of her book *Feminism and Deconstruction.* Elam's "Ms. en abyme" is obviously a ludic pun on the deconstructive trope of *mise en abyme*: the "condition of 'women' would be the *mise en abyme,* a structure of infinite deferral" of representations (27). Thus "Ms. en abyme" is a ludic description of woman (Ms.) as indeterminate, destabilizing: a desiring Ms. who is cited and reiterated in what Elam says is an "infinite regression that I specifically call the '*ms. en abyme*'" (28). Elam argues for "the importance of this abyssal indeterminacy for feminism" because it renders "the subject/object positions assumed by representation . . . infinite and ultimately incalculable" (28, 29). But such a deconstructive feminism in the abyss is not the revolutionary project that Elam claims. It reduces the condition of women to questions of indeterminate representations and substitutes an infinitely undecidable feminine—that is, an endless chain (an abyss) of citationalities—for a historical and materialist knowledge for praxis: knowledge of the causal relations of social totality (the forces and relations of production) necessary for social transformation. The "Ms. en abyme," the maverick feminist and their other cited identities are post-al rearticulations of a very familiar figure: the anarchist whom Emma Goldman celebrated, the feminine that brings down patriarchy by defying hierarchies. Goldman, like Butler and Cornell, regards power (namely domination, not exploitation) to be the dynamic of the social and of subjectivities. The history that this anarchist maverick feminist is supposed to break with is the history of revolutionary struggle that is Marxism. The maverick feminist is one who anarchistically acts to subvert (in the classic anarchist model) the authority of the state and disciplinary regimes of power *without* transforming the economic structure this power sustains.

Ludic theories of power in feminism are primarily aimed at displacing any centralized or systematic exercise of political, social, or symbolic authority. These theories, however, take the state (not capital) to be the primary arena for the exercise of centralized power. For instance, the Foucauldian analytics is fundamentally antistatist, with its critique of juridical and sovereign theories of power and substitution of diffuse, dispersed and antiauthoritarian theories of power. The state in Foucault and in ludic feminism is an ahistorical source of power. However, the state, as Marx and Engels have indicated, is the "committee for managing the common affairs of the whole bourgeoisie" (*Communist Manifesto* 57). In place of any systematic authority—which derives from control of the means of production—ludic theorists seek to reconstitute power as, in and of itself, nonauthoritarian and decentralized. What is at stake in these diverse anarchic-ludic theories of power is that they all rewrite power as an abstract form of domination, which remains abstract no matter how specific and local a particular effect of power. This anarchic-ludic understanding of power is always already abstract because it is cut off from the economic: it is defined as autonomous from the relations of production, thus severing its relation to *exploitation*. As Foucault asserts, "[P]ower is not primarily the maintenance and reproduction of economic relations, but is above all a relation of force" (*Power/Knowledge* 89). Force is essentialized in Foucault and remains an ahistorical, abstract entity. Power is, in short, an abstract relation of force severed from the relations of production.

We see the anarchism of post-al politics perhaps most clearly expressed in the claims being made for radical democracy by ludic leftists. Stanley Aronowitz—who represents himself as a "new" New Left person and, as such, almost by definition a feminist—rejects socialism and the old Left, in large part, for its sexism and substitutes radical democracy as an effective politics of liberation. He argues, "I do not intend to renounce socialism as a strategy of economic change, but I do contend that it can no longer remain a guiding principle for a movement of social emancipation" ("Situation" 43). Why? Because the issue of emancipation, in this ludic-anarchic logic, is severed from actual economic exploitation: it becomes marginalized as the special problem of a largely suppressed socialism. As Aronowitz makes quite clear, social questions and the "goal of freedom (sexual, gender, ecological, and individual)" are considered sovereign and separate from "more economic and social equality" and issues of class—that is, they are quite separate from economic exploitation (44). However, as I have demonstrated throughout this book, social questions and the goal of freedom are not at all sovereign and separable from the material conditions of economic exploitation. Goals of freedom are themselves historical: environmental (Green) freedom becomes a goal only after a certain level of economic development has been reached. As Marx says, humanity always "sets itself only such tasks as it is able to solve" (*Contribution* 21). In addition, goals are class goals: the class that has already achieved economic freedom sets itself the goal of sexual freedom, but sexual freedom, which is so important in the West, is not one of the primary goals of freedom in developing countries. The goals of freedom for each class are fundamentally the (different) *effects* of exploitation arising from the relations of production. But the focus of radical democracy and the broad Left, including ludic theorists, is on the more general issue of freedom from constraint, freedom from an abstract, centralized authority: the pursuit of radical democracy, according to Aronowitz, "can only be consonant with ideological and economic heterogeneity and the decentering of political authority" ("Situation" 44).

Of primary concern in anarchic-ludic politics is not human emancipation from economic exploitation but that "human emancipation, if that term may be employed at all in the post-communist era, may be antagonistic to highly centralized authority and power" (44). In other words, in post-al politics, the issue of human emancipation is largely displaced and put in question—becoming more a matter of skepticism. If addressed at all, it is largely reduced to a problem of individual freedom, an antagonism to "centralized authority and power" without even asking how that centralized authority is related to the ownership of the means of production. This in turn becomes one of the main alibis for dismissing socialism because of its "authoritarian political legacy." But this simplistic ludic opposition of emancipation and authority completely rejects the revolutionary necessity of appropriating the power and authority of the state (the executive committee of the owners of the means of production) for social transformation. It focuses so exclusively on the (bourgeois) priority of individual freedom from *any* constraints on desires and differences that it denies the revolutionary necessity of appropriating power to end the ways in which the individual desires and differences of the few are used to exploit the many. Let us not forget the *revolutionary* uses of state authority, for example, in the People's Republic of China, to (until recently) successfully eliminate the most severe socioeconomic exploitation of women—including female infanticide, indenture, sexual slavery and prostitution—and provide women with extensive health care, education, and economic opportunities. However, the recent counterrevolution in China and (re)turn to market economy has meant *less* state authority exercised on these issues in order to promote the emergence of privatization and "free" enterprise. This is creating a severe deterioration in the condition of women in all areas: much higher unemployment for women; a debilitating decline in health care for women, and the revival of female infanticide, indenture, sexual harassment, abuse; and the slave trade in women.

The maverick, ludic feminist entirely occludes the historical necessity of the class struggle over power—that is, the revolutionary struggle to wrest power away from the owners of the means of production and end the exploitative divisions of labor around gender, sexuality, race, nationality. In the anarchic-ludic logic such struggle is a nonissue, since power, as I have already discussed, is seen as nondeterminate and immanently generating its own local sites of resistance. Liberation is seen as freedom from authority, from regulation, from any constraints on the free play of the possibilities of (sexual) differences. It is reduced to a cultural politics confined to superstructural practices and severed from the material relations of production. Such a post-al freedom (postauthority, poststate, postclass, post-production) is disturbingly close to the demands (desires) of the new aggressive entrepreneurial anarchism of late capitalism that is so evident in the backlash against health care reform in the United States and the increasing strength of right-wing politics and racism both in the United States and in Europe. This entrepreneurial anarchism is passionately, even violently, committed to a completely unfettered freedom for the individual to pursue profit unconstrained by the state and any obligation to the social good. Ludic feminists, obviously, do not necessarily sanction such entrepreneurial objectivities. Cornell's ethical feminism, for instance, seeks to theorize an ethical good, but she understands this good as "the equitable honoring of faces," by which she means a reciprocal recognition of the other. In other words, Cornell's understanding of the good, of justice, as I have already demonstrated, is a matter of (non)representation isolated from the relations of production. Cornell's ethics, like the post-al politics of other ludic feminists, is quite unable to challenge the effects of entrepreneurial anarchism. Instead, the *effects* of ludic claims for the unrestricted play of (sexual) differences, for the unrestricted freedom of individual desires reinforce this aggressive individualism. There is very little difference—in their *effects*—between maverick feminists and free-market entrepreneurs in late capitalism.

For all its complicity with entrepreneurial anarchism, ludic theory is haunted by Marx and historical materialism—a haunting that Derrida examines in his text *Specters of Marx*. As I have already had occasion to note, the title marks what Derrida says is "a certain haunting obsession that seems to me to organize the *dominant* influence on discourse today. At a time when a new world disorder is attempting to install its neocapitalism and neoliberalism, no disavowal has managed to rid itself of all of Marx's ghosts" (37). However, ludic theory, including much feminist theory, has expended enormous energy and effort to dismiss Marx and Marxism. I have already shown that this is the case with Gayle Rubin and Donna Haraway. But it is also the subtext of the work of such other feminists as Butler, Cornell, Cixous, and Irigaray, as well as of theorists as diverse as Baudrillard, Lyotard, and Foucault. Foucault, for instance, declares that "As far as I'm concerned, Marx doesn't exist. I mean the sort of entity constructed around a proper name, signifying at once a certain individual, and the totality of his writings, and an immense historical process deriving from him" (*Power/Knowledge* 76). But such proclamations have not dispensed with Marxism, nor with the revolutionary struggle and "immense historical process deriving from him." In fact, the work of all these theorists continue to be haunted by the specters of Marxism. For, as Derrida proclaims, "There will be . . . no future without Marx, without the memory and the inheritance of Marx" (*Specters* 13). For Marxism *is* the theory of emancipation in global, patriarchal capitalism, and there is no emancipatory future, no emancipatory politics, without Marxism.

We see the *undeniable* necessity of Marxism precisely in the ludic efforts to deny it. This contradiction is especially evident in Butler's "Poststructuralism and Postmarxism," which is yet another effort to suppress historical materialism and with it a revolutionary understanding of emancipation. Written as a review of Drucilla Cornell's *The Philosophy of the Limit* and of an essay by Ernesto Laclau called "Beyond Emancipation," Butler's text is an argument in favor of an unprincipled, pragmatic, post-al politics of "politically practicable possibilities" following what she finds to be the "impossibility" of Marxism and the "unrealizability of the Good and/or

Emancipation" (10–11). While Butler marks a difference between her own more Nietzschean-Foucauldian approach and the more Derridean approach of Cornell and Laclau, her discussion of these texts is largely approbatory and quite exemplary of the ludic logic and its post-al politics. As Butler sums up these related positions:

> For Cornell, the unrealizability of the Good, as she calls it, is the very condition of the possibility for the ethical relation; for Laclau, the unrealizability of "emancipation" is the condition of the possibility for a political field mobilized and expanded through antagonism; and for me, the loss of the subject as center and ground of meaning has been, still is, the condition of the possibility of a discursive modality of agency. ("Poststructuralism" 8)

This valorization of unrealizability derives in large part from the Lyotardian incredulity toward narratives or metanarratives—especially what Butler refers to as "the apparent failure of Marxist teleologies" (3). According to Butler, "Marxist versions of history" have lost "credibility" not because "this version of history has played itself out, has taken place, and is now over" but rather because "belief in the possibility of such a history ever taking place, regardless of its temporal placement in past, present, or future, is now in permanent crisis" (3).

What is this Marxist version of history Butler considers implausible? It is the historical materialist understanding of the forces of history as "the history of class struggles" (*Communist Manifesto* 55). It is an understanding of history not as narrative, not as contingencies, not as the desires of individuals, but as the process in which "the material productive forces of society come into conflict with the existing relations of production," which have turned "from forms of development of the productive forces . . . into their fetters" (*Contribution* 21). This then, according to Marx, "begins an era of social revolution. The changes in the economic foundation lead sooner or later to the transformation of the whole immense superstructure." For it is in the "ideological forms" of the superstructure that "men become conscious of this conflict and fight it out" (21). The historical materialist explanation of history is a theory of social struggle and change—what Cornell dismisses as messianic history and Laclau as eschatological history (Butler, "Poststructuralism" 3). But historical materialism is not messianic, nor idealist, utopian belief; rather, it is a concrete *praxis:* it is a critique of the *existing* relations of production and exploitation in order not just to interpret the world (the goal of ludic theorists), as Marx says in his famous Thesis XI, but to *change* it ("Theses" 5). Laclau's attack on Marxism as eschatological is an alibi for positing history as aleatory: as the effect of haphazard forces of the market. If eschatology is the real question here, then it is radical democracy that is the outcome of an eschatological historiography.

It does not matter to Butler and other ludic theorists whether historical materialism effectively explains "historical reality," whether such history "has taken place" or will ever take place. Rather what counts is whether the stories, the (meta)narratives are believed; whether they are credible. According to Butler, "that narrative," constituting Marxist theories, "can no longer be told with the degree of plausibility that it once had . . . To claim that belief in a certain version of history is no longer possible is simply to claim that the narrative that tells and enacts that history is no longer plausible" (3–4, n. 1). Under the guise of truth ("believability"), Butler is, of course, reinscribing the pragmatic subject of the entrepreneurial bourgeois. Believing is subjective and, as such, privileges consciousness. In other words, under the cover of believing, Butler puts forth a social theory in which the consciousness of the subject makes (narrates) the world—a reassuring view of history for the ruling class. Butler is also positing history as a narrative, a story that one (consciousness) tells about the past. It is a telling that not only narrativizes the past but also activates and constructs the very belief that sustains it and lends it credibility. Butler, in a somewhat contradictory move, is also reducing history to *ideology:* to a series of representations that produces its own legitimacy. What counts is not the truth of the narrative or the validity of its explanation of the real—poststructuralists have largely bracketed both—but its ability to construct its own legitimacy in the telling.

Aside from her reinscription of the humanist consciousness of the entrepreneurial bourgeois subject, Butler's theory of history (like that of Cornell and Laclau) is largely an orthodox adoption of the deconstructionist position of history as narrative and narrative as textual troping—as the play of *differance*. However, Butler also seeks to integrate a Foucauldian notion of history into her theory. Foucault (as he first articulated in "Nietzsche") displaces the historical materialist theory of history—as the history of necessity—with a history of contingencies. Genealogy is, to be brief, an account that substitutes the logic of aleatory contingencies for necessity; this move is undertaken in the name of providing a progressive theory of history: a history without origin and teleology, that is, without "arche" and "telos." At the core of Foucault's genealogy is his discussion of "event":

An event, consequently, is not a decision, a treaty, a reign, or a battle, but the reversal of a relationship of forces, the usurpation of power, the appropriation of a vocabulary turned against those who had once used it, a feeble domination that poisons itself as it grows lax, the entry of a masked "other." The forces operating in history are not controlled by destiny or regulative mechanisms, but respond to haphazard conflicts. (154)

In Foucault, then, history is the unfolding of the haphazard, aleatory, and contingent. As such, it is basically "the appropriation of a vocabulary turned against those who had once used it." In other words, history is reduced to a discursive vocabulary used against those who have been in power. In this move Foucault replaces materiality with discourse and exploitation with domination. Furthermore, he mystifies the history of exploitation—which has a rigid clarity in terms of its violent and cruel division of people into classes—by turning it into the trope of the "masked other." If the history of exploitation is masked, it is only in so far as the dominant ideology misrepresents and tries to bury the systematic relations of class violence and the exploitative division of labor beneath the multiplicity of seemingly disparate events. However, no event is haphazard in historical materialism: nothing happens without being connected to other social and economic practices. Foucault's method of eventalization, as he calls it in a later interview ("Questions" 76), ends up being just another mode of ideological mystification. The crux of eventalization, according to Foucault, is "making visible a *singularity*"—an isolated, contingent particularity—in order "To show that things 'weren't as necessary as all that'" (76); rather, they are aleatory, reversible, diffuse. Foucault does claim that "eventalization means rediscovering the connections, encounters, supports, blockages, plays of forces, strategies and so on" (76). However, he understands these connections in terms of a "pluralization of causes" that are basically discursive and noncausal in their reversibility and multiplicity. Eventalization, in other words, traces out haphazard and contingent linkages within the superstructure by excluding any connections between events and the base, that is, the relations of production. The popularity of Foucault's genealogy in feminism and the ludic knowledge industry derives, in large part, from the power of this protocol of ludic reading—this genealogy or eventalization—to mask the rigid divisions of class struggle.

History as the history of class struggles is not the assertion of a historical constant or "extra-historical . . . economic mechanism," as Foucault characterizes "de-eventalized history" ("Questions" 76, 78). As Marx argues in his critique of Proudhon's idealist understanding of history, "[T]he economic forms in which men produce, consume, and exchange are *transitory and historical*," not constant (Tucker 138). A materialist understanding of history is a complex, dialectical theory of historical changes and development: the very thing that Butler's reading of history as story, as discourse, attempts to occlude. For Butler, history is not the forces of ongoing struggles but rather the "narrativizability of the past," and some of these stories, notably Marxism, become a "history which is no more"—again, not because "this version of history has . . . taken place, and is now over" but because it is simply no longer credible ("Poststructuralism" 3). In positing history as narrative, as discursive event, as contingent, reversible effects of dissimulating power, Butler, Foucault, and other ludic theorists may have "grasped the fact that men [and women] produce cloth, linen, silk," but what they have

> not grasped is that these men [and women], according to their abilities, also produce the *social relations* amid which they prepare cloth and linen. Still less [have they] understood that men [and women], who produce their social relations in accordance with their material productivity, also produce *ideas, categories*, that is to say the abstract ideal expressions of these same social relations. Thus the categories are no more eternal than the relations they express. They are historical and transitory products. (Tucker 140)

In contrast to the specific material relations of the Marxist understanding of history, ludic theorists revive a form of ("negated") Hegelianism, which in its "very impossibility" and "failure" becomes the "condition of . . . democratic contestation" for Laclau and "guarantees the ethical relation as ethical" for Cornell. But this revival of Hegelianism also resurrects the same old idealism as Butler demonstrates in her discussion of their work ("Poststructuralism"). Laclau substitutes for the historically specific relations of class struggle what is, in effect, an "eternal" category of abstract antagonism "between the claims of universality and the claims of difference," as Butler puts it (5). Similarly, Cornell defines the ethical in terms of an (eternal, transhistorical) unrealizability that Butler characterizes as "the radically unachievable relation to the Other" (5), in which Cornell substitutes a "mystical," "masked" "Other"—a "feminine," that Butler notes "must . . . remain impossible . . . unrealizable" (5)—for the historically specific others produced by class struggle and the divisions of labor. This artic- ulation of post-Marxist history is, itself, based on conflating the failure of Hegelianism with "the failure, the impossibility, of a certain version of pro- gressive history," that is, Marxism (6). In so doing, ludic theorists occlude the Marxist rejection of Hegelian idealism. Instead, they reessentialize his- tory as an (eternal) epistemological category and suppress history as the concrete history of class struggles in patriarchal capitalism.

The poststructuralist position, according to Butler, posits *"a future which is in principle unrealizable. The promise of history is one that is des- tined to be broken"* ("Poststructuralism" 4). In making such claims, ludic theories are mystifying history as an abstract, eternal category, an eternal present whose "future . . . is in principle" (essentially) unrealizable, and whose promises—of equality, emancipation, well-being—"are destined to be broken." Such a notion of history becomes little more than an alibi for the status quo. It attributes the historically specific *failures of patriarchal cap- italism* to an abstract, essential failure of history in itself, and in so doing, offers a subtle apologetics for free-market anarchism. It suppresses the "real," objective contradictions and class conflicts in capitalism. This essen- tialization of capitalism is particularly evident when Butler declares that "In the unrealizability of history resides its promise," for any effort, accord- ing to Butler, to realize history "would foreclose contestation, difference, alterity" (6). Such a logic reifies an eternal category of contestation and dif- ference that is always already necessary.

What does this mean when we leave ludic mystification—what is this eternal category of "contestation, difference, alterity" that cannot be fore- closed or ended? It is, of course, the struggles over the exploitation of *other* people's labor; it is *class* contestation. This ludic legitimization of the *"unre- alizability* of the end of history," of the end of contestation, and the impos- sibility of emancipation is nothing short of the legitimization of the unreal- izability of the *end of capitalism*—an alibi for continuation of the existing relations of class exploitation and class privilege. Especially significant here is Cornell's position, in which the "very difference, gap, incommensu- rability between the realizable and ideal," according to Butler, generates an "infinite striving" (7). Cornell substitutes the ethical—as an unrealizable, infinite striving—for a socially transformative politics. In so doing, this (former) socialist feminist not only abandons the socialist revolution to overthrow existing class privileges and relations of production but also argues against the revolution ever arriving, for that would end the "infinite striving that failure somehow motivates" (7). This is the bourgeois hope that the revolutionary "letter never arrives at its destination"—that is, the place of its own class privilege.

Ludic theory leaves us, then, with a version of history as abstract and idealist as Proudhon's Hegelianism. Marx's critique of Proudhon is just as appropriate today to make of ludic theorists: "[I]ncapable of following the real movement of history, [they] produce a phantasmagoria . . . it is not history but old Hegelian junk, it is not profane history—a history of man—but sacred history—a history of ideas" (Tucker 138). Cornell's notion of messianic history and Laclau's notion of eschatological history both refer, according to Butler, to "Marxist teleologies." But it is ludic theorists rather than historical materialists who construct a utopian, messianic, sacred history of an eternal, unending present of infinite striving over differences. This is an abstract, static notion of social development as multiple and diverse in its details but as unchanging and unchangeable in its fundamental structure. It valorizes the permanence of class conflict—and thus its own class privilege—in its claims for the necessity of unending antagonism: the permanence and inevitability of capitalism. It is not that the future—specifically a nonexploitative, socialist future—is unrealizable, but the end of capitalism is, for these theorists, impossible and unthinkable, and for many, even undesirable.

Butler is largely approbatory of this valorization of unrealizability, particularly Laclau's argument, as she writes, "that certain freedoms and possibilities are opened up by the failure of a conventional sense of emancipation" whose "foundations are exposed as contradictory and untenable" (8). For Butler such a "postfoundationalist sense" of emancipation "will be *citational:* its use will be "provisional and revisable . . . Indeed the writer of 'emancipation' will not know in advance for what purposes or in what direction the term will come to signify" (8). In her claims to "redeploy emancipation" Butler seeks to "mark off the 'playful' use of the category from the serious and foundationalist one" (8). She substitutes, in other words, a playful citationality of emancipation as a sliding, unlocatable, reversible trope for the "serious foundationalist" meaning of emancipation as a *struggle concept* necessary to the *praxis* of ending the exploitation of people's labor. This amounts to a *ludic* emptying of emancipation of any concrete meaning as specific revolutionary possibility; instead it becomes an abstract, floating impossibility. But emancipation—*as the historically specific project of freeing people from the exploitation of the relations of production in capitalism*—is neither unrealizable nor impossible. It is important to recall Marx's observation here: "Mankind thus inevitably sets itself only such tasks as it is able to solve, since closer examination will always show that the problem itself arises only when the material conditions for its solution are already present" (*Contribution* 21). It is the task of historical materialism to provide this closer examination that not only shows us the problem but also how "the material conditions for its solution are already present."

Butler, however, offers a Nietzschean-Foucauldian solution to the "valorization of unrealizability," which she argues is subject to the Nietzschean critique: "[I]deals, defined as the unattainable and inapproximable, are a deformation of the will to power . . . which turns back upon itself, defeats itself, and valorizes and romanticizes that self-defeat as its own constitutive necessity" (8). Butler does not contest the unrealizability of emancipation, with which she is largely in agreement, but rather its romanticization as a condition of possibility. She thus poses instead "the more Nietzschean query: how is it that the unrealizability of the Good and/or Emancipation has produced a paralyzed or limited sense of political efficacy, and how, more generally, might the fabrication of more local ideals enhance the sense of politically practicable possibilities?" (10–11). Butler's solution to the "paralyzed . . . political efficacy" of post-al politics, in short, is more of the same. In advocating "the fabrication of local ideals," she is merely rehearsing and elaborating on Lyotard's little narratives and Foucault's eventalization. She offers her assertion of a Foucauldian approach as "the site for a certain unbridling of utopian faith post-Marx" (11). Butler claims this is "a deviation *from* Hegel, a repetition forward" (11). But this is just another return to the same old bourgeois idealism, the same "old Hegelian junk," that historical materialists have been struggling against for more than a century. As Lenin argued, "Thousands of shades of varieties of philosophical idealism are possible and it is always possible to create a thousand and first shade; and to the author of this thousand and first little system . . . what distinguishes it from the rest may appear to be momentous. From the standpoint of materialism, however, these distinctions are absolutely unessential" (*Materialism* 275). Butler's thousand-and-first shade of difference from the idealism of Laclau or Cornell is indeed unessential. What matters are the consequences of their post-al politics, and this is indeed the same: to render the emancipation of women and other oppressed peoples from the exploitation of capitalism *impossible*.

CHAPTER 5

Excess-ive Bodies: Essentialism, Indeterminacy, and Retrofeminism

The question of the body has become the central issue in ludic feminism: not only is it the main concept through which most postmodern feminist theory critiques the idea of the subject as the subject of consciousness (Cartesianism) or the subject of the unconscious (Freudianism), but it is also the primary concept through which feminism deconstructs the established binaries of Western metaphysics. The body, in short, has become the most recent site of discursive struggle and the primary ground for much of the most recent ludic feminism. Not only does Judith Butler articulate feminism as a theory of the (discursive) "matter" of bodies, but Elizabeth Grosz calls for a "corporeal feminism": a feminism focused on the specificity of bodies.[1] Grosz argues that

> If women are to develop autonomous modes of self–understanding and positions from which to challenge male knowledges and paradigms, the specific nature and integration (or perhaps lack of it) of the female body and female subjectivity and its similarities to and differences from men's bodies and identities need to be articulated. (19)

Grosz's book belongs to the genre of feminist theory that I have described in the preface: a genre devoted to an autonomous mode of knowing women by women, an affirmation of what she calls "pure difference." I have argued throughout this book that there are no autonomous forms of knowing. All arguments for the autonomy of knowledge of sexuality, race, environment, and so on offered by the new social movements are part of a larger upper–middle-class theory that localizes the globality of knowledge through which social differences are articulated materially and historically, and it does so in order to serve the interests of specific groups. The body has now become the ever-more-specific site of this local (autonomous) knowledge.

What are the consequences of the contestations between ludic and historical materialist feminism for understanding and rethinking such fundamental issues in feminist cultural studies as the politics of the body and the problem of essentialism? The body is the primary site for new articulations of cultural understanding not only for a wide range of feminist theorists but also for ludic postmodern critics in general. The body has become the privileged zone of inquiry throughout ludic postmodern knowledges, as evident in the writings of Foucault, Barthes, Deleuze, Guattari, Bourdieu, and others. Andrew Ross proclaims a "new generation" of intellectuals who "appeal to the liberatory body, and the creativity of consumption" (11). A diverse range of ludic writers are more and more following Foucault, for whom, as John Fiske argues, the "body replaces the subject" (161). Grosz is even more explicit on this point: the body is "the very 'stuff' of subjectivity" (ix), and her goal is to show that "all significant facets and complexities of subjects, can be as adequately explained using the subject's corporeality" (vii). The body, corporeality, in short, is the new site of an ever-more-localized and localizing autonomous knowledge cut off from the social relations of production. Thus Fiske argues for a cultural studies of "everyday life" that deals not with subjects but with "the body [as it] enters into immediate, performed relationship with the different settings or spaces it inhabits" (162). However, there is a complicity, as I will argue, between this ludic corporeality and the efforts of transnational corporations to recall women from the workforce. What is presented as a progressive move in ludic theory is, in fact, a reactionary one: an attempt to preserve the material and ideological interests of the dominant class through a new rhetoric and a new theory.

Bodies and/as Concepts

Perhaps more than any other issue, the body bridges the considerable differences dividing feminism today, and we find humanist feminists like Adrienne Rich, socialist feminists like Nancy Hartsock, and ludic feminists like Jane Gallop all attempting to "think through the body" as a new basis for a feminist social dynamic. In fact, Grosz reads all of contemporary feminism in terms of how the body is theorized. Her typology is helpful in outlining some of the diverse ways the body is understood.[2]

In Grosz's typology there are three modes of dealing with the body in feminism. She calls the first category "egalitarian feminism" and includes Simone de Beauvoir, Shulamith Firestone, Mary Wollstonecraft, "and other liberal, conservative, and humanist feminists" (15). This group is concerned with the "specificities of the female body . . . menstruation, pregnancy, maternity, lactation, etc." (15). It naturalizes a biological determinism of women's bodies, Grosz argues, as either limiting "women's capacity for equality" or generating unique kinds of "knowledge and ways of living" (15). "Social constructionism" is the second category, which "includes probably the majority of feminist theorists today: Juliet Mitchell, Julia Kristeva, Michèle Barrett, Nancy Chodorow, Marxist feminists, psychoanalytic feminists, and all those committed to a notion of the social construction of subjectivity" (16). Grosz defines this group as also maintaining a form of biologism—"a biologically determined, fixed, and ahistorical notion of the subject" (16–17). She argues that it retains the mind/body dualism and codes it as "the opposition between the realms of production/reproduction (the body) and ideology (mind)" (17). This is, to my mind, a distorted reading of social constructionism, especially the farcical rewriting of basic Marxist feminist assumptions, which derives from her own ahistorical rendering of materialism as, in effect, the "raw materials," that is, the raw matter, of bodies (21). I have already demonstrated that what passes for materialism in ludic feminism is little more than matterism. Grosz distorts the base/superstructure model in terms of an absurd biologism, arguing that "biology provides a self–contained 'natural' base and ideology provides a dependent parasitic 'second story'" (17). Of course, in ludic discourses, story does not mean level so much as it means fiction—an ungrounded narrative. By making biology the natural base, Grosz not only erases the historical materialist theory of subjectivities, in which bodies *and* consciousness are *together* historically produced and determined by the social relations of production and class struggles, but also turns dialectics into a silly dualism.

Grosz is herself largely aligned with the third category, sexual-difference feminists, among them Irigaray, Cixous, Spivak, Gallop, Moira Gatens, Vicki Kirby, Butler, Schor, and Wittig (17). Grosz defines this group as "concerned with the *lived body*, the body insofar as it is represented and used in specific ways in particular cultures" (18). It puts forth, in short, a notion of the "body as social and discursive object, a body bound up in the order of desire, signification, and power" (19). However, as I have argued, power and the social in the works of these feminists, including Grosz herself, are understood as primarily discursive processes within the superructure and severed from the historical materiality of the divisions of labor and relations of production. Grosz thus focuses her corporeal theory on "the specificity of bodies . . . [T]here is no body as such: there are only *bodies*—male or female, black, brown, white, large or small—and the gradations in between" (19). What she leaves out of this typology of specificity is quite telling: she omits *bodies in and of labor*.

This valorization of the specificity, the concreteness, of bodies informs nearly all feminist theories of the body. One of the main questions, then, for a transformative feminist politics and culture critique is, what is the political effect of these rewritings of knowledge and everyday culture through the specificities of the body? Do they disrupt and transform knowledge practices and relations of exploitation in patriarchal capitalism, or do they reproduce the divisions of labor and subjectivities necessary to patriarchal capitalist oppression, in spite of their subversive agenda?

Obviously, there is considerable diversity in the way feminists understand the body, ranging from Butler's citationality of the body to Paglia's fetishization of the procreative power of female sexuality. Having already discussed Butler's rearticulation of the matter of the body as itself the performativity of discourse or citationality, my focus here is on those feminist theories that revive the corporeality and givenness of the body.

To be precise: the body in feminist theory is seen as the site of the concrete, the specific, the particular, in opposition to abstraction, which is considered masculinist and phallogocentric. As Rich puts it, women's

> need to begin with the female body—our own—[is] understood . . . as locating the grounds from which to speak with authority *as* women. Not to transcend this body, but to reclaim it. To reconnect our thinking and speaking with the body of this particular living human individual, a woman. Begin . . . with the material, with matter, mma, madre, mutter, moeder, modder . . . Pick up again the long struggle against lofty and privileged abstraction. (213)

We are all well aware, since it has become a commonplace of both feminist and postmodern discourses, that abstraction marks the hierarchical dualism dominating Western rationalism in which the abstract, the ideal, the concept, and mind are privileged over the concrete, the material, experience, and the body. And as Nancy Hartsock writes in *Money, Sex, and Power*,

[I]t is not accidental that women are associated with quasi–human and nonhuman nature, that woman is associated with the body and material life, that the lives of women are systematically used as examples to characterize the lives of those ruled by their bodies rather than their minds. (241)

Diverse feminists thus share a commitment to overturning this hierarchal dualism dominating the binary other, whether nature, woman, or men and women of color. Thus Jane Gallop begins her *Thinking through the Body* by decrying the "systematic mind–body split that is killing our children," and she quotes Rich: "Culture: pure spirit, mind . . . has . . . split itself off from life, becoming the death–culture of quantification, abstraction, and the will to power which has reached its most refined destructiveness in this century" (2). Abstraction, in short, comes to represent the alienation and destructiveness of dominant modes of knowing—especially the primacy of concepts—in Western thought.

In opposition to this "alienating abstraction," feminists posit the body as an anticonceptual, material knowledge that is both disalienating and creative. For many humanist feminists, such as Rich, Susan Griffin, and Andrea Dworkin, the *experience* of the female body—what Sandra Harding has described as "female embodiment . . . Menstruation, vaginal penetration, lesbian sexual practices, birthing, nursing and menopause . . . bodily experiences men cannot have" (661–62)—is seen as locating women in a specific, particular, material knowledge of daily life and involving them in creative, nondominating relations of nurturing and connection with others. Female embodiment is considered to overcome masculinist, rationalist dualism, for as Hartsock argues, a "unity of mental and manual labor . . . grows from the fact that women's bodies, unlike men's, can be themselves instruments of production" (*Money* 243). Thus, Hartsock seeks to base an unalienated production with its "erotic possibilities" and a "reunderstanding of power and community" on women's "bodily, sensual, creative" experiences, especially those of "maternal sexuality"—"coitus, parturition, and lactation" (255–57). She argues that "the body—its desires and needs, its mortality . . . would be given a place of honor at the center of the theory": both feminist standpoint epistemology and a specifically feminist historical materialism (259). The body, in short, has become such a privileged site of nonalienating, concrete, unifying experience that even a complex theorist like Nancy Hartsock bases her feminist historical materialism—with its theory of women's labor, of power, and epistemology—in the end all on the female body: on what, in the end, is understood as a form of biological essentialism.

Hartsock's feminist materialism reverses the very relations of historical materialism. Instead of critiquing how the body—that is our experiences and understanding of the body, how we make the body intelligible— is produced through the political economy of social relations, she grounds her theory of social relations on a biology and erotics of reproduction: on the menstruation, pregnancy, lactation of the female body as if these were self–evident, invariable, essential processes. But are these bodily processes natural, material grounds for social relations? Or are they always already mediated and thus constructed, made intelligible, and experienced through the structuring of the symbolic order and the operation of the political economy of social relations according to the divisions of labor and demands of the mode of production? In other words, is the meaning of lactation, for example, in the experience of lactation (its physical bodiliness, its sensuousness), or is the meaning in the way that experience gets read in a given social formation on the basis of the frames of intelligibility and labor practices that society produces on the basis of the existing mode of production?

Currently, lactation and breast feeding are being revalorized in advanced capitalist countries, especially among the middle and upper middle classes. A recent spate of scientific studies and media stories in the West, for example, are proclaiming the nutritive and health benefits of mother's milk and breast feeding. One report declares in its headline "Mother's Milk Found to Be Potent Cocktail of Hormones" and goes on to claim that "The latest studies of peptides and other hormones in milk offer yet another reason why, whenever possible, mothers should breast–feed their babies" (Natalie Angier, *New York Times*, 24 May 1994, C1, C10). The power of breast milk "is so evident that in Sweden, at least, 'it's considered unethical to feed infants anything but human milk,' said Dr. Neuringer. After the birth of a child, a woman is given plenty of time off from work to nurse an infant. For those who cannot nurse, there are banks of human milk, just as there are blood banks. And the comparison is apt, for both are rivers of life" (C10).

Significantly, these studies validating breast feeding—and the corporeality of the subjectivity of mother—are appearing at a time of considerable unemployment and corporate attempts to downsize the labor force— including managerial and professional positions—in the United States. It is also a time of a corporate and small-business backlash against providing social and medical benefits to workers, as reflected in the increasing employment of temporary workers without benefits, and in business opposition to universal health coverage. The renewed valorization of breast feeding and maternal care, the celebration of the "intensities of flows" of the body in such texts as Grosz's *Volatile Bodies*, are complicit with the political status quo in that they contribute to current efforts to recall women from the labor force and are linked to other regressive efforts to reinstate domesticity, the traditional family and the regime of the social as composed of specific bodies.

In the neocolonies of global late capitalism, however, the ideological construction of such corporeal practices as lactation is often quite otherwise. The political economy of breast feeding is very different, for example, in the Alto do Cruzerio of northeastern Brazil, a poverty-stricken region of "cloying sugarcane fields amid hunger and disease" (Scheper–Hughes, *Death* 31). Nancy Scheper–Hughes examines the "'political economy' of emotions" in this region, focusing particularly on "culture and scarcity, both material and psychological, and their effects . . . on 'maternal thinking'" (*Death* 341, 15; see also "Death"). Northeastern Brazil, according to Scheper–Hughes, accounts for a quarter of "all childhood deaths in Latin America," deaths in large part attributable to the "precipitous" decline in breast feeding, from 96 percent in 1940 to less than 40 percent in 1975; it has since decreased further (*Death* 316–17). Scheper–Hughes argues that "a fairly direct and positive correlation exists between infant survival and breast feeding," yet "each generation of mothers in the Third World is less likely than the previous one to breast–feed offspring. This is especially true of rural migrants to urban areas, where wage labor and the work available to women are incompatible with breast–feeding" (*Death* 316–17). As one Alto woman described her work situation, "Her *patroas* would never allow her to enter their homes if they even suspected that she were lactating. '*Da nojo* [It's disgusting]!' Irene exclaimed . . . One could not run the risk of suddenly having a wet blouse, she explained, in the middle of serving the family meal: 'It would make everyone lose their appetites'" (323). The choice to bottle–feed, for most women engaged in wage labor, is not a matter of desire but of economic necessity; it is really no choice at all.

Moreover, the transition from semisubsistence peasants to wage laborers has also involved the extensive commodification of food, including infant food (323). The United States played a leading role in the commodification of baby's milk, dumping its excess dairy production in the

Third World in the 1960s in the form of free powdered milk under the auspices of Food for Peace. It thereby fostered, as Scheper–Hughes notes, "a powdered–milk dependency in the populace, which Nestle and other companies took advantage of when the free distribution ended in the 1970s" (322) in order to mass-distribute their infant formulas, which have become one of the primary food commodities—and by far the most expensive—among the Alto families, "consuming about a fifth of their weekly income" (318).

The changing relations of production in northeastern Brazil, which have brought not only wage labor and the commodification of food but also extreme hunger and scarcity, have produced radical changes in the ideological representation and meaning of lactation and baby's milk. Many women of the Alto, nearly all of whom suffer from acute hunger and overwork, perceive their breast milk as bad, according to Scheper–Hughes, and "described it as salty, watery, bitter, sour, infected, dirty, and diseased . . . as 'unfit' for the infant" (326). For these women, "human milk appeared blue, thin, watery" in contrast, to the rich, strong infant formulas they offer to their "often small, puny infants" in the form of a "heavy, thickened 'pap'" (325). Moreover, the provision of infant formula plays a crucial role in demonstrating paternity and establishing the child's legitimacy. With the transition to wage labor, marriages have become "less formal, more consensual, and more transitory in the shantytown . . . [T]he definition of a 'husband' . . . is a functional one. A husband is the man who provides food for his woman and her children," especially the expensive infant formula (323). It is, in short, the father, rather than the mother, who has now become the source, the provider of baby's milk. As the father arrives "bearing the prestigious purple–labeled can of Nestle . . . a woman will say to her newborn . . . 'Clap your hands, little one; your milk has arrived!'" (323–24). In northeastern Brazil, then, women are called to stop breast feeding, and this is validated by "commonsense" knowledge and economic practices. In the United States, however, women are recalled from the labor force to breast–feed, and science provides the evidence for the naturalness of such practices. Both Brazilian and U.S. women are provided with knowledges that affirm the practices that capitalism needs.

Contrary to the scientific as well as the romanticized claims for breast feeding among the middle and upper middle classes, especially in overdeveloped countries, breast milk is neither self–evidently perceived as healthy nor universally recognized as a "river of life." Nor are women's bodies universally experienced as the source of creative, sensuous unity and redemption from alienating relations of production as claimed by feminist–standpoint epistemologists and ludic writers like Irigaray and, in her more recent ludic work, Iris Young. For instance, Young, following Irigaray, writes that in a

> woman–centered experience of breasts . . . the breasted body becomes blurry, mushy, indefinite, multiple . . . A metaphysics generated from feminine desire, Luce Irigaray suggests, might conceptualize being as fluid rather than as solid substances, or things . . . Fluids surge and move, and a metaphysic that thinks being as fluid would tend to privilege the living, moving, pulsing over the inert dead matter of the Cartesian World view. (*Throwing* 192–93)

Such valorized meanings are, to a large degree, the privilege of prosperity: they are class specific. For the superexploited women living at the "foot of the cane"—at the foot of global capitalism—the body is where "the contradictions of the social order are reproduced in the disquieting image of needy, hungry, dependent women who must withhold their milk from their babies to keep from being devoured by them first" (Scheper-Hughes, *Death* 326). It is not women's bodies that redeem alienating production but rather the exploitative relations of production in capitalism that produce women's alienation from their own bodies.

But such a historical materialist understanding of the body is rejected by most feminists. How, then, does the body function in feminism, particularly ludic feminist discourses? As I have already mentioned, the body is posited as the opposite of abstraction, of conceptuality, but the body as it circulates in feminist theory is a *concept:* a specific historically produced articulation or way of making sense of experience. Adrienne Rich makes this dilemma especially clear.

> Perhaps we need a moratorium on saying "the body." For it's also possible to abstract "the" body. When I write "the body," I see nothing in particular. To write "my body" plunges me into lived experience, particularity: I see scars, disfigurements, discolorations, damages, losses. (215)

Rich, in other words, recognizes that the body is itself a concept, an abstraction, but she is, I think, wrong in thinking we can overcome this abstraction if only we can make the body more particular, more specific, "my body," my scar, my color. We are back again to the bourgeois isolate, the monad so necessary to capitalist patriarchy: the specific, local, me cut off from any understanding of the operation of the social relations of exploitation.

This isolated individualism grounded in the concept of bodily particularity not only connects various feminists to each other but also to ludic postmodernism, as Nancy Miller clearly demonstrates in *Getting Personal*, when she ties Rich's claims for bodily specificity to Roland Barthes's "individualism" and her own "limited personalism" (xiv). Translating from an interview Barthes published just before his death, Miller tellingly points out that, "invited to comment on the new conformity and the failure of all protest movements in France, Barthes remarks that 'the only effective marginalism is individualism'" (xiii). Miller goes on to claim that this

> individualism—refashioned—could be understood as radical and not a return to a petit–bourgeois liberalism. Barthes writes: "The mere fact, for instance, of thinking my body until I reach the point at which I know that I can think *only* my body is an attitude that comes up against science, fashion, morality, all collectivities." (xiii)

Despite her assertions of radicality, Miller quite accurately shows that for all their differences—which she describes as "Rich's commitment to the political, to militancy, to the collective; Barthes's complete resistance to all of the above" (she quotes him as saying "I've never been a militant and it would be impossible for me to be one . . . I don't like militant language")— Rich and Barthes as well as herself are united by this bodily revitalization of the bourgeois monad in all its dehistoricized and isolated particularity. As Miller argues,

> [W]hat joins them . . . is the sense they share of the ways in which one's own body can constitute an internal limit on discursive irresponsibility . . . The autobiographical act . . . can like the detail of one's (aging) body, produce this sense of limit as well: the resistance particularity offers to the grandiosity of abstractions that inhabits what I've been calling the crisis of representativity. (xiii)

This idea of the body as resistance has become, by now, the commonplace of ludic and much post-al left thinking. Paul Julian Smith, for instance, in *The Body Hispanic*, argues that "resistance is to be found not in transcendental imperatives but in bodies and their very particular pleasures" (125).

But as Greg Dawes points out in his critique of Smith, "While this may indeed be a *symbolic*, micro-political form of resistance, it is difficult to see it as disturbing the status quo"—it is "an *individual* solution to a *socio-structural* problem." (13)

The concept of the body as antiabstract—whether in feminism, more generally, or in ludic feminism, specifically—continues to be trapped in the hierarchal dualism it is used to contest. The body is not so much a unifying experience as it is simply reversed—or subjected to an inversion, as Grosz calls her corporeal project (vii). Instead of privileging mind, contemporary feminism privileges body; instead of reifying abstractions, it reifies the concrete. The mind–body split still operates, and women are still located in the body, abstracted as *corporeality*. Only now it is women who confirm our place there in the name of change. Certainly such a move alters some of the *ideological* relations of privilege—it valorizes what the dominant order denigrates—but it does not overthrow the relations of production underlying oppressive dichotomies: it is merely a discursive reversal of the privileged terms. The exploitative and alienating relations of production that determine ideological binaries remain intact, only now they are concealed behind a false monism of the body. Grosz is quite aware of this impasse and attempts to find a discursive solution to this materialist contradiction—calling the new forms of binaries produced out of such a reversal noncontradictory (18).

We need to examine more closely how ludic feminists have articulated the body. What are the aporias and limits of their thinking? Jane Gallop's *Thinking through the Body* is a lesson text for us to use in addressing this question, not only because it is considered by many to be a primary discussion of the subject, but also, and perhaps more important, because its contradictions and confusions so vividly enact the contradictions over the body in ludic feminist theory at this historical moment.

In *Thinking through the Body*, Gallop contests what she calls the "mind–body split . . . exemplified in an opposition between philosophers and mothers" (8)—which is another (ludic) way of writing the opposition between idealists (philosophers) and materialists (mothers). Gallop begins by drawing on Roland Barthes to posit the body as a "bedrock given, a priori to any subjectivity."

> Not just the physical envelope, but other puzzling and irreducible *givens*, arising from the "body" if that word means all that in the organism which exceeds and antedates consciousness or reason or

interpretation. By "body," I mean here: perceivable givens that the human being knows as "hers" without knowing their significance to her. In such a way a taste for a certain food or a certain color, a distaste for another, are pieces of the bodily enigma. (13)

The body, in short, is a form of perceivable, that is, *sensuous* "givens"—the *matter*—of an organism. The primary marker of this material sensuousness, for Gallop, is predilection (or taste), which "indicates a bodily enigma; it points to an outside—beyond/before language" (16). In other words, it is through taste and predilection that we know (experience) the unrepresentable, uninterpretable bodily enigma: the material givenness of the body in excess of language, of textuality. In my discussion of theories of materialism, I have already argued that in ludic feminism the material—as outside of the discursive—is the matter of the body, which is perceived to be autonomous from the letter. Like Butler, Gallop has reached the boundary limit of poststructuralist theories of signification and seeks an outside, beyond/before language in the matter of the body. However, unlike Butler, who insists on the performativity, the citationality, of the materiality of the body, Gallop returns to a concept of the experience, the givenness of bodily materiality.

Gallop's text is fraught with contradictions: on the one hand, she asserts the poststructuralist position on textuality and the crisis of referentiality, and on the other hand, she affirms the body as referent and valorizes the experience of the body. For example, in discussing the work of Irigaray, she argues that

belief in simple referentiality is . . . politically conservative, because it cannot recognize that the reality to which it appeals is a traditional ideological construction, whether one terms it phallomorphic, or metaphysical, or bourgeois, or something else. The politics of experience is inevitably a conservative politics, for it cannot help but conserve traditional ideological constructs which are not recognized as such but are taken for the "real." (98–99)

This is a clear statement of the ideological politics of referentiality and experience, but the question is, does it also end up being a description of Gallop's own politics? Her critique of the phallus in Lacan, for example, is located in the experience of her own desiring body and her valorization of the "spectacular," "erect penis" (129–32). She argues against the Lacanian distinction between phallus and penis and for the penis as referent: according to Gallop, the *"phallus*, the signifier in its specificity . . . is always a reference to *penis"* (128). To disconnect penis and phallus—that is, to erase the penis as referent for the phallus—Gallop contends, leads to "one of the weaknesses of the Lacanian orthodoxy [which] is to render *phallus* transcendental, an originary name, not dependent on penis and its contingencies" (128). Yet she is also ambivalent about the referentiality of the penis, claiming that "the penis, through the contingencies of experience, can become the sign of the phallus—sign as opposed to referent" (128). She objects to what she sees as the Lacanian construction of an "unreachable, unspeakable referent" for the phallus and instead claims "to insist on bodily masculinity," on the "erect penis"—that is, on "the experience of heterosexuality" and on "locating thinking in a desiring body" as a way of rendering the "idealized, transcendent phallus . . . impossible" (129, 131, 132). In other words, Gallop both decries the conservative politics of referentiality and asserts the givenness, the materiality of the body as the excess-ive outside, the *referent* locating the idealized phallic signifier, thereby reinstating the very referentiality that she disclaims: a referentiality that, to use her own words, "conserves the traditional ideological constructs" of patriarchal capitalism and does not offer us a possibility for an emancipatory politics.

Gallop does not resolve these contradictions or overcome them by thinking through the body. Rather, she tries to simply dissolve them by uncritically juxtaposing quite opposing positions (like Grosz's notion of noncontradictory binaries) and declaring both equally valid: "[E]verything matters," she claims, "everything is real *and* everything is textual, mediated, interpretable" (90). This inclusive logic passes for complex, subtle thinking among ludic theorists, but it is little more than an evasion. It does not move beyond binaries (such as the mind–body split and idealism–materialism), nor does it overcome the contradictions in the social relations of production producing these ideological dichotomies and phallogocentrism. Grosz, for example, attempts to overcome binaries by declaring, "I will deny that there is the 'real,' material body on one hand and its various cultural and historical representations on the other. It is my claim throughout this book that these representations and cultural inscriptions quite literally constitute bodies and help to produce them as such" (x). The *represented* and *representation* are one and the same: a new mystical

monism or noncontradictory binary that solves a fundamental binary—
produced in the material relations—in terms of a discursive ludic imaginary.

Gallop's ludic logic simply elides contradictions. She claims that "to
read for and affirm confusion, contradiction is to insist on thinking in the
body in history. Those confusions mark the sites where thinking is literally
knotted to the subject's historical and material place" (*Thinking* 132). "Confusions," for Gallop, in–and–of–themselves, mark the historical, material
validity—the authenticity or "truth"—of her thinking through the body
simply because they are embodied. Embodied thinking, for Gallop, supposedly escapes the mind–body/idealism–materialism split, by being
simultaneously located in both sides of the divide, in all the conflicting confusions. The question of *how* or *why* the body (the "subject's historical and
material place") is socially produced in the way it is—the question of *how
and why these confusions, contradictions are produced; what are their effects and
their relation to the social totality (to the relations of production)*—is entirely
suppressed.

By uncritically affirming the givenness of these confusions, she reproduces the ideological binaries and obfuscation in which the subject is
already located. For Gallop these confusions—her inability, for example, to
"disentangle the desire for a male body . . . from . . . 'the Lacanian Phallus'";
the inability to know *"our* 'wants'"* because they "are alienated in language"—are the result of her "difficulty in moving beyond the phallus"
(132). Her difficulty, in short, is the impossibility of the ludic logic moving
beyond the cul–de–sac of an idealized matterism, which Gallop articulates
as the dichotomy between the "idealized phallus" and the reified penis as
"an attribute of an embodied subject" (132). Her ludic affirmation of confusions in the name of the "subject's historical and material place" becomes
an alibi for avoiding the difficult issues of the subject's actual historical and
material construction in the unequal relations of production. Gallop, in
short, posits a kind of "embodied" knowledge—an anticonceptual knowledge located in an uncritical affirmation of the experience of the desiring
body *as it is*—that celebrates the pleasures and perversities of desire without confronting either the social production or the consequences of those
desires. In contrast, a historical materialist reading contends that desires
are determined in the social relations of production. Similarly, it reads the
phallus as also a social entity. The meaning of the phallus, for historical
materialists, does not reside in any secure ground, such as the physicality
of the penis, nor in an idealized symbolization. The meaning of the phal-

lus—like the construction of desires—is basically a matter of power produced in the site of production.

No emancipatory politics can be based on an affirmation of confusion,
as Gallop claims. Rather, revolutionary struggle requires a clear and rigorous explanatory critique of the social production of the body, its desires
and pleasures. Gallop, however, asserts the ludic position of theory as play:
which, for her, embraces the endless, conflicting play, disruptions, and perverse pleasures of both significations and the excesses of "irrational bodily
materiality" (47). "Theorizing," Gallop says, "is precisely endless, an eternal reading of the 'body' as authorless text full of tempting, persuasive significance, but lacking a final guarantee of intended meaning" (13), because
the body, for Gallop is "insubordinate to man–made meaning" (18). The
ludic theory as play, as I argued in chapter 1, not only insists on incoherence but also reads conceptuality as a form of violence: the violence of
totalizing reason. It seems to be progressive in its opposition to rationalism,
but it validates the existing world and suppresses theory as a site of social
struggle—as a political practice.

The limits of a ludic feminist antitheory theory are especially evident
in Gallop's claims for the disruptive potential of the body. The conflict, as
she points out in her discussion of the Marquis de Sade, is "between rational order, that is, 'philosophy' and irrational bodily materiality . . . [T]here
is always some disorderly specific which exceeds the systematizing discourse" (47) and disrupts the mastering impulse of knowledge. Thus in her
discussion of *Justine* and *The New Justine* Gallop claims that

> The pedagogical examination which attempts to regulate the student
> on the basis of external rules, of the teacher's rules, is messed up by the
> *règles*, the rules, flowing from within. The bodily, fluid, material, fem-
> inine sense of *règles* [as "woman's bloody (menstrual) 'rules,'" or
> period] undermines the Sadian pederastic pedagogue's attempt at
> exact examination, at subjugation of the pupil to his rational, master-
> ful rules. (52)

This is a rather exemplary ludic reading of Sade: it exposes rationalism's
violence toward the body and celebrates the body's uncontainable excess.
But what is its political effectivity? It may disrupt the dominant rational
categories, but does it move beyond a local, subversive annotation? Does it
transform them? Gallop asserts that "the really disturbing violence is not
physical violence but the physical as it violates the rational categories that

would contain and dominate it" (18). In other words, in a very ludic move, she proposes that what is disturbing is not the violent exploitation and abuse of the body, but the body's violation of rational categories. She does not mean a revolutionary act of resistance by the body as agency of conscious social change, but rather the excessive, disorderly, irrational details and predilections of bodily matter (its fluids, menses), which passively escape rational logic. This celebration of the body as seepage, as an excessive deregulation of the "mechanics of the solid" (which is masculinism), is becoming the new commonplace for many ludic feminists following Irigaray (e.g., Grosz 203–4). The sensuous matter of female bodily fluids is deregulating not only because its materiality is considered to be outside language, as Gallop contends, but also because the body is seen as divided by its differences from itself: the body as fragmented, nomadic details that escape knowing.

In her reading of Sade, Gallop not only textualizes violence, rendering it discursive, but uses a concept that conceals its own conceptuality—the concept of the irrational, fragmented, desiring body in excess—to subvert the linguistic categories of discursive, rational violence. Through a parodic play and linguistic reversal she posits cognitive violence (reason) as the most oppressive and represents disturbing violence as liberating, in that it disrupts rationalism. In other terms, bodily seepage disrupts the mechanics of solids. She occludes what is historically and materially really disturbing violence: both physical violence (rape, torture, battery, killing, all frequently done to women) and *economic violence*—poverty, starvation, destitution, the denial of basic resources and dignity of life, but also the harsh conditions of the working day for most people. The economic and physical harm in patriarchal capitalism of, for example, the sex trade or migrant labor camps—both of which are reviving forms of indenture—become unintelligible in Gallop's ludic rewriting of violence, as does the violence of the threat of immediate layoffs and loss of essential health coverage.

We need to keep in mind that the texts Gallop is attempting to disrupt through the tropic excess and violence of a textual body are ones in which teachers and fathers sexually assault, physically abuse, cut up and murder mothers and daughters. This is not merely some pornographic fantasy, some libertarian rationalism gone amuck, this is the reality of innumerable women today. According to Catherine MacKinnon, only 7.8 percent of women in the United States have *not* been sexually assaulted or harassed in their lifetime (*Feminism* 6). Moreover, only 17 percent of all rapes and attempted rapes are committed by strangers; the majority, then, are committed by men the victims know (247). Women of color ("specifically . . . Black women") are raped four times as often as white women (82).³ Even more disturbing, domestic violence—physical, sexual, and verbal abuse of a woman by her (male) partner—is now so widespread that the American Medical Association has declared it "a public health problem that has reached epidemic proportions." The AMA asserts that "nearly one quarter of women in the United States 'will be abused by a current or former partner some time during their lives,'" and that "each year about four million women are assaulted by husbands or lovers . . . across all racial, ethnic, religious, educational and socioeconomic lines" (Carol Lawson, "Violence at Home: 'They Don't Want Anyone to Know,'" New York Times, 6 August 1992, C1). But the ludic textualization of violence that Gallop is articulating ends up erasing the political economy of the body in the social relations of exploitation and turning resistance into a tropic game.⁴

In what way does Gallop's excessive body transform the mind–body split or move beyond the materialism–idealism dichotomy? It merely reinscribes woman in the same place she has also been in the patriarchal hierarchy: in the unknowable, unrepresentable, bloody body opposing concepts. The anxiety over concepts in ludic postmodernism and humanist feminism is, to my mind, especially counterproductive for an emancipatory politics. This anticonceptuality is based on a rather idealist, Hegelian notion of the concept that Gayatri Spivak has helped to disseminate in postmodern feminism. Spivak critiques the concepts of property and money in Marx for "the concept's self–possession in its definition" ("Speculations" 32). The concept is seen as an identitarian approximation to an ideality—a "self–proximity" and "self–possession" that is then deconstructed into metaphor, into a differential chain of signifiers. But concepts are not self–proximating idealities; they are historical: they are, in short, the effects of the relations of production. As such, concepts are not only unavoidable; they are also a necessary means for social change. Thinking the body, thinking experience without concepts is impossible: concepts are the historical mediating frames of intelligibility through which we know the world. Experience—which is put forth as liberation from concepts/thinking by ludic feminists (such as Gallop) and cultural feminists (as different as Susan Griffin and Camille Paglia)—is itself intelligible only through the mediation of concepts. The issue here is not to romantically dismiss concepts but to question how we theorize and use them.

Gallop, however, does not so much contest concepts as abandon them. When she is forced to recognize that *jouissance* is a principle, that is, a concept, it loses its unsettling, disruptive features for her, and she essentializes it as "a 'general rule,' a 'fixed form' . . . 'strong, muscular, and phallic.'" In its place, she substitutes the weaker, "mediocre and unworthy word, pleasure" (*Thinking* 123–24), whose conceptuality is still veiled for her. Like Adrienne Rich, who abandons the concept of the body for the details of "my body," Gallop and other ludic feminists flee in the face of concepts, taking refuge in the autobiographical and the local, anecdotal details of differences: as if the local were not local precisely *because* of its relation to the political economy of the social totality.

I believe a politically effective feminism needs to refuse to essentialize theory and concepts as masculinist and dominating or to seek refuge in an anticonceptual, biological, biographical, textual, or performative body. Nor can it acquiesce to the pervasive and universal (in spite of its seeming particularity) ludic displacement of concepts and the theories they help construct into an indeterminate chain of differences. For theory is not in and of itself controlling; rather, it is the specific historical uses of theory and concepts in the struggles over exploitative socioeconomic relations that can be oppressive. And indeed, theory has been largely the province and property of the privileged, hegemonic gender, class, and race: concepts have been used in the name of a transhistorical reason to establish and maintain an oppressive patriarchal and racist hierarchy of knowledge. But we need to critique theory and show its historical limits and then reunderstand it as a site of class struggle. "Theory," as Marx says, can become "a material force" (*Early Writings* 251). It is especially important that we engage in the materialist retheorization of theory as the historical frames of intelligibility and conceptual strategies through which we know the operation of socioeconomic oppression in the world in which we live. For it is through the struggle over theory, the critique of the limits and uses of existing modes of knowing and the effort to construct new frames of intelligibility, that we can produce emancipatory knowledges (rather then merely subversive pleasures) and thus generate the new subjectivities necessary to transform the world.

It is, therefore, more productive to move beyond the upper–middle–class antirationalism of ludic critics to focus on a materialist feminist reunderstanding of concepts. As I discussed earlier, it is necessary that feminism not fetishize an identitarian Hegelian notion of concept as a moment of rational plenitude, in which the signifier and the signified correspond without difference. Instead, we need to understand concepts as struggle concepts: as historical, material practices through which the subject engages the social contradictions produced by the exploitation of surplus labor in patriarchal capitalism. Concepts, in other words, are historical matrices of intelligibility that display the relations among apparently disconnected entities and thus enable us to grasp the logic of exploitation underlying seemingly isolated experiences of individuals in culture. Concepts allow us to perceive the way experience is produced and thus empower us to change the social relations and produce new nonexploitative experiences and collective subjectivities. The aim of such conceptual knowledge, then, is not contemplative reflexivity or cognitive delight—the joys of knowing—but explanatory critique: a critique that explains the conditions of possibility of ideological and social practices in patriarchal capitalism and thus points to ways that they can be transformed by overthrowing the underlying relations of production. Concepts, contrary to the "bodism" of Gallop, are not simply philosophical, epistemological, and cognitive but rather are historical maps of social struggles, as they have been articulated in the arena of ideology and, more specifically, the scene of theory.

These struggles have meant that women, people of color, and oppressed classes historically have been restricted in their ability to produce theories and concepts as well as silenced by the dominant regime that excludes and discredits the knowledges they do construct. In large part they have been denied access to those cultural and institutional subject positions and practices—such as education (including literacy), philosophy, and theory itself—through which individuals are enabled to produce and legitimate new concepts (in short, to be heard). Patriarchal capitalism has used the practices of theory and institutions of knowledge to try to keep those whose labor it exploits from entering into the struggle over theory and producing new modes of intelligibility that would reconceptualize reality in nonexploitative ways. One of the most recent (and pernicious) forms of this deeducating of women, workers, people of color, and the (neo)colonized has been antitheoretical theory itself. In a politically damaging move, theory is used to argue against theory, to delegitimate concepts productive for social struggle and to dissuade women from theorizing, from offering explanatory critiques. As Nancy Hartsock has quite rightly pointed out:

> Somehow it seems highly suspicious that it is at the precise moment when so many groups have been engaged in "nationalisms" which involve redefinitions of the marginalized Others that suspicions

emerge about the nature of the "subject," about the possibilities for a general theory which can describe the world, about historical "progress." Why is it that just at the moment when so many of us who have been silenced begin to demand the right to name ourselves, to act as subjects rather than objects of history, that just then the concept of subjecthood becomes problematic? Just when we are forming our own theories about the world, uncertainty emerges about whether the world can be theorized. ("Foucault" 163–64)

Feminist thus must ask, what are the consequences of grounding feminist politics in a biological, textual, or performative body that is posited as anti-conceptual? Does this not reproduce the dominant regime of patriarchal capitalist ruling class and its control over theory, as well as perpetuate the historical marginalization of women from the struggle over concepts?

What was consciousness raising if not a grassroots struggle by women to contest the hegemonic concepts that concealed the relations of domination underlying their disparate experiences, their effort to produce new concepts that revealed the operation of patriarchal and capitalist social relations: concepts that constructed new subjectivities for women?[5] Feminism, in fact, has long had a history of producing and rearticulating struggle concepts—from sexual politics, sexual harassment, reproduction, wages for housework, date rape, and gender to the concept of Ms. itself. To ludically put Ms. "en abyme" (as Elam does) is to occlude and trivialize efforts to produce transformational knowledge. These struggle concepts have made it possible to make intelligible as historical and social effects those practices that have been previously thought of as inevitable, thus opening up those practices to the possibility of intervention and social change. The concept of date rape, for instance, allows women to make distinctions and thus help to transform those practices that deny women equal power in the production of agency and the determinations of their own bodies. Date rape marks a social relation in which the ideology of patriarchal capitalism blocks women from signifying their autonomy and resisting the sexual appropriation of their bodies. It operates by a perverse semiotics that translates a woman's "no" (her self-determination) into another signifier, "yes" (legitimating sexual appropriation and violence). No needs to be recognized not as the playful slippages of a signifier without a signified—a self-divided signifier that actually means its other (i.e., yes)—but as a signifier related through the social struggles of women to a decided signified: stop the violence!

Date rape, like many other feminist struggle concepts, has, of course, become the site of considerable contestation in the backlash against women and feminism, as is demonstrated by Katie Roiphe's *The Morning After* and the responses to it. One of the disturbing consequences of an anticonceptual, localizing ludic logic is that its antirationalism actually functions hand in glove with dominant power structures in the reaction against feminism and women.[6] By severing the connections of concepts, tropes, and practices to the larger social relations of exploitation, ludic postmodernism and feminism have played a significant role in opening up the ideological space for counterfeminism. Specifically, ludic logic has greatly facilitated the reactionary appropriation of feminist and leftist principles. In translating fundamental social relations into an indeterminate play of differences and signifiers without decidable referents—that is, without determinate connections to objective conditions, specifically the reality of the working day—ludic thinking makes it very easy to turn liberatory concepts and principles against the emancipation of women, often in the name of feminism. The ludic indeterminacy of meaning also makes it very difficult to argue against this appropriation and to insist on the social reality of exploitation that this counterlogic obscures.

Retrofeminism as Farce

In short, the antirationalism put forth as liberation from domination by ludic postmodernism, and more specifically, the anticonceptual bodism of ludic feminism, has generated its own supplementary others, which, like all supplements, involve "two significations whose cohabitation is as strange as it is necessary" (Derrida, *Grammatology* 144). The supplement of ludic feminism is that signification of feminism which, in the name of feminism, perpetuates the backlash against the fundamental principles and strategies of feminism as an emancipatory theory and practice. I would call this *retrofeminism* and include here the writings of such reactionary authors as Camille Paglia, Katie Roiphe, Naomi Wolf, Rene Denfeld, V-Girls, and Christina Hoff Sommers. In spite of their often vitriolic opposition to postmodernism (especially in the case of Paglia), these retrofeminists have clearly taken advantage of the ludic anticonceptuality and destabilization of meanings to assign quite different meanings to key feminist concepts: retromeanings that undermine the emancipatory effectivity of feminism.

If any concept is always already divided by its difference and no difference is more valid than its other, ludic logic not only validates all other meanings, it has no grounds for contesting them. The political and philosophical myopia of ludic feminism has made it impossible to evaluate differences. In other words, by isolating the play of differences from the fundamental structures of exploitation, ludic feminism renders all differences local, incommensurate, and ostensibly the same: that is, having the same or equal value because one cannot be privileged above the other. Ludic feminism is thus unable to choose (judge) between democracy and its other, fascism, except on the very limited grounds of the seemingly free play of differences. Recall, for example, Drucilla Cornell's ludic notion that "justice *remains,* as beyond our description, as the call of the Other" (*Beyond Accommodation* 113). Nor can ludic feminism challenge the way retrofeminists translate the very meaning of feminism into its other: turning a liberating feminism into victim feminism. They blame feminism for *causing* women's oppression, for producing victims. Wolf, for instance, in her counterfeminist *Fire with Fire,* claims victim feminism compels "women to identify with powerlessness even at the expense of taking responsibility for the power that they do possess"; instead she calls for women to "develop a vision of femininity in which it is appropriate and sexy for women to use power."

Similarly, retrofeminism turns the empowerment of women into its other. Empowerment no longer means the collective ability to transform economic, political, and cultural conditions affecting women because, according to Wolf, economic *opportunity* is already here. All that stands in women's way is their "lack of a psychology of female power to match their new opportunities." In short, all women need to do is realize their innate *feminine power.* What is variously called the "new-power" feminism, "sexual-agency" feminism, "sexual-empowerment" feminism comes down to variations on the notion of an innate, individual feminine power deriving from the female body, a primarily sexual, sexualized, and sexualizing feminine power. There is surprisingly little difference between retrofeminists like Wolf and such advocates of traditional femininity as Georgette Mosbacher (whose fame derives largely from her marriage to Texas oil millionaire and Republican power broker, Robert Mosbacher) and New Age feminists like Marianne Williamson—all three of whom appeared together to promote their books to a luncheon of society women at New York's 21 Club and to participate in the broad cultural move to counterfeminism.[7] As noted by two critics who witnessed the event, all three advocate the power of "sheer feminine will" in their books (Wolf's *Fire with Fire,* Mosbacher's *Feminine Force,* and Williamson's *A Woman's Worth*), and all are putting forth "empowerment as the ultimate form of do–it–yourself therapy"

(Futrelle and Tanenbaum 34, 33). The ways in which this new feminism of feminine, sexual empowerment reinforces the backlash against feminism is clearly demonstrated in *Esquire*'s popularization of these feminists and their counterconcepts as "do-me" feminism. *Esquire* asserts that "do-me feminists are choosing locker-room talk to shift discussion from the failures of men to the failures of feminism, from the paradigm of sexual abuse to the paradigm of sexual pleasure" (Friend 50).

The exemplar of backlash feminism is Camille Paglia, who has been one of the inaugurators of many of the positions of retrofeminism, notably attacks on victim feminism and on the struggle concept of date rape. But she is especially representative of ludic and retrofeminism's bodism: she is the *outrageous* exemplar of all the diverse claims for a power located in the female body: its sexuality and reproductive function, its hormones, fluids, and bodily rhythms. A number of popular genealogies of the new retrofeminism of sexual empowerment trace its main principles back to Paglia. Clare McHugh, for instance, writing on Naomi Wolf, argues that "*Fire with Fire* echoes the work of several prominent feminist thinkers, including most recently, the ideas advanced by Wendy Kaminer in her 1990 book *Fearful Freedom: Women's Flight from Equality* and by Camille Paglia, the author of *Sexual Personae*" (47). Tad Friend, in his *Esquire* article, argues that "do-me" or sexual-agency feminism draws the genealogy for its politics of sexual pleasure and criticism of feminism from "iconoclast" Paglia, with her "gay–male view," and the "gay–and lesbian movement" (55). He points out that "when the counterattack began to get attention, it was thanks to a woman who" viewed "sex as dark, violent, and shot through with male prerogative"—Paglia (55). This double genealogy of Paglia and the gay and lesbian movement is an especially telling one: for, one of the main inaugurators of a queer politics of pleasure and desiring is, of course, Gayle Rubin, and Paglia's discourse of sexual determinacy—her claims for the power of the procreative imperative—are the other of Gayle Rubin's insistence on the priority of lust.

At the core of all these diverse theories of female power and pleasure is the reification of the (anticonceptual, arational) female body: variously understood as natural, biological, experiential, or textual, but in all cases as innately sexual. Many of these critics naturalize the body and its sexuality as always already gendered, always already feminine. Female sexuality (whether articulated in terms of significations of desires or reproductive function) becomes the root of women's natures or subjectivities and sets the parameters of their lives. Many of these theories of feminine power participate in a retrofeminism that is both a backlash feminism and a New Age feminism: a burlesque of cultural or spiritual feminism in the conjuncture of late capitalist patriarchy. The outrageous performances of Camille Paglia are only the most powerful and perverse examples of this New Age, backlash retrofeminism, with its farcical resurrection of a mystical, biological, natural female power located in the particularities of women's sexual body: her bodily fluids, hormones, and reproductive functions.

Paglia vehemently declares herself a feminist: "The historical record will show that I am one of the great feminists of the twentieth century" (Wolcott 301), and she hails herself as the "successor to Simone de Beauvoir" (Stanfill 29). Her feminism combines individual libertarianism, legislative equality, and an unavoidable determinism of the biologically sex-differentiated body—determined especially by hormones. As she describes herself,

> I'm part of the Sixties generation that sought freedom of speech and self–expression and full development of our personalities. Feminism is a late outgrowth of the Sixties, and what I'm arguing is that while it began with laudable aims it quickly rigidified into a kind of ideology which has become oppressive and needs another revolution. So I as a feminist support 100 percent the feminist social activist agenda, which means that we must seek full legal and political equality for women. What I'm saying is that many of the problems that are going on between the sexes are rooted in biology, or in emotion, or in the psychodynamics of the mother–son relationship . . . things not subject to legislation. The failure to note this has led to a lot of chaos today. ("What's Wrong" 4)

She is determined to rectify this failure and reform feminism.

Thus, in the *name of feminism* and on behalf of the daemonic, procreative power of the female body, Paglia engages in ruthless attacks on feminists and feminism. Her writings and performances (public lectures, interviews, talk–show appearances) are deeply misogynist and rancorous. She is outrageously aggressive, even offensive, in asserting a bodily, biological basis for sex differences and the inescapable force of a brutal pagan female nature–body, which she uses to justify male domination, violence, and superiority in Western culture. She quite fiercely insists on fixing women back in place in the patriarchal hierarchy, in the same unknowing and unknowable bloody body opposed to concepts that Gallop gives us; only Paglia takes the rehearsal of the mind–body split much further, resurrecting the old truisms of woman as natural barbarian and man as civilizing creator. Paglia is, of course, positing an ahistorical notion of a pancultural patriarchy, thereby eclipsing the historical specificity of patriarchal capitalism.

Paglia is in the forefront of the cultural shock troops carrying out the backlash against feminism in patriarchal capitalism. As a self–proclaimed feminist carrying out a one–woman vendetta against feminism, she is doing the work of patriarchal capitalism to erase not only feminism but issues of emancipation and social justice. Paglia, in short, is a patriarchal feminist—one whose discourses reproduce patriarchal power, privilege, and exploitation in late capitalism. For most patriarchal feminists these effects are unintended, even resisted. Paglia, however, actively, intensively argues for the necessity, the civilizing value and greatness of patriarchy and against the "propaganda, tenth–rate crap" and "evil" of academic feminism ("What's Wrong" 4, 6).

Her burlesque of these positions has made Paglia a cultural sensation: not only through her outrageous writings but also because she, herself, has become a notorious text constantly performing these views.[8] While letters to the editor call her a "pit viper on a bad day" (Fitzgerald 36) and "the self–styled Morton Downey Jr. of American Academia" (Breitenberg 36) leading critics (mostly male) herald her as "an intellectual Joan of Arc" (Stanfill 30). Harold Bloom, whose own misogynous theory of literary history (*The Anxiety of Influence*) serves as a main theoretical basis for *Sexual Personae*, claims her book is "provocative, it is stimulating, it is brilliant, it is original, and it compels one to rethink the entire question of the literary representation of human sexuality" (Stanfill 30). In the pages of *Raritan*, which is quickly becoming the organ of neoconservative intellectuals, William Kerrigan writes, "[I]t is an amazing book, a rude punch in the tender stomach of the new sanctimoniousness" of feminism and political correctness (134–35). Both Kerrigan and the reviewer for the *Nation* find "the time is right for such a book" (Edmundson 897).

Many feminists, however, have been caught off guard by Paglia's "scorched–earth attack" (Teachout 7). Instead of thinking the time is right for Paglia's texts—with their outmoded notions of biological femaleness, Medusan mothers, natural hierarchies, and apocalyptic rhetoric—most have comfortably thought the time had past when such ideas would be taken seriously, not to mention celebrated in leading cultural forums. Feminists have, by and large, treated her as a cultural joke—a buffoon of patriarchy whose silliness is mostly unintended because she is a premodernist confused in the intricate labyrinth of postmodernity (which she rants against at every opportunity).[9] But Paglia, I would argue, is not so much premodern as a perverse inversion—an outrageous, quite effective, and very telling burlesque—of the assumptions and strategies informing ludic postmodernism. Paglia is the other of ludic postmodern feminism. Her impact on the new generation of retrofeminists, from Naomi Wolf to Susie Bright, is considerable. Yet feminist theorists have treated her as irrelevant for the most part.

The common feminist response has thus been to dismiss Paglia as "crackpot anti–feminism" (Caryn James, "Feminine Beauty as a Masculine Plot, *New York Times*, 7 May 1991, C18). Sandra Gilbert sums up the feminist astonishment at Paglia's prominence: "The strangeness of [her] book is such that I would not have expected it to be a subject of debate . . . It has the quality . . . of an idiot savant" (Stanfill 30). The point, however, is to examine the cultural politics of this strangeness—what historical, economic, and political forces produce it?

More often than not, feminists have refused to read Paglia at all, in effect to ignore her. Bloom recounts a telling story to Stanfill of two women at Yale, "one a faculty member, the other a graduate student," who were "so deeply offended" by *Sexual Personae* that they returned the book to the bookstore, demanding their money back, because "it was ideologically unacceptable" (24). Feminists cannot afford to ignore Paglia, to return her texts unread. Instead, we need to ask what are the political effects of such crackpot extremism, such strangeness, even idiocy? The issue is not whether her texts are ideologically acceptable (they are unquestionably offensive and misogynist), but what are their ideological uses; what work are they doing for patriarchal capitalism? In short, why are Paglia's text and Paglia herself having such cultural resonance at this moment, when a post–cold war conservatism is triumphing and feminism is itself increasingly turning toward an affirmative cultural studies focused on individual libidinal and bodily liberation?

Patriarchal capitalism is currently mounting a powerful counterassault on feminism, as Susan Faludi's *Backlash* so massively details—from the raw violence of the pro-life campaigns and much of the media to the more nuanced writings of counterfeminists and to attacks on political correctness. Paglia is in the vanguard of the cultural and intellectual post–cold war battle against feminism. Her texts demonstrate the highly effective strategy that a postmodern, patriarchal, late capitalism is using to resecure gender divisions of labor and unequal access to social resources.

Feminism has effectively discredited much of the commonsense and taken-for-granted assumptions in the ideology of patriarchal capitalism in the West. Ideology in its post-Althusserian meaning is a system of cultural representations and sense making through which we (mis)recognize and live in the world. Thus in order to reproduce and secure its meanings and constructions of reality, the ideology of patriarchal capitalism has to repair the damage feminism has done to its fundamental concepts; it has to resurrect the truisms and stereotypes of its common sense as natural and inevitable. But it cannot do so simply as a return to more traditional ideological modes. Late capitalism has been discarding those aspects of its ideology that have become dysfunctional. In their place, it is appropriating ludic postmodern forms and strategies, such as irrationalism, parody, excess, sensationalism, sensuousness, the primacy of the libidinal body, and fragmented, multiple subjectivities, to resecure its hegemony.

Paglia is instrumental in this project of ideological renaturalization. The very crackpot extremism of her texts articulate a strategy of *the logic* of the *outrageous*, which is the dangerous supplement of the ludic logic of the excessive. In this logic, sensationalizing, parodic assertions revive a nostalgia for the power of patriarchy in capitalism, resurrect worn-out or discredited assumptions of gender divisions and inequality, and represent these as natural and inevitable. While not new, this logic is newly privileged in postmodern patriarchy as a primary practice, and Paglia is one of its exemplary practitioners. The logic of outrageousness is the supplementary other of the ludic logic of excess: both try to subvert the prevailing cultural meanings, and they do so by asserting an extreme or excessive individualism or particularism that destabilizes the clarity and dependability of an established meaning or stand. In ludic theory, excessive particularism leads to undecidability. In the logic of outrageousness, it leads to a farcical revival of irrationalism: especially the overthrow of progressive meanings by turning them into their obverse and the literalization of discredited ideological myths and clichés.

We can see the logic of outrageousness operating not only in Paglia's revival of sexual determinism but also in, for example, the pro-life movement's farcical replaying of the 1960s sit-ins and protest demonstrations, and in such films as *The Silence of the Lambs*, which literalizes sexual transvestism. The film's brutalization of women is so extreme and sensational (skinning women and donning their skins as a form of transvestite dress) that ordinary sexual violence such as date rape seems not very serious by comparison. The outrageous does the social work of rendering everyday violence natural and commonplace.

Paglia claims her method in *Sexual Personae* "is a form of sensationalism" (xiii), and her readers are well aware that her cultivation of the outrageous informs all her texts (including her own actions—several interviewers report that she "beat up" a male student, or as she says, "kick[ed] him in the ass," after he insulted her when she was teaching at Bennington College (B. Rich 32; Stanfill 27). Her writing and speaking are a series of proclamations and provocations, serving up a sensationalized validation and burlesque of nearly every patriarchal myth, cliché, and truism feminism has argued against. Sensationalism, then, is the name of the strategy Paglia uses to *represent* the metaphysics of masculinity: to literalize the tropes of patriarchal capitalism. They are all here, circulating throughout the book: the monstrous mother-destroyer (as the Great Mother, Medusa, Gorgon); the misogynist identification of women with a primeval, destructive nature and man with intelligence, as the creator and preserver of beauty, order, and civilization itself. The book is permeated by all the old gendered binaries disputed by feminists and poststructuralists alike. The male is Apollonian, culture, art, order, form, conceptualization, sky cult; the female is Dionysian, nature, primeval, chthonian, miasmic, formless, bodily, earth cult. Moreover, she not only valorizes capitalism as "an art form," but she also describes it as a masculine, patriarchal achievement, "an Apollonian fabrication to rival [female] nature" (38).

Paglia literalizes misogynist myth, reasserting the truth and naturalness of claims feminists have shown to be outrageous fabrications. In fact, she opens *Sexual Personae* by stressing the "truth in sexual stereotypes" (xiii). The stereotype—the embodiment of outrageousness—is for her the articulation of the (sexual) instinct of the *volk*. She thus claims, "Mythology's identification of woman with nature is correct," (12) or "[M]an justifiably fears being devoured by woman, who is nature's proxy" (16), or again, "Nature gives males infusions of hormones for dominance in order to hurl them against the paralyzing mystery of woman" (24). Feminists have treated such utterances as cultural jokes because feminists have so fully exposed them as constructions of ideology. Patriarchal capitalism can continue to assert such representations only by embracing their outrageousness, flaunting them in the face of feminist disapproval, and thus reviving their cultural circulation.

Paglia represents these stereotypes of male and female nature in a farcical and parodic manner that reinvigorates them. Because these are the commonplace assumptions of patriarchal capitalism, she enlivens the already familiar by turning them into burlesque, making them seem witty, original, and even fresh to those who depend on these assumptions for their (mis)recognition of reality. One of the more notorious examples is Paglia's farcical resurrection of a bodily, biological "explanation for the male domination of art, science, and politics, an indisputable fact of history" (p. 17), and I will quote at some length to give a full sense of Paglia's outrageous logic. Male domination, for Paglia, is

> based on an analogy between sexual physiology and aesthetics. I will argue that all cultural achievement is a projection, a swerve into Apollonian transcendence, and that men are anatomically destined to be projectors . . . The male projection of erection and ejaculation is the paradigm for all cultural projection and conceptualization . . . Women have conceptualized less in history not because men have kept them from doing so but because women do not need to conceptualize in order to exist . . . Culture is man's iron reinforcement of his ever-imperiled private projections . . .
>
> Concentration and projection are remarkably demonstrated by [male] urination . . . [which] really *is* . . . an arc of transcendence . . . Women, like female dogs, are earthbound squatters. There is no projection beyond the boundaries of the self . . . Without [man's concentration and projection], woman would long ago have absorbed all of creation into herself. There would be no culture, no system, no pyramiding of one hierarchy upon another. (17, 20–21)

Clearly this is not philosophical argument nor history but a pastiche of argument as bizarre farce—Marx's statement that history repeats itself "the first time as tragedy, the second as farce" (Marx, *Eighteenth Brumaire* 15) is quite apt for reading Paglia. She not only turns the conventional notions of natural sexual difference, grounded in biological bodies, into farce, she also burlesques traditional concepts of feminine and masculine. It is ironic that feminism now has to struggle against the resurgence of many of patriarchy's most pernicious assumptions and stereotypes—this time as farce. But we should not delude ourselves: farce has socially real and politically dangerous effects.

It is the social function of outrageousness to justify the social injustices and exploitation of patriarchal capitalism; it confirms and validates the debasement and objectification of women and resecures the gender divisions of labor. By so relentlessly identifying women with a violent, destructive, formless, miasmic nature and base animality manifested in their bodies, Paglia can proclaim women the negators and destroyers of culture. In order to create art or social order, the procreative (female) nature/body must be violently suppressed and abandoned. Thus she sees male homosexuality, as she argues in *Sexual Personae*, as "the most valorous of attempts to evade the femme fatale and to defeat nature" and create culture. For woman to create, on the other hand, she must engage, according to Paglia's reading of Emily Dickinson in *Sexual Personae*, in "self-hermaphrodization . . . an emptying out of female internality" and in "masculinizing her(self) into abstraction" (641)—which Paglia valorizes as a sadomasochistic undertaking in Dickinson. Paglia is reproducing here the same dichotomy between the masculine conceptuality and the anticonceptual female body, that we find in Gallop and other feminists.

Through such representations, Paglia erases the entire history of women's labor, denying the reality that patriarchal capitalism is built on the exploitation of women's productivity. The only labor, the only power, Paglia allows women is that of birth, and even that is degraded. Negating women's creative and productive labors, she represents culture as a male creation, as irrevocably patriarchal, and ends up justifying the inevitability and value of patriarchy itself. "Everything here," she tells Stanfill, "the whole thing is a creation of men. And the feminists are really deluded, with their heads up their ass, if they don't know this" (28).

As bizarre as these statements are, eminently respectable presses and journals legitimate them by publishing them. They are championed by some of the most prominent literary critics. Chief among these is her mentor, Harold Bloom, who tells Stanfill, "I am not yet ready to pass on the banner to her, but she looks to me like the best candidate around for that inevitable moment when the aged Bloom must totter off the mountain and cast the mantle of Elijah on the next person" (25).

Farce is also its own mode of validation: it is a performative speech act that puts these scandalous proclamations beyond critique-al scrutiny. How can we take seriously a history based on ejaculation and the biology of urination? We do not need to. The logic of the outrageous works by preventing serious attention, by displacing critique. It works by titillating, eroticizing, and enthralling; it is a pornographic logic of simulated experience. Just as the excitement of an erotic image compels the viewer to suspend critical judgment so as not to interfere with the pleasure of the experience, so the pleasure of Paglia's texts reproduces the pornographic elation in the degradation of women through a sensational and imagistic prose. It is important to note here how closely related the strategies of Paglia's outrageous, pornographic logic of pleasure are to the parodic, libidinal logic of ludic postmodernism, which similarly displaces any critical, conceptual understanding by privileging the sensuous, visual pleasure of the text and the ironic, subversive, lustful pleasures of bodily acts. In both cases—despite the very different intent—the displays of pleasure simply redeploy the existing relations of exploitation in new ways. How subversive and liberating are ludic performances, pleasure, and affirmations of the libidinal in their effects? What difference is there, in effect, between Gallop's valorization of the titillating pleasures of (textual) excessive bodies in her readings of the Marquis de Sade and Paglia's outrageous valorization of excessive, destructive female bodies and the "profanation and violation [that] are part of the perversity of sex" (*Sexual Personae* 24)?

Because many feminists see exploitation rather than pleasure in this pornographic logic of the outrageous, it may be difficult for us to see how effective it is in titillating and enthralling readers, recuperating them uncritically into a series of pernicious assumptions of patriarchal capitalism. But we need only turn to the reviews of *Sexual Personae* to see this effect. One especially dramatic demonstration is Duncan Fallowell's piece in *The Spectator*. He is unable to critically evaluate, or even, as he admits, review the book; he can "only attempt to digest it" (34). He is seduced by the book: "She sexualises everything and the result is a revelation. Our entire culture emerges throbbing and moist from beneath its marmoreal carapace of critical highmindedness." The review, then, consists of a litany of sensuous descriptions of Paglia—the person and text collapsing into one "enthralling" text—"she can be acute ... devastating ... spectacular ... disturbing" and so on. Each of these is followed by a quote from one of her "magnificent extemporisations." Thus he says, "She can be breathtaking: 'There is no female Mozart because there is no female Jack the Ripper.'" He consumes (and in turn reproduces) such statements without any critical or moral awareness; he simply relishes and savors the titillating pleasure of her sensational claims for male superiority and articulations of female debasement and degradation.

Fallowell's reading of Paglia abandons critique for the pleasures of experience. In doing so, it points up the danger in some feminists' own willingness to give up critique (as masculinist) and instead to found feminism on experience alone. Paglia's text and the way it is read show how urgently feminism needs critique not experience in order to reread the culture of late-capitalist patriarchy.

Paglia's texts reproduce the latent logic of the ideology of postmodern patriarchal capitalism: the deployment and expansion of a *pornographization* of superstructural forms to promote the social relations of exploitation. The basic strategy in Paglia's texts is a *pornography of ideas.* Like pornography, she uses eroticization, scandal, titillation, and fetishization to establish gendered/sexual hierarchies of domination, violence, and exploitation. This is especially clear in her fascination with sadomasochism, especially the Marquis de Sade. Her fetishization of sadomasochism and Sade is simply the other side of the ludic feminist fetishization, as in Gallop or in current ludic modes of lesbian sadomasochism (Meese, Rubin): both reify the violent excesses and extremes of libidinal libertarianism. For Paglia sadomasochism permeates Western art and culture since romanticism, particularly in its decadent moments. She then extends this excessive, sexually violent decadence to all of late romanticism and even to American romanticism, thus enabling her to reread Emily Dickinson as "the female Sade" (624).

Following Sade, she finds that "violence is the authentic spirit of mother nature" (235) and that hierarchies and domination are inevitable—man's way of defending himself against violent, devouring mother nature. This leads Paglia to condemn those (like Rousseau) who "seek freedom by banishing social hierarchies" and to proclaim "My theory: when political and religious authority weakens, hierarchy reasserts itself in sex, as the archaizing phenomenon of sadomasochism" (234). This is a pornographic logic that absolves the dominator from responsibility for exploitation and violence. It subverts historical reality, erasing the actuality of hierarchies of gendered class differences resulting from the social relations of production and sexual divisions of labor. Instead she grounds hierarchies and differences in innate bodily hormones, in the opposition of female and male natures.

I have pointed out some of the complicities between Paglia's avowed antipostmodernism and ludic postmodernism. But I want to stress here that the emphasis in both on sensual experience (whether textual or bodily); on parody, outrageousness and excess—with their concurrent abandonment of conceptuality and critique—have helped to reinscribe repression and exploitation in social relations. Paglia and Gallop are each other's supplement: they are constitutive of each other. There is little difference in effect, for example, between Gallop's Foucauldian erasure of the dominated and Paglia's naturalization of the inevitability of domination: both render irrelevent the revolutionary struggle against domination and for emancipation.

Paglia's retrotheory is the supplement of Cornell's utopian theory. Both violently erase the material and historical: one idealizes the past and the other fantasizes about the future. What is erased is the present—the temporality in which capitalism intensifies its efforts to increase the rate of profit by extracting the free labor of others. Retrotheory, then, is a ludic reversal, an outrageous blaming the victim, in which female/mother nature is held responsible for the violence and social injustice against women, and patriarchy is presented as women's protector and benefactor. Paglia is quite specific about this in her comments on rape: as she says in *Sexual Personae*, "Rape is a mode of natural aggression . . . Rape is male power fighting female power . . . [and] Society [that is, patriarchy] is woman's protection against rape, not, as some feminists absurdly maintain, the cause of rape" (*Sexual Personae* 23). Or as she says in the interview, "What's Wrong with Feminism?": "[M]en have provided material sustenance and protection and security to women and children throughout history. The number one barrier against women being raped was in fact men" (6). This reversal is no small feat: Paglia turns the entire historical understanding of women's position within patriarchy upside down in a bizarre burlesque of the actual conditions of women's lives. She depicts women as desiring and needing patriarchy and ends up proclaiming: "[I]t is patriarchal society that has freed me as a woman" (*Sexual Personae* 37).

Perhaps even more damning, Paglia eliminates the possibility and even necessity of social change. For Paglia, "[T]here are no nonexploitative relationships" (*Sexual Personae* 2). Freedom—the elimination of social hierarchies—only unleashes the inherent violence of nature. This is an apologia for a new post–cold war fascism: if exploitative relations are natural and inevitable, our only protection from them are social hierarchies, like Apollonian patriarchy, which constrain the sexual violence of (female) nature and subsume it into making cultural things, order, and beauty. She makes no bones about her fascination with strong, charismatic personalities and the totalitarian, "fascist political power" of ancient Egypt (59), grounding Western civilization. Nor does she conceal her contempt for liberal social freedoms and the democratic common man, represented by Charlie Chap-

lin's Little Tramp (171). Her Alice-through-the-looking-glass reasoning justifies the way things are and condemns any need for change and social justice, since change will only make things worse.

The appeal of Paglia's pornographic logic, its ability to revive discredited concepts, and the success of *Sexual Personae* all suggest that outrageousness will become an increasingly common strategy to use against
feminism and other radical struggles for social justice. Paglia proves that
excess and outrageousness are commodifiable and highly profitable: the
book has by now gone through several reprintings in hardcover at Yale,
and the paperback rights were "bought by Vintage for a rumored $65,000,"
according to Stanfill, which as she notes is "an unusually high amount for
a university press book" (24). Yale's publication and promotion of Paglia's
text is an instance of the complicity of the knowledge industry with the
patriarchal capitalist social order; while university presses frequently
refuse to publish radical critiques on the ground that they are not scholarly,
Yale has no problem publishing Paglia's outrageous text. Moreover her
paperback publisher has also brought out a collection of her occasional
essays, including her attacks on feminism, called *Sex, Art, and American
Culture.*

Paglia's texts as well as those of other retrofeminists are part of the
current crisis in feminism over the very nature of feminism for a new generation—or perhaps more accurately, a new configuration—of women:
what is being called third-wave feminism. While this term is commonly
associated with the younger feminist writers and activists, like Susan
Faludi and Rebecca Walker, and especially with such new radical activist
groups as WAC (Women's Action Coalition), WHAM (Women's Health
Action and Mobilization), as well as other groups like Third Wave (sponsored by the Ms. foundation; see Cathering Manegold, "No More Nice
Girls: Growing Wave of Radical Feminists Do Not Just Want to Have Fun,"
New York Times, 12 July 1992, 25, 31), Paglia violently rejects such connections (particularly to Faludi) and instead proclaims, "*I* am the Third Wave"
(Wolcott 303). She fashions herself as the champion of a new feminism—
manifested by Madonna—and seeks to "reform feminism, to critique it
from within" ("What's Wrong" 4). And indeed, as I have already indicated,
she has had considerable impact on the emergence of a backlash feminism
that is highly critical of feminism. Paglia's criticisms of feminism, postmodern discourses, and progressive politics, however, are hysterical, vitriolic diatribes that rely heavily on ad hominem attacks and character assas-

sination.[10] She openly declares, "I'm part of the backlash. But the backlash is not coming from feminism's success but rather from feminism's excesses, its failure to change and critique itself" (Paglia and Gordon 79). Paglia, in short, criticizes academic feminism for inducing "a posture of resentment toward the world and a resentment towards history and culture, so that you are forced to see culture as a simplistic scenario of male oppression and female victimage" ("What's Wrong" 6).

What is fundamentally at stake in the rejection of feminism as victim feminism by Paglia and other retrofeminists is the conviction that there is no oppression—as Ruby Rich states, "When pressed, she admits that she can't really conceive of oppression as an operative category in the U.S. today" (30). Retrofeminism is largely the province of the privileged, who—in their localized experience—indeed find little oppression. For most, what matters is the state of their own pleasures and desires. Catherine MacKinnon is quoted by *Esquire* as saying, "The sexual-agency people don't want equality, they just want better orgasms" (Friend 56). By denying oppression, retrofeminists and other counterfeminists deny that women are being exploited—sexually, economically, socially, in short, by anything other than their own (feminist-induced) psychology of powerlessness. They thus deny the need for any social change: all that is required, as Wolf makes clear, is a feminine will. Paglia simply dismisses women as agents of social change of any kind. As she tells Stanfill, "[W]omen are content with things as they are. Women lack the violent aggression to change, to revolutionize" (28). The reason, of course, is our biological bodies: "[P]hysically and psychologically, [women] are serenely self-contained" because they do not ejaculate or project their fluids beyond the boundaries of the self.

What then is feminism for Paglia if it is not resistance to gender and sexual oppression or the struggle to transform patriarchal capitalism? The answer is Madonna:

Madonna is the true feminist. She exposes the puritanism and suffo-
cating ideology of American feminism, which is stuck in an adolescent
whining mode . . . Madonna has a far profounder vision of sex . . . both
the animality and artifice . . . [she] embodies the eternal values of
beauty and pleasure . . . Through her enormous impact on young
women around the world, Madonna is the future of feminism.
("Madonna—Finally, a Real Feminist," *New York Times*, 14 December
1990, A28)

Paglia's vision of feminism is a burlesque of the ludic feminist valorization of the feminine and reification of a highly individualistic libertarianism, privileging the erotic pleasures ("beauty") and consumption (commodification) of the sexed/sexual body. Her uncritical affirmation of Madonna as the liberatory, pleasureful exemplar of feminism and her exclusion of issues of oppression and economic exploitation is little different from the antimaterialist, postpolitical stance of an affirmative, feminist cultural studies, as in Constance Penley's popular study of a genre of fan magazines on *Star Trek* called "slash zines" because they eroticize the relationship between Kirk and Spock and are designated by a code with a slash, "K/S." Her analysis of the creation and consumption of slash zines is a pleasureful affirmation of "what women *do* with popular culture, how it gives them pleasure, and how it can be consciously and unconsciously reworked to give them *more* pleasure" (488).

Paglia's feminine/feminist burlesque is primarily an alibi for patriarchal capitalism. It resurrects the bourgeois monad in its vehement individualism: as she tells Steven Petrow in the *Advocate:* "I despise the idea of community—period" (76). She dismisses the revolutionary collective politics of Marxism because "Marxism is a flight from the magic of person and the mystique of hierarchy. It distorts the character of western culture, which is based on charismatic power of person" (*Sexual Personae* 36). Capitalism, on the other hand, with its "teeming multiplicity of . . . products is an Apollonian correction of nature . . . Our shiny chrome automobiles, like our armies of grocery boxes and cans, are extrapolations of hard, impermeable western personality" (37). Paglia's feminist manqué is profoundly antiemancipatory, miring women in an alienating individualism and subjecting them to the tyranny of the "intractable physical laws of her own body . . . [T]he female body is a chthonian machine . . . [I]t has one mission, pregnancy" (10).

It is not enough, however, to criticize Paglia; we also need to critique-ally engage her feminist defenders and to expose the consequences of their underlying assumptions.[11] One especially telling defense—a letter to the editor written by Jane Gorman—is worth quoting and interrogating at some length, for she finds a revolutionary potential in Paglia's discourse. Gorman condemns feminist critiques, such as the one I am offering here, for their refusal to incorporate the wisdom of her text or "to integrate the messages from the unconscious." She argues that "Paglia's associational thinking and her access to the underbelly of things places her in a revolutionary position in relation to a feminist ideology characterized by worn definitions of power, facile dualism and a refusal to wallow in the mire (or dance with the angels) of the unconscious" (4). It is worth noting here the parallels to Cornell's calls for a subversive, utopian feminism based on a "new choreography of sexual difference" (*Beyond Accommodation* 96). Obviously Cornell would oppose Gorman's biologism, but there is certainly a shared commitment on the part of both critics to dance with the unconscious, the unrepresentable feminine as the utopian and revolutionary project of feminism—a supplementary relation, in short, between Cornell's maverick feminism and Gorman's revolutionary feminism. Gorman supports Paglia's claims that patriarchy created civilization "in reaction to the incredible subterranean power of women" and "freed [Paglia] as a woman." She is "amazed" that feminists cannot seriously engage Paglia's idea that the history of civilization is based on ejaculation and the biology of urination and sees this refusal as a denial of difference. She then claims that "the rejection by feminists in the Academy of the gravity and the glory of the female connection to rhythms, blood, earth, swamps, and smells results in a disembodied and reactive vision. Their denial of women as creative destroyers of the projectile artifices of culture is antirevolutionary." While Gorman does not recognize the large number of academic and ludic feminists who also celebrate this "glory" as a subversion of masculine rationalism, masculine culture, her New Age retrofeminism is, again, supplementary to their ludic valorization of the "leaking," seepage of the female body and its fluids (Grosz 203–4).

The contradictory logic both of this defense and Paglia's own discourse are historical and symptomatic of a retrofeminism that attempts to overcome the revolutionary aspects of socialist and materialist feminism by reifying experience in the body—the seemingly irrevocable imaginary and psychic determinations created by anatomical differences ("women squat and women inwardly lubricate. Men play their piss and jism trajectory games," in Gorman's words). Gorman, like Paglia, substitutes a matter of the body for materialist social relations based on women's labor and thereby erases the exploitation of both women's bodies and their labor. This reification of the body and bodily matter, of course, is not confined to New Age retrofeminism but, as I have made clear by now, circulates throughout feminism, from Gayle Rubin's valorization of bodily lust to Hartsock's and Harding's affirmations of female bodily fluids.

What is at stake here is nothing less than the articulation of revolutionary feminism: is it to be theorized in terms of the subterranean and the unconscious—Cornell's unrepresentable feminine—as these are mystified

in the figure of the body, or is revolutionary feminist knowledge and political practice to be understood in the historical materiality of the social relations of production shaping and determining women's bodies and their
experiences, their lived relations—conscious and unconscious—to their
bodies? In short, is feminism becoming "fem-mystic" (or "fem-mystique")
rather than critically producing itself as a socially transformative political
practice?

Gorman's claims for a revolutionary aspect to Paglia's texts raise the
issue of revolution over what and for whom. She, like many ludic critics,
seems to think that the purpose of revolution is to release the forces of the
unconscious, the forces of desire. In other words, the purpose of revolution,
for Gorman, as for ludic and retrofeminists alike, seems to be nothing more
than psychic (spiritual) enrichment of the monadic bourgeois individual in
late capitalism. Such a revolution will not change the system of exploitation
in patriarchal capitalism one bit: it will not end the suffering of women; it
will not stop the global social, economic, sexual oppression and violence
against women. It merely ends up protecting these practices by diverting
attention away from the structured relations of exploitation, especially the
gender division of labor, toward the seemingly pregiven, transcendental—
natural or textual—experiences (pleasures) of the body: "the gravity and
the glory of the female connection to rhythms, blood, earth, swamps, and
smells." In terms of the fundamental consequences of their theories for
social change, there is little difference between ludic and retrofeminists.
Their different theories are much more similar than they would first appear
to be. While ludic feminists tend to textualize women's relation to the particularities of the female body, its rhythms, fluids, desires (e.g., Kristeva's
semiotics of the "chora") and retrofeminists try to naturalize and literalize
this connection, many ludic feminists, like Gallop and Rubin, have begun
to embrace these two conflicting ways of valorizing women's embodiment.
This has led, as we saw in Gallop's arguments, to a fetishization of conflict,
confusion, and incommensurability in order to justify holding such contradictory positions.

Retrofeminism and ludic feminism shift the site of struggle from
socioeconomic emancipation to the sensuous maximizing of bodily pleasures and the libidinal liberation of the individual. They displace the social
collective with the bourgeois monad and erase the political through the
violent reinscription of the body. Yes, violent. Because no matter how feminine and antimasculine such an exquisitely embodied form of self salva-

tion may seem, its salvation and pleasures are only at the cost of suppressing the harsh realities of those millions of women (in our own cities and globally) who do not have the luxury of such bodily connections but are forced by economic necessity to rent their uteruses and sell their eggs, their kidneys, and other body parts to feed themselves and their children. Such self-salvation is not, by any means, a societal transformation: in its celebration of the exquisite, subterranean pleasures of the individual in her body (whether understood as nature or semiotics), it violently excludes any understanding, or even awareness, of the way women's bodies and unconscious are historically produced *and* exploited by the social relations of production.

This New Age, retrofeminism in "respectful and ambivalent *relationship* with the formless, the miasmic and the animal nature of being," as Gorman puts it, a feminism that seeks to "wallow in the mire (or dance with the angels) of the unconscious" (4) is not a feminism that can produce the radical historical and social understanding of systematic relations of exploitation that operate across diverse societies. But then neither can ludic feminism, with its affirmative relation to the unconscious of desire, lust, and unrepresentable feminine *jouissance*. Neither form of feminism can effectively intervene to end the killing and disappearance of 100 million women globally through such social practices as infanticide; denial of adequate food and health care to female (but not male) children, and bride or dowry murders (Sen; N. Kristof, "Stark Data on Women: 100 Million Are Missing," *New York Times*, 5 November 1991, C12). The political unconscious operating to maintain these social practices is not a subterranean fear of women's natural, miasmic reproductive powers, nor is it the semiotic suppression of sexual desires and differences. Rather, it is the effect of the ideology of patriarchal capitalism as it harnesses the unconscious fears and desires of individuals, recruiting them—women and men alike—to act on behalf of the socioeconomic interests of the relations of production, specifically the gender divisions of labor and access to social resources. (After all, it is most often women who are compelled to murder and starve their own daughters.)

What Gorman, Paglia, and other retrofeminists evoke as a revolutionary feminism is simply counterrevolutionary: a concerted, reactionary effort to take back the gains of feminism in the last several decades. What is tired and worn-out is not the feminist use of power or the politically necessary recognition of the historical reality of binaries: revolutionary feminism abandons its materialist understanding of the historical categories of oppressor and oppressed and its struggle against the exploiter at its own peril. What is tired and worn-out is reification of the body and natural/textual experience, not only by retrofeminism but also by ludic feminism, both of which rework the centuries-long patriarchal appropriation of women's bodies and labor that has always been used to put women in their place, that is, to place them in nature so the culture of men can proceed without any serious threat from women. Such reification of bodily experiences excludes women from social relations and from any agency in social transformation. New Age feminism, in particular, reduces women to primordial miasmic formlessness, turning them into what Maria Mies calls "the last colony" (Mies, Bennholdt-Thomsen, and von Werlhof) so that the civilization built on the real, material, social oppression of women's labor and the raw material of their bodies can continue.

In the name of women's mystic, subterranean, amorphous, procreative, natural power, such a counterrevolutionary feminism negates women's social power. Women's power does not lie in their mystified, colonized state, in their primordial, miasmic bodily fluids, nor does it lie in its supplementary other—in ludic feminism's utopian dream of an excessive, unrealizable feminine. These are all fantasies that perpetuate the ideology of patriarchal capitalism. Instead, women's power is, I believe, historically constructed out of collective social struggle based on historical understanding and political critique of the systematic relations of exploitation deriving from the mode of production and appropriation of surplus labor.

This commitment to collective critique and struggle against the systematic relations of exploitation, particularly the gendered division of labor, is just as antithetical to ludic feminism as it is to New Age retrofeminism. One of the consequences of the critique of Paglia's politics of the outrageous is that it points up the limits of ludic feminism's own liberatory claims and highlights the problematic class politics of both. Ludic feminists like Gallop, Rubin, or Butler, just as much as New Age feminists, power feminists, sexual-agency feminists, move the site of struggle away from socioeconomic emancipation to the arena of bodily pleasures and an individual libidinal liberation in which gender and sexuality become marks of a flexible, shifting discursivity or bodily performance, on the one hand, or an essentialist biologism and bodism, on the other. For all their differences, retrofeminism and ludic feminism participate in and help articulate the emergent forms of postmodern patriarchal capitalism, in which the irrational, parodic excesses, and sensuousness of the (natural/performative/discursive) body are used to dissolve issues of social justice and emancipation.

Essentialism, Again

Many feminists, particularly ludic feminists, will resist my conclusion that the discourses of the body in such diverse feminisms produce similar *effects* in occulting the exploitative relations of global patriarchal capitalism and suppressing emancipatory struggles. Their objections rest largely on the claim that New Age feminism, power feminism, and much sexual-agency feminism are *essentialist*—tying the body to both a naturalism and biologism—whereas ludic feminism posits itself as moving beyond essentialist dichotomies (essentialism-difference; essentialism-constructivism). "Deconstructing essentialism" is, for example, part of the central tenet of Drucilla Cornell's *Beyond Accommodation* (4), and Judith Butler claims her strategy of performance and citationality, through which the body is materialized, "is no longer constructivism, but neither is it essentialism" (*Bodies* 8). An increasing number of ludic feminists—particularly those whom Elizabeth Grosz has described in her category of sexual-difference feminists, including Irigaray, Cixous, Gallop, Butler, and Schor—claim to displace the essentialist understanding of the body as biologically given through their attention to the specificity and plurality of differences of the "lived body" (Grosz 18). Grosz herself offers a more "subtle" version of the ludic deconstruction of essentialism; she argues that "one is always implicated in essentialism even as one flees it" (23). Essentialism, for Gross, is supplementary: [T]he opposition between essentialism and constructionism," she says, "seems to me a false one: constructionism is inherently reliant on essentialism" (213 n. 20). This logic leads Grosz to a position of indeterminacy: the body is a "borderline concept that hovers perilously and undecidably at the pivotal point of binary pairs" (23). This "indeterminable position" of the body is for Grosz a "powerful strategic term to upset the frameworks" of binary pairs, for "dissolving oppositional categories" (24). In fact, indeterminacy is increasingly becoming the preferred ludic strategy for what Teresa de Lauretis calls "the way out—let me say, the sublation—of the contradictions in which are caught these two mainstream feminist views" of essentialism and constructionism (difference) ("Upping" 262). But indeterminacy is not the way out of oppositions—or rather it is *not the way* that leads to any revolutionary transformation of the exploitative social relations producing oppositions. It simply provides a conceptual stalemate—a deferment of the encounter with the social contradictions produced in the social relations of production. Deferring is itself a strategy for maintaining the status quo through a pseudophilosophical maneuver ("bordering").

Perhaps the fullest articulation of the indeterminacy of essentialism is put forth by Diana Fuss in her *Essentially Speaking*. Her discussion is especially revealing of the limitations of this ludic logic. Fuss begins by making the important point that "in and of itself, essentialism is neither good nor bad, progressive nor reactionary, beneficial nor dangerous. The question we should be asking is not 'is this text essentialist (and therefore "bad")?' but rather, 'if this text is essentialist, *what motivates its deployment?*'" (xi). The point that essentialism is not in essence progressive or reactionary is a necessary one for feminist politics, but the question it raises for feminism is not so much one of "motivation and deployment" but one of historical use and effect. What are the historical *uses* and economic and political *effects* of essentialism? What is its relation to the struggles over the divisions of labor and access to social resources? Are they used to reinforce or to transform the existing social relations of production? The important difference in a historical materialist understanding of the issue is the move away from the ludic emphasis on motivation, which is the revival of intention, to a concern with *praxis* and its effects—the way the discourse is used, regardless of the motivations for its deployment. This difference between intention and effect is a fundamental difference between a ludic and a resistance postmodern feminism. For ludic feminists the issue of motivation is becoming the determining criteria for evaluating the politics of a theory or practice, and this is especially evident in the turn toward ethics in much postmodern feminism, especially in the work of Cornell. Resistance postmodern feminism, as I have indicated, looks beyond good intentions to critically understand the actual historical consequences of a specific knowledge or practice and the way it relates to the systematic relations of exploitation. Resistance postmodern feminism is concerned, in short, with politics rather than ethics, with consequences, not intentions.

The debate over essentialism in postmodernism is a wide-ranging one, and it may be useful to include here the observations of others, and not only feminists, on the question. Gerald Graff, for instance, has recently written that the claims for antiessentialist theories or textual practices as "*inherently* subversive" and the corresponding critiques of essentialism are "the ultimate descent into the politics of silliness" (174). He goes on to add that this line of critique is itself essentialist, a kind of anti-essentialist essentialism. It assumes, in effect that essentialism (as well as any appeal to the natural, the objective, etc.) always and everywhere has the same (sinister) political consequences, irrespective of the contexts in which it functions. What is essentialist, in other words, is to imagine that an idea has its political coloration *in itself*, instead of acquiring that coloration from the way it is used, or the effect it has, in a specific context or situation. To be sure, essentialism (like any other *ism*) always has some political effect, but *what that effect is* cannot be deduced from the idea itself but only from an examination of how the idea operates in a particular social conjuncture. Appealing to essences (or to the natural, the objective, etc.) is often a way of rationalizing coercive social practices, but not necessarily always. In the recent American and South African racial struggles, to take just one example, the idea that there is an essential human nature that racist regimes violate has had an important "oppositional" effect. (175)

It is important to stress here that the political nature or essence of a concept is determined by the *effects* of its *uses* in a specific situation and not by the intentions motivating its use, since consequences can be quite different from those intended.

To argue for the strategic uses of essentialism for political struggle does not mean reifying identity or difference-between as natural or ontological categories. Instead, we need to understand essences as historically constructed concepts produced out of social struggle: concepts constructed out of and necessary to both the maintenance of hegemonic social relations and the fight against them. It is thus necessary to critically examine the uses of essentialism in recent feminist reformulations. Have they turned historical concepts into metaphysical fictions and epistemological categories to be deconstructed by rhetorical strategies, and what are the consequences of doing so? Fuss's *Essentially Speaking* is an especially telling exemplar for such an analysis. However, before critiquing Fuss's articulation of essentialism, I need to briefly distinguish my argument for the revolutionary uses of essentialism from Spivak's well-known phrase "the strategic use of essentialism." Spivak has, herself, reconsidered the strategy as "too risky a slogan in a personalist, academic culture" because it "gives a certain alibi to essentialism" ("In Word" 128). At the same time she "reminds feminists who want so badly to be anti-essentialists that the critique of essence à la deconstruction proceeds in terms of the unavoidable usefulness of something that is very dangerous" (129). But Spivak's ambivalence about essentialism rehearses the very same individualism and ahistoricism that she warns against. She posits essence/essentialism as another epistemological category that can be deconstructed by rhetorical strategies (and as dangerous insofar as it is not deconstructed) rather than as a historical construct produced out of social struggle and necessary to revolutionary praxis. Moreover, she largely discards "the idea of a *strategy*" because of the way it has been appropriated and deployed in what she calls a "personalist culture" (129), which is, in short, opportunism—the ideology of the middle class in capitalism. Instead she calls for vigilance in "building for difference" (128), which is largely a localist project of intervention in particular institutions. What is missing from both Spivak's original call for "the strategic uses of essentialism" and her reconsideration is a historical understanding of the material conditions producing binaries or essences and their usefulness in constructing class consciousness in the struggle against the exploitative social relations that binaries legitimate.

The rhetorical deconstruction of essentialism as an epistemological category is perhaps most fully developed by Fuss. She proposes a new way out of the dichotomy of essentialism and constructionism through a deconstructive reading of each term as divided from within by its other: thus she finds, on the one hand, "differences *within* essentialism" (*Essentially Speaking* xii) and, on the other, that "essentialism is *essential* to social constructionism" (1). Fuss's deconstructive reading of the conflicts over essentialism and constructionism has influenced a number of ludic feminists; however, there are serious problems politically with the way she theorizes essentialism and its other. Fuss engages in a deconstructive double move that does not so much think a way out of the dichotomy as simply obscure the binary hierarchy.

Her strategy is "to work both sides of the essentialist/constructionist binarism at once, bringing each term to its interior breaking point" (xiii). In doing so, she demonstrates that "the bar between essentialism and constructionism is by no means solid and unassailable" (xii). If the distinctions between the two terms are not "solid and unassailable," then the terms themselves cannot be coherent, self-contained identities or have stable meanings. Instead, they are divided by *differance*: each term of the binary is divided by its other within—by its supplement. In other words, those entities we take to be the same—that is, identical with themselves and marked by their differences from (between) others—are shown instead to be *supplementary* to their others and different within themselves. Each term is reversible with its other. Thus essentialism is not a pure essence but partakes in the difference of its supplement: constructionism. Fuss argues, "[T]here is no essence to essentialism . . . [E]ssence *as* irreducible has been *constructed* to be irreducible" (4). Similarly constructionism is traversed by its other and thus is "fundamentally dependent upon essentialism" (xiii). I would agree that essences are constructed, but there is a fundamental difference between my notion of constructed and Fuss's. For Fuss, constructed means textualized, articulated through the discursive regime. For me, constructed means constructed in the class struggle over the rate of profit and the ratio of surplus labor to necessary labor. In short, for me, essence, in its postmodern sense, is alienated historical reality, and alienation is the effect of estranged labor (Marx, *Economic Manuscripts*). But Fuss displaces the historical understanding of essence with the logical cognitivism of a ludic deconstructionism and turns constructionism itself into a rhetorical ploy.

This move is especially clear when she revives John Locke's binary oppositions to help her "distinguish between *kinds* of essentialism" (4). She thus articulates a difference within essentialism—between "real" and "nominal" essence (4)—that also "corresponds roughly to the broader oppositional categories of essentialism and constructionism" (5). "Real essence," Fuss argues, "connotes the Aristotelian understanding of essence as that which is most irreducible and unchanging about a thing," whereas "nominal essence signifies . . . a merely linguistic convenience, a classificatory fiction" (4). Through such logical associations, Fuss imbricates constructionism in the linguistic. At the same time she is also putting forth (nominal) essence as linguistic and discursive, particularly when she specifies that "essence is a sign, and as such historically contingent" (20). While Fuss occasionally refers to history, as in this instance, or makes claims to historicize, the logic of her own analysis is quite ahistorical. She reads history and the social discursively—as the effect of textual difference—on the one hand, and ontologically, on the other, but never *historically:* that is, as the effects of systematic relations of social contradictions brought about by the clash of the forces of production and the relations of production. In short, she offers an epistemological and discursive reading of both essence and constructionism, thus reducing them to rhetorical practices and eliding their historical reality and effectivity.

Fuss's dehierarchization of the binaries essence/constructionism follows a deconstructive double move—what Derrida calls a "double science" (*Positions* 41)—that does not simply overturn the hierarchy; rather, such "dislodging writing" (reading), Derrida claims, "mark[s] the interval between inversion, which brings low what was high, and the irruptive emergence of a new 'concept'" (42). In Derrida's dislodging or bifurcated writing, deconstructing such binaries as speech/writing "releases the dissonance of writing within speech, thereby disorganizing the entire inherited order" (42) and marks a new concept—what Derrida calls "arche-writing" (*Of Grammatology* 65–73): a form of protowriting that is the very condition of both speech and writing. In other words, the enabling condition of any meaning making, whether speech or writing, is the differing, deferring play of signifiers and it is unveiled by the deconstructive dislodging that releases (the "irruption") of the new concept marking it—"archewriting," "archetrace" ("Differance" 12). Similarly Fuss's deconstructive reading strategy—her "bifurcated writing"—"releases the dissonance" of constructionism (difference) in essence and of essence (the irreducible) in constructionism. In doing so, she elicits the "irruptive emergence of a new 'concept'": what we can call, following Derrida, a protoessence or arche-essence that goes largely un(re)marked in her text and is the condition for both essentialism and constructionism. Fuss, in short, reinscribes a new form of essentialism—what we can call a ludic essentialism—into the agonistics of difference in feminism, and this arche-essence, in Fuss's logic, marks the play of *differance*, difference-within. Thus Fuss's dislodging of the binary constructionism/essentialism as supplementary—that is, as founded on an (arche-essence)—is basically another way of asserting the priority of *differance*, of difference-within. Essence divided by difference is itself a play of difference: essence, as she says, "is a sign" (20) and thus is a textual play of signifiers, an arena of *differance*. She then reads identity as divided by difference and critiques those who would relocate "difference *outside* identity, in the spaces *between* identities," and thus "ignore the radicality of the poststructuralist view which located differences *within* identity," which is her own position (103).

By insisting on the supplementary relation of essence and difference, Fuss, like any deconstructionist, engages in a paradoxical logic. For essence as what is irreducible—as what is already given—is, in effect, a return to the ontological. By continually citing the irreducible essence in constructionism (as in her readings of Lacan, Derrida, and Wittig), Fuss is stopping the unending slippage of *differance* that is the mark of her discursive readings of both constructionism and essence. For instance, she argues that

"contradiction" emerges as the "always already" of deconstruction, its irreducible inner core without which it could not do its work. It is *essential* to deconstruction, and as such it runs the risk of reification and solidification . . . [W]e cannot do without recourse to irreducibilities. (18)

This notion of essence as an "irreducible inner core" is not so much a matter of taking "the risk of essence," as Fuss says (18), but rather risks resurrecting ontology—an inner core based on the inherent being of the thing or concept—and eliding history. What is privileged or taken for granted as irreducible is itself a product of the struggle over social contradictions determined by the relations of production. While Fuss does attempt to articulate the irreducibility of essence as constructed, she tends to mean by this a discursively (linguistically) constructed ("nominal essence"). Even when she articulates a social constructionism, the social remains an unspecified, already given set of discursive differences (a notion that has its full theoretical articulation in Laclau and Mouffe): an ahistorical essence (ontology). Similarly, her understanding of history, as I have already suggested, is discursive—history as sign, as semantics (4)—or another form of ludic essentialism: history as series of particular, multiple localities, an already given context.

Fuss's deconstructive logic does not so much sublate these contradictory, binary oppositions as rhetorically *dissolve* one into the other while, at the same time, reasserting their opposition. The critic's position in relation to this epistemological paradox is, as Fuss writes of herself, one that "balances precariously between the two" (40). In short, what begins as an attempt to politicize and reunderstand the agonistics over difference and essentialism continually falls back into the cul-de-sac of deconstructive indeterminacy, and we are left oscillating in the circular logic of the closed circuit between discursive and ontological categories, enmeshed in the local pluralities of differences-within. Fuss's logic elides the historical contradictions and social struggles brought about by the forces and relations of production. She thereby obscures the historicity of constructions (differences) as enactments of social struggles and of essences as their effects. Fuss does not so much resolve the agonistics in feminism over essentialism and constructionism as displace it onto an undecidable circuit of rhetorical strategies and epistemological ambiguities.

Grosz's notion of corporeal feminism and her call for a "nondichotomous understanding of the body" (21) deploys much the same deconstructive indeterminacy we find in Fuss's discourse. Grosz understands the body in supplementary terms: "as the threshold or borderline concept that hovers perilously and undecidably at the pivotal point of binary pairs. The body is neither—while also being both" (23). At the core of Grosz's supplementary logic is what she calls "the pure difference that constitutes all modes of materiality" (208). Grosz argues for a "notion of corporeality" that "refuses reductionism, resists dualism, and remains suspicious of . . . holism" (22). However, by positing an absolute, pure difference as the core of all materiality, subjectivity, and sexed bodies, Grosz is, in effect, putting forth a ludic essentialism grounded in the *arche-essence* of an absolute, ahistorical ontological difference—one that is largely articulated through discursive practices. She goes even further and equates this pure (ontological) difference with material difference itself when she asserts a "pure, that is, material difference" (190). For all her discursive detours and disclaimers, Grosz ends up asserting an extraordinarily reductive, panhistorical, and universalizing theory of the body as based on pure (ontological) difference—an ontological difference that is concealed under the ludic reification of difference as an endless, open proliferation of multiplicities. Such a theory of absolute pure difference no more sublates dualism and essentialism than does Fuss's deconstructive reading. Instead, like Fuss and other ludic feminists, Grosz's understanding of (pure) difference reifies one side of the binary, difference-within, while suppressing the other, difference-between.

Moreover, this (pure, ontological) difference appropriates materiality itself. Like Gallop and other ludic critics, Grosz attempts to assert "a materiality or a material specificity and determinateness to bodies," and these bodily materials "exert . . . resistance or recalcitrance to the processes of cultural inscription" (190). Materiality, in this ludic sense, is that which resists inscription by language. But following the conflicting, indeterminate logic that has become the commonplace of ludic thinking, materiality is itself reduced to the pure (ontological and discursive) difference that constitutes it. Thus for all her claims for a theory of the historical specificity of *"bodies*—male or female, black, brown, white, large or small" (19)— Grosz erases the real historical, material specificity of bodies: the materiality constituted not by an abstract, pure (ontological or textual) difference but by the historical struggles over the relations of production and divisions of labor and property. We see this erasure of materiality, for example, in her experiment with a "Deleuzian feminism" (180) in which she deploys Deleuze and Guattari's binary of the "rhizomatic" and "arboreal," in spite of her own injunctions against dualities. The outcome of her experiment is predictable: although there are "problems" with such a project, nonetheless, a feminist rhizomatics can be developed. In it, the arboreal (the systematic understanding of society, as in historical materialism) is put aside in the interest of a "rhizomatics"—a concrete, specific, discontinuous, heterogeneous understanding of bodies in terms of their "intensities and flows" (160–83). Bodies in such a rhizomatics are assemblages of differences, "fragments of a desiring machine" (167–68). These "assemblages or machines" ("desiring machines")—as Grosz summarizes Deleuze and Guattari's thinking—"are heterogeneous, disparate, discontinuous alignments or linkages" (167). They have (and here she quotes Deleuze and Guattari directly) "neither base nor superstructure" but follow the "imperative of endless experimentation, metamorphosis, or transmutation"; they "are essentially in movement, in action" (167–68). Such a theory of bodies, and thus of subjectivities, as the effects of transhistorical, endlessly metamorphosing assemblages of differences or desiring machines does not displace base and superstructure but is profoundly idealist in its articulation of bodies *only* in terms of superstructural processes.

What is omitted here is the *determined* materiality of the body as the effect of class struggles brought about by the forces and relations of production making up the *base* of society. From the beginning of her book, Gross reduces base and superstructure to just another metaphor among other metaphors that she reads as having "all presumed a certain mastery of and exteriority to the object—the body, bodies" (23). Instead, she calls for what are in effect supplementary "metaphors and models that implicate the subject in the object" (23): such as Deleuze and Guattari's rhizomatic metaphor of a desiring machine with its "destratification," "demassification of the great division of social power in culture." While Grosz is uncomfortable with aspects of Deleuze and Guattari's theory and warns that this "demassification . . . must at first sight appear to undermine the power and justification of various oppressed groups . . . and their struggles," she still argues that Deleuze and Guattari are "rendering more complex the nature and forms that these oppressions take" (173). But this greater subtlety is an alibi for erasing the historical materiality of the production and exploitation of bodies. It saturates bodies so fully in the local permutations of differences-within that their determinate connections to the class struggles over the relations of production are entirely suppressed—as is the objective reality of bodies as *laboring bodies*. While Grosz argues that the rhizomatic of Deleuze and Guattari only *seems* to "undermine the power and justification of various oppressed groups—women, the working class, people of color, gays and lesbians, religious or cultural minorities and their struggles" (173), in fact, the rhizomatic, along with the ludic essentialism of her trope of pure difference, does indeed undermine the struggles of the oppressed. It does so by fetishizing difference-within as a means for metamorphosing binary oppositions and deconstructing dualities. But as I have argued earlier, binary oppositions and essentializations are historical constructs produced out of class struggle and necessary for the revolutionary transformation of the fundamental structures of exploitation in society—in short, for the transformation of the relations of production and divisions of labor and property in patriarchal capitalism.

CHAPTER 6

Women and/as
the Subaltern

Several years ago, in the course of a discussion on what has happened to the political Left in the West, especially in the United States, Robert Fitch observed that one of the most visible changes has been the Left's preoccupation with questions of the Third World, or postcoloniality. The Left, as he said, "having gotten rid of those 19th century heirlooms" of socialism

> needed to replace them with something to avoid the embarrassment of empty space—preferably something without sharp edges. Third World workers and peasants fit in quite well. Didn't they deserve our attention more than the workers in our own society? In absolute terms, weren't they even poorer and even more oppressed? Besides, relationships with them were easier to maintain. They were located in convenient out-of-the-way places so you hardly ever saw them. And if asked why we didn't support workers in our own communities, we could always answer that we were anti-imperialists and that the truly deserving workers were outside our reach. So the new internationalism of the left meant that support for Third World struggles gradually tended to replace, rather than reinforce involvement in struggles at home. (18–19)

In other words, this new preoccupation with postcoloniality is far from being the mark of the Left's internationalization and growing involvement in the plight of the oppressed workers in the world. Instead, it is a strategy of evasion and containment of class struggle.

In fact, Fitch goes on to say that

> by and large, special concern with labor, class and the transformation of society has been displaced intellectually by the "posts-." With the advent of postindustrialism, postmodernism, post-Marxism or what-

ever, the assumption appears to be that here in the U.S. we are all bourgeois, or could be with suitable government programs and affirmative action. (19)

The important point here is that the Left, by and large, feels defeated in the capitalist world and has succumbed to the prevailing logic or ideology of the bourgeoisie. It has thus lost the initiative to deal with the "home" problems (rampant sexism, racism, economic devastation and its global exportation) and has instead turned to the safely distant "other"—particularly the subaltern.

This shift and the "pleasure" the "other" often generates for the Left as an escape from the home difficulties of labor and class is vividly demonstrated by New York City's 1993 Labor Day parade. The parade

celebrated cross dressing and Caribbean ethnicity with much more gusto than it showed for working men and women or union solidarity.

At a time when wages are stagnant or falling and when practically every politician recognizes the big issue to be jobs, jobs, jobs, what does the perfunctory marching mean? Is class struggle truly over? . . . Or is it simply a case that drag queens and West Indians throw much better parties? (Michael T. Kaufman, "Of Marching and Labor and a Few Onlookers," *New York Times*, 8 Sept. 1993, B3)

In the face of such contradictions we need to ask whether the growing interest in feminism and postmodern cultural studies with issues of coloniality/postcoloniality[1] is a mark of international activism and a global retheorization of the understanding of exploitation or merely a means of running away from the problems at home. The issue is whether feminism should attend to the (discursive) politics of truth and explore the axes of power-knowledge relations—particularly regarding the "other"—or whether, as Marx argued, we should engage the economics of untruth involving ourselves in relation to a common humanity.

In other words, there are two fundamentally different ways of understanding postcoloniality. The first, and by far most prevalent, mode is a ludic engagement with postcoloniality as a regime of power-knowledge relations; it foregrounds the problems of representation and is part of the project exploring the discursive politics of truth.[2] In contrast, the second mode does not take postcoloniality to be simply a problem of cultural politics, as Foucauldian genealogy proposes, but instead understands it as basically an economic issue that has to be explored in the context of the international division of labor. This second mode poses the problem of the economics of untruth in the relations of metropole and periphery.[3]

While postcoloniality understood as cultural politics is necessary, it is, to my mind, a very limited project. The more productive and politically effective undertaking is one that sees postcoloniality as the articulation of the international division of labor. To say this does not mean I am dispensing with the problems of representation, knowledge, or truth, but I am arguing that these cannot be understood separate from the political economy of labor. The related issues of postcoloniality, Third World women, and women of color are becoming the predominant arenas of Western feminist concerns. Prominent feminist theorists—from Donna Haraway and Elizabeth Meese to Gayatri Spivak—increasingly focus their recent work on questions of postcoloniality.[4] The major anthologies of feminist theory in the last few years, such as Marianne Hirsch and Evelyn Fox Keller's *Conflicts in Feminism*, Elizabeth Weed's *Coming to Terms*, and Judith Butler and Joan Scott's *Feminists Theorize Politics*, all have significant discussions of Third World women, and a number of anthologies such as Chandra Mohanty, Ann Russo, and Lourdes Torres's *Third World Women and the Politics of Feminism*, Sidonie Smith and Julia Watson's *De/Colonizing the Subject*, and Inderpal Grewal and Caren Kaplan's *Scattered Hegemonies* are entirely devoted to these issues.

My concern here is to ask some difficult and, for many, quite discomforting questions about the political and social effects of the way postmodern feminist theorists are engaging the postcolonial, specifically the subaltern. I will be carrying out this inquiry through a critique of several exemplary texts, notably Gayatri Spivak's "Can the Subaltern Speak?" (which an interviewer in *Socialist Review* called her "most famous [or notorious] work" and a "major contribution to this discussion" [Donald Lowe, Michael Rosenthal, and Ron Silliman, "Introduction," to "Gayatri Spivak" 83]) as well as Elizabeth Meese's turn from poststructuralism to postcoloniality in her *(Ex)tensions*.

Feminist and postmodern encounters with the Third World see themselves as postimperialist. However, imperialism in their writings is an extension of ludic semiotics. It does not mean a regime of the division of labor and transfer of wealth from the periphery to the metropole; instead it means a discursive domination in which the other is prevented from speaking for herself. Imperialism, in other words, is not understood as a historical articulation of capitalism but rather is turned into a "semiotic violence" silencing the voice of the other: instead of a military-economic practice, imperialism becomes a trope. In a recent essay, "Postcolonial Culture, Postimperial Criticism," W. J. T. Mitchell articulates the ludic idea of imperialism quite clearly. He claims that we are in "the process of 'decolonization,' a term that suggests as its necessary corollary some related transformations in the corresponding centers of empire, a 'deimperialization'" (13). But such an assumption confuses the end of one specific stage of imperialism (nineteenth-century territorial colonialism) with the end of imperialism as a global system of exploitation. In fact, imperialism—that is, the international division of labor and appropriation of economic and natural resources benefiting First World countries at the expense of Third World societies—is thriving under new guises and by other means, such as the international debt structure, "free trade" or "export processing" zones and the practices of multinational corporations, creating what Annette Fuentes and Barbara Ehrenreich have called the "global factory." Most recently, it has expanded to Eastern Europe under the guise of helping emergent democracies, where a highly skilled labor force is subjected to novel strategies of exploitation. Nor has the West abandoned direct military coercion and territorial occupation—witness the invasions of Vietnam, Grenada, Panama, the Falkland Islands, and the military occupation of parts of Iraq and of Haiti.

The automatic assumption of the deimperialization of the center is itself an act of concealed imperialism. However, beginning from this assumption, Mitchell goes on to argue that there is a "cultural reconfiguration . . . overwhelmingly evident in the global cultural relations of the First, Second and Third Worlds" (14): a "reconfiguration and relocation of cultural and critical energy, reversals of center and margin, production and consumption, dominant and emergent forces, reversals in traditional divisions of cultural labor such as 'criticism' and 'creative writing'" (13). And what is this profound reversal? "The commonplace," he says, which "is simply this: the most important literature is now emerging from the former colonies of the Western empires . . . the most provocative new criticism is emanating from research universities in the advanced industrial democracies, that is, from the former centers of the 'Western empires'—Europe and the United States" (14). If this is "the commonplace," as Mitchell claims, of current knowledges, that the creative energies and articulations of experience are to be found in the former colonies, but that the theories, interpretations, and criticisms—the master knowledges—we use to make sense of them are the products of the research centers of the former empire, then there is little if any deimperialization going on (even in the discursive, ludic sense of imperialism). On the contrary, even in his own account, the old relations of domination and exploitation are reproducing themselves in new forms. In his model, for example, the margin (the "former colonies") provide the "raw material" of experience ("creative writing"), and the "former center" (the "advanced industrial democracies") the finished product. It is assumed here that the First World has grown out of the experiential innocence and naïveté needed for the make-believe worlds of creative writing in the same way that it has grown out of low-technology practices: critical theory is high-tech cultural work largely unavailable to the Third World.

These old power-knowledge relations are largely reproducing themselves through two moves that have serious implications for postmodern feminist theory, which is often complicit in these strategies. The first is to read contemporary criticism—by which Mitchell means postmodern "antifoundationalist" discourses such as pragmatism and deconstruction that "come to the Third World from the First"—as "subvert(ing) the imperial economy that supports it, 'decentering' the very structure of discursive authority" (16). But this claim for the "postimperialist subversiveness" of antifoundational discourses is itself an abstract, universalizing notion that erases their specific historical uses and effects. For instance, the deconstructive insistence on discursive indeterminacy is not postimperialist or even subversive in its effect when it puts under erasure the certainty and truth value of the political principles distinguishing the discourses of the African National Congress and those of neo-Nazi and apartheid white supremacists. Second, such a concept of "postimperialist criticism" or knowledge can only be maintained by restricting the arena of subversive intervention to that of the discourses or representations of empire, in short, to cultural politics—which is another way of repeating what I have already suggested: imperialism in ludic theory is a semiotic regime and not "the highest stage of capitalism," as Lenin put it. This ludic "postimperialism" requires that we follow Mitchell's injunction "to resist," as he says, "the notion that this relationship"—"between First World Critical movements and literary developments in the Second and Third Worlds"—"reflects the traditional economic relations of imperial centers and colonial peripheries" (17). In short, what Mitchell calls a "rhetoric of decolonization from the imperial center" is only possible if we suppress the global economic realities of the international division of labor and its articulation through the construction of significations, representations, and subjectivities.

Most feminist inquiries into postcolonialism and the subaltern see themselves, like Mitchell, as participating in postimperialist knowledges and producing a subversive "rhetoric of decolonization from the imperial center." But in doing so, many feminists frequently participate in the same uncritical and ahistorical notion of deimperialization maintained by essentializing the political effects of discursive performances and, more important, at the cost of suppressing the economic relations—in short the labor relations—between center and periphery, between overdeveloped and underdeveloped countries, and, not least, between Western feminists and the subalterns they study.

Gayatri Spivak seems well aware of this issue in her essay "Can the Subaltern Speak?" in which she insists on situating the possibility/impossibility of postimperialist knowledges in the West within the international division of labor, for, as she says, "Western intellectual production is, in many ways, complicit with Western international economic interests" (271). In current postcolonial dicourses, particularly concerning the subaltern, "the first-world intellectual," according to Spivak, "masquerad(es) as the absent nonrepresenter who lets the oppressed speak for themselves" (292). In other words, the seemingly compassionate gesture to let the subaltern speak, to give voice to the other, is not only paternalistic but relies on an illusory transparency that occludes the continuing historical privilege and economic collaboration of the "benevolent Western intellectual" in the international division of labor. Spivak's concern in the essay is, thus, to deconstruct the way "the intellectual is complicit in the perisitent constitution of the Other as the Self's shadow"—and by Self, with a capitalized "S," she means the continued perpetuation of the sovereign subject of Western imperialism in which the Other, the subaltern, is repeatedly re-constituted as the different/the Other of U.S./Europe (280). "This S/subject," according to Spivak, "belongs to the exploiter's side of the international division of labor" (280). These efforts to give voice to subaltern subjects operate, Spivak argues, through a ruthless dislocation of "motives (desires), and power (of knowledge)" from the economic situation, which is put "under erasure" by Western intellectuals (280).

In developing this argument, Spivak devotes much of her critique to a deconstruction of the interview between Michel Foucault and Gilles Deleuze called "Intellectuals and Power." Her interventions in this text are of considerable importance to feminist and postcolonial critics in the U.S. academy since most of their discourses on the empowerment of the Other are heavily indebted to this text. This interview has also had considerable influence on the new formation of the post-al intellectual (as different from the Marxist universal intellectual). In his recent book, *Representations of the Intellectual*, Edward Said denounces the universal intellectual—the partisan of causes—and instead advocates that intellectuals should abandon "political absolutism" (a code for Marxism) and simply maintain a state of constant alertness and steady realism (a code for pragmatism). The post-al intellectual is a pragmatic, postideological, vigilant reader of social practices and not a revolutionary person fighting for truth and justice, since these are "absolutes." In the interview, Foucault and Deleuze propose what is, in effect, a new theoretical model for deconstructing the idea of theorist as universal intellectual—that is, for displacing the relationship between the intellectual, who traditionally would articulate theoretical knowledges for the masses, who would then follow these knowledges. As Foucault said, "[T]he intellectual discovered that the masses no longer need him to gain knowledge: they *know* perfectly well, without illusion; they know far better than he" (Foucault and Deleuze 207). And Deleuze states, "[A] theorizing intellectual, for us, is no longer a subject, a representing or representative consciousness. Those who act and struggle are no longer represented . . . Representation no longer exists; there's only action" (Foucault and Deleuze 206). The point of this retheorization and the project of empowerment following from it tries to establish an equal relationship between the intellectual and the people, specifically the subaltern.

But such equality is illusory. For, as Spivak argues, the intellectual's rewriting of theory as a "relay of practice" in which "the oppressed can know and speak for themselves" reintroduces an irreducible "Subject [capital 'S'] of desire and power" and a

> self-proximate, if not self-identical, subject of the oppressed. Further, the intellectuals who are neither of these S/subjects, become transparent in the relay race, for they merely report on the nonrepresented subject and analyze (without analyzing) the workings of (the unnamed Subject irreducibly presupposed by) power and desire." (Spivak, "Subaltern" 279)

In short, the efforts to give voice to the subaltern, not only reinstate an essentialized Subject of power but also "romanticiz[e] the subaltern," as she says in the *Socialist Review* interview, constituting them as unified subjects immune from "all of the complications of 'subject production' [that] apply to us" but do not "apply to them" ("Gayatri Spivak" 90). Moreover, this transparency of the intellectual marks for Spivak the place of economic interest and "is maintained by a vehement denegation"—by which she means the intellectual's refusal to acknowledge his/her own economic interestedness.

This blindness becomes especially apparent in her critique of Foucault's notion of power, which underlies this postcolonial theory of empowering the Other. In his discussion with Deleuze, Foucault invokes a geographical discontinuity to displace the Marxist notion of exploitation—and the corresponding necessity of collective economic struggle—with his own notion of diffuse power that allows for multiple resistances based on alliance politics. But such a notion of decentralized power, Spivak quite rightly argues, not only erases "the real mark of 'geographical (geopolitical) discontinuity' [which] is the international division of labor," but it is itself "made possible by a certain stage of exploitation . . . and is geopolitically specific to the First World" (289). Foucault's argument that a new mechanism of power emerges in the seventeenth and eighteenth centuries—one that he says is "absolutely incompatible with the relations of sovereignty . . . and is more dependent upon bodies and what they do than upon the Earth and its products" (*Power/Knowledge* 104)—is, Spivak contends, "secured *by means* of territorial imperialism—the Earth and its products—'elsewhere'" ("Can the Subaltern" 290). In other words, this new diffuse, asystematic mechanism of power put forth by Foucault and grounding most postcolonial politics of empowering the subaltern is, in fact, historically dependent on a sovereign and systematic exercise of economic and military coercion elsewhere and not just then but also now. For Foucault is blind, Spivak maintains, not only to the "first wave of 'geographical discontinuity'"—and here she points out that the "real mark of 'geographical (geopolitical) discontinuity' is the international division of labor" ("Subaltern" 289)—but Foucault also "remain[s] impervious to its second wave in the middle decades of our own century" ("Subaltern" 290), by which she means the global economic and military domination of American imperialism that ushered in, as she quotes Mike Davis, the "new era of commercial liberalism" ("Subaltern" 290). It is this imperialist-based commercial liberalism that supports contemporary bourgeois notions of discursive freedom.

Spivak's deconstruction of the concealed, ongoing imperialist politics of Western representations of the subaltern is an important critique. The outcome of such a project is a necessary one for feminist/postcolonial critics: as Spivak says, "[T]o confront [subalterns] is not to represent . . . them but to learn to represent ourselves" (288–89), or, as she also says, "the task of the first-world subject of knowledge in our historical moment is to resist and critique 'recognition' of the Third World through 'assimilation'" (292).

Spivak's blindness to the relation of subsistence labor and capital accumulation leads, I believe, to a serious slippage in her analysis of the representation of the subaltern woman, in which she herself occludes the political economy, the labor relations of representation, by substituting a discursive politics that textualizes the subaltern and reduces imperialism to a ludic semiosis.[5] Thus we find Spivak's analysis of suttee, or widow burning in India, as what she calls the "exemplum of the woman-in-imperialism," almost entirely confined "within discursive practice" (305). She posits the other woman, the subaltern, as a silent, unrepresentable excess outside labor relations and circulating instead in a discursive circuit in which "the figure of the woman disappears," according to Spivak, "into a violent shuttling which is the displaced figuration of the 'third-world woman' caught between tradition and modernization" (306) and concludes "there is no space from which the sexed subaltern can speak" (307); "the subaltern cannot speak" (308). This impossibility of speaking is seen as the rule of imperialism, but such a move dematerializes imperialism itself. Thus, although on the surface Spivak's move seems progressive, it is a reactionary move that dematerializes imperialism.

This conclusion is the result of her reinscribing, in the end, the very discursive politics and problematic notion of empowerment that she effectively critiqued earlier in her text. For the question she asks, then answers in the negative, "Can the Subaltern Speak?" is itself a misplaced question for a materialist postcolonial critique. To pose the problem of the subaltern with "can she speak?" is simply to reify the project of giving a voice to the Other as the primary political agenda and to mistake a discursive empowerment for a social and economic enablement. This displacement, however, is widely shared in feminist and postcolonial discourses. As bell hooks writes, the process of gaining a voice is "a metaphor for self-transformation . . . for women of oppressed groups . . . coming to voice is an act of resistance. Speaking becomes both a way to engage in active self-transformation and a rite of passage where one moves from being object to being subject. Only as subjects can we speak" (*Talking Back* 12). Without denying the importance of these struggles to speak, we need also to recognize that such an agenda reinscribes the autonomous individual of bourgeois ideology in which speaking, coming to voice, is largely understood as a voluntaristic act of free will and consciousness, presupposing a coherent, self-identical subjectivity outside the history of labor. The discourse of empowering voice, in short, reduces the struggles for emancipation and the end of exploitation to a discursive freedom that equates democracy with speaking, with free speech. In doing so, it displaces *material democracy*—the equal access of all to social and economic resources—and substitutes verbal empowerment for economic and social enablement and individual expression for collective social struggle to transform existing social relations of production.

The question "Can the Subaltern Speak?" blocks the more pressing questions for the subaltern: what are the effective knowledges and modes of collective subjectivity the subaltern needs to transform the economic and political conditions of her life, to intervene in the international division of labor? Freedom is not the effect of speaking but the result of collective praxis: freedom is freedom from necessity, and that will not come about without changing the dominant institutions. The silencing of the subaltern is not simply the effect of domination but rather the economico-historical effect of exploitation. If we examine the anecdote, as Spivak calls it, that provoked her despairing conclusion that "the Subaltern cannot speak," we find the subaltern speaking all along. The incident as originally described by Spivak is as follows:

> A young woman of sixteen or seventeen, Bhuvaneswari Bhaduri, hanged herself in her father's modest apartment in North Calcutta in 1926. The suicide was a puzzle since, as Bhuvaneswari was menstruating at the time, it was clearly not a case of illicit pregnancy. Nearly a decade later, it was discovered that she was a member of one of the many groups involved in the armed struggle for Indian independence. She had finally been entrusted with a political assassination. Unable to confront the task and yet aware of the practical need for trust, she killed herself. ("Subaltern" 307)

Our political understanding of her "puzzling" suicide—that it was an alternative to carrying out a political assassination for the anticolonial struggle—is the result of a letter she had left. As Spivak says, revising her view of the incident in the *Socialist Review* interview, "[T]his woman took good care to speak, and look at what happened . . . She left a letter that was dis-covered . . . even when, whether showing her political impotence or her political power, she tries to speak and make it clear, so that it would be read one way, the women in the family—radical women—decide to forget it" ("Gayatri Spivak" 89). In other words, the subaltern is not mute, as Spivak claims, although her speaking is suppressed.

Spivak reads this as "an unemphatic, ad hoc, subaltern rewriting of the social text of *sati*-suicide" ("Subaltern" 308), but if we move beyond the bounds of "discursive practice" in which Spivak has confined her analysis, we find that this incident raises other issues for us. Not the least is the ques-tion of the historical subjectivities and knowledges available to Bhu-vaneswari that would enable her to intervene to transform the economic and political relations of imperialism—that would enable her, in short, to participate in the armed struggle of the anticolonial struggle. Her suicide would suggest that these collective subjectivities and new frames of under-standing were not fully available to her and/or that the social and ideolog-ical contradictions of her specific situation did not allow her to fully take up this new position. *Why not?* The emphasis on her voice, her autonomous, self-evident, voluntary speaking, or, on the other hand, a dis-cursive suppression of her free speech, covers over and conceals the mate-rial and ideological issues of her struggle to build and enact a revolution-ary subjectivity for herself and actively transform the colonial relations of exploitation.

The problematic of her failed struggle is all the more apparent when we contrast this incident to the Telangana People's Struggle in Hyderabad a decade or so later when subaltern women—illiterate peasants, bonded laborers, and even middle-class women like Bhuvaneswari—joined in armed resistance against the extremely oppressive feudal social and eco-nomic conditions under the princely reign of the Nizam, kept in power as subservient allies by British colonial rule and the imperialist economic regime (Stree Shakti Sanghatana 1). These struggles enabled the women to unite collectively in their villages to oppose the atrocities of the landown-ers and their police; to fight with the guerrilla squads; and even to become squad commanders and barefoot doctors. The question for these women, these subalterns, is not simply one of coming to voice (although many did), nor of voice as an unmediated expression of an already given conscious-ness and experience. Rather the question is, what enabled these women to struggle on their own behalf, to engage in the revolution to transform the division of labor and the limited access to social resources oppressing them? In short, what enabled them to become collective subjects in the social and economic struggle for emancipation?

A crucial part of this answer, I believe, is the collective development of materialist explanatory critiques, by which I mean those practices and struggle concepts through which the subject develops historical knowledge of the social totality and her own subjectivities. She acquires, in other words, an understanding of how the existing social institutions (such as motherhood, family, poverty) have in fact come about and how they can be changed. The question is not simply one of knowing or speaking but a matter of the *kind* of knowing that provides guidelines for revolutionary praxis and demystifies the historical situation. Critique, in other words, is that knowledge-practice that historically situates the conditions of possibility of what empirically exists under patriarchal-imperialist-capitalist labor relations and, more importantly, points to what is suppressed by the empirically existing: what could be (instead of what actually is). Critique indicates that "what is" is not necessarily the real or true but rather only the existing actuality that is transformable. The role of critique in postcolonialism and resistance postmodern feminism is exactly this: the production of historical knowledges that mark the transformability of existing social arrangements and the possibility of a different social organization, an organization free from exploitation. Historical materialist critique, as I suggested earlier, is a mode of knowing that inquires into what is not said, into the silences and the suppressed or missing, in order to uncover the concealed operations of power and underlying socioeconomic relations connecting the myriad details and seemingly disparate events and representations of our lives. It shows how seemingly disconnected zones of culture—including the privileges of Western intellectuals and the suffering of subalterns—are in fact linked through the highly differentiated and dispersed operation of a systematic logic of exploitation and international division of labor informing all practices in societies globally under imperialist late capitalism. In sum, historical materialist critique disrupts that which represents itself as what is, as natural, as inevitable, as the way things are, and exposes the way "what is" is historically and socially produced out of social contradictions and how it supports inequality. Critique enables us to not only *explain* how class, race, gender, and imperialist oppression operate so we can change it but also to collectively build the emancipatory subjectivities we need to carry out the revolutionary struggle.

While there were serious limits on the forms of historical critique available to the women in the Telangana People's Struggle, especially regarding issues of gender, the social and political enablement of these women is deeply indebted to the knowledges and subjectivities made available to them through collective practices of critique, particularly as disseminated in political education classes. According to members of the feminist collective Stree Shakti Sanghatana, which has written the history of these women and their resistance, "All the women refer to the (Communist) Party or the Sangham as the basis and the cause of their liberation" (Kannabiran and Lalitha 186).

> They were taught to read and write and discuss political questions. Political classes were held for them . . . The knowledge they gained as a result of these classes gave them the tools to understand their own social reality . . . the ideological framework provided by the Party helped the women to analyze their situation, process their knowledge and make sense of their surroundings . . . The opportunity to act, the power to fight for control over their own lives gave the women an identity, a sense of enormous strength and wisdom. (185)

As was the case for the subalterns in the Telangana Uprising, the Marxist tradition of historical materialist critique has been one of the most productive sites for developing a historical explanatory critique, but it is, of course, not necessarily the only site. If we resist romanticizing the subaltern, we find that the conditions of exploitation and their situation in the division of labor have led them to produce forms of materialist critique. This is quite evident in Rigoberta Menchú's autobiographical history of the struggles of subalterns in Guatemala—the collective struggle of Indians, peasants, and *ladinos*—against the landowners (Menchú, *I*). Menchú is a revolutionary leader of the CUC, the Peasant Unity Committee, and a Nobel Peace Prize winner. In discussing the Indians' tradition of centuries of resistance to the colonial domination of Whites (the Spanish) in Guatemala, she points to, at the very least, a nascent materialist critique informing that tradition: a fundamental understanding of the division of labor and colonial exploitation based on it. When an Indian child is forty days old, she/he is initiated into the community in a collective ceremony that locates her/him in the history and knowledges of the people. First, according to Menchú, the "parents make a commitment. They promise to teach the child to keep the secrets of our people," then toward the end, the people say "Let no landowner extinguish all this, nor any rich man wipe out our customs. Let our children, be they workers or servants, respect and keep their secrets" (12). And again when the child is ten years old, another ceremony, according to Menchú, "reminds them that our ancestors were dishonoured by the White Man, by colonization" (13). Such traditions clearly mark not only a critique of the class and labor relations of colonialism but also its cultural politics: for the subaltern to speak, to reveal the secrets of her identity to the colonizer, to us, is to make these vulnerable to the colonizers', to our, appropriation and assimilation, even commodification, of them.

This critique was even more strongly developed out of the specific material conditions of exploitation of her family and village at the hands of the landowners, so that Menchú repeatedly tells how her father, an illiterate peasant who helped found and lead the CUC, would say, "[M]y children there are rich people and there are poor. The rich have become rich because they took what our ancestors had away from them, and now they grow fat on the sweat of our labour. We know this is true because we live it every day, not because someone else tells us" (121). But this is not a self-evident, transparent experience. What Menchú calls "seeing things more clearly" or having "clarity of thought" comes from the long painful struggle of what she specifically identifies as "criticism and self-criticism" (166) from days and nights of discussion among the *compañeros*. It is through such critique and discussion that she and other members of the CUC are able to overcome the historical barriers of racial oppression and discrimination between the Indians and *ladinos* (those of mixed Spanish and Indian blood) and to see as Menchú says that "our poverty united us . . . the root of our problems lay in the ownership of the land. All our country's riches are in the hands of the few" (166).

I want to return here to the problem of how Western feminists engage these discourses of the subaltern by critiquing Elizabeth Meese's "benevolent" and "compassionate" reading of Rigoberta Menchú's story in her book *(Ex)tensions.* Meese's reading is located in what she calls "feminism's double bind . . . that it cannot speak 'for' other women, nor can it speak 'without' or 'apart from' other women." Instead, echoing the Foucault-Deleuze discourse on intellectuals, she says, "[I]t must create a space where women who are not these white, middle-class Anglo-American or European feminists can speak or write" (98). The unsaid of this ludic postmodern project of empowering the other, the subaltern, to speak is not to empower them to speak *for themselves,* for, as Menchú makes clear, the subaltern *already* speaks *for* herself and *to* other subalterns. The hidden agenda is to empower the subaltern to speak to *us.* Is this just another form of imperialist appropriation masquerading as a decolonizing gesture? For all Meese's thoughtful and compassionate care—and she is both caring and careful—the end result of her encounter with the subaltern is the reinscription of the Western feminist as the sovereign subject of imperialism. This is not a personal inadequacy of Meese but rather the historical limits of the ludic discourses of empowerment, which reduce collectivity to sentimentalization. Her project is firmly located in the discursive politics of desire and power that Spivak so severely critiqued in Foucault and is thus subject to the same limitations.

Meese's aim is to "recuperate the experience of the feminist project's desire for writing the other woman" (101), or more specifically to write herself and Western feminism in a benevolent or, as she says, "compassionate," relation to the subaltern. She thus ends her writing by declaring, "[M]y own desire for feminism and (with) a Quiche Indian woman . . . if she can grow to love the *ladino compañero*, Yanero might she someday learn to love the feminist theorist?" (128). But why should she? As Meese quickly acknowledges and passes over at the beginning of her text:

> The undeniable complicity of the United States government in Guatemala's ongoing regime of political murder and oppression cannot be separated from my position as writer and my production of the Quiche Indian as both the tragic victim and the courageous opponent of my country. (100)

The historical materialist analysis of imperialism is reduced here to confession and compassion and a world-historical relation is trivialized as a woman-to-woman empathy. It is in such sentimentalizations that ludic feminism becomes complicit with imperialism. Sentimentalization occludes an explanatory critique (as guidelines for praxis), replacing it with empathy (an empathy that mysteriously develops by the sheer power of will) for the "victim," who somehow is supposed to understand "courageous" acts across diverse cultural differences. Ludic feminism exists, in other words, in a relation of complicity with the imperialist political and economic exploitation of Menchú and her people in the international division of labor. However, rather than critically interrogate and intervene in that systematic circuit of labor relations and exploitation, Meese displaces it by substituting a circuit of discursive desires and differences. Colonialism thus becomes largely a discursive arena from which the economic and certainly the international division of labor almost entirely disappear.

In a deconstructive move Meese repeatedly tries to put under erasure the binary oppositions of Western/Third World feminism; self/other; feminism/*machismo*, Indian/*ladino*, rich/poor. She sees Menchú as exemplary in "crossing over the oppositions, contradicting the contradictions" (113). For Meese, in other words, Menchú is an excessive subject, and her radicality is this ludic excessiveness. Menchú breaks the categories ("contradicting the contradictions") and thus qualifies herself as the radical other—as courageous victim. Meese is especially concerned with Menchú's relation as an Indian/Indianist to the *ladinos* who have historically exploited and racially discriminated against Indians—the crossing over, in short, of barriers of racial discrimination. For Meese the "structural position (of the ladino) resembles (that of) the feminist theorist." She thus enacts a textual transfer: if Menchú can "cross-over" and learn to "love the *ladino*," she can learn to "love the feminist theorist"—Meese, you and me, thereby absolving us of our complicity and privilege in the concealed circuit of the imperialist division of labor and economic appropriation. For Meese, imperialism is ended by an act of "love" across borders. Thus Meese claims that

> Rigoberta Menchú's struggles to liberate the racial or ethnic term from economic and moral connotations of the opposition are instructive to feminist criticism as it negotiates other (con)founding oppositions such as masculine/feminine, political/personal. Her contribution to the discussion of *ladinos* is the retrospective awareness ("afterwards we realized") that *ladinos* can be human (like Indians) good and bad depending on how they behave rather than on any essential (blood) nature. This is a profoundly un/settling awareness for the revolutionary who needs to be clear about who the enemy is. (116)

But there is an equally unsettling aporia here on the part of the feminist desiring not to be complicit with the enemy: after what did Menchú change her understanding of *ladinos*? For Menchú, the man who taught her "to love *ladinos* a lot" (165) was "a teacher, who worked with the CUC," and taught her Spanish; he was "an intellectual," "a *compañero* who had taken the side of the poor, although I have to say that he was middle class. He was someone who'd been able to study, who had a profession and everything. But he also understood clearly that he had to share these things with the poor, especially his knowledge" (165, 166). Menchú's friend is the person Marx and Engels so clearly described in the *Communist Manifesto*:

[I]n times when the class struggle nears the decisive hour, the process of dissolution going on within the ruling class, in fact within the whole range of old society, assumes such a violent, glaring character, that a small section of the ruling class cuts itself adrift, and joins the revolutionary class, the class that holds the future in its hands. Just as, therefore, at an earlier period, a section of the nobility went over to the bourgeoisie, so now a portion of the bourgeoisie goes over to the proletariat, and in particular, a portion of the bourgeois ideologists, who have raised themselves to the level of comprehending theoretically the historical movement as a whole. (64)

Unlike Meese, whose discursive desiring erases her understanding of her position in the international division of labor, Menchú's *compañero ladino* is an intellectual who has recognized and broken with his own class position and joined in solidarity in the struggle to overthrow the system producing his own privilege and exploiting Menchú. And like her he has educated himself and others into the struggle through critique, for it is in the context of discussing her relation to *ladinos*, in general, and this *compañero ladino*, in particular, that Menchú stresses the "lengthy discussions" and "times for criticism and self-criticism" (166). Thus, it is not Menchú's experience that spontaneously empowers her; rather, it is a historical and materialist intervention that enables her.

It is the historicity of this economic and revolutionary reality and the necessity for a historical materialist critique that Meese's textual substitutions occlude, displacing these with "love" (ludic desire). For Meese the "crossing over" of the boundaries of Indian and *ladino*, marked by the "*ladino/compañero* opposition," is a "shifting nominalization" in which the "definitions of the oppositional terms refuse to stay put, to stay on the respective sides of the divide" (116–17), and later she again states that the "'unwieldy,' confounded category of the *compañero ladino* . . . [is] neither strictly one nor the other, terms and identities which refuse to stay put in the very space of [Menchú's] own speaking" (119). Such rhetorical slippages finally allow her to claim these "odd hybrids, the *compañero ladino*, the feminist man, the (com)passionate U.S. feminist theorist—each an instance of being neither one thing nor the other, somehow both in an uncanny identity of man and woman, enemy and friend" (121–22). The uncanny, rhetorical indeterminacy of these binary oppositions, may discursively free the "(com)passionate U.S. feminist theorist" from the material realities of the imperialist division of labor, with its binary oppositions of exploiter and exploited, but it will do little to emancipate Menchú and other subalterns—like the mothers and children of the Alto do Cruzeiro of northeastern Brazil—from the real conditions of starvation, torture, and death that they face in their material struggles against the landowners and global capitalism supporting them.

Postcolonial theory and subaltern studies have brought to contemporary feminism a crucial dimension that had been missing from it: an understanding of the situation of women of color and a recognition of the problematics of race. However, what seems "progressive"—a gesture of solidarity between First and Third World women—remains simply a gesture. It is a gesture that substitutes affinity, and more often sentimentality, for a sustained, viable, and material collectivity. My argument throughout this book has been that the "progressive" gestures of contemporary ludic feminism remain hollow and simply discursive because they substitute the freedom of pleasure for the founding freedom: *freedom from necessity*. The freedom of pleasure, the freedom to pleasure oneself, is the specific freedom of the upper middle class, particularly in the First World.

In their theories and discussions of women of color, ludic feminists commonly point to an array of issues from phallocentrism and unrestrained patriarchal domination to religious factors. But few have taken into account the way that these factors, which are said to be the cause of oppression of women of color, are intimately related to the problem of the distribution of resources in the world, the international division of labor, and the world-historical situation of the proletariat in general. For example, one of the causes routinely pointed to as the source of the oppression of women in the Third World is the question of religion, especially Islamic fundamentalism. In ludic discourses, however, Islam is essentialized as a series of discursive practices without ever relating these practices to the historical situation of transnational capitalism. Muslim women, whether in Bangladesh, Indonesia, Iran, India, or Bosnia, are subjected to the regime of superexploitation because historical conditions have turned Islam into an ideology that promises to solve—in the religious imaginary—the material problems in which these countries are involved as a result of imperialism, the highest stage of capitalism. As Marx wrote, "*[R]eligious* suffering is at the same time an *expression* of real suffering and a *protest* against real suffering . . . The abolition of religion as the *illusory* happiness of men [and women] is the demand for their *real* happiness" (*Early Writings* 244). Any understanding of women and Islam, in other words, requires a critique of the historical relations between the ideological practices of Islam and the relations of production of global capitalism and Western imperialism.

The fundamental point for a socially transformative feminism is that sentimentalizing the other; mystifying the seemingly, unrepresentable, unknowable alterity of the other, or reifying the situation of the other as local (separate, distinct, and thus isolated) cannot be substituted for material struggle *in solidarity with the oppressed.* However, ludic feminists have taken refuge from the necessity for material struggle in the ludic motto that one should not speak for the other. In so doing, they have left the other in exile from common humanity. Drucilla Cornell, for example, insists on an "ethical feminism" that "would demand the recognition of each one of us in her singularity, not in the commonality we share *as persons as defined by a particular context (Beyond Accommodation* 113). But the particular context that Cornell denies is, in fact, the *global material context* of the laws of motion of capital. We need to be critique-al indeed of "ethical" claims to deny the commonality—that is, the relations that explain the welfare of the few and the misery of the many—in global capitalism.

In short, the other that dominates ludic feminism—whether in Cornell's notion of mimesis, Butler's strategy of citationality, Spivak's notion of subalterity, Gallop's view of the body, Grosz's trope of pure difference, Meese's "desire for feminism and (with) a Quiche Indian woman"—all provide sites for arguing for otherness as the space in which the self is one more time isolated from the collectivity in the name of respect for uniqueness and specificity: what Cornell calls "honoring . . . singularity." But this notion of the other has reduced ludic feminism to a reactionary defense of monadic individualism that is so profitable for transnational capitalism. In his essay, "Identity, the Other, and Postmodernism," Jorge Larrain is critical of the way (ludic) postmodernism "reduces otherness to pure difference and opposition, [and] it understands otherness as an incommensurable world of its own." He warns that this leads to "another form of racism," for "postmodern discourses . . . although allowing the other to speak for itself, do not want anything to do with it because it is constructed as totally different, as belonging to an alien world. The other may be acknowledged in its right to exist but it is suspected as culturally invasive and so different as to be inferior or unacceptable" (278).

For historical materialist feminists the other is not only *not other,* it is inseparably linked to "us" in our common humanity and in the universal struggle to end the exploitation of all oppressed peoples. Thus, feminism in the third wave, if it is going to be at all relevant to the lives of the world's women, must reunderstand the other not as "pure difference"—as "absolute alterity"—but as the basis for a new international collectivity. Feminism cannot be other than international. International, not in the ludic sense of the cosmopolitan, the commodification and appropriation of the other (the desire for the other), but international in the collective commitment to the revolutionary struggles to end the exploitation of all peoples—to end the exploitative regime of profit and with it the unequal global division of labor and distribution of wealth. Feminism in the third wave needs to be a historical materialist feminism: feminism as the theory and praxis of freedom—above all, freedom from necessity.

Notes

1. As I explain in this chapter, I make a distinction between *critique-al*, which is a mode of historical-materialist analysis implicating practices in the social relations of production, and *critical*, which is an ahistorical form of evaluation and judgment according to abstract norms.

2. For recent feminist efforts to engage the problem of ideology critique, see Silverman, *Male Subjectivity;* Hennessy, *Materialist Feminism;* Assiter, *Althusser;* and my forthcoming book *Patriarchal Narratives.*

3. For a more extended critique of the ideology of romance see my "Romance of Patriarchy" and forthcoming book *Patriarchal Narratives.*

4. Behind my argument here is Louis Althusser's thesis that "Philosophy is, in the last instance, class struggle in theory" (*Essays* 143).

5. On the ethical subject of pleasure/*jouissance* see especially Foucualt, Deleuze and Guattari, Barthes, and the significant feminist reworking of this issue in Cixous, Irigaray, and Butler.

6. Paglia's controversial comments on rape are collected in her *Sex, Art, and American Culture,* and Roiphe's views are developed in her *Morning After.* I critique the retrofeminism of Paglia and Roiphe in chapter 5.

7. MacKinnon elaborates on her views on rape in Bosnia in her "Turning Rape."

CHAPTER 2

1. The related concepts of "post-al" and "post-ality" are more fully articulated by Mas'ud Zavarzadeh in his "Post-ality: The (Dis)Simulations of Cyber-capitalism."

2. In self-revision, Rubin now calls this repudiation more of a correction than a "huge rejection" and decries the "current neglect of Marx," but neither of her revisions alters the profound displacing effect her work has had ("Sexual Traffic" 67, 90).

3. The exemplary of this deregulated subject of desire can be found in the post-al celebration of "perversity"; see, for example, Rubin's "Catacombs."

4. See Lyotard's "Sublime" and, more extensively, *Lessons.*

5. One of the main articulations of the debate on dual-systems theory is Sargent, *Women and Revolution;* also see Weinbaum, *Curious Courtship.* For other perspectives, see Vogel, *Marxism,* and Delphy, *Close to Home.*

6. Following Maria Mies and other dependency theorists, I am using the terms *overdeveloped* and *underdeveloped* here to indicate the historically linked relations among these zones: relations that, as Mies explains, are "based on exploitation and oppression . . . in which . . . one pole is getting 'developed' *at the expense* of the other pole, which is in the process of getting 'underdeveloped'. . . Overdevelopment and underdevelopment' are, therefore, the two extreme poles of an inherently exploitative world order, divided up and yet linked by the global accumulation process or the world market" (39). Second, I am using the term *zones* rather than countries since these zones, both over- and underdeveloped, obviously cut across national boundaries: for instance, underdeveloped zones of subsistence labor and extremely limited access to social resources clearly exist in the United States in many inner cities and among migrant farmworkers.

7. Sivanandan is, in many ways, an effective critic of the bourgeois politics of postmodernism, post-Marxism, post-Fordism, and New Times, but in the end his own politics suffers from the same limits: it ultimately breaks with historical materialism and, like Cornell West's politics, collapses into "race matterism." In "All That Melts into Air Is Solid," his perceptive critique of New Times is undermined by his own misreading of the current situation of capitalism and his displacement of the relations of production when he proclaims, "Capital had been freed from Labour" (4).

8. To argue, as many Marxists do, that racism is a historical product of capitalism is not to say that earlier societies did not have slavery or oppression, but rather to be more historically specific about the basis of that oppression. As C. L. R. James points out, "[H]istorically it is pretty well proved now that the ancient Greeks and the Romans knew nothing about race. They had another standard—civilised and barbarian—and you could have a white skin and be a barbarian and you could be black and civilised" (quoted in Alexander 5). In other words, as Peter Alexander argues "[T]hey justified [oppression] in terms of culture, not race" (5), while "Racism itself took shape in the course of the development of capitalism . . . [and] assumed three successive forms, the *racism of slavery,* the *racism of empire,* and *anti-immigrant racism*" (6). Also see Callinicos, *Race and Class.*

9. The concept of class process they use here is based on the notion of class developed in Resnick and Wolff's *Knowledge and Class.*

CHAPTER 3

1. In using the term *late capitalism,* I follow Ernest Mandel, who articulates *stages* in capitalism without positing any break. See his *Late Capitalism.*

2. It is interesting to note that Lazarus's critique of postmodernism, "Doubting the New World Order," is published in *Differences,* one of the main forums for ludic postmodern feminism.

3. I have used Moi's translation of this passage because it is clearer; for the

full English translation of Irigaray's text see her *This Sex Which is Not One*, trans. C. Porter, 78.

4. On the question of essentialization in Irigaray, see, for example, Whitford; Moi, *Sexual/Textual* and "This Essentialism." I address the problem of essentialism in ludic feminism more fully in chapter 5.

5. I have debated this issue with Mercer as a discussant to his paper and put forth this critique in more detail in the published commentary (see Mercer 443).

6. This supposed inability to account for gender, for instance, is the critique Teresa de Lauretis makes of Louis Althusser's theory of ideology in her *Technologies of Gender*.

7. In this argument, Foucault puts forth three reasons against ideology, with economic determinism being the third. His other two objections include the concept that ideology is standing in opposition "to something else which is supposed to count as truth" and to its reference "to something on the order of a subject."

CHAPTER 4

1. In addition to these feminists, Foucault's considerable impact on feminism is evident in the writings, for instance, of Sawicki; Bartky (see especially chap. 5); Butler; Martin; the more recent work of Eisenstein, such as her *Female Body*; Weedon; and Diamond and Quinby.

2. My concern here is to critically engage Butler's more recent theorizations in *Bodies That Matter*. I have already discussed her earlier articulation in *Gender Trouble* of the "performativity" of gender in my "Ludic Feminism." It is important to note, however, that in her move from *Gender Trouble* to *Bodies That Matter*, Butler largely supplants her earlier notion of performativity by citationality and displaces gender by sexuality.

CHAPTER 5

1. In addition to the works discussed here, also see Eisenstein, *Female Body*; Jacobus, Keller, and Shuttleworth; Wilcox, McWatters, Thompson, and Williams; and Sappington and Stallings.

2. The typology is, however, problematic and, I find, quite ironic: Grosz's argument is based on the necessity of moving away from categories, dualisms, binaries, but at the heart of her book lie some of the most conventional typologies—complete with categories, abstractions, exclusions, and inclusions.

3. The work of MacKinnon and other interventionist feminists is frequently delegitimated and excluded by ludic feminists for being essentialist, as demonstrated in the criticisms by Haraway in her "Manifesto" and Cornell in *Beyond Accommodation*. Another telling example of this ludic feminist exclusion

is a recent experience of mine. One of my essays on resistance postmodern feminism was rejected by two editors of a special issue on feminism and postmodernism for two main reasons: first, my critique of ludic postmodernism, and second my use of MacKinnon's statistics on rape in developing a materialist postmodern critique of Jane Gallop's ludic feminist celebration of the Marquis de Sade (I have included part of that material here) because, as the editors said, MacKinnon's statistics "are after all embedded in a highly polemical argument many of whose essentializing premises don't seem at all compatible with yours!" MacKinnon's statistics are also commonly discredited, even by those on the post-al left, as the distortions of a "crackpot"—such views are themselves distortions of the careful arguments of a committed position. The issue here for resistance postmodern feminism is to question and critique this blanket rejection of radical, interventionist feminist theories, such as those of MacKinnon, as "essentializing," "totalizing," or even "crackpot," and to recognize the way such exclusion participates in the reactionary ludic postmodern attack on systematic critiques of gender exploitation and oppression.

4. The ludic politics of pleasure as liberatory is becoming an increasingly common stance in feminist cultural studies, even at the cost of displacing real and representational violence against women. See, for example, Laura Kipnis's apologia for *Hustler* magazine as subversive over against the puritanical ("serious," nonludic) feminism of the antipornography movement. Her piece is yet another instance of the largely affirmative approach in Grossberg, Nelson, and Treichler.

5. Consciousness raising should not be trivialized as a resistance to conceptuality and rationality, nor, in a reactionary move, should it be reduced to an operation aimed at recovering woman's transhistorical and essential experience. A celebration of transhistorical and nonconceptual experience is as politically damaging to feminism as is a commitment to an equally transhistorical "reason."

6. Ludic feminists have, as a matter of routine, assumed that reason is masculine and that Marxism is the emdodiment of such masculine rationality. Such an assumption is, of course, part of the poststructuralist mythology. Marx and Engels always argued that reason is a struggle concept—it is the means for forging concepts that can provide explanatory and transformative critique. They were, in fact, quite aware of the distortion and misuse of reason. In his famous letter to Ruge (September 1843), Marx specifically addressed the issue, stating that "Reason has always existed, only not always in reasonable form" (Tucker 14). Engels, in the opening pages of his *Socialism*, discussed the way reason was deployed, in the Englightenment, by philosophers as a device for naturalizing property rights and added:

> We know today that this kingdom of reason was nothing more than the idealized kingdom of the bourgeoisie; that this eternal Right found its realisation in bourgeois justice; that this equality reduced itself to bourgeois equality before the law; that bourgeois property was proclaimed as one of the essential rights of man; and that the government of reason, the

Contract Social of Rousseau, came into being, and only could come into being, as a democratic bourgeois republic. The great thinkers of the eighteenth century could, no more than their predecessors, go beyond the limits imposed upon them by their epoch. (Tucker 684)

7. Part of this cultural move to counterfeminism includes the way mainstream feminists are also erasing basic feminist concepts—most commonly the cognitive dissolution of patriarchy itself. For instance, Gloria Steinem, in an interview, terms the new *Ms.* "postpatriarchal" (Deirdre Carmody, "*Ms.* Magazine Prepares for a Life without Ads," *New York Times*, 5 March 1990, C10). Also see MacCannell.

8. See, for example, Stanfill; B. Rich; as well as Paglia's own essays, such as "Madonna," "Ninnies," and "Academe," and her interview-conversations with Neil Postman (Paglia and Postman) and with Suzanne Gordon (Paglia and Gordon). She has been profiled in *New York* magazine, *Vanity Fair*, and *People* magazine; pictured on the *Village Voice's* front page Wanted poster "For Intellectual Fraud"; featured in the *New York Times*, both on its op–ed page and in the book review's front-page guest column; covered in the *Chronicle of Higher Education* and printed on its opinion page; featured as writer of "Guest Opinion" column for *Playboy*; published by the most prestigious presses; presented at the most important cultural sites; and heard on the *Donahue Show* and on London's *Late Show*. She has lectured at the New York Public Library, at Harvard, and on campuses throughout the country. In short, Paglian texts have been prominently circulated, widely lauded, and hotly contested in a variety of cultural forums. Her book has even been optioned for television by producers who hope to make her "a demonic female alternative to the late Joseph Campbell," according to Stanfill (24).

9. See, for example, her pieces "Ninnies" and "Academe."

10. For examples of Paglia's vitriolic and ad hominem attacks, see especially her "Return," "Ninnies," and "Nursery-School Campus."

11. Paglia's feminist defenders include, for example, the former art critic for the *Boston Phoenix*, Rebecca Nemser, who resigned her position over the publication's banning of her laudatory profile-review of Paglia, which was subsequently published in the *Boston Review*. Nemser writes, "I've been told that it's anti-feminist to admire Paglia. But I admire her precisely because I *am* a feminist. I like to hear a strong woman's voice, whether it's the voice of Camille Paglia or Catherine MacKinnon, Aretha Franklin singing R-E-S-P-E-C-T . . ." (3).

CHAPTER 6

1. The current engagement with issues of coloniality/postcoloniality is deeply indebted to the work of Fanon, although Fanon often becomes the "unsaid" of these discourses. For some of the recent articulations of the concept

of postcoloniality, see Mishra and Hodge; Appiah; Ashcroft, Griffiths, and Tiffin; Spivak, *Post-Colonial Critic;* and special issues of journals such as *Social Text* 31–32 (1992) and *Polygraph* 4 (1990), as well as, the anthologies by Williams and Chrisman and by Ashcroft, Griffiths, and Tiffin, *Post-colonial.*

2. The genealogy of postcolonialism as discourse or cultural politics traces itself to the earlier works of Fanon, while the materialist understanding of postcoloniality is shaped in part by the later works of Fanon. For discussions of the relation of cultural politics to Fanon, see especially Parry; Bhabha, "Remembering Fanon" and "What Does the Black Man Want"; and Feuchtwang. Also of importance is Memmi's *The Colonizer and the Colonized.* Some of the key texts addressing coloniality/postcoloniality in terms of dicourses or cultural politics include those of Bhabha and of Trinh Minh-ha; much of the writings of Spivak as well as many of the essays in Mohanty, Russo, and Torres; Eagleton, Jameson, and Said; Tiffin and Lawson; Niranjana; JanMohamed; Gates; JanMohamed and Lloyd; Said; Anzaldúa; Parker, *Nationalisms and Sexualities;* Petersen and Rutherford; Alcoff; Smith and Watson; Grewal and Kaplan; and such special issues of journals as *Neocolonialism, Third World Literary and Cultural Criticism, Discourse of the Other, New Americanists 2, Writing after Colonialism, Colonial Discourse,* and *Identities.* A neoconservative exemplar is Pascal Bruckner's *The Tears of the White Man.* For a critique of these discourses, see Ahmad.

3. Materialist critiques of coloniality and postcoloniality (although they rarely use the term) begin with Marx, *On Colonialism;* are developed by Lenin in *Imperialism;* and are continued more fully in such Marxist critiques as Vakhrushev and Woddis. More recent materialist critiques include such texts as Amin, *Eurocentrism* and *Empire of Chaos;* Mies; Mies, Bennholdt-Thomsen, and von Werlhof; Makhosezwe; Fuentes and Ehrenreich; Enloe; Miliband and Panitch; and the special issue *Reflections on Racism.*

4. See, for instance, Haraway, "Manifesto" and *Primate Visions;* Meese; and Spivak's work since 1985.

5. This slippage from the economic to discourse, from a materialist critique to a tropological reading, informs most of Spivak's writings. See not only the texts and interviews collected in *In Other Worlds* and *The Postcolonial Critic,* but also "Imperialism," "Naming," "Three Women's Texts," and "Woman in Difference." Spivak especially thematizes and textualizes the economic in her reading of Devi's stories.

Bibliography

Abelove, Henry, Michele Aina Barale, and David Halperin, eds. *The Lesbian and Gay Studies Reader*. New York: Routledge, 1993.

Adams, Parveen, and Elizabeth Cowie, eds. *The Woman in Question, m/f*. Cambridge: MIT Press, 1990.

Ahmad, Aijaz. *In Theory: Classes, Nations, Literatures*. London: Verso, 1992.

———. "The Politics of Literary Postcoloniality." *Race and Class* 36, no. 3 (1995): 1–20.

Alcoff, Linda. "The Problem of Speaking for Others." *Cultural Critique* 20 (winter 1991–92): 5–32.

Alexander, Peter. *Racism, Resistance, and Revolution*. London: Bookmarks, 1987.

Allison, Dorothy. *Skin: Talking about Sex, Class, and Literature*. Ithaca, N.Y.: Firebrand Books, 1994.

Althusser, Louis. *Essays in Self-Criticism*. Trans. Grahame Lock. London: New Left Books, 1976.

———. "Ideology and Ideological State Apparatuses." In *Lenin and Philosophy and Other Essays*.

———. *Lenin and Philosophy and Other Essays*. Trans. Ben Brewster. New York: Monthly Review Press, 1971.

———. "Marxism and Humanism." In *For Marx*, trans. Ben Brewster. New York: Vintage, 1970.

———. *Philosophy and the Spontaneous Philosophy of the Scientists and Other Essays*. Ed. Gregory Elliott. Trans. Ben Brewster et al. London: Verso, 1990.

Althusser, Louis, and Etienne Balibar. *Reading "Capital."* Trans. Ben Brewster. 2d ed. London: New Left Books, 1977.

Amin, Samir. *Empire of Chaos*. New York: Monthly Review Press, 1992.

———. *Eurocentrism*. New York: Monthly Review Press, 1989.

Anzaldúa, Gloria, ed. *Making Face, Making Soul, Haciendo Caras: Creative and Critical Perspectives by Women of Color*. San Francisco: Aunt Lute Foundation, 1990.

Appelbaum, Richard, and Harry Chotiner. "Science, Critique, and Praxis in Marxist Method." *Socialist Review* 9, no. 4 (1979): 71–108.

Appiah, Kwame Anthony. "Is the Post- in Postmodernism the Post- in Postcolonial?" *Critical Inquiry* 17 (winter 1991): 336–57.

Aronowitz, Stanley. *The Crisis in Historical Materialism: Class, Politics, and Culture in Marxist Theory*. 2d ed. Minneapolis: University of Minnesota Press, 1990.

———. *The Politics of Identity: Class, Culture, Social Movements.* New York: Routledge, 1992.

———. "The Situation of the Left in the United States." *Socialist Review* 93, no. 3 (1994): 5–79.

Ashcroft, Bill, Gareth Griffiths, and Helen Tiffin. *The Empire Writes Back: Theory and Practice in Post-Colonial Literatures.* London: Routledge, 1989.

———, eds. *The Post-Colonial Studies Reader.* London: Routledge, 1995.

Assiter, Alison. *Althusser and Feminism.* London: Pluto Press, 1990.

Balbus, Isaac. *Marxism and Domination: A Neo-Hegelian, Feminist, Psychoanalytic Theory of Sexual, Political, and Technological Liberation.* Princeton: Princeton University Press, 1982.

Baldi, Guido. "Thesis on Mass Worker and Social Capital." *Radical America* 6, no. 3 (1973): 3–21.

Barrett, Michèle. *The Politics of Truth: From Marx to Foucault.* Stanford: Stanford University Press, 1991.

———. *Women's Oppression Today: The Marxist/Feminist Encounter.* Rev. ed. London: Verso, 1988.

———. "Words and Things: Materialism and Method in Contemporary Feminist Analysis." In *Destabilizing Theory,* ed. Michèle Barrett and Anne Phillips, 201–19.

Barrett, Michèle, and Anne Phillips, eds. *Destabilizing Theory: Contemporary Feminist Debates.* Stanford: Stanford University Press, 1992.

Barrios de Chungara, Domitila. *Let Me Speak! Testimony of Domitila, a Woman of the Bolivian Mines.* New York: Monthly Review Press, 1978.

Bartky, Sandra Lee. *Femininity and Domination: Studies in the Phenomenology of Oppression.* London: Routledge, 1990.

Bataille, Georges. *The Accursed Share; An Essay on General Economy.* Vol. 1. New York: Zone Books, 1991.

Baudrillard, Jean. "Consumer Society." In *Selected Writings,* ed. Mark Poster. Stanford: Stanford University Press, 1988.

———. *For a Critique of the Political Economy of the Sign.* Trans. C. Levin. St. Louis: Telos Press, 1981.

———. *The Mirror of Production.* Trans. Mark Poster. St. Louis: Telos Press, 1975.

———. *Simulations.* Trans. Paul Foss, Paul Patton, and Philip Beitchman. New York: Semiotext(e), 1983.

Beaud, Michael. *A History of Capitalism 1500–1980.* New York Monthly Review Press, 1983.

Beechey, Veronica. "On Patriarchy." *Feminist Review* 3 (1979): 66-82.

———. *Unequal Work.* London: Verso, 1987.

Bell, Daniel. *The Coming of Post-Industrial Society.* New York: Basic Books, 1976.

Benhabib, Seyla. *Critique, Norm, and Utopia: A Study of the Foundations of Critical Theory.* New York: Columbia University Press, 1986.

Benhabib, Seyla, and Drucilla Cornell, eds. *Feminism as Critique: On the Politics of Gender.* Minneapolis: University of Minnesota Press, 1987.

Benhabib, Seyla, Judith Butler, Drucilla Cornell, and Nancy Fraser. *Feminist Contentions: A Philosophical Exchange.* New York: Routledge, 1995.

Benson, Pamela. *Invention of Renaissance Woman*. University Park: Pennsylvania State University Press, 1992.

Benstock, Shari. *Textualizing the Feminine: On the Limits of Genre*. Norman: University of Oklahoma Press, 1991.

Benston, Margaret. "The Political Economy of Women's Liberation." *Monthly Review* 21, no. 4 (September 1969).

Bersani, Leo. *Homos*. Cambridge: Harvard University Press, 1995.

Bhabha, Homi. *The Location of Culture*. London: Routledge, 1994.

———. "Remembering Fanon: Self, Psyche, and the Colonial Condition." In *Remaking History*, ed. Barbara Kruger and Phil Mariani. Seattle: Bay Press, 1989.

———. "'What Does the Black Man Want?'" *New Formations* no. 1 (spring 1987): 118–23.

Bloom, Harold. *The Anxiety of Influence*. New York: Oxford University Press, 1973.

Boll, Eric. *A History of Economic Thought*. London: Faber and Faber, 1992.

Bordo, Susan. "Postmodern Subjects, Postmodern Bodies." *Feminist Studies* 18, no. 1 (spring 1992): 159–76.

Boyne, Roy, and Ali Rattansi, eds. *Postmodernism and Society*. New York: St. Martin's Press, 1990.

Breitenberg, Mark. "Letters." *New York Times Book Review* (21 June 1991): 36.

Brennan, Teresa, ed. *Between Feminism and Psychoanalysis*. London: Routledge, 1989.

Bridenthal, Renate. Review of *The Politics of Truth: From Marx to Foucault*, by Michèle Barrett. *Science and Society* 58, no. 2 (summer 1994): 218–20.

Bright, Susie. "Undressing Camille." *Out/Look* (spring 1992): 9–14.

Brodribb, Somer. *Nothing Mat(t)ers: A Feminist Critique of Postmodernism*. North Melbourne, Australia: Spinifex Press, 1992.

Bruckner, Pascal. *The Tears of the White Man: Compassion as Contempt*. Trans. William Beer. New York: Free Press, 1986.

Buechler, Steve. "Sex and Class: A Critical Overview of Some Recent Theoretical Work and Some Modest Proposals." *Insurgent Sociologist* 12, no. 3 (1984): 19–32.

Bunch, Charlotte, et al. *Building Feminist Theory: Essays from "Quest," a Feminist Quarterly*. New York: Longman, 1981.

Butler, Judith. "Against Proper Objects." *Differences* 6, nos. 2–3 (summer–fall 1994): 1–26.

———. *Bodies That Matter: On the Discursive Limits of "Sex."* New York: Routledge, 1993.

———. "Contingent Foundations: Feminism and the Question of 'Postmodernism.'" In *Feminists Theorize the Political*, ed. Judith Butler and Joan W. Scott, 3–21.

———. "Gender as Performance: An Interview with Judith Butler." *Radical Philosophy* 67 (summer 1994): 32–39.

———. *Gender Trouble: Feminism and the Subversion of Identity.* New York: Routledge, 1990.

———. "Imitation and Gender Insubordination." In *Inside/Out: Lesbian Theories, Gay Theories,* ed. Fuss, 13–31.

———. "Mbembe's Extravagant Power." *Public Culture* 5, no. 1 (fall 1992): 67–74.

———. "Poststructuralism and Postmarxism." *Diacritics* 23, no. 4 (winter 1993): 3–11.

———. *Subjects of Desire: Hegelian Reflection in Twentieth-Century France.* New York: Columbia University Press, 1987.

Butler, Judith, and Joan W. Scott, eds. *Feminists Theorize the Political.* New York: Routledge, 1992.

Calasanti, Toni M., and Anna M. Zajicek. "Reweaving a Critical Theory: The Socialist-Feminist Contributions." *Rethinking Marxism* 6, no. 4 (winter 1993): 87–103.

Callinicos, Alex. *Against Postmodernism: A Marxist Critique.* New York: St. Martin's Press, 1989.

———. *Race and Class.* London: Bookmarks, 1993.

Carby, Hazel. "The Politics of Difference." *Ms.,* September–October 1990, 84–85.

Carr, C. "Battle Scars: Feminism and Nationalism Clash in the Balkans." *Village Voice,* 13 July 1993, 25–26, 29–32.

Chinchilla, Norma Stoltz, "Marxism, Feminism and the Struggle for Democracy in Latin America." *Gender and Society* 5, no. 3 (1991): 291–310.

Christian, Barbara. "The Race for Theory." *Feminist Studies* 14, no. 1 (spring 1988): 67–79.

Cixous, Hélène. "The Laugh of the Medusa." In *Feminisms,* ed. Robyn R. Warhol and Diane Price Herndl. New Brunswick: Rutgers University Press, 1991. 334–49.

Cixous, Hélène, and Catherine Clément. *The Newly Born Woman.* Trans. Betsy Wing. Minneapolis: University of Minnesota Press, 1986.

Colonial Discourse. Special issue of *Social Text* 19–20 (fall 1988).

Connerton, Paul. *The Tragedy of Enlightenment: An Essay on the Frankfurt School.* Cambridge: Cambridge University Press, 1980.

Connor, Steven. *Postmodernist Culture: An Introduction to Theories of the Contemporary.* Oxford: Basil Blackwell, 1989.

Coontz, Stephanie, and Peta Henderson. *Women's Work, Men's Property: The Origins of Gender and Class.* London: Verso, 1986.

Cornell, Drucilla. *Beyond Accommodation: Ethical Feminism, Deconstruction, and the Law.* New York: Routledge, 1991.

———. *The Philosophy of the Limit.* New York: Routledge, 1992.

Cotter, Jennifer. "On Feminist Pedagogy." *Minnesota Review* n.s. 41/42 (fall 1993/spring 1994): 118–28.

Dalla Costa, Mariarosa, and Selma James. *The Power of Women and the Subversion of the Community.* Bristol, England: Falling Wall Press, 1972.

Daly, Mary. *Gyn/Ecology: The Metaethics of Radical Feminism.* Boston: Beacon Press, 1978.

D'Amato, Paul. "Famines Do Not Occur; They Are Organized." *Socialist Worker,* August 1993, 11.

Davis, Angela. *Women, Culture, and Politics.* New York: Random House, 1990.

———. *Women, Race, and Class.* New York: Random House, 1981.

Davis, Mike, with Sue Ruddick. "Los Angeles: Civil Liberties between the Hammer and the Rock." *New Left Review* 170 (1988): 37–60.

David, Miriam E. *The State, the Family, and Education.* London: Routledge and Kegan Paul, 1980.

Dawes, Greg. "On the Textualization of Sexuality and History in Hispanism." *Transformation* 2 (fall 1995).

de Lauretis, Teresa. "The Essence of the Triangle; or, Taking the Risk of Essentialism Seriously: Feminist Theory in Italy, the U.S., and Britain." *Differences* 1, no. 2 (1989): 3–37.

———. "Film and the Visible." In *How Do I Look? Queer Film and Video,* ed. Bad Object-Choices, 223–91. Seattle: Bay Press, 1991.

———. *The Practice of Love: Lesbian Sexuality and Perverse Desire.* Bloomington: Indiana University Press, 1994.

———. *Technologies of Gender: Essays on Theory, Film, and Fiction.* Bloomington: Indiana University Press, 1987.

———. "Upping the Anti (sic) in Feminist Theory." In *Conflicts in Feminism,* ed. Marianne Hirsch and Evelyn Fox Keller, 255–70.

Deleuze, Gilles, and Felix Guattari. *Anti-Oedipus: Capitalism and Schizophrenia.* Trans. R. Hurley et al. Minneapolis: University of Minnesota Press, 1983.

———. *A Thousand Plateaus: Capitalism and Schizophrenia.* Trans. Brian Massumi. Minneapolis: University of Minnesota Press, 1987.

D'Emilio, John. *Making Trouble: Essays on Gay History, Politics, and the University.* New York: Routledge, 1992.

———. *Sexual Politics, Sexual Communities: The Making of a Homosexual Minority in the United States, 1940–1970.* Chicago: University of Chicago Press, 1983.

Delphy, Christine. *Close to Home: A Materialist Analysis of Women's Oppression.* Trans. Diana Leonard. Amherst: University of Massachusetts Press, 1984.

Denfeld, Rene. *The New Victorians: A Young Woman's Challenge to the Old Feminist Order.* New York: Warner, 1994.

Derrida, Jacques. "Differance." In *Margins of Philosophy,* trans. Alan Bass. Chicago: University of Chicago Press, 1982.

———. *Of Grammatology.* Trans. Gayatri Chakravorty Spivak. Baltimore: Johns Hopkins University Press, 1974.

———. *Positions.* Trans. Alan Bass. Chicago: University of Chicago Press, 1981.

———. *Specters of Marx: The State of the Debt, the Work of Mourning, and the New International.* Trans. Peggy Kamuf. New York: Routledge, 1994.

———. *Writing and Difference.* Trans. Alan Bass. Chicago: University of Chicago Press, 1978.

Derrida, Jacques, and Geoff Bennington. "On Colleges and Philosophy." In

Postmodernism: ICA Documents, ed. Lisa Appignanesi, 209–28. London: Free Association Books, 1989.

Derrida, Jacques, and Christie McDonald. "Choreographies." In *The Ear of the Other,* ed. Christie McDonald. Trans. Peggy Kamuf. 1985. Lincoln: University of Nebraska Press, 1988, 163–86.

Diamond, Irene, and Lee Quinby, eds. *Feminism and Foucault: Reflections on Resistance.* Boston: Northeastern University Press, 1988.

Dionne, E. J. "The Idea of Equality Is Proving Unequal to the Demands of Today." *Washington Post National Weekly Edition,* 7–13 May 1990, 12–14.

Discourse of the Other: Postcoloniality, Positionality, and Subjectivity. Special issue of *Quarterly Review of Film and Video* 13, nos. 1–3 (1991).

Dobb, Maurice. *Studies in the Development of Capitalism.* New York: International Publishers, 1947.

Dreyfus, Hubert, and Paul Rabinow. *Michel Foucault: Beyond Structuralism and Hermeneutics.* 2d ed. Chicago: University of Chicago Press, 1983.

Drucker, Peter. *Post-Capitalist Society.* New York: HarperCollins, 1993.

Dunbar, Roxanne. "Female Liberation as the Basis for Social Revolution." In *Sisterhood Is Powerful,* ed. Robin Morgan, 536–53. New York: Vintage, 1970.

Eagleton, Terry. *Ideology: An Introduction.* London: Verso, 1991.

Eagleton, Terry, Fredric Jameson, and Edward Said, eds. *Nationalism, Colonialism, and Literature.* Minneapolis: University of Minnesota Press, 1990.

Ebert, Teresa. "Ludic Feminism, the Body, Performance, and Labor: Bringing *Materialism* Back into Feminist Cultural Studies." *Cultural Critique* 23 (winter 1992–93): 5–50.

———. "Patriarchal Narratives: Feminist Culture Critique after Post-al Politics." Book manuscript.

———. "The Romance of Patriarchy: Ideology, Subjectivity, and Postmodern Feminist Cultural Theory." *Cultural Critique* 10 (fall 1988): 19–57.

———. "Writing In the Political: Resistance (Post)modernism." *Legal Studies Forum* 15, no. 4 (1991): 291–304.

Edmundson, Mark. "Art and Eros." *Nation,* 25 June 1990, 897–99.

Eisenstein, Zillah. "Developing a Theory of Capitalist Patriarchy and Socialist Feminism." In *Capitalist Patriarchy and the Case for Socialist Feminism,* ed. Zillah Eisenstein, 5–40.

———. *The Female Body and the Law.* Berkeley and Los Angeles: University of California Press, 1988.

———. "Specifying US Feminism in the 1990's: The Problem of Naming." *Socialist Review* 90, no. 2 (1990): 45–56.

———, ed. *Capitalist Patriarchy and the Case for Socialist Feminism.* New York: Monthly Review Press, 1979.

Elam, Diane. *Feminism and Deconstruction: Ms. en abyme.* London: Routledge, 1994.

———. *Romancing the Postmodern.* New York: Routledge, 1992.

el Saadawi, Nawal. *The Hidden Face of Eve: Women in the Arab World.* London: Zed Books, 1980.

Engels, Frederick. *Anti-Dühring.* New York: International Publishers, 1976.

———. "The Funeral of Karl Marx." In *When Karl Marx Died: Comments in 1883*, ed. Philip Froner. New York: International Publishers, 1973.

———. *Ludwig Feuerbach and the Outcome of Classical German Philosophy*. New York: International Publishers, 1941.

———. *The Origin of the Family, Private Property, and the State*. New York: International Publishers, 1972.

———. *Socialism: Utopian and Scientific*. Peking: Foreign Languages Press, 1975.

Enloe, Cynthia. *Bananas, Beaches, and Bases: Making Feminist Sense of International Politics*. 1989; rpt. Berkeley and Los Angeles: University of California Press, 1990.

Fallowell, Duncan. "Between the Will and the Slime." *Spectator*, 28 July 1990, 34.

Faludi, Susan. *Backlash: The Undeclared War against American Women*. New York: Crown Publishers, 1991.

Fanon, Frantz. *Black Skin, White Masks*. New York: Grove, 1967.

———. *A Dying Colonialism*. 1965; rpt. New York: Grove Weidenfeld, 1967.

———. *Toward the African Revolution*. 1967. New York: Grove, 1969.

———. *The Wretched of the Earth*. New York: Grove Weidenfeld, 1968.

Felman, Shoshana. "Women and Madness: The Critical Phallacy." *Diacritics* 5, no. 4 (1975): 2–10.

Ferguson, Kathy. *The Man Question: Visions of Subjectivity in Feminist Theory*. Berkeley and Los Angeles: University of California Press, 1993.

Ferguson, Margaret, and Jennifer Wicke, eds. *Feminism and Postmodernism*. Durham, N.C.: Duke University Press, 1994.

Feuchtwang, Stephan. "Fanonian Spaces." *New Formations* 1 (spring 1987): 124–30.

Field, Nicola. *Over the Rainbow: Money, Class and Homophobia*. London: Pluto Press, 1995.

Firestone, Shulamith. *The Dialectic of Sex*. 1970, rpt. New York: Bantam, 1971.

Fish, Stanley. *There's No Such Thing as Free Speech . . . and It's a Good Thing, Too*. New York: Oxford University Press, 1993.

Fiske, John. "Cultural Studies and the Culture of Everyday Life." In *Cultural Studies*, ed. Lawrence Grossberg, Cary Nelson, and Paula Treichler. 154–73.

Fitch, Robert. "What's Left to Write?" *Voice Literary Supplement*, May 1989, 18–22.

Fitzgerald, John K. "Letters." *New York Times* (2 June 1991): 36.

Flax, Jane. *Disputed Subjects: Essays on Psychoanalysis, Politics and Philosophy*. New York: Routledge, 1993.

———. *Thinking Fragments: Psychoanalysis, Feminism, and Postmodernism in the Contemporary West*. Berkeley: University of California Press, 1990.

Folbre, Nancy. "Exploitation Comes Home: A Critique of the Marxian Theory of Family Labour." *Cambridge Journal of Economics* 6 (1982): 317–29.

———. "A Patriarchal Mode of Production." In *Alternatives to Economic Orthodoxy*, ed. R. Albelda, Christopher Gunn, and William Waller. Armonk, N.Y.: M. E. Sharpe, 1987.

———. *Who Pays for the Kids? Gender and the Structures of Constraint*. London: Routledge, 1994.

Foucault, Michel. *The Archeology of Knowledge and the Discourse on Language.* Trans. A. Sheridan Smith. New York: Pantheon, 1972.

———. *Discipline and Punish: The Birth of the Prison.* Trans. Alan Sheridan. New York: Random House, 1979.

———. "The Ethic of Care for the Self as a Practice of Freedom." Interview. *Philosophy and Social Criticism* 12, nos. 2–3 (1987): 109–31.

———. *The History of Sexuality.* Vol. 1. Trans. R. Hurley. 1978. New York: Vintage, 1980.

———. *Language, Counter-Memory, Practice.* Ed. Donald F. Bouchard and trans. Sherry Simon. Ithaca, N.Y.: Cornell University Press, 1977.

———. *Madness and Civilization: A History of Insanity in the Age of Reason.* Trans. Richard Howard. 1965. New York: Vintage, 1988.

———. "Nietzsche, Genealogy, History." In *Language, Counter-Memory, Practice.*

———. *The Order of Things: An Archeology of the Human Sciences.* 1970. New York: Vintage, 1973

———. "Politics and the Study of Discourse." In *The Foucault Effect,* ed. Graham Burchell, Colin Gordon, and Peter Miller, 53–72. Chicago: University of Chicago Press, 1991.

———. *Power/Knowledge.* Ed. Colin Gordon. Trans. Colin Gordon, Leo Marshall, John Mepham, and Kate Soper. New York: Pantheon, 1980.

———. "Questions of Method." In *The Foucault Effect.* Ed. Graham Burchell, Colin Gordon, and Peter Miller, 73–86.

———. "Truth and Power." In *Power/Knowledge,* ed. Colin Gordon. New York: Pantheon, 1980, 109–33.

———. "What Is Enlightenment?" In *The Foucault Reader,* ed. Paul Rabinow. New York: Pantheon, 1984, 32–50.

Foucault, Michel, and Gilles Deleuze. "Intellectuals and Power." In *Language, Counter-Memory, Practice,* ed. and trans. Donald F. Bouchard. Ithaca, N.Y.: Cornell University Press, 1977.

Fraad, Harriet, Stephen Resnick, and Richard Wolff. *Bringing It All Back Home: Class, Gender and Power in the Modern Household.* London: Pluto Press, 1994.

———. "For Every Knight in Shining Armor, There's a Castle Waiting to Be Cleaned: A Marxist-Feminist Analysis of the Household." *Rethinking Marxism* 2, no. 4 (winter 1989): 10–69 and 3, no. 2 (summer 1990): 124–44.

Fraser, N., and L. Nicholson. "Social Criticism without Philosophy: An Encounter between Feminism and Postmodernism." In *Feminism/Postmodernism,* ed. Linda Nicholson, 19–38.

Friend, Tad. "Yes." *Esquire,* February 1994, 48–56.

Fuentes, Annette, and Barbara Ehrenreich. *Women in the Global Factory.* Boston: South End Press, 1984.

Fukuyama, Francis. *The End of History and the Last Man.* New York: Free Press, 1992.

Fuss, Diana, ed. *Essentially Speaking: Feminism, Nature, and Difference.* New York: Routledge, 1989.

———. *Inside/Out: Lesbian Theories, Gay Theories.* New York: Routledge, 1991.

Futrelle, David, and Leora Tanenbaum. "Bootstrap Feminism." *In These Times,* 8 August 1994, 33–36.

Gage, Matilda Joslyn. *Woman, Church, and State.* 1893; rpt. Watertown: Persephone, 1980.

Gallop, Jane. *Around 1981: Academic Feminist Literary Theory.* New York: Routledge, 1992.

———. *The Daughter's Seduction: Feminism and Psychoanalysis.* Ithaca, N.Y.: Cornell University Press, 1982.

———. *Reading Lacan.* Ithaca, N.Y.: Cornell University Press, 1985.

———. *Thinking through the Body.* New York: Columbia University Press, 1988.

Gallop, Jane, Marianne Hirsch, and Nancy Miller. "Criticizing Feminist Criticism." In *Conflicts in Feminism,* ed. Marianne Hirsch and Evelyn Fox Keller, 349–69.

Garber, Marjorie. *Vested Interests: Cross-Dressing and Cultural Anxiety.* New York: Routledge, 1991.

Gates, Henry Louis, ed. *"Race," Writing, and Difference.* Chicago: University of Chicago Press, 1986.

German, Lindsey. *Sex, Class, and Socialism.* London: Bookmarks, 1989.

Gilligan, Carol. *In a Different Voice: Psychological Theory and Women's Development.* Cambridge: Harvard University Press, 1982.

Giroux, Henry, ed. *Postmodernism, Feminism, and Cultural Politics: Redrawing Educational Boundaries.* Albany: State University of New York Press, 1991.

Goldstein, Richard. "The Politics of Political Correctness." *Village Voice,* 18 June 1991, 39–41.

Gorman, Jane. Letter to the editor. *Women's Review of Books,* December 1991, 4.

Graff, Gerald. "Co-optation." In *The New Historicism,* ed. H. Aram Veeser. New York: Routledge, 1989, 168–81.

Gramsci, Antonio. *Selections from the Prison Notebooks.* Ed. and trans. Quintin Hoare and Geoffrey N. Smith. New York: International Publishers, 1971.

Grewal, Inderpal, and Caren Kaplan, eds. *Scattered Hegemonies: Postmodernity and Transnational Feminist Practices.* Minneapolis: University of Minnesota Press, 1994.

Grossberg, Lawrence, Cary Nelson, and Paula Treichler, eds. *Cultural Studies.* New York: Routledge, 1992.

Grosz, Elizabeth. *Volatile Bodies: Toward a Corporeal Feminism.* Bloomington: Indiana University Press, 1994.

Guha, Ranajit, and Gayatri Chakravorty Spivak, eds. *Selected Subaltern Studies.* New York: Oxford University Press, 1988.

Habermas, Jürgen. *The Philosophical Discourse of Modernity.* Trans. F. Lawrence. Cambridge: MIT Press, 1987.

———. *Toward a Rational Society: Student Protest, Science, and Politics.* Trans. Jeremy Shapiro. Boston: Beacon Press, 1970.

Hall, Stuart. *The Hard Road to Renewal: Thatcherism and the Crisis of the Left.* London: Verso, 1988.

———. "The Rediscovery of 'Ideology': Return of the Repressed in Media Studies." In *Culture, Society, and the Media,* ed. Michael Gurevitch et al., 56–90. London: Methuen, 1982.

———. "Signification, Representation, Ideology: Althusser and the Post-Structuralist Debates." *Critical Studies in Mass Communication* 2, no. 2 (1985): 91–114.

Hall, Stuart, and Jacques Martin, eds. *New Times: The Changing Face of Politics in the 1990s.* 1989. London: Verso, 1990.

Hamilton, Roberta. "Working at Home." In *The Politics of Diversity,* ed. Roberta Hamilton and Michèle Barrett, 139–53.

Hamilton, Roberta, and Michèle Barrett, eds. *The Politics of Diversity: Feminism, Marxism, and Nationalism.* London: Verso, 1986.

Hanninen, Sakari, and Leena Paldan. *Rethinking Ideology: A Marxist Debate.* Berlin: Argument-Verlag, New York: International General/IMMRC, 1993.

Hansen, Karen, and Ilene Philpson, eds. *Women, Class, and the Feminist Imagination: A Socialist-Feminist Reader.* Philadelphia: Temple University Press, 1990.

Haraway, Donna. "A Manifesto for Cyborgs: Science, Technology, and Socialist Feminism in the 1980s." 1985; rpt. in *Simians, Cyborgs, and Women,* 148–81.

———. *Primate Visions: Gender, Race, and Nature in the World of Modern Science.* New York: Routledge, 1989.

———. *Simians, Cyborgs, and Women: The Reinvention of Nature.* New York: Routledge, 1991.

Harding, Sandra. "The Instability of the Analytical Categories of Feminist Theory." *Signs* 11, no. 4 (1986): 645–64.

Harlow, Barbara. *Resistance Literature.* New York: Methuen, 1987.

Harrington, Michael. *Socialism.* New York: Saturday Review Press, 1972.

Hartmann, Heidi. "The Unhappy Marriage of Marxism and Feminism: Towards a More Progressive Union." In *Women and Revolution,* ed. Lydia Sargent, 1–42.

Hartsock, Nancy. "Foucault on Power: A Theory for Women?" In *Feminism/Postmodernism,* ed. Linda Nicholson, 157–75.

———. *Money, Sex, and Power: Toward a Feminist Historical Materialism.* Boston: Northeastern University Press, 1985.

Harvey, David. *The Condition of Postmodernity.* Oxford: Basil Blackwell, 1989.

Haug, Frigga. "Boys' Games and Human Work: On Gender Relations as Relations of Production." *Rethinking Marxism* 6, no. 3 (1993): 49–65.

———. "The Women's Question and the Class Question." In *Rethinking Ideology,* ed. Sakari Hanninen and Leena Paldan, 144–51.

Hegel, Georg W. F. *Phenomenology of the Spirit.* Trans. A. V. Miller. New York: Oxford University Press, 1977.

Heidegger, Martin. *Poetry, Language, Thought.* Trans. A. Hofstadter. New York: Harper and Row, 1971.

Heilbroner, Robert. *The Nature and Logic of Capitalism.* New York: Norton, 1985.

Hekman, Susan. *Gender and Knowledge: Elements of a Postmodern Feminism.* Boston: Northeastern University Press, 1990.

Hennessy, Rosemary. *Materialist Feminism and the Politics of Discourse.* New York: Routledge, 1993.

Hennessy, Rosemary, and Rajeswari Mohan. "The Construction of Woman in Three Popular Texts of Empire: Towards a Critique of Materialist Feminism." *Textual Practice* 3, no. 3 (1989): 323–59.

Hirsch, Marianne, and Evelyn Fox Keller, eds. *Conflicts in Feminism*. New York: Routledge, 1990.

hooks, bell. *Black Looks: Race and Representation*. Boston: South End Press, 1992.

———. "Essentialism and Experience." Review of *Essentially Speaking*, by Diane Fuss. *American Literary History* 3, no. 1 (1991): 172–83.

———. *Talking Back: Thinking Feminist, Thinking Black*. Boston: South End Press, 1989.

———. *Yearning: Race, Gender, and Cultural Politics*. Boston: South End Press, 1990.

Hunt, Lynn, ed. *The Invention of Pornography: Obscenity and the Origins of Modernity, 1500–1800*. Cambridge: Zone, 1993.

Huston, Perdita. *Third World Women Speak Out*. New York: Praeger, 1979.

Identities. Special issue of *Critical Inquiry* 18, no. 4 (summer 1992).

Irigaray, Luce. *Speculum of the Other Woman*. Trans. G. Gill. Ithaca, N.Y.: Cornell University Press, 1985.

———. *This Sex Which Is Not One*. Trans. Catherine Porter and Carolyn Burke. Ithaca, N.Y.: Cornell University Press, 1985.

Jacobus, Mary, Evelyn Fox Keller, and Sally Shuttleworth, eds. *Body/Politics: Women and the Discourses of Science*. New York: Routledge, 1990.

Jameson, Fredric. "*History and Class Consciousness* as an 'Unfinished Project.'" *Rethinking Marxism* 1, no. 1 (1988): 49–73.

———. *The Ideologies of Theory: Essays 1971–1986*. 2 vols. Minneapolis: University of Minnesota Press, 1988.

———. *The Political Unconscious: Narrative as a Socially Symbolic Act*. Ithaca, N.Y.: Cornell University Press, 1981.

———. *Postmodernism; or, The Cultural Logic of Late Capitalism*. Durham, N.C.: Duke University Press, 1991.

JanMohamed, Abdul. *Manichean Aesthetics: The Politics of Literature in Colonial Africa*. Amherst: University of Massachusetts Press, 1983.

JanMohamed, Abdul, and D. Lloyd. *The Nature and Context of Minority Discourse*. New York: Oxford University Press, 1990.

Jardine, Alice. *Gynesis*. Ithaca, N.Y.: Cornell University Press, 1985.

Jayawardena, Kumari. *Feminism and Nationalism in the Third World*. London: Zed Books.

Johnson, Barbara. Introduction to *Dissemination*, by Jacques Derrida. Chicago: University of Chicago Press, 1981.

———. *A World of Difference*. Baltimore: Johns Hopkins University Press, 1987.

Kannabiran, Vasantha, and K. Lalitha, "That Magic Time: Women in the Telangana People's Struggle." In *Recasting Women*, ed. Kumkum Sangari and Sudesh Vaid, 180–203.

Kant, Immanuel. *Critique of Practical Reason*. Trans. L. W. Beck. Indianapolis: Bobbs-Merrill, 1956.

Kaplan, E. Ann, ed. *Postmodernism and Its Discontents: Theories, Practices*. London; Verso, 1988.

Kerrigan, William. "The Perverse *Kulturgeschichte* of Camille Paglia." *Raritan* 10, no. 3 (1991): 134–45.

Kipnis, L. "(Male) Desire and (Female) Disgust: Reading *Hustler*." In *Cultural Studies*, ed. Lawrence Grossberg, Cary Nelson, and Paula Treichler, 373–91.

Kiss & Tell: Persimmon Blackbridge, Lizard Jones, and Susan Stewart. *Her Tongue on My Theory: Images, Essays and Fantasies*. Vancouver, B.C.: Press Gang Publishers, 1994.

Kollontai, Alexandra. *The Autobiography of a Sexually Emancipated Communist Woman*. Trans. S. Attanasio. New York: Schocken, 1975.

———. *Selected Articles and Speeches*. New York: International Publishers, 1984.

———. *Women Workers Struggle for Their Rights*. Trans. C. Britton. Bristol, England: Falling Wall Press, 1973.

Krentz, Jayne Ann, ed. *Dangerous Men and Adventurous Women: Romance Writers on the Appeal of the Romance*. Philadelphia: University of Pennsylvania Press, 1992.

Kristeva, Julia. *The Kristeva Reader*. Ed. Toril Moi. New York: Columbia University Press, 1986.

———. "Oscillation between Power and Denial." In *New French Feminisms*, ed. Elaine Marks. Amherst University Press, 1980, 165–68.

Kroker, Arthur, and David Cook. *The Postmodern Scene: Excremental Culture and Hyper-Aesthetics*. New York: St. Martin's Press, 1986.

Kruks, Sonia, Rayna Rapp, and Marilyn B. Young, eds. *Promissory Notes: Women in the Transition to Socialism*. New York: Monthly Review Press, 1989.

Kubitschek, Missy Dehn. "Pygmalion as Black and Female." *Socialist Review* 89 (1989): 147–53.

Kuhn, Annette, and AnnMarie Wolpe, eds. *Feminism and Materialism: Women and Modes of Production*. London: Routledge and Kegan Paul, 1978.

Kwant, Remy. *Critique: Its Nature and Function*. Pittsburgh: Duquesne University Press, 1967.

Lacan, Jacques. *Ecrits: A Selection*. Trans. Alan Sheridan. New York: Norton, 1977.

Laclau, Ernesto. "Beyond Emancipation." *Development and Change* 23, no. 3 (1992): 121–37.

———. "Building a New Left: An Interview with Ernesto Laclau." *Strategies* 1 (fall 1988): 10–28.

———. *New Reflections on the Revolution of Our Time*. London: Verso, 1990.

———. "Populist Rupture and Discourse." *Screen Education* 34 (spring 1980): 87–93.

———. "Transformations of Advanced Industrial Societies and the Theory of the Subject." In *Rethinking Ideology*, ed. Sakari Hanninen and Leena Paldan, 39–44.

Laclau, Ernesto, and Chantal Mouffe. *Hegemony and Socialist Strategy: Towards a Radical Democratic Politics*. London: Verso, 1985.

Landry, Donna, and Gerald MacLean. *Materialist Feminisms.* Cambridge, Mass.: Blackwell, 1993.

Larrain, Jorge. "Identity, the Other, and Postmodernism." *Transformation* 1 (spring 1995): 271–89.

Lash, Scott. *Sociology of Postmodernism.* London: Routledge, 1990.

Lather, Patti. *Getting Smart: Feminist Research and Pedagogy with/in the Postmodern.* New York: Routledge, 1991.

Lazarus, Neil. "Doubting the New World Order: Marxism, Realism, and the Claims of Postmodernist Social Theory." *Differences* 3, no. 3 (1991): 94–138.

Lefebvre, Henri. *The Critique of Everyday Life.* Trans. John Moore. London: Verso, 1991.

Lenin, V. I. *The Emancipation of Women.* New York: International Publishers, 1984.

———. *Imperialism: The Highest Stage of Capitalism.* New York: International Publishers, 1939.

———. *Materialism and Empirio-Criticism.* New York: International Publishers, 1970.

———. *State and Revolution.* Trans. Robert Service. New York: Penguin, 1992.

Lipietz, Alain. *Mirages and Miracles: The Crises of Global Fordism.* Trans. David Macey. London: Verso, 1987.

Lorde, Audre. "The Master's Tools Will Never Dismantle the Master's House." In *This Bridge Called My Back: Writings by Radical Women of Color,* ed. Cherríe Moraga and Gloria Anzaldúa, New York: Kitchen Table, 1983, 98–101.

Lourdes, Benería, and Martha Roldán. *The Crossroads of Class and Gender: Industrial Homework, Subcontracting, and Household Dynamics in Mexico City.* Chicago: University of Chicago Press, 1987.

Lowe, Donald, Michael Rosenthal, and Ron Silliman. "Introduction" to "Gayatri Spivak on the Politics of Subaltern." *Socialist Review* 90, (July–Sept. 1990): 81–83.

Luxemburg, Rosa. *Rosa Luxemburg Speaks.* Ed. Mary-Alice Waters. New York: Pathfinder Press, 1970.

———. *Selected Political Writings of Rosa Luxemburg.* Ed. Dick Howard. New York: Monthly Review Press, 1971.

Lyotard, Jean-François. *The Differend: Phrases in Dispute.* Trans. Georges Van Den Abbeele. Minneapolis: University of Minnesota Press, 1988.

———. *Lessons on the Analytic of the Sublime.* Trans. Elizabeth Rottenberg. Stanford: Stanford University Press, 1994.

———. *The Postmodern Condition.* Trans. Geoff Bennington and Brian Massumi. Minneapolis: University of Minnesota Press, 1984.

———. "The Sublime and the Avant-Garde." In *The Lyotard Reader,* ed. Andrew Benjamin. New York: Blackwell, 1989.

Lyotard, Jean-François, and Jean-Loup Thebaud. *Just Gaming.* Trans. Wlad Godzich. Minneapolis: University of Minnesota Press, 1985.

MacCannell, Juliet Flower. *The Regime of the Brother: After the Patriarchy.* New York: Routledge, 1991.

MacFarquhar, Emily. "The War against Women." *U.S. News and World Report*, 28 March 1994, 42–48.

MacKinnon, Catharine. *Feminism Unmodified: Discourses on Life and Law.* Cambridge: Harvard University Press, 1987.

———. *Toward a Feminist Theory of the State.* Cambridge: Harvard University Press, 1989.

———. "Turning Rape into Pornography: Postmodern Genocide." *Ms.*, July–August 1993, 24–30.

Makhosezwe, Bernard. *The Political Economy of Race and Class in South Africa.* Rev. ed. New York: Monthly Review Press, 1989.

Mandel, Ernest. *An Introduction to Marxist Economic Theory.* New York: Pathfinder Press, 1970.

———. *Late Capitalism.* New York: Verso, 1978.

Martin, Biddy. "Feminism, Criticism, and Foucault." *New German Critique* 27 (fall 1982): 3–30.

Marx, Karl. *Capital: A Critique of Political Economy.* Trans. B. Fowkes. Vol. 1. New York: Vintage, 1977.

———. *A Contribution to the Critique of Political Economy.* Ed. Maurice Dobb. Trans. S. W. Ryazanskaya. New York: International Publishers, 1970.

———. "Critique of Hegel's Doctrine of the State." In *Early Writings.*

———. *Critique of the Gotha Programme.* New York: International Publishers, 1966.

———. *The Communist Manifesto.* Ed. Frederic Bender. New York: Norton, 1988.

———. *Early Writings.* Ed. Quintin Hoare. Trans. R. Livingstone and G. Benton. London: Penguin, 1992.

———. *Economic and Philosophic Manuscripts of 1844.* In *Early Writings.*

———. *The Eighteenth Brumaire of Louis Bonaparte.* New York: International Publishers, 1963.

———. *Grundrisse.* Trans. Martin Nicolaus. New York: Vintage, 1973.

———. *On Colonialism.* New York: International Publishers, 1972.

———. "On the Jewish Question." In *Early Writings.*

———. *The Poverty of Philosophy.* New York: International Publishers, 1992.

———. *Theories of Surplus Value.* Pt. 1. Trans. Emile Burns. Moscow: Progress, 1969.

———. "Theses on Feuerbach." *Collected Works.* Vol. 5. New York: International Publishers, 1976.

———. *Wage-Labour and Capital and Value, Price, and Profit.* New York: International Press, 1976.

Marx, Karl, and Friedrich Engels. *Collected Works.* Vol. 3. New York: International Publishers, 1975.

———. *The German Ideology.* In *Collected Works.* Vol. 5. New York: International Publishers, 1976.

———. *Gesamtausgabe.* Vol. 1., pt. 2. Berlin: Dietz Verlag, 1982.

———. *The Marx-Engels Reader.* 2d. ed. Ed. Robert C. Tucker. New York: Norton, 1978.

Marx, Karl, Fredrick Engels, V. I. Lenin, and Joseph Stalin. *The Woman Question:*

Selections from the Writings of Karl Marx, Fredrick Engels, V. I. Lenin, Joseph Stalin. New York: International Publishers, 1951.

Matthaei, Julie. "Surplus Labor, the Household, and Gender Oppression." *Rethinking Marxism* 2, no. 4 (winter 1989): 70–78.

McAllister, Carol. "Global Economic Restructuring and Women's Experiences." *Bulletin in Defense of Marxism*, March 1994, 18–19, 34.

McGowan, John. *Postmodernism and Its Critics.* Ithaca, N.Y.: Cornell University Press, 1991.

McHugh, Clare. "The Prophet of Power Feminism: Is Naomi Wolf the Gloria Steinem of Her Generation?" *New York*, 29 November 1993, 44–50.

McRobbie, Angela. "Post-Marxism and Cultural Studies: A Post-script." In *Cultural Studies*, ed. Lawrence Grossberg, Cary Nelson, and Paula Treichler, 719–30.

Meese, Elizabeth. *(Ex)tensions: Re-Figuring Feminist Criticism.* Urbana: University of Illinois Press, 1990.

Meese, Elizabeth, and Andrew Parker, eds. *The Difference Within: Feminism and Critical Theory.* Philadelphia: John Benjamins, 1989.

Memmi, Albert. *The Colonizer and the Colonized.* 1965; rpt. Boston: Beacon Press, 1967.

Menchú, Rigoberta. *I . . . Rigoberta Menchu: An Indian Woman in Guatemala*, ed. Elisabeth Burgos-Debray. London: Verso, 1984.

Mercer, K. "'1968': Periodizing Postmodern Politics and Identity." In *Cultural Studies*, ed. Lawrence Grossberg, Cary Nelson, and Paula Treichler, 424–49.

Mies, Maria. *Patriarchy and Accumulation on a World Scale: Women in the International Division of Labour.* London: Zed Books, 1986.

Mies, Maria, Veronika Bennholdt-Thomsen, and Claudia von Werlhof. *Women: The Last Colony.* London: Zed Books, 1988.

Mies, Maria, and Vandana Shiva. *Ecofeminism.* London: Zed Books, 1993.

Miles, Angela. "Economism and Feminism: A Comment on the Domestic Labour Debate." In *The Politics of Diversity*, ed. Hamilton and Barrett, 168–79.

Miliband, R., and Leo Panitch. *New World Order?* New York: Monthly Review Press, 1992.

Miller, J. Hillis. *Theory Now and Then.* Durham, N.C.: Duke University Press, 1991.

Miller, Nancy. *Getting Personal: Feminist Occasions and Other Autobiographical Acts.* New York: Routledge, 1991.

Milner, Andrew, Philip Thomson, and Chris Worth, eds. *Postmodern Conditions.* Clayton, Victoria: Centre for General and Comparative Literature, Monash University, 1988.

Minh-ha, Trinh T. *When the Moon Waxes Red: Representation, Gender, and Cultural Politics.* New York: Routledge, 1991.

———. *Woman, Native, Other: Writing Postcoloniality and Feminism.* Bloomington: Indiana University Press, 1989.

Mishra, Vijay, and Bob Hodge. "What Is Post(-)Colonialism?" *Textual Practice* 5, no. 3 (winter 1991): 399–414.

Mitchell, Juliet. *Psychoanalysis and Feminism.* New York: Vintage, 1975.

———. *Women: The Longest Revolution.* New York: Pantheon, 1984.

———. "Women and Equality." In *Feminism and Equality,* ed. Anne Phillips, 2–43. New York: New York University Press, 1987.

———. *Women's Estate.* New York: Pantheon, 1971.

Mitchell, W. J. T. "Postcolonial Culture, Postimperial Criticism." *Transition* 56 (1992): 11–19.

Modleski, Tania. *Feminism without Women: Culture and Criticism in a "Postfeminist" Age.* New York: Routledge, 1991.

Moghadam, Valentine. "Revolution, Islam, and Women: Sexual Politics in Iran and Afghanistan." In *Nationalisms and Sexualities,* ed. Andrew Parker, Mary Russo, Doris Sommer, and Patricia Yaeger. 424–46.

———. "Socialism or Anti-Imperialism? The Left and Revolution in Iran." *New Left Review* 166 (1987).

Mohanty, Chandra, Ann Russo, and Lourdes Torres. *Third World Women and the Politics of Feminism.* Bloomington: Indiana University Press, 1991.

Moi, Toril. "Feminism, Postmodernism, and Style: Recent Feminist Criticism in the United States." *Cultural Critique* 9 (spring 1988): 3–22.

———. "Patriarchal Thought and the Drive for Knowledge." In *Between Feminism and Psychoanalysis,* ed. Teresa Brennan, 189–205.

———. *Sexual/Textual Politics: Feminist Literary Theory.* London: Methuen, 1985.

Morton, Donald. "Birth of the Cyberqueer." *PMLA* 110, no. 3 (May 1995): 369–81.

———. "The Politics of Queer Theory in the (Post)Modern Moment." *Genders* 17 (fall 1993): 121–50.

Mosbacher, Georgette. *Feminine Force: Release the Power.* New York: Simon and Schuster, 1993.

Mouffe, Chantal. "The Sex/Gender System and the Discursive Construction of Women's Subordination." In *Rethinking Ideology,* ed. Sakari Hanninen and Leena Paldan, 139–43.

Mullarkey, Maureen. "Hard Cop, Soft Cop." *Nation,* 30 May 1987, 720–26.

Negri, Antonio. *Revolutionary Writings: Working Class Autonomy and the Crisis.* London: Red Notes, 1979.

———. *Marx beyond Marx.* Amherst, Mass.: Bergin and Garvey, 1984.

———. "Worker's Party against Work."

Nemser, Rebecca. "Banned in Boston?" *Boston Review* 17, nos. 3–4 (1992): 3–4.

Neocolonialism. Special issue of *Oxford Literary Review* 13, nos. 1–2 (1991).

New Americas Press, ed. *A Dream Compels Us: Voices of Salvadoran Women.* Boston: South End Press, 1989.

New Americanists 2: National Identities and Postnational Narratives. Special issue of *boundary 2* 19, no. 1 (spring 1992).

Newton, Judith. "Family Fortunes: 'New History' and 'New Historicism.'" *Radical History Review* 43 (winter 1989): 5–22.

———. Historicisms New and Old: 'Charles Dickens' Meets Marxism, Feminism, and West Coast Foucault." *Feminist Studies* 16, no. 3 (1990): 449–76.

———. "History as Usual?: Feminism and 'New Historicism.'" *Cultural Critique* 9 (summer 1988): 87–122.

Nicholson, Linda. "Feminism and Marxism." In *Feminism as Critique*, ed. Seyla Banhabib and Drucilla Cornell, 16–30.

———, ed. *Feminism/Postmodernism*. New York: Routledge, 1990.

Niranjana, Tejaswini. *Siting Translation: History, Post-Structuralism, and the Colonial Context*. Berkeley and Los Angeles: University of California Press, 1992.

Norris, Christopher. *Uncritical Theory: Postmodernism, Intellectuals, and the Gulf War*. Amherst: University of Massachusetts Press, 1992.

———. *What's Wrong with Postmodernism: Critical Theory and the Ends of Philosophy*. Baltimore: Johns Hopkins University Press, 1990.

O'Brien, Mark. *Hope amidst the Horror: The Socialist Answer to the World*. London: Bookmarks, 1992.

Omvedt, Gail. "'Patriarchy': The Analysis of Women's Oppression." *Insurgent Sociologist* 13, no. 3 (spring 1986): 30–50.

Onimode, Bade. *Marxist Political Economy*. London: Zed Books, 1985.

Paglia, Camille. "Academe Has to Recover Its Spiritual Roots and Overthrow the Ossified Political Establishment of Invested Self-Interest." *Chronicle of Higher Education*, 8 May 1991, B1–2.

———. "Ninnies, Pedants, Tyrants, and Other Academics." *New York Times Book Review*, 5 May 1991, 1, 29, 33.

———. "The Nursery-School Campus: The Corrupting of the Humanities in the US." *Times Literary Supplement*, 22 May 1992, 19.

———. "The Return of Carry Nation." *Playboy*, October 1992, 36, 38.

———. *Sex, Art, and American Culture: Essays*. New York: Vintage, 1992.

———. *Sexual Personae: Art and Decadence from Nefertiti to Emily Dickinson*. New Haven: Yale University Press, 1990.

———. "What's Wrong with Feminism? A Conversation with Camille Paglia." Interview by Rich Baum. *Cornell Political Forum* 6, no. 1 (October 1991): 4–13.

Paglia, Camille, and Suzanne Gordon. "Face to Face" Interview. *Working Woman*, March 1992, 76–79, 106.

Paglia, Camille, and Neil Postman. "Dinner Conversation: She Wants Her TV! He Wants His Book!" *Harper's*, March 1991, 44–55.

Parker, Andrew. "Unthinking Sex: Marx, Engels, and the Scene of Writing." In *Fear of a Queer Planet*, ed. Michael Warner, 19–41.

Parker, Andrew, Mary Russo, Doris Sommer, and Patricia Yaeger, eds. *Nationalisms and Sexualities*. New York: Routledge, 1992.

Parry, Benita. "Problems in Current Theories of Colonial Discourse." *Oxford Literary Review* 9, nos. 1–2 (1987): 27–58.

Pecheux, M. *Language, Semantics, and Ideology*. Trans. H. Nagpal. New York: St. Martin's Press, 1982.

Penley, Constance. "Feminism, Psychoanalysis, and the Study of Popular Culture." In *Cultural Studies*, ed. Lawrence Grossberg, Cary Nelson, and Paula Treichler, 479–500.

Penley, Constance, and Andrew Ross, eds. *Technoculture*. Minneapolis: University of Minnesota Press, 1991.

Petersen, Kirsten Holst, and Anna Rutherford, eds. *A Double Colonization: Colo-*

nial and Post-Colonial Women's Writing. Mundelstrup, Denmark: Dangaroo Press, 1986.

Petrow, Steven. "Who Is Camille Paglia, and Why Is She Saying Those Terrible Things about Us?" *Advocate*, 26 January 1992, 74–76.

Phillips, Susan Elizabeth. "The Romance and the Empowerment of Women." In *Dangerous Men and Adventurous Women*, ed. Jayne Ann Krentz, 53–60.

Post-Colonial Cultures of Resistance. Special issue of *Polygraph* 4 (1990).

Poulantzas, Nicos. *Political Power and Social Classes*. Trans. T. O'Hagan. London: New Left Books, 1973.

Prescod-Roberts, Margaret, and Norma Steele. *Black Women: Bringing It All Back Home*. Bristol, England: Falling Wall Press, 1980.

Probyn, Elspeth. "Bodies and Anti-Bodies: Feminism and the Postmodern." *Cultural Studies* 1, no. 3 (October 1987): 349–60.

The Question of Postcolonialism and the Third World. Special issue of *Social Text* 31–32 (1992).

Rabine, Leslie Wahl. "A Feminist Politics of Non-Identity." *Feminist Studies* 14, no. 1 (1988): 11–31.

Ramazanoglu, Caroline, ed. *Up against Foucault: Explorations of Some Tensions between Foucault and Feminism*. London: Routledge, 1993.

Ranciere, Jacques. "The Concept of 'Critique' and the 'Critique of Political Economy.'" In *Ideology, Method, and Marx: Essays from "Economy and Society,"* ed. Ali Rattansi, 74–180. London: Routledge, 1989.

Ray, Peter. "It's Not Natural." *Living Marxism*, December 1992, 31–32.

Readings, Bill. *Introducing Lyotard: Art and Politics*. London: Routledge, 1991.

Reagon, Bernice Johnson. "Coalition Politics: Turning the Century." In *Home Girls: A Black Feminist Anthology*, ed. Barbara Smith, 356–69. New York: Kitchen Table, Women of Color Press, 1983.

Reed, Evelyn. *Problems of Women's Liberation*. New York: Pathfinder Press, 1969.

———. *Women's Evolution: From Matriarchal Clan to Patriarchal Family*. New York: Pathfinder Press, 1975.

Reflections on Racism. Special issue of *Thesis Eleven* 32 (1992).

Reiter, Rayna, ed. *Toward an Anthropology of Women*. New York: Monthly Review Press, 1975.

———. *Knowledge and Class: A Marxian Critique of Political Economy*. Chicago: University of Chicago Press, 1987.

Rich, Adrienne. *Blood, Bread, and Poetry: Selected Prose, 1979–1985*. New York: Norton, 1986.

Rich, B. Ruby. "Top Girl." *Village Voice*, October 1992, 29–33.

Roiphe, Katie. "Date Rape's Other Victim." New York Times Magazine (13 June 1993): 26–28, 30, 40, 68.

———. *The Morning After: Sex, Fear, and Feminism on Campus*. New York: Little, Brown, 1994.

Rooney, Ellen. *Seductive Reasoning: Pluralism as the Problematic of Contemporary Literary Theory*. Ithaca, N.Y.: Cornell University Press, 1989.

———. "Who's Left Out? A Rose by Any Other Name Is Still Red; or, The Politics of Pluralism." *Critical Inquiry* 12 (spring 1986): 550–63.

Rose, Margaret. *The Post-Modern and the Post-Industrial: A Critical Analysis.* Cambridge: Cambridge University Press, 1991.

Ross, Andrew. *No Respect: Intellectuals and Popular Culture.* New York: Routledge, 1989.

Rorty, Richard. *Consequences of Pragmatism, Essays: 1972–1980.* Minneapolis: University of Minnesota Press, 1982.

———. *Contingency, Irony, and Solidarity.* New York: Cambridge University Press, 1989.

———. *Philosophy and the Mirror of Nature.* Princeton: Princeton University Press, 1979.

Rowbotham, Sheila. *Women, Resistance, and Revolution.* 1972; rpt. New York: Vintage, 1974.

Rowbotham, Sheila, Lynne Segal, and Hilary Wainwright. *Beyond the Fragments: Feminism and the Making of Socialism.* Boston: Alyson Press, 1981.

Rubin, Gayle. "The Catacombs: A Temple of the Butthole." In *Leatherfolk: Radical Sex, People, Politics, and Practice,* ed. Mark Thompson. Boston: Alyson Press, 1991, 119–41.

———. "Thinking Sex: Notes for a Radical Theory of the Politics of Sexuality." In *Pleasure and Danger: Exploring Female Sexuality,* ed. Carole S. Vance, 267–319. Boston: Routledge and Kegan Paul, 1984.

———. "The Traffic in Women: Notes on the 'Political Economy' of Sex." In *Toward an Anthropology of Women,* ed. Rayna Reiter, 157–210.

Rubin, Gayle, with Judith Butler. "Sexual Traffic." Interview. *Differences* 6, nos. 2–3 (1994): 62–99.

Rustin, Michael. "The Politics of Post-Fordism; or, the Trouble with New Times." *New Left Review* 175 (May–June 1989): 54–77.

Saffioti, Heleieth. *Women in Class Society.* New York: Monthly Review Press, 1978.

Said, Edward. *Culture and Imperialism.* New York: Vintage, 1994.

Sangari, Kumkum, and Sudesh Vaid, eds. *Recasting Women: Essays in Colonial History.* New Delhi: Kali for Women, 1989; rpt. New Brunswick, N.J.: Rutgers University Press, 1990.

Sappington, Rodney, and Tyler Stallings, eds. *Uncontrollable Bodies: Testimonies of Identity and Culture.* Seattle: Bay Press, 1994.

Sargent, Lydia, ed. *Women and Revolution: A Discussion of the Unhappy Marriage of Marxism and Feminism.* Boston: South End Press, 1981.

Saussure, Ferdinand de. *Course in General Linguistics.* Trans. Wade Baskin. 1959; rpt. New York: McGraw, 1966.

Sawicki, Jana. *Disciplining Foucault: Feminism, Power, and the Body.* New York: Routledge, 1991.

Sayer, Derek. "Science as Critique: Marx vs Althusser." In *Issues in Marxist Philosophy,* vol. 3: *Epistemology, Science, Ideology,* ed. J. Mepham and D-H. Ruben, 27–54. Atlantic Highlands, N.J.: Humanities Press.

Sayers, Janet, Mary Evans, and Nanneke Redclift, eds. *Engels Revisited: New Feminist Essays.* London: Tavistock, 1987.

Scheper-Hughes, Nancy. *Death without Weeping: The Violence of Everyday Life in Brazil*. Berkeley and Los Angeles: University of California Press, 1992.

———. "Death without Weeping: Daily Life in Northeast Brazil." *New Internationalist* 254 (April 1994): 4–28.

Scheppele, Kim Lane. "Constructive Marxist Theory." *Rethinking Marxism* 2, no. 4 (winter 1989): 82–89.

Schneir, Miriam, ed. "Declaration of Sentiments and Resolutions, Seneca Falls." In *Feminism: The Essential Historical Writings*, 76–82. New York: Vintage, 1972.

Schor, Naomi. *Breaking the Chain: Women, Theory, and French Realist Fiction*. New York: Columbia University Press, 1985.

———. "Dreaming Dissymmetry: Barthes, Foucault, and Sexual Difference." In *Coming to Terms*, ed. Elizabeth Weed, 47–58.

———. "This Essentialism Which Is Not One: Coming to Grips with Irigaray." *Differences* 1, no. 2 (1989): 38–58.

Scott, Joan. "Deconstructing Equality-Versus-Difference; or, The Uses of Poststructuralist Theory for Feminism." In *Conflicts in Feminism*, ed. Marianne Hirsch and Evelyn Fox Keller, 134–48.

Segal, Lynne. "Whose Left? Socialism, Feminism, and the Future." *New Left Review* 185 (January–February 1991): 81–91.

Sen, Amartya. "More Than 100 Million Women Are Missing." *New York Review of Books*, 20 December 1990, 61–66.

———. *Poverty and Famines: An Essay on Entitlement and Deprivation*. New York: Oxford University Press, 1981.

Showalter, Elaine. "Toward a Feminist Poetics." In *The New Feminist Criticism*, ed. Elaine Showalter, 125–43. New York: Pantheon, 1985.

Sidel, Ruth. *Women and Children Last: The Plight of Poor Women in Affluent America*. New York: Penguin, 1986.

Silverman, Kaja. *Male Subjectivity at the Margins*. New York: Routledge, 1992.

Sivanandan, A. "Address to the 10th National Congress of Azanian People's Organisation." *Race and Class* 33, no. 2 (1991): 65–70.

———. "All That Melts into Air Is Solid: The Hokum of New Times." *Race and Class* 31, no. 3 (1989): 1–30.

Sloterdijk, Peter. *Critique of Cynical Reason*. Trans. M. Eldred. Minneapolis: University of Minnesota Press, 1987.

Smith, Adam. *The Wealth of Nations*. New York: Modern Library, 1985.

Smith, Dorothy E. *The Conceptual Practices of Power: A Feminist Sociology of Knowledge*. Boston: Northeastern University Press, 1990.

———. *Feminism and Marxism—a Place to Begin, a Way to Go*. Vancouver: New Star Books, 1977.

Smith, Paul. "Domestic Labour and Marx's Theory of Value." In *Feminism and Materialism*, ed. Annette Kuhn and AnnMarie Wolpe, 198–219.

Smith, Paul Julian. *The Body Hispanic: Gender and Sexuality in Spanish and Spanish American Literature*. New York: Oxford University Press, 1989.

Smith, Sharon. "Mistaken Identity; or, Can Identity Politics Liberate the Oppressed?" *International Socialism* 62 (spring 1994): 3–50.

Smith, Sidonie and Julia Watson, eds. *De/Colonizing the Subject: The Politics of Gender in Women's Autobiography.* Minneapolis: University of Minnesota Press, 1992.

Sohoni, Neera Kuckreja. "Where Are the Girls?" *Ms.*, July–August 1994, 96.

Soper, Kate. "Feminism as Critique." *New Left Review* 176 (July–August 1989): 91–112.

Spivak, Gayatri Chakravorty. "Can the Subaltern Speak?" In *Marxism and the Interpretation of Culture,* ed. Cary Nelson and Lawrence Grossberg, 271–313. Urbana: University of Illinois Press, 1988.

———. "Gayatri Spivak on the Politics of the Postcolonial Subject." Interview by Howard Winant. *Socialist Review* 90, (July–Sept. 1990): 81–97.

———. "Imperialism and Sexual Difference." *Oxford Literary Review* 8, nos. 1–2 (1986): 225–40.

———. "In a Word." Interview by Ellen Rooney. *Differences* 1, no. 2 (1989): 124–56.

———. *In Other Worlds: Essays in Cultural Politics.* New York: Methuen, 1987.

———. "Naming." Interview. *Stanford Humanities Review* 1, no. 1 (spring 1989): 84–97.

———. *Outside in the Teaching Machine.* New York: Routledge, 1993.

———. "The Political Economy of Women as Seen by a Literary Critic." In *Coming to Terms,* ed. Elizabeth Weed, 218–39.

———. *The Post-Colonial Critic: Interviews, Strategies, Dialogues.* Ed. S. Harasym. New York: Routledge, 1990.

———. "Speculations on Reading Marx: After Reading Derrida." In *Post-Structuralism and the Question of History,* ed. Derek Attridge, Geoff Bennington, and R. Young, 30–62. Cambridge: Cambridge University Press, 1987.

———. "Three Women's Texts and a Critique of Imperialism." *Critical Inquiry* 12 (autumn 1985): 243–61.

———. "Woman in Difference: Mahasweta Devi's 'Douloti the Beautiful.'" In *Nationalisms and Sexualities,* ed. Andrew Parker, Mary Russo, Doris Sommer, and Patricia Yaeger, 96–117.

Stanfill, Francesca. "Woman Warrior." *New York,* 4 March 1991, 23–30.

Stillman, Peter. "Marx's Enterprise of Critique." In *Marxism,* ed. J. R. Pennock and J. W. Chapman, 252–76. New York: New York University Press, 1983.

Stockton, Kathryn Bond. "Bodies and God: Postructuralist Feminists Return to Fold of Spiritual Materialism." In *Feminism and Postmodernism,* ed. Margaret Ferguson and Jennifer Wicke. Durham: Duke University Press, 129–65.

Stree, Shakti Sanghatana. *"We Were Making History": Women and the Telangana Uprising.* London: Zed Books, 1989.

Suleiman, Susan Rubin. *Subversive Intent: Gender, Politics, and the Avant-Garde.* Cambridge: Harvard University Press, 1990.

Szymanski, Albert. "Feminism: A Marxist Critique." In *Recapturing Marxism: An Appraisal of Recent Trends in Sociology Theory,* ed. Rhonda F. Levine and Jerry Lembcke, 194–222. New York: Praeger, 1987.

Teachout, Terry. "Siding with the Men." *New York Times Book Review,* 22 July 1990, 7.

Third World Literary and Cultural Criticism. Special issue of *South Atlantic Quarterly* 87, no. 1 (winter 1988).

Tiffin, Chris, and Alan Lawson, eds. *De-scribing Empire: Post-colonialism and Textuality.* London: Routledge, 1994.

Trotsky, Leon. *Women and the Family.* New York: Pathfinder Press, 1970.

Truong, Thanh-Dam. *Sex, Money, and Morality: Prostitution and Tourism in South-East Asia.* London: Zed Books, 1990.

Ulmer, Gregory. *Heuretics: The Logic of Invention.* Baltimore: Johns Hopkins University Press, 1994.

———. *Teletheory: Grammatology in the Age of Video.* New York: Routledge, 1989.

V-Girls. "Daughters of the ReVolution." *October* 71 (winter 1995): 121–40.

Vakhrushev, Vasily. *Neocolonialism: Methods and Manoeuvres.* Moscow: Progress, 1973.

Vattimo, Gianni. "Postmodern Criticism: Postmodern Critique." In *Writing the Future,* ed. David Wood, 57–66. London: Routledge, 1990.

Vogel, Lise. *Marxism and the Oppression of Women: Toward a Unitary Theory.* New Brunswick, N.J.: Rutgers University Press, 1983.

Voloshinov, V. N. [Mikhail Bakhtin]. *Marxism and the Philosophy of Language.* Trans. L. Matejka and I. Titunik. Cambridge: Harvard University Press, 1973.

Wall, Cheryl, ed. *Changing Our Own Words: Essays on Criticism, Theory, and Writing by Black Women.* New Brunswick, N.J.: Rutgers University Press, 1989.

Walby, Sylvia. *Patriarchy at Work: Patriarchy and Capitalist Relations in Employment.* Minneapolis: University of Minnesota Press, 1986.

———. *Theorizing Patriarchy.* Oxford: Basil Blackwell, 1990.

Warhol, Robyn R., and Diane Price Herndl, eds. *Feminisms: An Anthology of Literary Theory and Criticism.* New Brunswick, N.J.: Rutgers University Press, 1991.

Warner, Michael, ed. *Fear of a Queer Planet: Queer Politics and Social Theory.* Minneapolis: University of Minnesota Press, 1993.

Waters, Mary-Alice. *Feminism and the Marxist Movement.* New York: Pathfinder Press, 1972.

Weed, Elizabeth, ed. *Coming to Terms: Feminism, Theory, Politics.* New York: Routledge, 1989.

Weedon, Chris. *Feminist Practice and Poststructuralist Theory.* Cambridge, Mass.: Basil Blackwell, 1987.

Weeks, Jeffrey. "Capitalism and the Organization of Sex." In *Homosexuality: Power and Politics,* ed. Gay Left Collective, 11–20. London: Allison and Busby, 1980.

———. *Sex, Politics, and Society: The Regulation of Sexuality since 1800.* 2d ed. London: Longman, 1989.

Weinbaum, Batya. *The Curious Courtship of Women's Liberation and Socialism.* Boston: South End Press, 1978.

Weinberg, Steven. "Two Cheers for Reductionism." *Dreams of a Final Theory.* New York: Pantheon, 1992, 51–64.

Welsh, Diane, and Conners, Anne. Letter to *New York Times Magazine*, 20 June 1993, 8.

Whitford, Margaret. *Luce Irigaray: Philosophy in the Feminine*. London: Routledge, 1991.

Wilcox, Helen, Keith McWatters, Ann Thompson, and Linda R. Williams, eds. *The Body and the Text: Hélène Cixous, Reading, and Teaching*. New York: St. Martin's Press, 1990.

Williams, Patrick, and Laura Chrisman, eds. *Colonial Discourse and Post-colonial Theory: A Reader*. New York: Columbia University Press, 1994.

Williamson, Marianne. *A Woman's Worth*. New York: Random House, 1993.

Willis, Ellen. *No More Nice Girls: Countercultural Essays*. Hanover, N.H.: Wesleyan University Press, 1992.

Wittig, Monique. *The Straight Mind and Other Essays*. Boston: Beacon Press, 1992.

Woddis, Jack. *An Introduction to Neo-Colonialism*. New York: International Publishers, 1967.

Wolcott, James. "Paglia's Power Trip." *Vanity Fair* (Sept. 1992): 238–40; 300–303.

Wolf, Naomi. *Fire with Fire: The New Female Power and How it Will Change the Twenty-first Century*. New York: Random House, 1994.

Women's Labor. Special Issue of *Radical America* 7, nos. 4–5 (July–October 1973).

Wong, Nellie. "Socialist Feminism: Our Bridge to Freedom." In *Third World Women and the Politics of Feminism*, by Chandra Mohanty, Ann Russo, and Lourdes Torres, 228–96.

Wood, Ellen Meiksins. "Identity Crisis." *In These Times*, 13 June 1994, 28–29.

———. *The Retreat from Class: A New "True" Socialism*. London: Verso, 1986.

Woodiwiss, Anthony. *Social Theory after Post-Modernism: Rethinking Production, Law, and Class*. London: Pluto Press, 1990.

Writing after Colonialism. Special issue of *Social Text* 13–14 (1986).

Young, Iris. "Beyond the Unhappy Marriage: A Critique of the Dual Systems Theory." In *Women and Revolution*, ed. Lydia Sargent, 43–70.

———. *Justice and the Politics of Difference*. Princeton: Princeton University Press, 1990.

———. "Socialist Feminism and the Limits of Dual Systems Theory." *Socialist Review* no. 50–51 (March–June 1980): 169–88.

———. *Throwing Like a Girl and Other Essays in Feminist Philosophy and Social Theory*. Bloomington: Indiana University Press, 1990.

Young, Kate, Carol Wolkowitz, and Roslyn McCullagh, ed. *Of Marriage and the Market: Women's Subordination Internationally and Its Lessons*. 2d ed. London: Routledge, 1984.

Zaretsky, Eli. *Capitalism, the Family, and Personal Life*. New York: Harper and Row, 1976.

Zavarzadeh, Mas'ud. "'Argument' and the Politics of Laughter." *Rethinking Marxism* 4, no. 1 (1991): 120–31.

———. "Post-ality: The (Dis)Simulations of Cybercapitalism." *Transformation* 1 (spring 1995): 1–75.

Zavarzadeh, Mas'ud, and Donald Morton. *Theory, (Post)Modernity, Opposition:*

An 'Other' Introduction to Literary and Cultural Theory. Washington, D.C.: Maisonneuve, 1991.

————. *Theory as Resistance: Politics and Culture after (Post)Structuralism.* New York: Guilford Press, 1994.

Zetkin, Clara. *Selected Writings,* ed. P. Foner. New York: International Publishers, 1984.

Žižek, Slavoj. *Looking Awry: An Introduction to Jacques Lacan through Popular Culture.* Cambridge: MIT Press, 1992.

————. *The Sublime Object of Ideology.* London: Verso, 1989.

Index

Adorno, Theodor, 165
Ahmad, Ai jaz, 308n.2
Alcoff, Linda, 308n.2
Alexander, Peter, 304n.7
Allison, Dorothy, 218
Althusser, Louis, 63–64, 89, 219, 303n.4, 305n.6
Amin, Samir, 308n.3
Anzaldúa, Gloria, 308n.2
Appiah, Kwame, 308n.1
Aronowitz, Stanley, ix, 71, 222–23
Ashcroft, Bill, 308n.1
Assiter, Alison, 303n.2

Balbus, Isaac, 92
Barrett, Michele, ix, 24–25, 35–36, 50, 75, 129, 177
Barthes, Roland, 242–43, 303n.5
Bartky, Sandra, 305n.1
Base and superstructure, 38, 47–49, 110, 130–50, 171–73, 176–78, 182, 198–200, 219, 235–36, 281
Bataille, Georges, 172
Baudrillard, Jean, 56–58, 137–41, 172
Bell, Daniel, 105–6
Benhabib, Seyla, 36, 200
Bennholdt-Thomsen, Veronika, 79–82, 308n.3
Benstock, Shari, 27–28
Benston, Margaret, 98
Bersani, Leo, 64
Bhabha, Homi, 308n.2
Bloom, Harold, 257–58, 262
Body, 30–33, 81, 212, 219–20, 233–82
Bruckner, Pascal, 308n.2
Butler, Judith, xi, 24, 26, 29, 108, 122,

172, 185, 189, 209–220, 225–32, 273, 285, 303n.5, 305n.1, 305n.2

Callinicos, Alex, 110–13
Capitalism, 61, 65–66, 69, 74, 90, 100, 103, 105–7, 110–17, 130–52, 179–80, 195–97, 224, 230–31, 238–40, 251, 258–59, 268, 300–301
Christian, Barbara, 16
Cixous, Hélenè, 162, 166–67, 190, 303n.5
Class, 98, 102–3, 118–19, 131, 178, 205, 217–18, 223, 304n.8
Class consciousness, 177, 276
Class struggle, 40–41, 57–59, 64, 76–77, 108, 113, 117–21, 133, 136, 148, 150–51, 157, 171, 173–75, 196–97, 224, 230, 250, 277, 281, 283–84, 303n.4
Collectivity, 150, 153, 169–70, 272, 292, 293–95, 301–2
Consumption, 56–58, 137–40
Copelon, Rhonda, 22
Cornell, Drucilla, 26, 36, 150, 158–59, 165–66, 185–87, 189–209, 220, 224–32, 254, 265, 269, 273, 301, 305n.3
Cotter, Jennifer, 125
Critique, 3–7, 11–24, 43–44, 53–54, 63, 132, 153, 176–77, 226–27, 251, 263–64, 291–96, 299–300, 303n.1, 306n.6
Crosby, Christina, 121

Dalla Costa, Mariarosa, 98–99, 101
Daly, Mary, 28

Stallings, Tyler, 305n.1
Stanfill, Francesca, 262, 267, 307n.8
Steinem, Gloria, 307n.7
Stockton, Kathryn Bond, 32–34
Subaltern, 285, 288–301

Textuality, 39–40, 140–42, 158–60,
    162–63, 167–68, 172, 177, 182–84,
    186–87, 193–95, 199–203, 244–49,
    277–78, 291
Thebaud, Jean-Loup, 192–94
Theory, 14–23, 64, 186, 250–52, 289
Tiffin, Chris, 308n.2
Treichler, Paula, 306n.4
Triffin, Helen, 308n.1
Torres, Lourdes, 285, 308n.2
Totality, 49–50, 85–89, 160, 182–85,
    190–92, 197, 250
Value, 122
    exchange, 56, 64
    surplus, 40–41, 60–62, 79
    use, 64
Vakhrushev, Vasily, 308n.3

Vogel, Lise, 304n.4
Volosninov, V. N., 40, 120,
    174–75
von Werlhof, Claudia, 79–82,
    308n.3
Watson, Julie, 285
Weed, Elizabeth, 285
Weedon, Chris, 305n.1
Weeks, Jeffrey, 65–66
Weinbaum, Batya, 304n.4
Wilcox, Helen, 305n.1
Williamson, Marianne, 254
Willis, Ellen, 118
Woddis, Jack, 308n.3
Wolf, Naomi, 254
Wolff, Richard, 102–3, 304n.8
Wong, Nellie, 36–37

Young, Iris, 70–75, 241

Zaretsky, Eli, 97, 100
Zavarzadeh, Mas'ud, 303n.1
Žižek, Slavoj, 57–64